Never Fear the Spills

DAVID WILSON

Published in Australia by Sid Harta Books & Print Pty Ltd,
ABN: 34632585293
23 Stirling Crescent, Glen Waverley, Victoria 3150 Australia
Telephone: +61 3 9560 9920, Facsimile: +61 3 9545 1742

E-mail: author@sidharta.com.au

First published in Australia 2022
This edition published 2022
Copyright © David Wilson 2022

Cover design, typesetting: WorkingType (www.workingtype.com.au)

The right of David Wilson to be identified as the Author of the Work
has been asserted in accordance with the Copyright, Designs and Patents Act 1988.

All rights reserved. No part of this publication may be reproduced,
stored in a retrieval system, or transmitted, in any form or by any means without the prior written permission of the publisher, nor be otherwise circulated in any form of binding or cover other than that in which it is published and without a similar condition being imposed on the subsequent purchaser.

David Wilson
Never Fear the Spills
ISBN: 978-1-922958-02-0 (paperback)
978-0-6457244-0-0 (ebook)
pp552

Cover portrait of the author by Alexander Goudie
www.alexandergoudie.co.uk

ABOUT THE AUTHOR

Born in Dalby in 1947, David Wilson grew up on Mount Oscar Station just outside Clermont. Having matriculated, his initial instinct was to study medicine but when offered a scholarship in civil engineering his future path was decided. His early years as a graduate engineer were spent on projects around Australia but faced with losing his driver's licence for driving dangerously, he accepted a job in Singapore in the oil and gas industry. Later, David established an engineering office in London where he spent much of his time improving the written English of his colleagues, but *Never Fear the Spills* is his first published book. The book was spawned by a desire to impart some of his wisdom to younger generations of engineers. David now spends his days in retirement on the Sunshine Coast.

For Lockwood, my brave brother

Contents

About the author	iii
Contents	vii
Prologue	1
Introduction	6
Early Days	10
University	29
Graduate Engineer	48
Botany Bay	58
My Year of Living Dangerously	83
The Fasht al Arab	127
Jockstrap Inc	164
Bourdon Street	198
Paul Street	251
The Aramco Affair	282
RIP Bligh Engineering	305
CanOcean	319
Trent Eels	365
Freefall	389
Bontang Train F	421
Singapore Again	440
Bakrie Kvaerner Engineering	469
Bakrie Engineering	499

Bibliography 524
List of Acronyms and Abbreviations 526

Prologue

As I flew from London to Singapore on 8 January 1992, I wondered how it had come to this. For ten years my fortunes had been in a downhill spiral. Now the spiral was a nosedive.

It started in March 1981 with a telephone call from a friend in Aramco, formerly the Arabian American Oil Company. At the time, I was the managing director and major shareholder of thriving offshore oil and gas production facilities designer, Bligh Engineering. Aramco was our biggest client and we had designed some of the largest production platforms in the Persian Gulf. The Saudi Arabian Tax Department had advised Aramco we had been evading local taxes and instructed it to withhold payment of outstanding invoices pending resolution of the matter. Worse still, a substantial contract earmarked for award to us was diverted to a competitor. The Saudi claim was withdrawn fifteen months later, but with over fifty professional staff on the payroll it was impossible to continue without progress payments for ongoing work. The money was eventually released but my partners and I were forced into a fire sale and sold the company to CanOcean, a Canadian subsea engineering specialist, for a song.

The sale included a provision for me to remain with the

company for a further two years as projects director and I was happy to do so since the terms were generous. We even managed to secure another Aramco contract. But by 1983 the oil price momentum triggered by the Iran-Iraq war was dissipating and prices were falling. New business was scarce and CanOcean was struggling. The managing director resigned and I was offered the job. I declined and resigned in December 1985. It was a quixotic gesture. I should have stuck to the knitting but had decided to try something new.

Years earlier, during my second Christmas in England, I had met another Australian, Ansell Egerton, director of strategic planning at Rothmans International. Rothmans had investments in areas unrelated to cigarettes; it had tonnes of money and it was Ansell's job to screen the proposals that flooded in. One scheme of interest, but not to Rothmans, was a proposal for an intensive eel farm to be built alongside Drax Power Station on the River Ouse. The optimum water temperature for eel cultivation is 24 °C. The basic idea was to use waste heat from the power generation process to maintain this temperature in the farm waters all year round.

I read everything I could find about eels and eel farming. The literature even included accounts of recent projects in the UK that had failed. An earlier project at Drax was on track to meet its production target of 165 tonnes a year, only to be stymied by the 1984 miners' strike. Not to be deterred, I went to the Central Electricity Generating Board (CEGB), which was happy to take me on a tour of its power stations in the Trent Valley. In the wake of the oil price hikes precipitated by the Iran-Iraq war, waste heat utilisation had become a European community mantra. The CEGB was keen for the kudos but not the cost. It offered a site large enough for a 200-tonnes-a-year plant immediately to the north of the Ratcliffe-on-Soar Power Station in Nottinghamshire. Plans, a budget and a new company, Trent Eels PLC, followed close behind. Barney Cue, my financial advisor, had swiftly vetoed a facetious suggestion we call it 'The Electric Eel Company'. A prospectus to raise £350,000 was issued in October 1985. It was a flop. The brave investors who subscribed £20,000 got their money back.

I had just about purged eels from my system when I heard of a European community scheme providing soft loans for waste heat utilisation demonstration projects. I prepared a design and budget for a fifty-tonnes-a-year pilot plant and applied for a £75,000 loan, thinking it would be rejected and that would be the end of it. No such luck. The loan was approved contingent on raising capital of £150,000. I stumped up half by selling my flat in Holland Park Avenue. An assortment of friends put in the rest.

Construction commenced in March 1986. By September, when construction of all thirty-one tanks had been completed and fully stocked, it was evident the company would not meet its production targets. Trent Eels was on the road to bankruptcy. The local coarse fishermen were ropeable when the surviving eels were released into the Trent.

Then there were other disappointments—an attempt to buy a bankrupt fishing company in Punta Arenas in Chile and a failed proposal to develop a waste-to-energy plant for the Berkshire County Council. When the penny dropped and I knew I was in trouble, I sold my beloved George Stubbs engravings, *Dungannon* and *Sweetbriar*, back to the dealer. The money bought some time but in the early nineties jobs in oil and gas, the industry I knew something about, were few and far between. Regardless, I applied for anything that looked even remotely related. No response. Being forty-four hadn't helped either.

By December 1991, I could barely pay the rent for my small cottage in Nottinghamshire. Then, out of the blue, there was a call from an old friend aware of my predicament. He was passing through Singapore and Ipco Marine, which had just won a pipeline construction contract in Indonesia and was looking for a project engineer. Would I be interested? Well, yes, I would. A few days later Ipco's president, Charles Hardeman, called to confirm my interest and suggested I come to Singapore for a chat as soon as possible after New Year. This was it. Perhaps the tide would turn.

Ipco booked me into the Equatorial Hotel where I had stayed on my first stint in Singapore nineteen years earlier. I had known the company since my earlier days in Singapore when Sandy Sandford had started it after retiring as the Singapore Government's chief engineer. He too had experienced difficult times and Ipco had struggled until Sandy came up with the brilliant idea of building instant jetties from prefabricated jack-up modules. The company's fortunes flourished when he successfully installed the first off Yanbu in the Red Sea in 1977. He retired shortly thereafter, but over the years I had kept in touch with the company and vaguely knew Chuck Hardeman so was hopeful of salvation, even though it would mean being a lowly project engineer again.

On my arrival at Ipco's offices in Jurong next morning I was ushered into a conference room where I was introduced to, among others, Ray Hodgson, director of projects and George Klause, project manager. All I had been told was that the project was a large pipeline in Indonesia. Ipco Marine was, as its name suggests, a marine engineering and construction company. This was what I knew. I was an offshore pipeline engineer. I had not entertained the idea that this project could involve anything else. Within minutes it became clear it *was* something else. It was a contract for the design, supply and installation of a fifty-seven kilometre, thirty-six-inch-diameter cross-country gas pipeline from Badak to Bontang in East Kalimantan. Cross-country and submarine pipeline projects are chalk and cheese.

I interrupted Ray Hodgson's preliminary remarks and explained there had been a terrible mistake. They had my resume and should have known I had never been associated with a cross-country pipeline in my life. Silence. To Ray's credit he just said, 'wait a minute' and asked George Klause to leave the room with him. They were out for about ten minutes. I sat there anticipating a miserable return trip to London and the dismal prospects thereafter.

When they came back, Ray simply said, 'We don't have time to find anybody else. Do you want the job?

Introduction

The aftermath of the American Civil and Franco-Prussian Wars ushered in an era of unprecedented prosperity. The wars crystallised the innovations of the industrial revolution and peace fomented evolution and expansion. Railroads were built across North America. Steam supplanted sail in the Atlantic and the Pacific. The western world became a giant marketplace. Trade flourished, and with it, wealth and all the trappings—science, technology, architecture, art, music and literature. This was the Belle Epoque, and my grandfathers were born into it—my maternal grandfather, Bertram Knights, in Carbrooke, Norfolk, in 1882 and my paternal grandfather, Frederick David Gilmore Wilson, in Sandgate, Queensland, in 1893. Not everybody shared the wealth, so in 1905 Bert Knights immigrated to Australia. I have been to Carbrooke on a cold wet day and have no doubt he made the right decision.

All parties come to an end. The Belle Epoque finished the day the German Army marched into Belgium on its way to Paris in September 1914. During the four years that followed, forty million people were either killed or wounded and the accumulated wealth of the world all but destroyed.

Grandfather Dave was one of the forty million. He enlisted,

went to Gallipoli and survived but was then wounded in France. He was shot through the chest in an attack on German lines at Pozières in August 1916. Miraculously, he survived and after four months in various English hospitals returned home. Seven years later, he established Wilson & Wilson, a grain-trading firm, in Dalby on the Darling Downs, Australia's richest farming district. My father, Thomas David Addison Wilson, was born at this time.

In the meantime, the major western economies were doing their best to rebuild in the wake of the Great War. This wasn't easy. It's said the Great Depression started in 1929 with the Wall Street crash, but in Australia unemployment levels were high from the end of WW1 to the beginning of WW2. Despite these headwinds, Wilson & Wilson prospered. In 1938, my father was enrolled as a boarder at Church of England Grammar School in Brisbane, known affectionately as Churchie.

Meanwhile, Bert Knights, a carpenter by trade, married and thrived as a contractor in the St George district. His specialty was bridges and one he built across the Moonie River in front of the pub at Nindigully is still there. My mother, Adele, was three years old when Bert bought Billi Station, sixty kilometres south-west of St George. In my mother's account of her childhood, she wrote:

Our home was built by my father, who milled most of the timber on our property—mostly pine. It was a large double storey building with six bedrooms upstairs and a wide verandah all round. We always put our beds out on the verandah on hot summer nights. Since we had no refrigeration, there was a canvas water bag hanging on the rail of the verandah, which kept the water cool. Often at night we would get out of bed and throw water bombs at one another—just to cool off.

Following its WW1 defeat, Germany was forced to pay substantial compensation to the victors. This led to the hyperinflation that eventually propelled Hitler to power. If WW1 wasn't bad enough, twenty years later we were at it again. Only this time it was truly a world war, with fighting on every continent and in every ocean. The Japanese bombed Pearl Harbor in December 1941. My father enlisted in the RAAF in July 1942 and my mother did the same in September. They met soon after at the RAAF's Initial Training School in Kingaroy and later in Townsville. Dad was flying Mustangs and Kittyhawks in 86 Squadron and Mum was a WAAF transport driver. They married in Brisbane in March 1946 and settled in Dalby where my father joined the family grain-trading firm, Wilson & Wilson. I was born in April 1947.

Engineers learn to make estimates and it's my belief I was one of around sixty million babies born world-wide in 1947. In the great lottery of life, I did well. I was fit and healthy, had wonderful parents, was born in Australia and the timing couldn't have been better. The world had decided the destruction of the two world wars and the Great Depression had to be repaired. A monumental reconstruction commenced. It was an era that surpassed even the Belle Epoque, an age of unprecedented growth and wealth creation that lasted thirty years—*Les Trente Glorieuses* (The Glorious Thirty).

We can't manage our birth, but even before we mature we can take steps to influence our future. We can work hard to take advantage of our education. We can strive to learn as much as possible from our mentors in the formative years at work. More importantly, however, is to recognise the opportunities and pitfalls and react to achieve the best result. Marcus Brutus[1] said it best:

> There is a tide in the affairs of men.
> Which, taken at the flood, leads on to fortune;
> Omitted, all the voyage of their life
> Is bound in shallows and in miseries.
> On such a full sea are we now afloat,
> And we must take the current when it serves,
> Or lose our ventures.

This is the story of the ebbs and floods of a baby boomer.

Early Days

In June 2011, I flew out to Dalby for the 150th anniversary celebrations of the local state school. It was my first school and Miss O'Dea, my teacher in 1953, had taught my father in 1927. My memories of that time are dim, but by the time I left the school two years later, I was an avid reader. And I could write too, so she must have done a good job. Naturally, I read *Noddy*, *The Famous Five* and *Biggles*, but top of the pops were the Edward S Ellis books my father had read as a boy—*Ned in the Blockhouse*, *Ned in the Woods*, *Hunters of the Ozark*, *Deerfoot in the Forest*, *Deerfoot on the Prairies* etc. It was another world and another time, and I read them again and again. Thank you, Miss O'Dea.

The first family house I remember was on the outskirts of town by the aerodrome. Dad went to church on Sunday mornings. Grandfather Dave didn't but would come to our house to mow the lawn. If it was hot, he would take off his shirt. Forty years on, the scars from the bullet wound received in the attack on German lines at Pozières were still vivid, front and back. Dave had enlisted in July 1915 and shipped out for Egypt to join the 15th Battalion six weeks later. After a short spell on the Gallipoli Peninsula and further training in Egypt, the 15th was shipped to France in June 1916. They landed in Marseilles and made their way by train to Bailleul, where they underwent further training and savoured the local produce. Old Dave was promoted to lance corporal in charge of a Lewis gun team.

It was the Lewis gunners that led the 15th towards the German trenches between Pozières and Mouquet Farm in their first action on the Somme on the night of August 8th. In his *History of the 15th Battalion AIF 1914–1918*, Lieutenant TP Chataway described Dave's night as follows[2]:

> Captain Corrigan had only gone a few yards from the trench when he was hit by a piece of high explosive. Sergeant Farr, the senior NCO in 'D' Company, then took command of Corrigan's men and carried on ... 'C' Company with most of its NCOs intact was rapidly consolidating its position. On their extreme right a Lewis gun team under the command of Private Dave Wilson containing those splendid soldiers Privates Douglas Clarke, Archie Brown and George Goodfellow had overrun their objective, and, taking up a position forward of the new front line, held on to it until Wilson became a casualty with a bullet in the lung. They then fell back into their correct position taking Wilson with them.

What happened next is a mystery. C Company held its position until midday the following day and the time was used to evacuate the wounded, but somewhere in the maelstrom between Mouquet Farm and Albert, Dave was lost and posted missing. It came as no surprise the battalion that had suffered 1095 casualties over the eight months of the Gallipoli campaign had lost more than half its strength in one day on the Somme, with 90 killed and 370 wounded. We don't know how my grandfather was taken from the frontline to the rear through what must have been a dreadful bombardment, but he was and was shipped across the Channel to the Wharncliffe War Hospital, Sheffield, where he spent the next four months. Having recovered, he was sent home where he resumed his career as a stock and station agent.

His day at Mouquet Farm must have been a dreadful experience, but the wound was probably a blessing in disguise. Precious few of the men of the 15th who survived that day also survived Bullecourt, Messines, Polygon Wood, Hamel and the dozen or so other battles the 15th fought leading up to the Armistice. One of those who did, however, was Colonel (retd) Jack Corrigan. As a captain, he had also been wounded at Mouquet Farm but returned to duty after a speedy recovery. Not long after the war, he and Dave ran into each other at a fat cattle sale in Jandowae. Corrigan thought he had seen a ghost. He was sure Dave had disappeared in the mud at Mouquet Farm. They celebrated their reunion in a pub in Jandowae, now known as the 'Colonel's Pub'.

Despite having firsthand evidence of their sacrifices, it took me ages to appreciate our debt to our forefathers. I wonder why the bleeding hearts think everybody in the world has a God-given right to come to Australia. And why do they think we should become a republic? Perhaps so our great traditions, those of the English-speaking people, can be forgotten. But it is precisely those traditions that attract people from countries that don't have the rule of law or the robust institutions inherited from England.

One of my early memories is of the Queen's visit to Queensland in March 1954. Dad booked a suite in Lennons Hotel with a balcony overlooking the route planned for her procession through Brisbane. I don't recollect seeing the Queen that day but do remember arriving for breakfast in the hotel dining room *en famille* and Dad noticing two hapless Japanese businessmen minding their own business. There was quite a scene, and he would not allow us to take our seats until they had been ejected. Many years later, when the big Japanese trading houses took over, Wilson & Wilson's most important clients were Japanese and this brought a stream of Japanese visitors to our house in Myall Street. We even dined on Noritake. Time and trade heal.

In 1954, my father, in partnership with a family friend, Dan Beard, leased Mt Oscar Station outside Clermont. Early in 1955, the entire family—Mum and Dad, my younger brothers Lockwood and Christopher, and Winkie, our fierce fox terrier, embarked on an adventure that was to last five years. It could have been a new chapter from Edward S Ellis. Clermont is 600 kilometres north of Dalby. In those days, the roads were mostly gravel and the trip took two days but was worth every minute.

Mt Oscar is about twenty-two kilometres east of Clermont on what Ludwig Leichardt described as 'the downs of the Peak Range'. It was a brand-new station of 22 000 acres carved from Huntley Station immediately to the east. Huntley Creek, which rises in the Peak Range, flows through the property's open downs country, with its occasional stony ridges and sporadic stands of coolabah, bloodwood and ironbark. The twenty-six inches of monsoon rain that fall mainly in the summer months sustains the Blue and Mitchell grasses, suitable for sheep and cattle grazing.

Dad had spared no expense on our new home, built on the side of a ridge with views to Table Mountain twenty kilometres to the east. All four bedrooms opened to wide verandahs along the eastern and southern sides. The carpenter, Victor Stanley, was still painting when we arrived. He had not long landed from England and sported a David Niven moustache and a pipe that had turned his front teeth black. Later on, Mum would remind us to clean our teeth if we didn't want to them to look like Victor's.

There was no furniture, so initially we camped on the floor, but it was so exciting we didn't worry. There was so much to do. There was no electricity, no telephone, no stockyards, no airstrip, no stock, no cultivation and little or no fencing. But two years later when, in tears, I left for boarding school, it was all there.

It's hard now to imagine living without electricity, but it's been done for thousands of years and we were at Mt Oscar for at least six months before we got our thirty-two-volt system. It barely mattered. We were all so busy during the day that we were usually in bed by nightfall. From time to time, however, particularly if Dad was away, Mum would read to us by the light of a carbide lamp. I remember the floods of tears that accompanied the final pages of *The Old Man and the Sea* and virtually every page of Oscar Wilde's short stories, such as *The Happy Prince* and *The Selfish Giant*.

The cooker was a coal-fired Rayburn. It provided our hot water as well. There was also a Charles Hope Cold Flame refrigerator. This was an ingenious device that looked like an old-style refrigerator but instead of electricity burned kerosene. Not even an engineering degree from The University of Queensland has helped me to understand how that worked.

Not long after our arrival, we were given a Jersey cow, which gave us the milk we needed. When we were out of meat, despite loathing it, Dad killed a fat lamb. From time to time and for variety, lamb would be exchanged for beef from neighbours. Watermelons and squash grew profusely by the septic tank and eventually there was a flock of chickens and bantams. These also provided relief from lamb. On one memorable occasion, my brothers and I were sent out to catch and kill two chickens. Despite agreeing to a foolproof procedure, Lock very nearly succeeded in cutting off two fingers from my right hand with a tomahawk. After a two-hour drive to the Emerald hospital, I howled as they stitched them back together again. No local anaesthetic in those days.

Work commenced on the stockyards as soon as the house was completed. The great boom in wool prices stoked by the Korean War had passed, but even so, prices in 1955 were way above historical averages. So, Mt Oscar was to be stocked with sheep, and for this, stockyards were a necessity. They were located well to the west of the house and built post-and-rail style from rosewood, a local hardwood that lasts forever. Fifty years later, while returning to the Sunshine Coast from North Queensland, I took a nostalgic detour to my old home.

Unfortunately, the landing strip was no more. However, the house and yards were still there and from what I could see flying over, the yards were as sound as ever.

The landing strip was a top priority in the early days of 1955. There was a suitable site in front of the house and by April a strip had been cleared and graded, and Dad was able to fly his war surplus Stinson L5 up to Mt Oscar from Archerfield. Bush aviation was in its infancy in those days and Dad was a pioneer. He used the plane to travel to sheep sales as far away as Blackall and when the sheep eventually arrived and settled into their new home he used the plane to expedite mustering. There was never any lack of volunteer spotters from my brothers and me on mustering days.

We soon had ponies. Mum had grown up on a sheep station with horses. She knew how to look after and ride them, so we had a good teacher. We were not allowed saddles. Dad was concerned we might be caught in a stirrup in a fall and be dragged across a stony ridge. Consequently, we learned to ride bareback and it wasn't long before we could do a good day's mustering without saddles. A year or two later, the accountant expressed surprise that Dad was successfully managing 8000 sheep on a 22 000-acre property with just one stockman. 'I have four,' was the response, 'but only one on the payroll.' We were nine, eight and six years old. Child labour was alive and well, but I don't think it did us any harm.

As Mt Oscar was a sheep station, the main events of the year were the lambing season, marking the lambs, weaning them and shearing. All these activities, with the exception of lambing, required mustering, and from time to time mustering was required for drenching and spraying. So my brothers and I had plenty to do. Shearing was the most exciting time of the year. We didn't have a shearing shed so drove the sheep eight kilometres to Huntley. It had a twelve-stand shed powered by a single-cylinder horizontal diesel engine with a flywheel bigger than the Ritz. I can still hear the *thump thump thump* of it starting and the entire shed coming to life with the rattle of the overhead drive shafts powering the shearers at each stand. The shearers came with their own cook who produced the most delicious array of cakes and buns for morning and afternoon teas. It was so good that old Mr Templeton, Huntley's owner, would often come down from the main house to join us. Many years later, I discovered he was one of the founders of Qantas.

Not content with sheep alone on Mt Oscar, Dad went on to farm some of the land as well. The ill-fated Queensland-British Food Corporation had successfully planted thousands of acres of sorghum in similar country on Peak Downs, fifty kilometres to the south-east in the summer of 1948/49 only to have it cut down by frost the following May. Dad planted an experimental crop on a fifty-acre plot on the Huntley Creek flood plain. The sorghum shot up like a weed but was a magnet to the feral pigs in the district. Some were big and savage. We knew we had to keep well clear of them when out on our ponies. One morning I went down with Dad in the Land Rover to check the cultivation for pigs. We disturbed an enormous sow with a litter and somehow got between her and her babies. She charged and stoved in the driver's door as she hit us. I suspect Dad was quite pleased in a way because he knew we wouldn't mess around with the pigs after that. Despite our best efforts to deter them, there wasn't much left to harvest afterwards.

Being stockmen didn't exempt us from our studies. Lock and I were enrolled in the Primary Correspondence School in 1955 and Chris reluctantly enrolled a year later. Life in the bush was punctuated by the arrival of the mail truck each week. Sacks of potatoes, sacks of carrots, sacks of bread, groceries, jars of rum, spare machinery parts, drums of fuel and, in the mail, the reusable manila envelopes conveying the week's work from the correspondence school. Sunday was school day and as long as we finished our homework we were allowed out on our ponies for the remainder of the week. This was probably a lot easier for me than it was for Lock since I had been fortunate enough to have had two years with Miss O'Dea compared to his one.

A dearly beloved uncle, who came to visit each year bearing gifts of poetry, nurtured our cultural welfare. I still treasure *The Collected Verse of AB Patterson*, inscribed: 'Never fear the spills. Two shillings reward is offered per head for every poem of Banjo which can be recited with no mistakes. 27.4.55'. Every year when he came there would be a formal recital and we would be paid, even if there was the odd mistake. I still love reciting poetry and listening to spoken verse, particularly Shakespeare.

Another chapter in my education unfolded in the Clermont Hospital. Shortly after my eighth birthday, Molly, the expectant border collie, disappeared, presumably to deliver her litter in peace. We searched high and low until squeaking under the kitchen floor indicated she had delivered her brood under the lowest part of the house. Dad was away buying sheep, but despite Mum's warnings of snakes, spiders and bulldog ants, I waited until she wasn't looking and made my way towards the noises from the front of the house where the ground clearance was greatest. At first the going was easy, but well before I reached the litter I was having difficulties negotiating the narrowing gap between floor beam and ground. That's when I realised it wasn't mosquitos biting my right arm but redback spiders. The puppies then became the last thing on my mind.

The fever struck well before bedtime and Mum spent the night keeping me alive by keeping me warm. Fortunately, Dad arrived home first thing next morning and flew me into Clermont where Dr Farrelly, more amused than anything else, suggested a few days in the hospital for observation. I was admitted to a two-bed room where my companion was an old drover. Whatever ailed him didn't stop him talking or smoking, and being a drover, he rolled his own with one hand. It certainly took my mind off redback spiders and before long he had taught me to roll ready rubbed Navy Cut into a passable cigarette.

All good things come to an end. The fifth-grade syllabus included the nine times tables. This was not in Mum's vocabulary according to Dad. I would have to go to boarding school, and that's what happened. I was enrolled at Toowoomba Prep and started there in February 1957. We studied English, social studies, a mash of history and geography and arithmetic. This included vulgar fractions, which amused the grubby little minds of the fifth grade. We played cricket, rugby and tennis and went to chapel every day and twice on Sundays. Mr Fox, the tennis coach, insisted we never serve hard to the ladies or play deep to their backhands. Mr Mackay, the cricket coach, suggested if the field was in too close to wait for a loose ball, swing at it and let the bat go. There was also swimming and the manly art of boxing. I have never understood why it was necessary to stand your ground and face an antagonist giving you a black eye and a split lip.

But boxing did have its uses. I remember well the agony of lining up for the twelve shillings special allowance we received for our day at the Toowoomba Agricultural Show. As a Wilson, I think the only boys behind me in the queue were the Yeatses. I hope they haven't been scarred for life as well. Nevertheless, we were all off to the showground on the same bus, and the excruciating wait for the cash and Mr Smith's advice not to forget the agricultural and horticultural exhibits were forgotten as most of us bolted for sideshow alley.

I had spent the allowance well before lunchtime and faced a four-hour wait for the bus back to school. Socks down, shirttail out and disconsolate, I ran into Philip Best, a classmate in the same predicament. Shuffling unenthusiastically towards the horticultural exhibits that were free, we were sidetracked by a loud and rhythmic drumbeat, the clarion call to Jimmy Sharman's boxing tent. What a show—Mr Sharman himself haranguing the gathering from a stage erected over the entrance—banners emblazoned with portraits of the great aboriginal pugilists—the boxers dressed in their brightly coloured silk dressing gowns and soft leather boxing boots taking turns to beat the big bass drum.

The best part of the show was free and went for thirty minutes—perfect for two penniless boys. We were awestruck as the wily old showman raised the crowd to a frenzy, negotiating terms and stakes for matches between liquored-up locals and the limber members of his troupe. By the end of this process there were few punters who could resist a ringside ticket for those fights. As the lines for tickets formed, we wretchedly turned away for the flower tent.

'Hey, you boys!' boomed the megaphone, 'wanna fight?' We were shy but not shy enough to resist a place on that platform with the fighters. As the crowd bought their tickets, Mr Sharman explained to us that we were to be the curtain raiser and to fight like hell.

We were each fitted with the biggest pair of boxing gloves imaginable, stripped to our shorts and led into the ring by Mr Sharman, who introduced us to the crowd, which gave us more than enough encouragement as we battered each other for two rounds. The bout was declared a draw and the crowd was invited to throw their change into the ring for us. The split was thirteen shillings and a penny-halfpenny each, and we were allowed to watch the remaining fights. A day out to remember.

Boarders were required to write a letter home weekly. Unfortunately, my mother saved most of them. They consisted of a litany of cuts and bruises, pleas for more pocket money and tuck and a running commentary on the pet of the moment. The first letter home from Prep, dated 31 January 1957, reads:

Dear Mum and Dad,
It is alright here. There are plenty of games to play and everything. Just after you left I fell and cut my lip. The next day I was playing football and a boy tackled me and I fell on my knee and hurt my lip and front tooth but we still won. Will you send me my pencil case please? My pencils go every where in my desk.
    Lots of Love,
    from David

Lock followed a year later. This meant Chris had no playmates left at Mt Oscar. Nobody suspected a problem until the day Lock and I were returned to school after the first term vacation. As Mum and Dad got into the car to leave two miserable boys behind, Chris bailed up and refused to go. There was a hurried summit with the headmaster and Chris was enrolled at Prep, aged seven. Dad was very good at arithmetic, but I don't think even he could have imagined the cost of keeping three boys at boarding school and university for the next twelve years. Even if he had, he would not have hesitated a moment. It was not his style.

Around this time, there was a curious, and potentially catastrophic, incident. The plane was due for a mandatory inspection. Dad took the opportunity to fly Mum to Brisbane. The idea was to spend the night in Rockhampton on the way, but in any event, Dad was pleased to do so as there was a strange thud on the way, and he was keen to inspect the plane before going further. The inspection drew a blank, so they set off for Brisbane first thing next morning. There is a lot of tiger country between Rockhampton and Brisbane, and on the way, there were four more thuds, so the nervous aviator was relieved to land safely at Archerfield. Anstey Rose, who had issued the certificate of airworthiness three years before, soon found the problem. Five of the six bolts securing the propeller to the drive shaft had sheared. Dad handed the keys to Anstey and never flew again. A disaster had been averted. Who knows what the future would have been for us if that last bolt hadn't held that day.

The Mt Oscar idyll came to an end in 1959. Dan Beard and his wife had decided that they wanted to live there too. Up to this time they had mostly been living in Hong Kong. This was never going to work because Mum didn't get on with Dan's wife. So, Mum and Dad returned to Dalby. There were other forces at play as well. Grandfather Dave was nearing retirement and Mum was pregnant. It must have been very quiet at Mt Oscar without the boys. The move was wonderful for us though. Dalby is only an hour's drive from Toowoomba, so we were able to go home for the odd weekend, but more importantly, Mum and Dad often came for the day to watch our rugby matches. What a handsome couple they made, and I know I tried harder when my father was on the sideline. I wasn't the only one. In one match, another boy in the team had broken away, with his father running down the sideline shouting 'Pass it, pass it'. And he did—but to his father.

My sister, Sarah Jane, arrived in April 1960 and shortly after this we moved into our new home on Myall Creek. It was spacious, comfortable and surrounded by an acre of virgin scrub, which Mum eventually turned into an attractive garden dotted with jacaranda trees. To keep us warm during Dalby's frosty winter nights we had a large fireplace in the living room and an oil-fired Rayburn in the kitchen. Myall Creek flows 1600 kilometres south to the Great Australian Bight via the Condamine, Balonne, Darling and Murray Rivers. But because Dalby is only 347 metres above sea level, it's a very slow journey, so big rains cause big floods. The worst on record came through in February 1981, and a scene from a scratchy old black-and-white film taken from the house might have been mistaken for a storm at sea were it not for the odd gum tree waving in the gale. Fortunately, the water didn't come into the house. Mum was evacuated by a policeman on a tractor, but not before donning all her jewellery, including pearl earrings, which she didn't take off until she was home two days later. The rescuing policeman went home to find his house had been inundated while he was out helping others.

Nineteen sixty was also my last year at Prep. It was years before I could eat baked beans or apple crumble again. Apple seed husks were a prominent ingredient and we had no doubt they were actually the kitchen maid's fingernail clippings. But there was another legacy. On the first day of the eighth grade our form master, Mr Jordan, wrote a maxim across the top of the blackboard that remained throughout the year: *Success is 10 % inspiration, 90 % perspiration.* This was lost on many of us thirteen-year-olds. Perspiration made our underwear smelly because we only changed twice a week. Years later, however, I came to realise the truth in this saying. Not all of us have brains but we can all work, and with hard work it's possible to beat the lottery of life.

The next step was Churchie, my father's old school. From around 200 boys at Prep to some 1000 at Churchie, it was a big step, not just from a small school to a big one but from a modest curriculum to a much larger one. Churchie was to be the first phase in the transition from boy to man, and in this regard it was a well-oiled machine. It had everything—great classrooms and science laboratories, half a dozen sporting fields for rugby and cricket, tennis courts, a swimming pool, a well-equipped rowing shed, army and navy cadets and a chapel, where we went every day except Saturday and twice on Sunday.

The other great institution was the annual Gilbert and Sullivan production. Senior boys and teachers were cast in the main roles and the chorus was all boys. It was a very popular event with much amusement as dress rehearsals approached and the boys cast as girls had to start dressing up. In those days, rehearsals were held in an open shed called the Club Hut in the afternoons and were a popular distraction for boarders with nothing better to do. By performance time, many of us knew all the songs.

As a boarder, there was always something to do in the afternoons after school, depending on the season. Sport was considered important, but we were in no doubt our headmaster, a scholar himself, considered academic achievement to be the primary goal. I had won a swimming trophy at Prep but try as I might was nowhere near selection in the Churchie swimming team. But as I weighed less than forty-five kilograms, even when I left school, I was the ideal size for a coxswain and ended up coxing the first four.

On Friday afternoons we marched round as army cadets. I may have been the only boy who spent four years as a cadet without promotion, in stark contrast to my youngest brother Chris, who was the senior cadet underofficer in his last year.

My main achievement at Churchie was academic. I was by no means the school dux but did well enough in the public examinations to secure a place at university. Perspiration helps, and I was a keen reader, however, there is no doubt good teachers make an enormous difference. They engender enthusiasm for their subjects. For me, the best was Bill Milligan, who taught English for my last two years. He opened our minds and ears to Shakespeare, Blake, Burns, Coleridge and Keats. However, try as he did, he never did succeed with another of our set texts, Joseph Conrad's *Lord Jim*. Years later, older and wiser and living in Indonesia, the scene of the crime as it were, I tried it again. The result was no different. Joseph Conrad is hard work no matter how much you love English literature.

My greatest teacher was my father, who taught by example. He had been a keen and successful sportsman at school as a rower, rugby player and athlete. However, an injury received shortly after World War II when, having run out of fuel, he ditched a Kittyhawk on the beach just short of Merauke, gave him back problems until his dying day. Regardless, he was an excellent clay pigeon shooter and won the double rise sparrow event in the 1959 Queensland Centenary Championships. Following this, he was invited to represent Australia in an international competition but declined due to work commitments—more likely due to having to pay school fees. He was also a champion bridge player. We would often go to bridge tournaments in Brisbane or on the Gold Coast where, after a session, we would listen to Dad and his partner, Joe McGahan, discuss the hands they had played. Hours afterwards, they could both remember every card from every hand. But more importantly, Dad was a kind, gentle and generous father, who could never do enough for his family. We learned how to behave by osmosis.

It was around this time an offer was made for the family firm, Wilson & Wilson. It must have been on Dad's mind one day when he was driving me back to school. More than fifty years later, the conversation is still a vivid memory. We were not far past the racecourse on our way out of Dalby when he asked me if I had thought about what I would do at university. I didn't know and he didn't mind but suggested whatever I decided I should strive for self-reliance. Never depend on the whim of another. As part of the offer for Wilson & Wilson, Dad had been offered a permanent position on a regular salary. It must have been very tempting, but as a gambler and a free spirit, he couldn't bring himself to take the bait. The real bottom line was he would not have someone else telling him what to do.

Wordsworth wrote, *The child is father of the man*,[3] and character building was a constant theme at both Prep and Churchie. No opportunity was lost to instil the virtues of courage, self-reliance, hard work, honour and integrity. We got it in the classrooms, on the sporting fields, at school assemblies, on Anzac Day and, of course, in chapel. On leaving Churchie I decided, having been to chapel 2000 times, I had done enough. My doubts about the church were initially raised in 1959 after my grandmother died and was buried in Brisbane. Shortly afterwards, the rector of the church she attended in Dalby came round to remind her she hadn't paid her tithe. He must have been oblivious to the fact she'd died. My father was furious and never went to church again, apart from the odd wedding. Fast forward fifty years to the Royal Commission into Institutional Responses to Child Sexual Abuse. In its wake, the Church of England launched a witch hunt causing the names of Larry Loveday and Harry Roberts to be removed from buildings named in their honour. Their crime—not handling past allegations of sexual abuse in accordance with current practice. It's a fair bet neither Prep nor Churchie would exist but for the dedication of these giants. It's also a fair bet many illustrious alumni were inspired by them. Now they have been smeared by midgets—the same gutless midgets who were responsible for concealing perversion in their midst for generations.

University

My first turning point occurred not long after the results of the final school exams were published in January 1965. In our last year, we had been encouraged to think about an occupation. There was no such thing as a gap year then, so there was little time for contemplation. Dad had made it clear he didn't think there was much of a future on the land or in the family business and wanted us to go to university. Income potential figured prominently in choosing an occupation, although nobody would admit it. There was even a pamphlet ranking the earning potential of doctors, dentists, veterinarians, accountants etc. There were quite a few doctors in my extended family and doctors were top of the earnings table, so my disposition was to go for medicine. I applied for a scholarship known as a state fellowship. It would cover tuition fees and accommodation. My application failed but was returned with a note suggesting an application for an engineering fellowship would be successful. And so it was. So much for a calling. At the time I could not have imagined how significant this change was to be.

My late enrolment in the engineering faculty was accepted, so all that was needed for my new life was accommodation.

St Johns was the traditional campus college for Churchie old boys from the bush, but by this time there were no places there or at any of the other men's colleges at St Lucia. One place was available at Union College on Wickham Terrace in Brisbane CBD. It was traditionally home to advanced year medical and dental students, who spent most of their time in the neighbouring teaching hospitals, however, a new wing was under construction on campus at St Lucia and due to be opened in three or four months. It was Hobson's choice and I took it. It was a choice that brought me into contact with teachers who were important influences in my life.

The University of Queensland was the only university in Queensland in 1965. It enrolled its first students in 1911, when there were four faculties: engineering, classics, mathematics and medicine, and the classes took place in Old Government House at the Gardens Point end of George Street, Brisbane. In the aftermath of WW1, the demand for tertiary education pushed the fledgling facility to the limit. There was no room for expansion. The answer was a private bequest that enabled the purchase in 1927 of a 240-acre site at St Lucia. Construction of the sandstone centrepiece of the Great Court complex at St Lucia was completed in 1939, although the final stages of that complex at the heart of the campus were not completed until my graduation in 1970.

The new campus plan provided sites for six halls of residence or colleges. These sites were taken up by the colleges that had been established in the vicinity of George Street. But as World War II drew to a close, it became apparent more accommodation would be needed, both on campus and in town, where the new medical school and dental college had been established. And so, another war baby was born. Union College was established in 1947 in a rented building on Wickham Terrace. Max Hickey, professor of anatomy at the medical school was its first warden and it catered mainly for fourth-year-plus medical students from the country or interstate. But because the new building on campus was to be opened in the second term, there were a few freshmen in Wickham Terrace for the first term of 1965. I suspect it was something of a novelty for both Max and the older students. He had a fierce reputation among medical students, and everybody knew he didn't suffer fools, but he went out of his way to make us fledglings welcome. He lived alone in the college and often joined us for meals. On these occasions he would encourage us to take advantage of everything the university had to offer, not just our courses. He remained in Wickham Terrace when we moved into the new buildings on campus but was often there and no doubt responsible for attracting many of the wonderful tutors who joined us in St Lucia.

    The centrepiece of orientation week activities for freshman engineers was Professor Gordon McKay's welcome to the 500 students, of which two were women and less than one hundred would graduate four years later. He was a civil engineer and in his Scottish brogue reminisced fondly of his days in sewers. His most important message, and one completely forgotten by later generations, was: 'Engineers are those that build for ten shillings that which costs everybody else a pound'. That's why the Scots are such great engineers and bankers.

    All first-year engineers studied the same course regardless

of their eventual specialisation, be it civil, mechanical, mining, chemical or electrical. There were six subjects and the workload was brutal—lectures and tutorials every morning from 9 am to 1 pm and laboratory or technical drawing sessions on four afternoons from 2 to 5 pm. I suspect the strategy was to weed out the uncommitted at the first hurdle. And to assist this winnowing, there were the distractions of theatre, opera and rugby.

The University Dramatic Society, Dramsoc, did Brendan Behan's *The Hostage* in the Avalon Theatre on St Lucia Road during orientation week. I had taken part in various school theatre productions so couldn't wait to see a play with grown-ups and real girls. It was a shock. Here was the real drama missing from the cosy comedies put on at school. I joined Dramsoc as a stagehand. One of my first productions was *Rashomon*, which ran for a week and involved a horse. This placid animal was accommodated on campus in the Vet School and ferried back and forth each night by a vet student with a horse trailer. One night towards the end of the week the horse hadn't appeared. No mobile phones in those days, in fact, no phones at all at the theatre. With half an hour to go, I hitched a ride along St Lucia Road towards the Vet School and persuaded the bemused driver to take me all the way. I found our trusty steed and a halter and gave him the ride of his life for the mile back to the theatre, where we arrived in time for his entrance in the first scene. No manure to shovel off stage that night.

The first stage of the new Union College building on campus was completed early in the second term. Those of us from Wickham Terrace who wanted to be on campus moved in together with a substantial number of new entrants. The old guard had treated us youngsters very well so I left the old buildings with mixed feelings. But they were soon gone. Our new home may have been short on tradition, but it was long on style, form and function. It was designed by the university architect, Jim Birrell, who used off-form concrete, pivoting windows, imagination and a truly Australian setting to create a hall of residence to inspire generations of students. The facilities building and residential block were laid out to form a spacious courtyard nestled into a stand of mature gum trees, complete with kookaburras and currawongs. The rooms were comfortable, the food was reasonable and there was a common room with a full-size pool table and enormous fireplace—all this next to a sports field where we often played touch rugby or cricket in the evenings. It was to be my home for five years and I loved it.

My new neighbour, Warwick Gould, a first-year arts student, had a record player. This was a rare luxury but, rather than the Beatles and the Animals, he played Beethoven. I was not from a family that listened to classical music so it was a little disappointing at first, but I soon warmed to it, particularly his recording of Beethoven's Fourth Piano Concerto. One of Warwick's lecturers was Val Vallis, the poet, who had regular opera evenings at home. Val had an enormous collection and an encyclopaedic knowledge of opera and its legends. His great love was Verdi, but he had everything else as well. There would be Toscanini nights, Gigli nights, Leontyne Price nights or nights when we would listen to half a dozen recordings of the same aria and attempt to identify the singers.

Each campus college had its culture and naturally these were well developed in the older colleges since the early fifties. The new Union College was certainly heir to Max Hickey and the original college in Wickham Terrace, but the ties were tenuous as fewer than half a dozen students transferred from the Terrace to St Lucia. The architecture of the new college gave it spirit and when the second stage was completed in 1968, and Union became coeducational, a further dimension was added to its persona. I suspect, however, much of the culture developed in the new Union College was fostered by the tutors who came to reside there. They were mostly single people who lived and dined with the students and were usually happy to assist with coursework where possible.

The pioneer tutors were Dr Leo Howard and Dr Dick Staveley. Leo was a senior lecturer in the university's mathematics department and also gave several courses in the engineering department. Without his help, I would not have graduated. Dick Staveley was a senior lecturer in the economics department. He lived in one of the tutors' studies not too far down the corridor from me and Warwick Gould. Coincidentally, he was also a great friend of Val Vallis, loved opera and would often be at Val's opera evenings. Before moving into Union College, Dick had studied with Milton Friedman at the University of Chicago and often talked of the influence of Plato and Aristotle on modern economics. This, like pure mathematics, went straight over my head. Twenty years later, I was spending a lot of time in Chile where Hernan Buchi, Augusto Pinochet's finance minister, had transformed the economy. Buchi had also studied at Chicago with Milton Friedman. Perhaps Plato and Aristotle did influence modern economics.

Later extensions to the college saw the arrival of more tutors and mentors. When the warden's residence was completed in 1967, Max Hickey retired and Dr Harley Bradbury succeeded him. Like Max Hickey, Harley was also an anatomist but that's where similarities ended. Max was a flamboyant bachelor; Harley was a taciturn family man who had saved enough as a professional fisherman to put himself through medical school. The new warden's residence gave Union a new dimension. Harley and Betty, his wife, often asked students to dinner and if requested he would play his recording of Bruch's Violin concerto. An extension to the accommodation block completed in 1968 provided space for female students and an apartment duly occupied by the manager of the University of Queensland Press (UQP), Frank Thompson, and his stylish wife, Cyrelle. Despite being American, Frank had a passion for publishing new Australian poetry and, as a result, UQP became leader in that field in the sixties and early seventies.

My brother, Lockwood, enrolled in medicine and Union College in 1967. He had been stroke of the first four at school and there were enough ex-schoolboy rowers at Union to form a crew to compete in the Inter College Eights race that took place towards the end of the first term. Lock took the stroke seat and initially they trained in a shell borrowed from the university club. They showed early promise and somehow enough money was found to order a state-of-the-art shell, delivered just weeks before the race. Appropriately, it was christened 'Max', and it lived up to its name. Come the big day, Union College caught Emmanuel on the finish line and the race was declared a dead heat. It surprised us even more than it did the older established colleges. Mum and Dad were there. Max Hickey was there too. He didn't say much but you could tell he was delighted. It was Union's first result in an inter-college event. We had taken our place on campus.

Meanwhile, there were the trials of first year engineering. Maths, physics and chemistry had been interesting, intuitive and relatively easy at school, but in a slow-motion ambush we were introduced to concepts way beyond school level. Algebra and geometry were left behind for differential equations, complex numbers, vector analysis and much more, now forgotten. Organic chemistry was introduced to complicate the symmetry of inorganic chemistry, and then there was technical drawing. Nobody could make a mess of a clean sheet of cartridge paper quite as quickly as me. I gradually came to recognise the problems but was confident cramming before the exams would get me through, just as it had at school. As the exams approached, the cliff got steeper and steeper as I began to appreciate the sheer amount of work needed. I was trying to manage with less than four hours sleep. This continued into the exams and to stay awake I was taking methedrine. That was until I woke up one morning shouting and pulling the blanket over my head, dreaming I was being attacked by a room full of crows. I was so emaciated afterwards I could barely swim across the pool. Of course, it didn't work. I was at home the following January when the results were published, and I had failed. All Dad said was, 'Well, you will just have to do it again.' No mention of the fact I had lost my scholarship and he would have to pay for everything.

When do we begin to appreciate our parents' struggle to make life better for their children? For me, it was that dreadful day. I still hadn't appreciated the cost of sending three boys to boarding school for seven years, but as I lined up for my second attempt at first year, I was spurred on not just by my first-time failure but by the dawning realisation of the unnecessary extra burden I had placed on my father. Forewarned and with much youthful exuberance extinguished, I managed to pass the second time.

It wasn't all work and no play though. The year 1966 was a golden era for theatre at UQ, not just for Dramsoc but for associated organisations that could pack the Avalon, such as Willy Young's Architects Review and Bryan Nason's College Players. The year kicked off with the Inter Varsity Drama Festival, which hosted thirteen productions, including *A Singular Man, Bartholomew Fair, The Glass Menagerie* and UQ's *The Duchess of Malfi*. It was too much for the Avalon, so the Rialto Theatre in West End was hired for the job. Jack Kershaw, a final year architecture student, took on the role of stage director and asked me to be his assistant. It was a monumental effort and I'm still wondering how we managed to erect and light thirteen sets in thirteen days. Perhaps it was because the theatre relied more on performance than technology in those days.

Early in the second term, I successfully auditioned for the

title role in Dramsoc's production of Joe Orton's *Entertaining Mr Sloane*, scheduled to open in July. The play was a black farce complete with profanity, sadism, murder and bisexuality—perfect for a theatrical society that considered its duty was to shock. There was a polite review in the *Brisbane Telegraph* damming with faint praise, but it ran for a week and made a profit, so we were happy. I was stopped in Queen Street afterwards by a stranger who had enjoyed it, but I wasn't catapulted to fame, and apart from a few more minor brushes with the theatre, stuck to my studies.

Nineteen sixty-six also saw the dawn of protest in Queensland. Two years earlier, the Menzies government had decided conscription was the best way to provide cannon fodder for Australia's commitment to go all the way with LBJ in Vietnam. The war and conscription were fast becoming unpopular. It may have been the first war where the authorities found themselves unable to suppress photographs of mutilated soldiers and civilians and a countryside devastated by Agent Orange.

One day an odd student started appearing in the refectory at lunchtime. Standing on a table he denounced the war and conscription and encouraged draftees to burn their conscription cards. Initially he was ignored, but gradually larger and larger crowds gathered, and the orations moved from the 'refec' to a space outside. The speaker, Brian Laver, was soon joined by other capable speakers, including Dan O'Neil, who was a lecturer, and Angus Innes, a mature-age law student. They could never have anticipated their success. A year later, almost half the campus marched in protest along

Coronation Drive towards the city. The police managed to amass a force in Roma Street that blocked the march, but the damage had been done. The movement that eventually led to the election of Gough Whitlam in 1972, and moved on to apartheid afterwards, had been started.

To avoid the call-up ballot and almost certain military service in Vietnam, I signed up with University Regiment for six years. I was thrown out a year after joining, having been classed 'not officer material'. This immediately qualified me for the ballot. I shouldn't have been concerned; I have never won a raffle and on this occasion nothing changed. It was to be another thirty years before I went to Vung Tau to build a gas pipeline in the Mekong Delta.

Towards the end of '66, I bought a ticket for the Elizabethan Theatre Opera Trust's Brisbane season—*Don Pasquale, The Flying Dutchman* and *Girl of the Golden West*. *Don Pasquale* was a great disappointment and if I hadn't already paid for the other two, my first could well have been my last night at the opera. But *The Flying Dutchman* captured me from the overture and I have been hooked ever since.

Having passed first year, at last, it was time to choose a specialisation. The choices, in order of decreasing difficulty, were chemical, electrical, mechanical, mining and civil. It was not going to get any easier, so along with eighty per cent of my classmates, I chose civil. It was still difficult. For me, the greatest challenge was pure maths II. Fortunately our lecturer, Dr Leo Howard, was a Union College resident tutor, and having come from the bush was always more than happy to help a straggler. Goodness knows how much time he spent patiently coaxing me through basic concepts. He was such a kind man; I will never know whether I really passed the subject or whether he waved me through.

At the end of the year, Bryan Nason invited me to tour western Queensland with the College Players's new production of *The Beggar's Opera*. I was tempted, mostly because I was smitten by one of the actresses who was going. But because the tour clashed with my mandatory summer vacation employment with an approved engineering organisation, it was out of the question. Making the inevitable decision had taken time and, when at last I approached the faculty administration to apply for a position, there was only one left—Sydney-based Westminster Dredging Australia (WDA). Not exactly what I had had in mind. Dredging didn't sound much better than Professor McKay's sewers and I didn't have friends in Sydney.

I wasn't to know Westminster Dredging Australia was part of the Dutch Bos Kalis Group, the world's largest dredging contractor. Its offices were on the twenty-first floor of Goldfields House, looking down on Circular Quay and across to Bennelong Point, where the Sydney Opera House sails were taking shape. In 1967, Goldfields House was the second tallest building in Sydney. There was nothing like it in Brisbane. It certainly made a boy from the bush feel important, getting in that lift in the morning and going to the top, almost.

I was assigned to a team preparing a tender to dredge the Tamar River in Tasmania to improve navigation from George Town up to Launceston. Suddenly, engineering became interesting. There is a lot of hard rock in the bed of that river and I was launched into the world of rock drilling, explosives, grab dredges, bucket dredges, shipping schedules, weather, tides and a lot more. I didn't need pure maths II for this, but it did provide some shortcuts. As the deadline approached, it was all hands on deck tuning the estimate and preparing the submission. This included David Durack, the managing director, who was a member of the famous 'Kings in Grass Castles' family. He called me into his office on the evening of the bid due date. As it was too late to post the tender would I fly to Launceston in the morning and deliver it by hand? And from Launceston, would I join the company's survey vessel, *WDA Gannet*, in Port Phillip Bay on contract to the Melbourne and Metropolitan Board of Works? Yes and yes. My first 'overseas' trip and somebody else paying.

There wasn't a moment during that flight I wasn't terrified I would misplace the tender. However, in the taxi to the port authority's offices my thoughts turned to who might be there to receive me. The offices, with their elegant Corinthian columns, were impressive and there was a receptionist to match. I had barely finished announcing my business when she curtly pointed to the tender box and turned back to her switchboard.

With time to kill before my onward flight to Melbourne, I asked the taxi driver to take me to the Batman Bridge. Second year structural engineering had introduced the various bridge types, including the cable-stayed bridge, a new concept in the sixties. The Anzac Bridge between Pyrmont and Glebe Island in Sydney is a good example, however, the Batman

Bridge across the Tamar River, opened in 1968, is even better. Many of the orchards that had led to Tasmania being named 'the Apple Isle' were situated on the western side of the Tamar. The new bridge was built to improve access to the port of Launceston and onward shipment to European markets. That was until Britain joined the European Economic Community (EEC) five years later. Apple production was halved and 700 orchards went to the wall.

Melbourne's sewerage is treated in plants at Werribee, commissioned in 1897, and Bangholme, commissioned in 1975. The plant at Bangholme was in its early design stages in 1967, when the Melbourne Metropolitan Board of Works (MMBW) commissioned WDA to carry out seabed surveys in Port Phillip Bay in the vicinity of potential treated-water outfalls for each site. *WDA Gannet*, a purpose-built forty-foot hydrographic survey vessel, had been sent to Melbourne for the job. The survey team comprised party chief, Jerry Wardenburg, two sextant hands (Don Smith and me) and the boat driver who was a local. There was also an observer from the MMBW on weekdays. Jerry, Don and I stayed in a pub in St Kilda that wasn't too far from Brighton Marina, where we moored *Gannet* overnight.

The survey involved measuring water depths with a recording echo sounder on parallel lines around fifty metres apart across the required survey area. There was no GPS then—we used sextants to fix the vessel position at one-minute intervals. The party chief would call 'Fix' and mark the echo sounder roll with a fix number and plot the boat position from the sextant angles. It kept us all busy and at the end of the day we would adjust the echo sounder depths for tide level, transpose the depths to a chart and draw in the contours by hand.

It was a punishing routine. Melbourne can be hot in January and this one was particularly so. On the 31st, the temperature was over 43 °C. The high temperature was accompanied by strong winds that developed through the morning to the extent that even in the enclosed waters of Port Phillip Bay, survey operations were impractical since it was impossible to distinguish the seabed profile from the wave profile on the echo sounder record. We could, however, achieve three to four hours work daily by being onsite as soon as there was enough light to distinguish our survey beacons. This meant leaving the hotel at 4 am to be at Werribee at daybreak.

It soon became apparent that MMBW thought we should be doing more each day. It was a day-rate rather than a lump-sum contract, with standby payment clauses. This unhappiness came to a head one day when Jerry was advised our client would be sending a delegation to join us. It turned out to be an amusing day. First, one of their representatives arrived late for the 4.30 am departure, so by the time we arrived at Werribee the waves were already building. The jolly banter that accompanied our departure soon evaporated. At this stage, Don, my co-sextant hand and an ex-P&O steward, offered coffee all round. This improved morale for a moment until one by one the MMBW team started spewing. We had to turn for home and call it a day. Later, Don confessed to lacing their coffees with a little salt—apparently an old trick of the cruising line trade. A harmless joke perhaps a trifle overdone. Jerry wasn't amused but there were no more complaints.

I returned to Brisbane at the end of the summer break determined to be a civil engineer. The ten weeks or so with WDA had given me a taste for the business of engineering and a realisation that there was a lot more to it than turning complicated calculations into untidy drawings. Despite my resolve to avoid a repetition of my first-year failure, in the two years that followed there had always been the nagging spectre of another defeat. That was now gone. I could see the way forward; I could imagine a life beyond. I launched myself into third year with renewed vigour and it showed in my grades. There were even a few credits.

The big event of 1968, however, was the completion of extensions to Union College, which included a women's section, thus making it the first coeducational residential hall on the UQ campus. Union went from being the new college to the cool college. It certainly influenced some of the men who hitherto may have been less than presentable at breakfast. There were a few amorous liaisons. However, the most noticeable effect was the improved esprit de corps, particularly in intercollege sport where the men tended to respond favourably to support from the opposite sex.

At the end of the year, WDA offered me a vacation job in New Zealand—this time a real overseas trip. The Tauranga Harbour Board was in the process of turning its port into the largest in the country. WDA was contracted to dredge the entrance channel from seven to ten metres draught and was undertaking the work with *WDA Seven Seas*, a trailer suction hopper dredger (TSHD). These look a bit like old-time oil tankers with a deckhouse supporting the navigation bridge towards the stern and hoppers with bottom-opening hatches forward. The ship's main engines and pumps are housed below deck aft of the hoppers and materials, such as sand, silt, soft clay and gravel, are pumped from the seabed into the hoppers via a suction pipe (or pipes) that trails along the seabed as the vessel steams forward. Having filled the hoppers, the suction pipe is raised and secured on deck as the dredger steams to a suitable dumping site, usually remote from the dredging area, and discharges the load through the bottom opening hatches. *Seven Seas* had a hopper capacity of around 2000 cubic metres and was only about eight years old when it mobilised from Europe to Tauranga. Contemporary TSHDs have capacities up to 35 000 cubic metres.

The ship's officers, engineers and deck crew were predominantly professional seamen with seagoing qualifications. There was sufficient onboard accommodation for a delivery crew, however, during dredging operations only essential personnel such as the captain and the chief engineer remained aboard. The remaining crew members were accommodated onshore in Mount Manganui where we had our project office. The normal work week was six twelve-hour day shifts and five twelve-hour night shifts. Dredging works were suspended at 6 pm on Saturdays and on Sundays the marine engineers would carry out planned maintenance work, particularly on the dredging pump, which was so big a welder could quite easily hard face the entire impeller through an access manhole. On Saturday nights, it was customary for the day and night shifts to get together for a barbeque. On Monday mornings, the night shift from the previous Friday started as the day shift.

My job was to assist with frequent surveys of the dredging areas in the port and the dumping areas outside. Each survey resulted in a coloured contour map and cross sections that would be used to plan the work and lodge claims for progress payments. The survey vessel we had used in Melbourne, *WDA Gannet*, was shipped over for the job. However, rather than use sextants for position fixing we used a Decca Hi Fix system that measured distances from fixed transmitters to mobile receivers with low frequency radio signals. This provided horizontal control for the dredger and the survey boat, thus eliminating discrepancies that might have occurred had different systems been adopted for each vessel. Nevertheless, I was disappointed the sextant skills I had developed in Port Phillip Bay were never required again.

The interesting aspect of this job was our solution to dredging over the shallow sand bank that formed the northern perimeter of the harbour approach channel. Parts of it dried at low tide, but it was possible to safely dredge there on high tides with the hoppers empty. This was achieved by diverting the dredging pump discharge to a fifteen metre-long, 800-millimetre-diameter pipe suspended over the port side by an 'A' frame. Thus, the dredger could run along the bank starboard side at high tide, moving material from the shallows to deeper water in the channel where it could be safely dredged at any tide.

Once again, my newborn belief that life as a civil engineer

was what I wanted was reinforced. It promised an interesting life among interesting people. When the third-year results were published and I had to take a supplementary exam in my old nemesis subject, engineering maths B, WDA arranged for me to undertake the exam in Auckland rather than Brisbane. It was a generous gesture. But that wasn't all. On the condition I would pass the supplementary and my final-year exams the following November, I was offered a job on graduation. And that's exactly what happened.

Graduate Engineer

The university protest movement wasn't Australia's only legacy from the Vietnam War. Demand for nickel went through the roof. Tiny exploration companies were floated. Prospectors went out and, as Banjo Patterson put it, defied *the stings of scorpions and the bites of bull-dog ants*[4] to discover the new El Dorado. Sure enough, just as my final year was drawing to a close, an unknown miner, Poseidon Nickel Ltd, announced the discovery of a substantial nickel-ore body in Western Australia. Its shares, which had been trading at AU$0.80, were well over AU$200 when, as a brand-new site engineer for Westminster, I arrived in Cairns in February 1970. By then the country was gripped by an epidemic of speculation. The All Ordinaries Index went to an all-time high. If you couldn't afford Poseidon, you bought something else, and if you couldn't do that, you went prospecting. North Queensland was considered prime territory. Surely it was only a matter of time before a new Charters Towers or Mount Isa was discovered. Cairns was the epicentre of this activity. It crawled with geologists and swung to the beat of Creedence Clearwater Revival. They had the best parties because they were paid a fortune and liked spending it after weeks in the bush. I was more than miffed to discover graduate geologists' starting salaries after a three-year course were double that of graduate civil engineers after a four-year course. I shouldn't have worried. Poseidon crashed about six months later and their jobs followed soon after.

Many years later, I learned that one of my fox hunting friends in Leicestershire made his fortune as a messenger in an Australian stockbroker's office, spending his wages on Poseidon shares rather than beer.

Westminster's contract with the Cairns Harbour Board was to undertake maintenance dredging in the port's approach channel to a depth of eight metres. The board had its own dredger, *Trinity Bay*, which was built in Germany in 1912 but she was now feeling her age and unable to compete with the sugar plantation sediment washed down the river by the summer rain. Westminster had dredgers that could, so *WDA Seven Seas* was mobilised from Tauranga. *Seven Seas* could dredge and dump as much material from the channel in a day as *Trinity Bay* could move in a week. The channel was around thirteen kilometres in length and ninety metres wide, so the dredging was much simpler than it was in Tauranga and there was nowhere to go aground. *Seven Seas* could steam up and down at the ideal dredging speed of about three to four knots and, having sucked up its fill of spoil, sail for the dumping area in deeper waters offshore. The load and dump cycle was about three hours, so in a good week it could excavate around 80 000 cubic metres of silt from the channel.

Again, Decca Hi Fix was deployed to provide horizontal control for the project, but dredging companies are nothing if not adventurous. Laser technology was in its infancy, the first related patent having been issued in 1960. Westminster had been unable to resist the temptation to try out the latest in technical wizardry to improve dredging efficiency. This came in the form of lasers that could be set up onshore to generate parallel wafer-thin vertical beams along each side of the channel that could be seen well out to sea depending on the observer's elevation. Robbie Burns may well have been thinking of this experiment when he wrote of the 'best laid plans …'[5] When we, the survey team, had persuaded the captain of the dredge that looking into these lights would not send the crew blind or impotent, they started using them. The only problem was that the initial progress surveys showed deep furrows down each side of the channel and virtually no progress in the middle. Fixing this was quite difficult as whenever the dredger steamed close to the furrows the suction head tended to fall in, thus exacerbating the problem.

It took a month or two to adjust to life as a grown-up with a real job, a real salary and a company car—well, a Mini Moke. By this time, the job was going well, so something was bound to go wrong. It was a Friday night, and the younger members of our team were leaving the bar of the Great Northern Hotel in the Mini Moke. I was driving. We had learned from our new friends, the geologists, the Cairns police prided themselves on their drink driving conviction record, which was second to none in Queensland. As a Friday-night drinking driver, one had to be careful. Not long after we had taken off, I became aware of a following car. I headed for our project manager's flat, which was just down the road above the Hertz rental car park. I pulled into the yard, parked the car, jumped the fence at the back of the yard and made for the docks. *Seven Seas* was alongside for the night. The police would never find me there.

They didn't have to. They found me in the office the next morning. I was soon to learn of the farce that followed my flight. My colleagues, who were unaware of the following police, had assumed I was visiting our project manager so got out of the Moke and climbed the stairs to his apartment. The police were close enough behind to see this. They followed and arrested our hapless project manager, who was at the door greeting his unexpected visitors. Eventually, the police were persuaded they had an innocent bystander but only on the proviso that the real suspect came forward the following day. And he did. I told them that, busting for a pee, I had gone off looking for a lavatory. There wasn't much they could do apart from charging me with driving without due care and attention, culminating in an appearance in court, an article in the *Cairns Post*, a fine and drivers licence suspension for one month.

The work in the entrance channel finished by summer's end and *Seven Seas* went up the river to the local shipbuilders, North Queensland Engineers and Agents (NQEA), for an overhaul and repairs. All Westminster's senior personnel and ship's officers were transferred to other projects. The dredger's marine crew remained on board, and I was left to keep them busy chipping and painting above deck while NQEA got on with their work below. I was also seconded to the Cairns Harbour Board to monitor the progress of *Trinity Bay*, which was dredging the inner harbour area.

These assignments brought me into close contact with two institutions in Cairns in the early 1970s, which took me back to the days of pearl luggers and Lord Jim. The Burns Philp Ships Chandlery was a living museum—a corrugated iron shed with timber flooring from the Wharf Street entrance to the wharves at the rear, suffused all the while with the scent of tar and hemp. A mindboggling assortment of pulley blocks, shackles and general rigging hung from the rafters, and once you knew what you were looking for you could find anything from rosin, turpentine, tar, linseed oil, tallow, varnish, chain, rope, nails, nuts and bolts to tools and galley supplies. But whereas Burns Philp was commercial, the Cairns Harbour Board was not. It operated from an imposing oversized Queenslander on stumps to keep it clear of the spring tides and was surrounded by verandahs to keep it cool. The extraordinary feature was the men's lavatory block, where the cedar-panelled partitions between the WCs were no more than a metre high. This meant that during one's morning constitutional one could discuss business with a neighbour or just read the paper and have a smoke. And this was typical of the Cairns Harbour Board—the archetypal rent-seeking organisation that couldn't even manage its own dredger.

There were still high spots in the inner harbour and my job was to regularly survey the area with *Gannet*, locate the highs and present the information to *Trinity Bay's* captain. It was a slow process but this didn't matter too much as I was enjoying my independence in Cairns and the maintenance on *Seven Seas* was also taking longer than anticipated.

Eventually *Trinity Bay* managed to dredge the inner harbour to the required eight metres and NQEA completed its work on *Seven Seas*. Her next assignment was off Mackay where the approaches required maintenance dredging and I was to receive a lesson in man management. The deck crew on *Seven Seas* was from Newcastle upon Tyne. Geordies are a pugnacious lot at the best of times and these lads were particularly annoyed when I insisted they finish chipping and painting the deck winches during the voyage. When she left Cairns, I paid the bills and drove down to Mackay.

Seven Seas arrived a day later in the early evening. I met her as she berthed and picked up my old friend from Tauranga days, Tama, the Māori cook. You can be on the wrong side of everybody on a dredger except the cook. We went to a nearby pub for a few beers and dinner. As we were leaving, he went off to find the men's and we agreed to meet in the carpark. Who should be there when I arrived but two loud Geordie deckhands who had clearly been drinking in a different part of the pub. 'Look who's here laddie,' the leader yelled to his mate as he came at me, fists flying. I managed to retreat without any damage but thought I was in big trouble when I was grabbed from behind by the collar and hoisted to one side. No trouble at all. It was Tama. He was an enormous man and didn't like those Geordies any more than I did. He set to work on them, and it was terrifying. In the end, I had to stop him seriously hurting them. The police and the ambulance were called. Onlookers confirmed the two men in the ambulance had started the fight. After they had been patched up in the hospital, they were locked up in the police station. I vouched for them in the morning and they were released. No more trouble with the chipping and painting.

The Mackay job came to an end in October and I was

sent to Western Australia where Westminster had won a contract in Dampier. This was a new port from which the first shipment of iron ore from Australia to Japan had sailed four years earlier. Lang Hancock had first discovered iron ore in the Hammersley Range in 1952 but kept the discovery secret until a government embargo on iron ore exports was lifted in 1960. He then entered into an arrangement with Rio Tinto to develop the mine at Mount Tom Price. Rio Tinto in turn entered into an agreement with Japanese steel mills to sell sixty-five million tonnes of iron ore forward over sixteen years. This agreement secured the finance needed to build the mine, the railway to Dampier and the port, and the first iron ore cargo from Australia to Japan sailed in August 1966.

The project must have been a success because four years on Westminster's brand-new dredger, *WDA Endeavour*, built in the Evans Deakin yard in Brisbane, was mobilised from Sydney to dredge the approaches to a new ship loader to be built on East Intercourse Island. My job as hydrographic surveyor was to set up and maintain the horizontal control system for the project using Decca Hi Fix and to monitor the progress of the dredger by carrying out regular seabed surveys across the project area. Despite summer approaching and days with temperatures in excess of 40 °C not unusual, this wasn't a bad job in Dampier. But from time to time it was necessary to attend to onshore survey stations and this could be uncomfortably hot. Few cars had air conditioning installed in those days and it was a toss-up whether one drove with the windows up or down. But early in December, there was an incident that saved me from the worst of the Dampier summer.

Endeavour was a 1600 cubic metre trailer suction dredger capable of dredging to a depth of twenty-three metres. When dredging, it steamed at about three knots in a prepared pattern in the dredging area with the lower end of the suction pipe scraping along the seabed. The dredged spoil was pumped into its hull and, when full, the suction pipe was hauled inboard for the trip to deeper waters offshore where the hull doors were opened to dump the spoil. Then the cycle was repeated. To ensure the dredging pump was always positively primed, the pump room in the dredger was located below the water line. Since pump maintenance was a regular necessity, a gate valve was installed in the hull upstream of the pump. This valve could be closed to allow access to the pump whenever required and was normally closed when the pump was not in use.

Endeavour worked six twelve-hour day and five twelve-hour night shifts a week, with Sunday being a maintenance day. Saturday was barbeque or pub night. As for the Mackay job, on Monday mornings, the night shift from the previous Friday started as the day shift. During dredging, most of the wear and tear is sustained by the teeth on the bottom of the trailer suction pipe and the main pump impeller, so on Sundays these were the main items on the agenda. Impeller life is prolonged by 'hard facing'. This involves laying beads of hard steel over the mild steel impeller blades using a simple welding technique and special welding rods. Access to the pump impeller is via a hinged access cover in the pump casing secured by ring bolts.

On a particular Sunday morning in December, I was out,

as usual, on the survey vessel running a progress survey over the dredging area. This was a tedious task made even worse by a hangover in 40 °C temperatures. The SOS came mid-morning: 'Bring the launch alongside immediately'. I was happy to abandon the survey and headed off towards *Endeavour*, which I was surprised to see was under way rather than at anchor. As the gap closed, I was even more surprised to see the ship's dinghy towing in its wake with a man at the bow and a cleaver in his hand. By this time, *Endeavour* was at full tilt heading for the beach about a mile away. I tried to manoeuvre alongside but the superintendent waved me off and over the radio explained what was happening.

As usual, first thing on Sunday the welder had gone down to the pump room to hard face the impeller. He loosened the ring bolts on the pump casing access cover and, as usual, water poured out. It always did, as there was always water in the pump, even when the gate valve to the sea was closed. But that Sunday it wasn't. The pump operator, in his rush to go on leave at the end of the Saturday shift, hadn't closed it. The welder hammered the ring bolts free. By the time he realised what was happening, it was too late. He couldn't shut the access hatch but managed to close the pump room compartment door as he escaped. This isolated the main ship engines but flooded the electric operator on the gate valve. By the time he had raised the alarm, attempting to close the gate valve from the bridge might have blacked out the entire ship, so the captain decided to beach it and did. The man in the dinghy was the cook. In the panic, he jumped into the dinghy, taking a cleaver with him to cut the towline, just in case.

As soon as *Endeavour* was aground, they tried closing the gate valve and it worked. It made it easier to pump the water out and float her, but the repairs were to take months. I was sent back to Sydney and the next time I saw *Endeavour* was in Botany Bay, two years later. Dampier is no place to be in the cyclone season and, having escaped, I was not in a hurry to return. Back in Sydney in Westminster's offices in Goldfields House on Circular Quay, I noticed The Maritime Services Board (MSB) of New South Wales was advertising for construction engineers for a new port development in Botany Bay. I responded and after an interview was offered a job. My interviewers could barely disguise their interest in my experience on dredging projects. Marcus Brutus again.[1]

> There is a tide in the affairs of men.
> Which, taken at the flood, leads on to fortune;
> Omitted, all the voyage of their life
> Is bound in shallows and in miseries.
> On such a full sea are we now afloat,
> And we must take the current when it serves,
> Or lose our ventures.

Botany Bay

In between Dampier and Sydney, I was able to join the family at Alexandra Headland for our traditional summer break. We had done this since the early sixties, when Mum and Dad had decided Surfers Paradise was too exciting for three teenage boys. We usually made the journey from Dalby to the coast on the first Saturday after Christmas, where for ten years or so we would spend a fortnight at Shemara Court on Alexandra Headland. In those days, it was a prominent landmark with panoramic ocean views and short walks to the surfing beaches at Alexandra Headland and Mooloolaba. There were twelve units at Shemara and many of them were taken by families we knew, such as the Martins and the Tonges. Over the years, we got to know many of the others. Indeed, the Sunshine Coast, as it came to be known, with its sleepy beachside environment, became not just part of Wilson family life but home away from home for countless families from Brisbane and Queensland's south-east.

Dad was in his element. He loved surfing and parties. Days at the beach usually started with the early surf at Mooloolaba followed by rum and milk and ham, eggs and tomato on toast with as many of Dad's friends as he could muster. The next set piece was the morning swim, also at Mooloolaba, which began to assemble at around 10.30 am. A procession of beach umbrellas, surfoplanes and towels assembled family by family in much the same spot each day. There was no set pattern to the afternoons. It depended on the weather. If it was hot, as it can be in January, staying in the surf was a good option; otherwise there was tennis, golf, water skiing, sailing on the Maroochy River and fishing. Dad was a keen fisherman and many years later it was the tailor fishing at Warana Beach that ultimately persuaded Mum and Dad to build their retirement home on Oceanic Drive.

There were few, if any, restaurants on the coast in those days and even fewer pubs. You had to be over twenty-one to go into a pub anyway. So in the evenings we made our own fun. There was usually a barbeque somewhere and often those gatherings would progress to dancing to the music of the day—Beatles, Stones, Creedence and Elton John. Otherwise, there was the drive-in picture show and associated adventures.

Bronzed, refreshed and enthusiastic, I took off for Sydney travelling light—brain only, no laptops, no iPads, no mobile phones. I pack more for a weekend these days. I had maintained contact with an old friend from UQ Dramsoc, Hilary Furlong, who offered me a room in her flat in Elizabeth Bay across from the Rushcutters Bay Cruising Yacht Club, less than ten minutes' walk to King's Cross and less than twenty minutes by bus or train to the Maritime Services Board offices on Circular Quay. It could not have been a better place to start manoeuvres in Sydney.

By 1970, the MSB was struggling to provide the facilities

needed in Port Jackson to accommodate the increasing drafts of bulk carriers for oil, coal and wheat. At the time, the port's main channel had been dredged to fourteen metres and the maximum depth available in the wharves at Darling Harbour and White Bay was eleven metres. The solution was to develop a new port at Botany Bay to accommodate ships drawing up to twenty-one metres. This was a challenge first recognised by Arthur Philip in 1788. He had been advised by Sir Joseph Banks to establish the new colony by Botany Bay but was disappointed. Despite its expanse, approximately six kilometres in diameter, Botany Bay was shallow and exposed. With an average depth of less than five metres at low tide and a spring tidal range of 1.25 metres, it offered no safe anchorage. A week later, Arthur Philip moved to Port Jackson. These days, this decision would require a parliamentary public works committee review.

Following extensive investigations, including the construction of a hydraulic model the size of one and a half football fields, it was decided to locate the new port on the bay's eastern side. The first stage of the development involved dredging the port entrance channel and basin to a depth of twenty-one metres, reclaiming 300 acres of port and industrial land and constructing a 1400-metre-long armoured embankment to protect the reclaimed land southwest from Bumborah Point. At the time, there were two oil refineries in Botany Bay, the Caltex Refinery at Kurnell on the south side and the Total (Boral) Refinery at Matraville on the north side. Crude oil deliveries for both refineries came in via the Caltex tanker terminal at Kurnell. Total's crude was pumped from there to Matraville in a twenty-two-inch-diameter subsea pipeline. This pipeline crossed the proposed new port entrance channel so had to be removed to facilitate the dredging. It was to be replaced by a multi-products single-point tanker mooring to be installed in Yarra Bay. Spoil from the dredging for the turning basin for this mooring would be used to extend the Kingsford Smith Airport's main runway, some 1500 metres into Botany Bay. This was an epic plan and as a young engineer I was fortunate to become a part of it. I was to learn a lot about harbour and marine civil works in the next two years.

Frits de Wit was the MSB's Botany Bay Port Development project engineer and I joined his team in the board's offices on Circular Quay on 2 February 1971. Work didn't commence on-site until July, but there was plenty to do evaluating preliminary designs for the wharves and port layout. Not long after my arrival, a time-share computer terminal was installed in the office. I learned Fortran IV, and the sheet pile analysis programme I developed saved a lot of work, but I was pleased when we moved out to our site office at Bumborah Point.

My social life in Sydney didn't enjoy such a good start. While in Cairns I had gone riding on Trinity Beach with the wife of a geologist doomed to weeks in the bush searching for the new El Dorado. Girls will be girls—she seduced me. Later, she had returned to Sydney where she was staying with her parents in their northside harbour mansion. Boys will be boys—I called, and we met for dinner. It had been an enjoyable evening until she lured me down to the boat shed where we got into a clinch and she asked me to marry her (even though she had one husband already). This was too much and I bailed up. She became terribly upset and jumped into the harbour, threatening to drown herself. I followed, trying to mollify her, all the time expecting the lights to come on in the big house and a confrontation with an irate father. Fortunately, the harbour cooled us both down, there were no lights, and we managed an uncomfortable adieu.

Chastened by this narrow escape, I sought solace with old friends from UQ Dramsoc days. Don Batchelor was stage manager for *Hair*, which had been running at the Metro Theatre in Kings Cross for two years. This was just round the corner from the flat, so I would often go down there for a beer or two after the show. Jane Harders was always busy on radio or in various plays around town and eventually took the role of Janet in *The Rocky Horror Show* when it opened in Glebe a few years later. Nevertheless, whenever possible we would meet for dinner or go to a play. Hilary Furlong, my flatmate, who worked in casting in The Australian Opera, mentioned the company's new season was coming up soon and would I like to be a spear carrier in *Turandot*? And be paid for it! Well, yes, I would. My theatrical career was taking off with no effort at all. The first of twelve performances was on May 8th.

If I hadn't been hooked on opera before, my spell in that wonderful production in The Elizabethan Theatre, Newtown, did it. *Turandot* is a strange opera with a twisted moral. It is a tragedy with a happy ending wherein the hero, Calaf, falls in love with and eventually wins over the villain, Turandot, but not before Calaf abandons the servant girl, Liu, to her fate as she is tortured by Turandot's henchmen. As one of the guards restraining Donald Smith as Calaf during the torture scene, I was less than yards away from Joan Carden as she sang Liu's last aria, 'Tu, che di gel sei cinta'. This is one of the most beautiful in opera and may be the last aria Puccini wrote before he died in 1924. Joan Carden certainly did it justice.

Later in the season, I performed further spear-carrying duties in *Figaro* and *Nabucco*. The latter is an old-school fire-and-brimstone story with a more-or-less happy ending wherein the Hebrews are saved from annihilation when Nabucco the Assyrian undergoes an eleventh-hour conversion. My performance didn't go smoothly. I was called in at the last minute, so there was little time for rehearsal. Act Two opens with Abigaille, Nabucco's adopted daughter, surrounded by lackeys and complaining bitterly about her lot. I was a kowtowing lackey downstage facing the audience so missed the cue to exit stage left for the soprano's lament 'Anch'io dischiuso un giorno'. Abigaille was supposed to have the stage to herself as she delivered this tender soliloquy. My presence wasn't noticed for a few bars and it was some time before I realised the urgent whisperings from the wings were for my benefit. The soprano, the famous Gwyneth Jones, would not have appreciated the audience titters as I crabbed towards the wings during what was supposed to be one of her most poignant moments.

Around this time there were several occurrences that, although inconsequential at the time, were to have a significant impact on my future. While taking a Saturday afternoon walk across Rushcutters Bay Park, I stopped to watch a rugby game. The supporters of the team in blue seemed friendly so I approached them and having learned they were of the Colleagues Rugby Club, whose home field was not far away in Rose Bay, asked if they were looking for players. They were and invited me to attend practise the following Tuesday night. This I did and a week or two later started playing as a breakaway in the club's second or third team. Shortly thereafter, Hilary Furlong's lease in Elizabeth Bay expired. To be closer to the MSB's offices on Circular Quay, I moved into the Port Jackson Hotel at the northern end of George Street in The Rocks, cradle of Australian civilisation. Norman Lindsay, author and illustrator of Australian classic, *The Magic Pudding*, has left numerous sketches inspired by scenes from this neighbourhood.

Less than a week later, while having a beer after rugby practice, it transpired one of the front rowers in my team, Chris Egan, was living in a hotel in The Rocks, not 500 metres away from the Port Jackson. The Captain Cook Hotel was at 33 Kent Street on a corner with High Lane. Its licensee, Dick McMahon, and his partner, Peter Ryan, of Golden Sheaf fame, had bought the hotel some three months previously. To avoid having to accommodate casual guests, Dick had filled the hotel's accommodation with acquaintances at a nominal weekly rent. There was a spare room, and to make sure I got it I moved in that night. It was June 1971 and the beginning of my friendship with Dick McMahon.

Dick had been a sales representative for Philip Morris so was a relative newcomer to the pub trade. He probably hadn't appreciated the effort involved in running an operation from

10 am to 10 pm, Monday to Saturday. The lunchtime trade was mainly city professionals. Some of them came back for a beer after work while waiting for the traffic to subside. Thereafter it was mainly dock workers. The permanent inmates were an eclectic bunch. Chris Egan was a solicitor's clerk, 'Tex' Saddington had the NSW sales rights for Slendertone weight loss machines, 'Rooster' Martin was the NSW rep for Gilby's Gin, and Gordon 'Bleu' was the Irish chef who stayed from time to time and produced tasty and wholesome bar lunches. Then there were two attractive barmaids who only stayed occasionally. They were professionals and knew how to chivvy the punters along without getting into too much trouble. Neva had very long legs and wore hot pants. Aideen was from Ireland.

With the benefit of Google Earth Street View, I can see the hotel is much as it was fifty years ago. Our accommodation was upstairs and I had the room on the High Lane corner looking south across Kent Street to the Ranvet Laboratory where Percy Sykes invented potions to keep racehorses racing. To the north over High Lane, there was a fish and chip shop with an upstairs flat. Ranvet is no longer there but the fish shop is, albeit with a slightly grander name, Fish at the Rocks. The footpaths on the northern and eastern sides of the hotel were sheltered by a continuous awning. From time to time there would be a party in the accommodation quarters and on these occasions the awning would be used by people in various stages of undress for inter-room access. These nights must have been amusing for the woman in the flat above the fish shop less than ten metres away.

Meanwhile, back at the MSB, a $32 million contract for stage one of the Botany Bay port development had been awarded to the Atkinson-Leighton Joint Venture in April. Atkinson International was an offshoot of the Guy F Atkinson Company from USA and would be the manager of the project, with Leighton Contractors as the Australian partner. They awarded a subcontract to Amsterdam Ballast-HAM Dredging Joint Venture for the dredging. A separate contract was awarded to IHC Holland for the supply and installation of the single point mooring (SPM) in Yarra Bay. IHC built the SPM in Sydney from a design prepared by a subsidiary organisation, Single Buoy Moorings Inc, now known as SBM Offshore. Rock dumping for the 1400-metre armoured embankment initiating from Bumborah Point commenced in July 1971. Frits de Wit's four-man project team moved from the MSB's head office to a site office on Bumborah Point in mid-August. Frits was the MSB's nominated site representative. His assistant was Trevor Todd, whose focus was the embankment and land reclamation behind. Jack Langby was an experienced site inspector, whose priority was to ensure the concrete tribars providing the outer armouring for the embankment were manufactured to specification. My job was to monitor the dredging works and the installation of the SPM. This meant I needed to be available on weekends and would need my own transport.

I had always hankered after a motorcycle and thought that, at age twenty-four, if I didn't buy one then I never would. And, besides, my salary had recently been raised to $7000 a year, so I could afford it. I bought a second-hand two-stroke

Yamaha 250, which was delivered to the site at Botany Bay where Trevor Todd, having observed it would be a handful for a learner, gave me some rudimentary lessons. For a week or so I practised riding up and down Bumborah Point Road, which had little traffic in those days. At the end of that week, I rode all the way home after work. It seemed like a great moment and, being a Thursday, an excuse for another Captain Cook–type party for which planning was unnecessary.

The next morning, slightly hungover but still excited by the novelty, I jumped on the bike and headed for Botany Bay—down Argyle Street, south along George, east along Circular Quay and south into Phillip Street to be stopped by a red light at the Bridge Street intersection. Traffic queued behind. The light turned to green and as I took off, I stalled. It took several feverish attempts to restart and by the time I had done so the lights were red again. Nobody had been able to pass. The indignation behind was palpable. After an age there was another green light. There was no way I was going to stall it again. Lots of throttle, drop the clutch and away I went, not south along Phillip Street but straight up. I landed on my back with the bike on top. I was winded but had nothing more than a few bruises. A bystander helped me and the bike off the road. The traffic moved away. Perhaps they felt compensated for the inconvenience. The helpful bystander handed me a card. I glanced at it. What do you say to somebody who has given you a 'Jesus Saves' card? Not much, except 'thank you'. I managed a conventional take off and headed south for Botany Bay and the SPM.

The SPM was chosen because of the many advantages it

offered over other tanker berth types, such as multi-buoy moorings and wharves. The most important feature was that tankers could be moored and unmoored with minimal tug assistance and, having moored, could swing freely with wind and tide while loading or discharging. When not in use, the polypropylene mooring lines and floating hoses could do the same. When discharging, the cargo flows from tanker to the buoy via the floating hoses and from there to shore via under-buoy hoses connected to a subsea pipeline. The body of the Botany Bay buoy was a 9.5-metre cylindrical doughnut divided into six watertight compartments. It was to be anchored to the seabed by six anchor chains, each attached to a fifteen-tonne anchor.

It would be a first for Australia and, of the twenty or so installed worldwide at the time, the first with a three-product swivel, meaning it could accept crude oil, black refined products, such as fuel oil and white refined products, such as naphtha. Despite its promise, the SPM installation was dogged with difficulties and though only a small element of the port development project it became a major headache leading up to its commissioning in May 1972, and afterwards.

The problem for the buoy during its installation was there were too many cooks and nobody in charge. Since the dredging for the SPM basin (to fifteen metres) had to be completed before the mobilisation of the dredging for the port entrance channel, it was undertaken by French contractor, Société Nationale des Travaux Publics (SNTP), with its trailer suction dredger *Atlantique*. At the time, SNTP was under contract to the Commonwealth Department of Works on the Kingsford Smith Airport runway extension. It beggars belief, but before the SPM basin dredging was finished, the Total refinery had installed the submarine pipelines out to the SPM, and IHC Holland had laid the mooring chains and anchors. This meant *Atlantique* was trying to dredge around the pipelines and the chains to finish the job. Fortunately, it didn't damage the new pipelines, but it did dislodge chains, which meant it was difficult tensioning them properly when the buoy arrived.

In October 1971, in an effort to meet a contractual milestone, IHC launched the buoy and towed it from Port Jackson around to Botany Bay before it was completed. They deluded themselves that the outstanding work, which included fitting the turntable and swivel and completing some of the painting, could be just as easily completed onsite. That is rarely the case and certainly not the case on a buoy bobbing around off La Perouse two kilometres in from the entrance to Botany Bay. It was directly in the path of swell produced by dominant winds from the south and, if this wasn't enough, the wave pattern generated by reflected waves from the new embankment became even more confusing and disruptive for any work except on calm days, which were few and far between.

IHC muddled on. A floating crane was mobilised to install the turntable, which incorporated a small jib crane, and this was used to finetune the anchor chain tensioning so that the buoy was accurately positioned directly over the pipeline end manifold (PLEM) on the seabed. Four submarine hoses were installed to connect the product swivel on the turntable to the PLEM. Finally, the floating hoses and mooring lines were connected to the turntable and the buoy was ready. Everybody and his dog were out to watch *ST Texaco Bombay* berth on Mayday, 1972, in perfect weather and conditions. Everything went according to script. The 167-metre, 23 334-deadweight tonnage (DWT) tanker discharged 16 000 tonnes of naphtha at 260 tonnes per hour and left three days later without incident.

The contract had not gone well for IHC, but it had taught me a lot about working in a marine environment. IHC's diving contractors taught me to dive with scuba and Hookah gear, and the MSB was happy for me to do this after I had passed the appropriate medical examination. This skill was not only useful in Botany Bay but a great asset on future projects in East Kalimantan, the Persian Gulf and the Red Sea.

SPMs are now an industry standard in suitable locations. The site chosen for this buoy in Botany Bay was not. It's unlikely it would have been suitable for any mooring given its proximity to the new embankment downwind from the dominant weather. It made tanker captains nervous and waves reflected from the embankment confused the sea state and necessitated a tug in attendance or engines slow astern to avoid impacts between tanker and buoy. The floating hoses and mooring lines were also a problem without a tanker on the mooring. They needed constant repair and replacement, and spares were not immediately available. But this was one of the first SPMs installed worldwide and certainly the first in Australia, so it was not well known that these moorings need to be in open water where tankers have unlimited manoeuvring space and can vacate the berth in a hurry without tugs, if necessary. Despite its problems, the SPM served its purpose until 1985 when it was decommissioned along with the Total refinery.

Having commissioned the SPM, it was now time to remove the twenty-two-inch-diameter submarine pipeline connecting the Caltex refinery at Kurnell to the Total refinery at Matraville. This would enable the completion of the port entrance channel dredging. The line was around four kilometres long and had a 1.5-inch-thick concrete coating providing sufficient weight to keep it submerged when empty. The plan was to cut the pipe on the southern side of the entrance channel and pull the northern half of the line out piece by piece with a twenty-five-tonne winch installed on the Matraville side of the bay. This would have been a routine task were it not for an accident that miraculously didn't kill anybody.

A massive concrete foundation approximately 150 metres from the water's edge on the pipeline alignment was prepared for the winch weeks before the operation. The plan was to pull the pipe from the bay in fifty-metre sections. The pull was rigged as a double tackle with two twenty-five-tonne capacity twin sheave blocks around fifty metres apart. This configuration meant there were four wires pulling the pipe from the bay instead of one. The scene was set to begin the pull in late September. The winch was started, and the wire was tensioned just enough to enable a final check of the rigging and instrumentation before gradually increasing tension to the estimated level deemed necessary to move the pipe. The safe working load for the 1.5-inch-diameter steel wire rope was about twenty tonnes, so in theory it was possible to exert an eighty-tonne pull on the pipe. The reading on the load cell was approaching seventy tonnes when the winch began to struggle. The pipe held fast. The load cell vibrated and the strain in the wire was there for all to see. The cast of assorted riggers, welders and plant operators instinctively moved back. If the winch operator had held the tension at this level the pipe may well have broken out from the seabed, but he didn't. He gave it a little more. There was an explosion and a vicious wire dance. It wasn't apparent at the time but the explosion was the twin sheave block nearest the pipeline disintegrating. The pent-up energy in the 200 metres of wire strung between the blocks was released in a malevolent hissing pirouette. That nobody was cut in half was a miracle. The job was completed weeks later with bigger gear. With the pipeline gone there was no impediment to completing the entrance channel dredging and the 300-acre port land reclamation.

As mentioned earlier, rock dumping for the core of the reclamation commenced in July 1971. The original idea for the core was sandstone, but this was later changed to basalt for its superior durability and availability around Sydney. This rock core was extended south-west from Bumborah Point along the required alignment by dumping rock on the seabed, laying a construction road on top and extending by dumping more. By late September, the embankment core had reached 500 metres of its eventual 1400-metre length. The cutter suction dredger, *HAM 211*, arrived from Dampier and started pumping sand into the reclamation area at around

2000 cubic metres an hour. At this rate, the project was creating around ten acres of port land a month. The cutter suction dredger, with its limited mobility, worked in the area immediately to the south of the reclamation. From there it was possible to pump its spoil directly into the reclamation via a floating pipeline. Later in October, a trailer suction dredger, *Willemstad* started dredging the entrance channel and dumping its spoil adjacent to *HAM 211* for transfer onto the reclamation.

My job was to monitor these operations and the monthly survey of the reclamation quantities. I normally did this on days when weather prevented work on the SPM, and as this was around fifty per cent of the time, it worked well. The additional benefit was I knew *HAM 211* people from Dampier days, and in July 1972 *Endeavour* arrived from Dampier having completed its repairs and the job, so it's fair to say client/contractor relations on the Botany Bay project were cordial. Early in 1973, Ian Hanson, HAM's works manager, gave my brother Chris a job as a deckhand on the *211*. A year later, Chris had muscles and more than enough money for an odyssey to England where he was to spend ten years.

Concrete tribar manufacturing commenced offsite in a yard at Taren Point in August 1971. In November, a casting yard was established onsite just off Bumborah Point Road on the reclamation. This provided excellent access for the dozens of ready-mix trucks required for each pour. At twenty-five tonnes apiece, the tribars were and still are massive. The process involved creating a reinforcing steel cage, assembling reusable steel formwork around the cage using spacers to ensure a minimum of one inch of concrete cover over the reinforcing steel, pouring the concrete, waiting a week or so for the concrete to set, removing the formwork, weighing and inspection.

Inspection was the killer. Jack Langby was ruthless. If he found any sign of the reinforcing cage on or near any surface, the entire tribar was condemned. He redlined hundreds—all twenty-five tonnes each. There was no way to repair them; they were taken away and scrapped. This was not a trivial requirement. Inadequate concrete cover over reinforcing steel exposes the steel to corrosion, particularly in a marine environment. Corroded steel expands and in doing so spalls off its concrete cover, thus exposing more reinforcing and so on, and those tribars were to be the first line of defence against the big seas that roll in from time to time. Forty-five years on, they are still doing their job, a monument to an inspector who didn't compromise for anybody. These days Jack's job would be done by a team of ineffectual QA/QC functionaries whose only interest is to delay projects because they are paid-by-the-hour consultants.

Atkinson-Leighton started placing tribars on the face of the embankment in January 1972. It was a dangerous operation requiring precise communication between diver and crane operator when placing underwater units. By March, the tribar armament on the embankment extended 200 metres from Bumborah Point. Its efficacy was demonstrated in a storm that tested the wall with waves in excess of three metres. The tribars were untroubled but sections of the rock core, construction road and reclamation beyond the protection of the tribars were breached, with ten-tonne rocks thrown from the core with apparent ease.

Dad was in Sydney for a few days in August and was able to visit the site. The night before had been wild, the embankment had been damaged and although there was a tanker on the SPM, the crew had been unable to connect the hoses. It was a day that vividly illustrated the challenges of the project. I introduced Dad to my colleagues, and Frits de Wit graciously made kind remarks about my progress and application. Apart from a visit to my office in London a few years later, it was the only time Dad saw at firsthand what I was doing. It may not have been quite what he had in mind for me, but it would do for now. I think he would have preferred me to have remained in Australia and done exactly what he wouldn't do, that is, work for somebody else.

Meanwhile, the Captain Cook Hotel had attracted an interesting clientele. As CBD office space became scarce in the early seventies, many companies moved to the city fringe. This included the northern end of Kent Street, and Dick McMahon concentrated on wooing the lunchtime trade from the professional offices moving to the neighbourhood. Perhaps the most prominent was IBM. There was also the Esso office managing its new oil and gas developments in the Bass Strait. Another was Global Engineering from Tulsa, Oklahoma, owned by larger-than-life Colonel Sanders lookalike, Ray Olsen. They were Esso's process engineers responsible for the front-end engineering that was to provide the design basis for those early platforms and pipelines. They mostly wore alligator-skin boots and shoestring ties. We got to know them well as many were away from home and enjoyed the after-work scene in the Captain Cook. They were my first contacts with the upstream end of the oil and gas industry that was to become my life, and in the years to come, I often ran into them in the more remote parts of the world.

While life in the Captain Cook was fun for the inmates, it was hard work for Dick. His morning started well before seven in the cellar, rearranging beer kegs and flushing the delivery lines to the bars. And that was just the start of preparations for the daily opening at 10 am. In addition to the upmarket lunchtime and evening trade, there was the wharfie trade, which trickled up from Darling Harbour as morning and evening shifts came to an end. The pub was busy from the off to 'Last rounds please' at 10 pm. By that time, Dick was usually out on his feet, but every now and then after the doors were closed, he would suggest a trip to his old stamping grounds in North Sydney. He had been a Joey's boy, where his crowning achievement had been selection as scrum half for the first fifteen. From there, he joined Philip Morris as a travelling salesman, continuing his rugby with the Mossman Club on winter weekends. One of the places still open in North Sydney at that time of night was Dionysus, a steakhouse with a bar in a vast basement in Alfred Street. The food was good, and the atmosphere created by the music of the time—Elton John, *Tiny Dancer*; Carole King, *It's too Late*; Rod Stewart, *Maggie May*; and Aretha Franklin, *Bridge over Troubled Water*—meant there were always people there late at night. Dick knew many of them, including Robin Preston, one of the owners, and on my first visit there she came over for a brief hello as we ordered dinner.

Fifty years on, I still remember being mesmerised as this goddess came our way. As Dick introduced us, I was captivated by her grace and might have made an ass of myself, but before I could, she gently said 'hello' and resumed her exchange with Dick. Then she returned to the bar, and I spent the rest of the night trying not to gaze at her—long dark hair, brown eyes, softly spoken and beautifully dressed. She was truly Aphrodite in a Dionysian cave. In the following weeks Dick began to realise why I was so keen to revisit Dionysus at such regular intervals. He was amused and suggested I might as well fall for Monica Vitti. Robin had an estranged husband and a small daughter and didn't need a poodle.

I miss the days when I was prepared to take a chance. In the ensuing weeks, my regular attendance at Dionysus paid off and one evening I remember just as well as the first, I invited her to the theatre. She accepted. For months afterwards, love trumped everything, but headwinds began to blow. Robin had other interests—her daughter and a new restaurant she was starting in St Leonards, designed to capture the TV studio market. I wasn't mature enough to find a way around them and it all came to nought. That was that. I never saw her again and she won't know I still think of her.

In March 1972, two more Americans came into the Captain Cook for lunch. They may have been related to Victor Kiam, because they enjoyed Gordon Bleu's lunch so much they came back the next day and made Dick an offer for the hotel he couldn't refuse. I don't think he told them owning a hotel meant working twelve hours a day, seven days a week—or about the vomiting drunk suffering a heart attack he had resuscitated by mouth to mouth one night.

We, that is, the assorted residents, had to leave. The solution was a large house for rent in Parsley Road, Vaucluse. The team of Dick, Chris Egan, Tex, Rooster and I moved in. Aideen came too. The neighbours weren't amused, particularly those on the southern side. It's a small world. They came from Dalby, knew Mum and Dad and didn't think their grand life in Vaucluse should be interrupted by our parties. Their misery was short lived. Dick's infatuation with a girl who had gone to London a year or so earlier got the better of him, and a month after we had moved in, he bought a ticket for London and left. Piece by piece, the team crumbled and a month or so later a good friend of Dick's, Paul Enemark, offered me the attic of his house in Reserve Street, Annandale, and I was more than happy to accept. Paul was from the world of advertising, which was new to me and interesting. He also had an encyclopaedic knowledge of racing and racehorses, which may be why he rarely had a bet.

Life away from work wasn't all ribaldry and decadence. My association with the Australian Opera had only increased my appetite for the theatre in all its forms, and Sydney had it all. My main interest was opera, and it was fun seeing the singers I had come to know in 1971 in their new roles in the magnificent 1972 season—*Lucia*, *Rigoletto*, *Cav and Pag*, *Forza*, *Rosenkavalier* and *Fidelio*. But there was more. The ABC had a subscription concert series that included a 'youth series', for which I was still eligible and went to every concert

I could. There was ballet season, which I didn't enjoy so much and still don't, apart from *Romeo and Juliet*. Then there was the theatre where I was able to keep up with old friends from Brisbane. I remember seeing Jane Harders as a particularly venomous Lady Macbeth.

After an apprenticeship of about a year on the Yamaha 250, I traded it in on a Honda 500 Four. This was a grown-up tourer, and just before Easter in 1973 I took the bike up to Brisbane on the train, rode out to Dalby and spent a few days at home. Then I rode back to Sydney. It's a 1000-kilometre trip and I did it in just over eleven hours, including stops for fuel, during which it was necessary to re-tension the drive chain as well. I was becoming an overenthusiastic bikie and was flattered to be invited to join a group of real motorcyclists who were off to Bathurst for the Easter races. They rode proper bikes—Laverdas, Moto Guzzis, and Nortons, but stooped to include a Japanese bike on this occasion as I was distantly related to one of the group, Guy Hayes.

The racing was fun and despite the fact we were camping the weather was perfect. On the Monday, we headed north for lunch at a winery near Mudgee and, uninhibited by the blood-red wine, headed home. We came into Sydney on the Pacific Highway and the closer to home the faster we went. I was trying to keep up with Guy on his Laverda 650. What a noise it made. But it wasn't the bike that made him faster than me; he was a much more experienced rider. It all came unstuck at an intersection near the Ryde Hospital. Guy had gone through a green light, which changed to amber. A Mercedes Benz coming from the opposite direction turned right, thinking I would stop. I couldn't, I was going too fast. I tee-boned it and said goodbye as I went over the top and felt my boots brush the handlebars.

The details came to light afterwards. I came to rest nearly one hundred metres from the collision. The next thing I remember was coming to in an operating theatre or something similar. Given the nature of the accident they may have been expecting internal injuries. There was an apparition in a white coat standing over me with a terrifying syringe. I passed out again. Later, I woke again in a recovery ward with a traffic policeman bending over me with a notebook. His left arm was in a cast from bicep to wrist. He was quite pleasant and I asked him how he had injured his arm. Trying to stop his bike falling off its stand. My only injury, apart from all-round muscular aches and pains, was a small cut to my upper lip. My gear had saved me—full-face Bell helmet, leather jacket, leather gauntlets and sturdy leather boots. It was all a write-off, as was the bike. The car had been towed away. Fortunately, the driver was uninjured.

The policeman asked me a few questions and left without saying much. Regardless, I knew my riding/driving days were numbered as this offence, no matter what the charge, would undoubtedly tip me over the edge to suspension, given the demerit points I had already accumulated for speeding. Guy Hayes rescued me from the hospital and took me to his home where I lay helpless on the floor for at least three days, with Guy manhandling me backwards and forwards to the loo.

Had I been lucky or unlucky? Depends on one's point of view. But having returned to work, my luck certainly took a turn for the better. IHC Holland, the SPM contractor, had a subsidiary in The Hague called RJ Brown and Associates (RJBA). It was a specialist submarine pipeline design consultancy. Its Singapore office was recruiting for a new project in New Zealand and in a week or so the RJBA boss in Singapore would be transiting through Sydney on his way to New Plymouth. Would I be interested in meeting him for an interview? Yes. Arrangements were made for us to meet in the transit lounge at Mascot at 6.30 am on 15 May 1973. It was three weeks since the accident. My relationship with Harold Myles, IHC's manager in Sydney, had not always been smooth but he must have given me a good reference because the meeting with my new boss, Art van Lent, was little more than a formality. As I was to learn later, Art was not interested in small talk. We shook hands on a salary of US$1000 a month and I agreed to make my way to New Plymouth as soon as possible.

I didn't like the idea of leaving the Botany Bay project before its completion, but it would have been difficult working there without a driver's licence. I could spend a year or two out of Australia and come home with a clean slate. Frits de Wit couldn't have been more helpful and gave me leave to tidy up my affairs in Sydney and to go home for farewells. He had been a tremendous mentor for a fledgling engineer such as myself, and even though he may have thought he had failed, I have never forgotten his methodical approach to any task regardless of complexity.

The Total refinery at Matraville was closed in 1985. There was no longer any need for the SPM, so after thirteen years' operation, Australia's first SPM and my first tangible creation, was decommissioned. Port Botany was eventually opened in 1979. It now handles around 1700 ships a year. In 2013, I took a ride on a container ship from Singapore to Sydney via Jakarta and Freemantle. The voyage ended in Port Botany. Forty years on, I could tell Jack Langby's tribars were as good as new and ready for another forty years.

On 23 May 1973, four weeks after my extraordinary escape from the collision in Ryde, I was on a Boeing 707 heading for Auckland. For the next two years, the police sergeant in Dalby would call on my father with a summons for me to appear in the court on a charge of dangerous driving. It was never served. I was to live abroad for the next twenty-nine years.

My Year of Living Dangerously

I can still remember how excited we students were in 1967 with the breaking news of Israel's first victories in the Six Day War. Ariel Sharon became a hero, crude oil prices shot through the roof and, but for brief spells, have never looked back. As I left Australia six years later, I wasn't to know that for the next year or so I would work on a kaleidoscope of projects that would launch me into the oil and gas industry in an era striving to diversify energy supply away from the Middle East. All this was made possible by crude oil prices sustained at record levels by relentless conflict in that part of the world.

The first project was the Maui gas field. When it was discovered, thirty-four kilometres off New Zealand's Taranaki coast in 1969 with reserves of 3.8 trillion cubic feet (Tcf) of gas, equivalent to 660 million barrels of oil, it was considered a monster. But in a seismically active area in the Tasman Sea in water 110 metres deep, the gas would not be easy to come by. The seas surrounding the North Sea oilfields, under development at the time, were benign by comparison. The Maui project would push technical boundaries to the limit and the financial risk, even with oil at record levels, was palpable. Financing was eventually achieved when the New Zealand

Government entered into a thirty-year take-or-pay contract for the gas in exchange for fifty per cent ownership of the field.

The main players in the team assembled by Shell BP Todd (SBPT) to develop the field were Global Engineering, process design; Earl and Wright, jacket design; and RJ Brown and Associates, pipeline design. Because the field was rich in hydrocarbon liquids, such as propane and butane, these were to be separated offshore. Therefore, there would be two export pipelines, a thirty-inch-diameter pipeline for the dry gas and a ten-inch-diameter pipeline for the valuable liquid by-product. RJBA's tasks were to undertake a survey to select the best route for the pipelines, bearing in mind they had to cross a known fault line in a seismically active area and to design a concrete weight coating for the pipelines that would ensure their integrity during installation and operation. My job was to assist RJBA's senior surveyor, Joe Moll, with the offshore survey work.

It was exciting. After an overnight stopover in Auckland, I took a local flight and arrived in New Plymouth early the next morning. Joe was there to meet me and took me into town where I was checked into the Devon Motor Lodge, the go-to place for all the new arrivals on the project. We then went straight to the SBPT project office where I met Paul Dantz, our RJBA team leader. He was busy preparing lattice charts for the pipeline survey area. This was a high priority if the survey was to avoid the worst of winter in the Tasman Sea, and it was already the end of May.

The best route for a pipeline is the shortest unless there is a compelling reason for a detour. Since the pipelines had to start at the platform, the purpose of the survey was to find an acceptable landfall closest to the platform and then to carefully survey the straight line from there to the platform location. Paul and Joe had examined the available maps and photographs, visited the area and decided the coastline between the Cape Egmont lighthouse and Opunake offered several landfall options. The priority would be to undertake a reconnaissance survey to pick the best.

The survey vessel chartered for the job, *RV Acheron*, was a seventy-six-foot ex-fishing boat with a wooden hull, twin Cummins diesel engines, accommodation for fourteen and a captain, Alex Black, who oozed common sense, and later, when we did encounter wild weather, made us feel safe if not well. The wooden hull was considered important to minimise interference with the electronic equipment.

The equipment and technicians needed to maintain, deploy and operate it had arrived by the end of May. The key to any survey is reliable and accurate horizontal control (navigation). Nowadays, this is readily supplied by a GPS system. In 1973, there were barely any satellites let alone GPS. The latest technology available for a job of this type was the Motorola Range Positioning System (RPS). This system measured the precise distance between a series of shore-based transmitters set up on permanent trig stations to the north and south of Opunake and a receiver attached to the mast of *Acheron*. With this data and the pre-prepared lattice charts, it was possible to continuously monitor and plot the position of the survey vessel and the equipment used to gather the data necessary for the pipeline design.

This equipment included a fathometer, side scan sonar and shallow seismic profiler.

The fathometer continuously measured and recorded the distance to the seabed from a transducer rigged over the side of the survey vessel. The instrument produced a continuous paper record annotated every minute or so with a position fix from the RPS. The water depths recorded offshore would later be corrected for tidal rise and fall using data from the tide gauge recorder in New Plymouth. This data would then be used to create a contoured hydrographic chart to record features identified from the side scan sonar and seismic profile records.

Side scan sonar records are produced by transducers housed in each side of a tow fish towed astern the survey vessel by an umbilical rigged to maintain the fish at a height above seabed between ten and twenty per cent of the swath width. In deeper water the typical swath width was 300 metres (that is, 150 metres on either side of the vessel). In shallower waters this would be reduced to 150 metres. The instrument produces a continuous picture of seabed features within the swath, such as shipwrecks, rock outcrops or debris that might influence pipeline route selection.

Shallow seismic profiles are produced by generating a sound pulse and recording the echoes returned from the seabed and the varying geological layers to a depth of around sixty metres below the seabed. These records could be used to interpolate strata between known boreholes. The shallow seismic profiling sound source generator was located on a small catamaran towed around fifteen metres astern the survey vessel on the port side. The hydrophones used to receive the return echoes were towed fifteen metres astern on the starboard side.

To survey a predetermined area the survey vessel runs a series of parallel straight lines at around five knots with all the survey instruments running, that is, horizontal control, fathometer, side scan sonar and shallow seismic profiler. The line spacing is determined by the width of the side scan sonar swath, around 300 metres in the deeper water and less inshore. Every minute or so, the position of the vessel is recorded as a 'shot point' and the shot point number is annotated on each of the paper records to facilitate the onshore data reduction process.

The first week of the survey was plagued by bad weather and equipment failure. *Acheron* had to operate from New Plymouth, a good four-hour trip north of the survey area. Often, she would leave port in reasonable weather only to return as it deteriorated. Joe Moll was a seasoned sailor but the technicians manning the equipment were not so lucky and were often *hors de combat* before any work had been done. Eventually, on June 1st, the weather improved enough for *Acheron* to operate nonstop for sixty hours until they ran out of lattice charts. They covered the inshore area from the Cape Egmont lighthouse south to a sandy beach just to the west of Oaonui. Joe Moll could tell from the side scan sonar records that this beach would be an ideal landfall for the pipelines, and this was confirmed when the records were examined in greater detail in New Plymouth. The added advantage was this beach offered the shortest route from the Taranaki coast to the proposed Maui platform. The remaining challenges were to survey the route to the platform location and make a careful examination of the Egmont fault zone crossing, with a view to determining whether future earthquakes posed any unacceptable risk at that point.

My job during this period was to look after the onshore RPS transmitters, which meant lugging twelve-volt car batteries over sodden paddocks in the driving rain. But this was to change. Joe's wife fell ill in Singapore and was admitted to hospital, so Joe left to be with her. Paul asked me to take over as party chief on *Acheron* and I was delighted to do so—anything to avoid lugging batteries, even if I wasn't so sure how I would respond to the sea conditions. It was blowing a gale as Joe left, but on the afternoon of June 6th (D Day) Charlie Mallowes, the lighthouse keeper, rang to say he thought the weather was improving. By evening we had prepared enough navigation charts to complete the inshore survey off the beach at Oaonui and make a comprehensive survey of the fault zone. We went aboard *Acheron* at 9 pm and eventually left New Plymouth at 4 am, when Alex Black thought we had a reasonable chance of doing some work. The sun was rising over Mount Egmont as we arrived at the fault zone—a ready reminder of the way home in an emergency. Fortunately, the weather exceeded expectations and in the next twenty-four hours we were able to run all the lines planned to cover the fault zone and a thirty-four-kilometre line from the coast at Oaonui to the platform location.

The preliminary plots were encouraging. We were able to identify the Egmont fault line well below the seabed on numerous shallow seismic records and to establish there was no visible sign of the fault on the seabed. There was no evidence the fault presented any credible threat to the pipelines. The line we had run from the tentative landfall, across the fault and all the way to the platform, was also free of any feature or obstacle that might necessitate a deviation from a simple straight line.

Bob Brown (RJ Brown of RJ Brown and Associates), who was in town to schmooze the client, was over the moon. We could not have handed him a better present than the shallow seismic records that defined the Egmont fault. Later, I was to discover Bob was like a big kid with submarine pipelines and associated toys. In retrospect, it can be seen that the surge in oil prices was luring the industry into deeper and deeper waters, so the pipelines had to follow, and Bob was one of the leaders in promoting innovations such as semi-submersible pipe-lay vessels, pipeline trenching ploughs, high strength steels and automatic welding that propelled pipelines from waters thirty to 300 metres deep between 1960 and 1980.

We pressed on with the preparation of navigation charts, which would enable us to run a further five lines out to the platform to provide a surveyed corridor 1500 metres wide. We were able to run another thirty kilometres of survey lines on June 11th, in ideal conditions off Oaonui. At about 3 pm a southerly breeze began to disturb the glaze on the water. Twenty minutes later, we were hauling in and securing the gear in a three-metre swell. An hour later, we were on our way home in force-seven conditions and very pleased to be alongside after an extremely rough four-hour trip.

By 9.30 the next night, conditions had improved

sufficiently for us to head out to the survey area. We deployed the equipment in marginal conditions, which got worse as we ran lines out to the platform location and back inshore to Oaonui, where we retrieved the gear and went home. We were stuck in New Plymouth for the next five days. The elation that followed confirmation of a textbook pipeline corridor dissolved into gloom as it looked as if our weather window had gone and we might be stuck in New Plymouth for the rest of the winter. We were shaken out of our misery by an earth tremor that rattled the crockery, a novelty for us visitors but hardly worthy of comment from the locals. But it did mean that at the next available opportunity we could rerun survey lines over the fault zone to detect any possible ground shift.

Just when we thought we might never finish, Charlie Mallowes called from the lighthouse to say the weather was moderating. We had pre-plotted every possible navigation chart that might be required and took off from New Plymouth late on June 18th, determined to finish the work, come what may. A week later we had. Altogether we ran around 400 kilometres of survey lines. We surveyed a complete corridor from Oaonui out to the platform location. The maximum tidal range on the Taranaki coast is 3.7 metres, but normal ranges is 2.3 metres, so we used the high tides to run lines as close as possible to the proposed landfall beach. We ran north-south lines across the platform location and found the wellhead on the seabed with the side scan sonar, thus demonstrating the accuracy of the Motorola RPS. We were even able to mimic survey lines that had been run across the Egmont fault zone before the earth tremor of the week before.

There was no evidence of any change. Almost fifty years later, the pipelines are still there and still working, so we must have done something right.

Back in New Plymouth, we were very pleased to unload the equipment from *Acheron* knowing we had all the deep-water data necessary to design and build the pipelines. It had not been easy. None of us in the survey crew had escaped the misery of seasickness, particularly in the final week when we had been determined to soldier on in marginal conditions.

The last outstanding item of field work was to take levels on the beach at Oaonui within the proposed pipeline corridor. We engaged a local land surveyor and, with a low spring tide, Paul Dantz and I accompanied him to the site. The idea was for me to take a survey rod to those places on the beach where we wanted levels and for the surveyor to observe and record the levels. I wore a wetsuit, which enabled me to wade out into the water almost as far as *Acheron* had been able to approach the beach on high tides. Unfortunately, I became overzealous and was swept out in a rip. I was never concerned for my safety as the wetsuit was quite buoyant and I'm a reasonably strong swimmer, but I was swept a long way south and it took almost two hours to get back to my distraught colleagues who had almost given me up. We never did recover the survey rod.

It took three months to issue the survey report—a month for data processing and a further two drafting the thirty detailed maps required to present the data. Although I was involved in checking the mapping, I had time to assist Paul Dantz, who had begun to prepare preliminary designs for the pipelines. This was my introduction to submarine pipeline design and I had a very good teacher. If Paul wasn't enough, Bob Brown spent a week with us in mid-August to review our approach and make a presentation to potential contractors. His enthusiasm was infectious and thirty years later when I designed my last pipeline (a thirty-two-inch-diameter crude oil pipeline across Siberia) I would ask myself 'How would Bob do this?'

Although those of us remaining in New Plymouth after the survey were busy, there was time for rugby, golf and parties, and there is no doubt the locals were keen to make us feel at home. SBPT had its own rugby team, and I was invited to join. It was wonderful playing rugby on the luxurious sward of a Kiwi rugby field where you can fall with impunity and still have bloodless knees and elbows. The English Rugby Team, including Fran Cotton, Andy Ripley and Roger Uttley, toured New Zealand in September. The tour included a game against the Wellington representative side at Athletic Park. We, that is, the SBPT team, were invited to play a curtain-raiser against Shell Wellington. What a day! We beat them and I scored a try. As it happened, it was to be my last game. In mid-October I was on my way to Singapore and playing rugby in a sauna was not my idea of fun.

The Maui gas field went into production in 1979. By 1985 it was producing 300 million cubic feet of natural gas a day, enough to fire a 2000-megawatt power station. Its anticipated life was thirty years. In 2016 it was still producing around forty million standard cubic feet a day (MMscfd), still a valuable addition to New Zealand's energy mix.

My next project assignment was associated with the

latter stages of the development of an extraordinary project in what is now known as West Papua. The Dutch, clearly aware of its rich mineral and energy resources, held on to Dutch New Guinea long after Indonesian independence was acknowledged by the United Nations in 1949. Eventually, in 1962, after a dodgy referendum, the province became part of Indonesia and was called Irian Jaya. The name was changed to West Papua in 2003.

As the story goes, a seismic survey run by Royal Dutch Shell in the 1960s showed extremely promising results in the Sele Beach area, sixty kilometres south of Sorong. The geophysicists involved pleaded in vain for an exploration drilling program. Eventually they resigned, having secured from Shell an option to purchase the lease and the seismic records. They formed a company and called it Petromer Trend. Irian Jaya No.1, their first exploration well, tested at 63 000 barrels a day and was less than three kilometres from the navigable waterway leading into Sele Beach. It was the biggest oil-producing well in Asia by far. Their second well came in at 20 000 barrels a day.

Sele Beach and its jungle hinterland receive three metres of rain a year. Civil works were a muddy nightmare but, apart from that, the development was simple. Crude oil production from the wells flowed under wellhead pressure through eight-inch-diameter pipelines to a simple gas-oil separator plant and flare constructed at Sele Beach. Storage was provided by a tanker permanently moored in the protected waterway off the beach. Export tankers were to moor alongside and load directly from the storage tanker.

If the Petromer Trend discovery hadn't been enough for its shareholders, just imagine their delight in October 1973 when the Yom Kippur War pushed crude oil from US$20 to US$50 a barrel. And now they were close to their big pay day. The first shipment of around 150 000 barrels would be worth US$8 million. Alas, how swiftly delight turns to despair! Just weeks before the big pay day, *MS Hoegh Pride*, a hapless cargo vessel delivering project material and stores, strayed outside the Sele Beach channel markers and went aground. She drew 9.5 metres. Lloyds of London advised Petromer Trend they would not insure their crude oil cargoes until a licensed hydrographer had proved Sele Beach Channel was at least ten metres deep.

RJBA Singapore was appointed to run the survey. The main project in the Singapore office at the time was the design of a forty-eight-inch-diameter submarine pipeline from Royal Dutch Shell's refinery on Pulau Bukom to a new SPM to be installed in the harbour to the south-west of the refinery. Pulau Bukom is a small island only five kilometres south-west of the main island of Singapore. For survey support on this project, RJBA had appointed a newly formed company, United Surveyors. Its founder and owner, Commander Tan Choo Haw, was a retired officer from the Malaysian Navy. He was also a licensed hydrographer, knew exactly what was needed to satisfy Lloyds and had agreed to do the work. I had arrived in Singapore from New Plymouth on 20 October 1973 (towards the end of the Yom Kippur War) and was to accompany him.

We left on the four-stage 2700-kilometre journey to Sele Beach in a twin engine Beechcraft, *Volpar*, on November

2nd. The first leg to the west coast of Borneo and Pontianak, where we refuelled, took just over two hours. The next leg east to Balikpapan took just over three hours. In those days, the lush green cover over Kalimantan was unscathed. Years later, vast tracts of these forests and savannah had been burned and cleared for transmigration and coconut oil plantations. Transmigration was the forced migration of poor families from Java to less densely populated areas of the Indonesian Archipelago. The coconut oil plantations were industrial affairs usually developed by the Chinese friends of President Suharto's wife, Ibu Tien, otherwise known as Madam Ten Percent. Next stop was Manado on the northern tip of Sulawesi where we spent the night. Manado has enjoyed a European presence since the early part of the sixteenth century and is famous for its beautiful Eurasian women. We were only there overnight, and it goes without saying those beauties stayed well away from our seedy hotel, which was heaving with Japanese coconut oil traders.

We took off for Jefman Airport at 5 am the next day. Built by the Japanese on a tiny island in 1944, it was used as a forward base to attack the Americans after they had seized Biak about 480 kilometres away to the east. Coincidentally, Jefman was even closer to another WW2 island airport, Middleburg, built later in 1944 by the Americans. It was a reminder that six weeks after the atomic bomb was dropped on Nagasaki, my father took off from Ross Airbase near Townsville in a Mustang he was delivering to Labuan Airbase off the west coast of Borneo. He flew the 5000-kilometre trip outbound via Merauke, Hollandia, Middleburg, Morotai and

Zamboanga. The return trip in a Kittyhawk was not quite as successful. Just short of Merauke he ran out of fuel and landed on a beach where he was rescued by locally based Dutch aircrew. Years later, when I had learned to fly myself, I appreciated what an epic journey that had been in a single engine aircraft with no more than the most rudimentary navigation aids in a region where the weather can turn violent in minutes.

Petromer Trend's loudmouth redneck foreman was there to meet us in the *Ruby*, our survey vessel for the next week. As we motored down the approach channel to Sele Beach, we passed the hapless *Hoegh Pride* still aground and still out of the channel. It would be a long wait for a suitable rescue tug to steam the 3000 kilometres from Singapore. At Sele Beach we were welcomed by Petromer Trend's friendly Australian area manager, John Naylor. He showed us to our basic accommodation hut, the company mess and to the assortment of buoys, weights and wires being assembled to enable us to sweep the approach channel. All the footpaths around the camp were corduroy, a continuous raft of small logs floating on mud. If it wasn't raining in the camp, it was going to rain.

Choo Haw had prepared a large map of the approach channel, complete with all the channel markers, to be our basic navigational aid for the survey. Having settled into the camp, we took a longboat and went out to the channel to verify the positions of the markers. Fortunately, they were all in the expected locations. *Ruby* had an echo sounder, so the next day we used her to run a series of transverse lines, around one hundred metres apart, across the approach channel. We plotted the results the next morning and found no highs in the channel above the minus-ten-metre contour. There was a high degree of probability the channel was clear of obstacles. All that was necessary now was to sweep it along its three-kilometre length to prove it beyond doubt. This was to be done by towing a wire along the channel suspended between two boats at ten metres, plus a tide allowance below the waterline. This took a day, and the following evening we flew back to Singapore from Sorong.

The Gulfstream twin turboprop had the range to take us back to Singapore nonstop. All was well until we approached Kalimantan and, in the darkness, could see lightning flashes in the distance. There was no need for the pilot to instruct us to fasten our seatbelts. At first, there were the usual bumps, but as we flew into the cloud, which reached way above the ability of the aircraft to avoid it by climbing, everything changed. We were surrounded by lightning, which illuminated and amplified the surrounding chaos. The plane would suddenly drop into an apparent void, leaving the sound of the engines far behind. When it seemed the fall would never end, the sound of the engines caught up as they regained traction and fought to recover lost altitude. Then it would start all over again and I don't think there was a man on that plane who wasn't terrified or who was sure we would make it to Singapore. Clearly we did, and with all the flying I have done since, I'm pleased to say I have never experienced anything remotely like it.

All in all, this trip had taken a week. Petromer Trend was

soon to load its first crude oil cargo, which was sold to Shell's Pulau Bukom Refinery in Singapore. Everybody except *Hoegh Pride's* insurers were delighted. Art van Lent was so delighted he gave me a US$1500 bonus, way in excess of a month's pay, so I was rolling in cash and self-esteem. I lashed out on a camera. It is said a picture is worth a thousand words, and certainly this camera and those that followed produced photographs that vividly recall some precious moments. On the other hand, I blame the camera for releasing me from the discipline of diary writing, which is regrettable.

Tan Choo Haw invited me to lunch to meet Janice, his Australian-born Chinese wife. As a young Malaysian naval officer, he had been seconded to the Queensland Harbours and Marine's hydrographic survey vessel, *Trigla*, which was surveying the Great Barrier Reef in the early seventies. He had met Janice during a run ashore in Cairns. Sailors are fast workers because they must be, so he proposed then and there, and she accepted. She met us on the steps of a now long-gone dim sum restaurant on the corner of Orchard and Scotts Roads, and I was bowled over as this attractive Chinese woman greeted us in a broad Australian accent. Perhaps that was the attraction for Choo Haw.

A week later, I was on my way to Saudi Arabia. Oil is never found in places like Rome, however on this occasion I had to go there to get a Saudi entry visa. In those days, international travel gave you a lesson in geography. There were stopovers in Bangkok, Karachi (I've never been since) and Athens. The Athens stopover was four hours and, assuming I would never be there again, I got off the plane, woke a sleepy immigration official who stamped my passport and found an English-speaking taxi driver agreeable to taking me to the Acropolis. Dawn was breaking as we arrived at the main gate at the western end of the complex. The taxi driver talked to a guard who waved me through and there I was, completely alone, clattering around this ancient precinct I had thought existed only in history books. Of course, the Parthenon was in pieces but the elements still standing told the story. I was so overwhelmed I didn't even take a photograph. Later, I took my first ever photograph looking out over the Odeon of Herodes Atticus, where Maria Callas sang *Leonora* in 1957. My flight was leaving at 9 am, but there was still time to pass by the Tomb of the Unknown Soldier safeguarded by a pair of Greek soldiers in traditional uniforms promenading their odd goosesteps.

My Olympic Airways flight landed at Rome Ciampino around midday. Signor Platania, the moustachioed fixer, found me in arrivals and drove me to the Hotel Mediterraneo on the Via Cavour in his Fiat Bambino. I was to wait there while he took my passport to the Saudi Embassy and arranged the visa. He would be back in time to take me back to the airport to catch my Middle Eastern Airlines flight to Beirut later that night. The hotel concierge, who appeared to be complicit in these arrangements, suggested that rather than sit around the hotel I should take the afternoon tour of Rome. This included, of course, the Coliseum and the Trevi Fountain, familiar to most Americans and Australians, not as locations from renowned historical texts, but as scenes from *Ben Hur* and *La Dolce Vita*. The highlight of the tour, however, was St Peter's Basilica. Here again, this was not so familiar to me as the great architectural masterpiece it is, but more because just eighteen months earlier a deranged Hungarian-born Australian geologist had taken a geological hammer to Michelangelo's *Pieta*. Perhaps the Poseidon meltdown had unhinged him.

Back at The Hotel Mediterraneo there was a message from Signor Platania advising the visa would not be ready for two days, I was booked into the hotel for another two nights and would be flying to Dhahran via Beirut on Friday night. Having toured Athens and Rome in a day, I was tired, so went up to my room for a snooze before dinner. Needing a pee, I stepped into the bathroom to be confronted with a loo and a bidet. I had never encountered the latter but having been so impressed with my first day in Europe concluded this sophisticated society fitted their bathrooms with urinals, so I used it accordingly. Then I flushed it all over the ceiling.

With two days to kill and having done the tour, I was free to walk Rome. This included a visit to the monument to Vittorio Emmanuel II, who became the first king of a unified Italy in 1871. Countless opera nights at Val Vallis's house during university days had taught me the connection between Giuseppe Verdi and Vittorio Emmanuel. The catchcry for the Italian unification movement that eventually crowned him was '*Viva Verdi*' (*Vittorio Emanuele Re d'Italia*), and '*Và pensiero*', the Hebrew slaves' chorus from *Nabucco*, became their anthem. Indeed, when Verdi died in 1901, this haunting lament was taken up by the crowds lining his funeral procession through Milan.

Walking up the Via del Corso from the Piazza Venezia I was drawn to the Via Condotti. I had stepped onto another planet. This was 1973. There was no such thing as McDonald's or the litter of tourists in promotional tee-shirts, cargo shorts and sandals. Without exception, man and woman, everybody in that street had stepped out of *Vogue Magazine*. Not one fat one. They were immaculately turned-out men and women in elegant suits and gleaming shoes, out shopping on a Friday morning. My sense of being out of place as I walked through Gucci was confirmed when I priced a scarf I thought might be a nice present for Mum. 16 000L (approximately US$30). No way. Fortunately, as we grow up, we learn giving is so much more rewarding than receiving.

My first three days in Europe had taught me a lot, but there was more to come. I was one of three passengers on the Middle East Airlines 707 bound for Beirut that evening. It was an eerie feeling sitting in a plane with 200 empty seats. Beirut, the beautiful gateway to the Middle East, was heading for the abyss. Palestinian refugees had been pouring into refugee camps since the Six Day War and these camps had nurtured the kidnappers who had massacred the Israeli Olympic team in Munich in September 1972. The Israelis retaliated by bombing the camps, even though some were on the outskirts of Beirut. Barely a month later, the Yom Kippur War made matters worse. But the airport was still working and after a three-hour stopover I was on my way to Dhahran, Saudi Arabia. It was 17 November 1973. Those very wars that were tolling the knell of parting day[6] for Beirut were to push oil from US$20 to US$50 a barrel and spur an oil and gas

El Dorado in the Persian Gulf that would see me travelling helter-skelter to that region for the next ten years.

Many of the projects contributing to the El Dorado were gas-gathering projects. It was no longer the 'oil' industry, it became the 'oil and gas' industry, and I had fallen into it from a motorbike. As we descended into Dhahran, it was impossible not to notice the proliferation of flares burning in the darkness. In 1973, associated gas, the gas trapped in crude oil reservoirs that escaped as pressures reduced during the production process, was flared. Oil at US$50 a barrel changed that. It didn't take people long to realise the value of that wasted gas, and ten years later there was barely a flare in sight.

The Yom Kippur War promoted worldwide efforts to diversify production away from the Middle East, however, Aramco, the Arabian American Oil Company and the world's largest producer, was not about to lose its market position. At the time, it was producing around seven million barrels a day. One of the projects adopted to improve this, by some 200 000 barrels a day, was to install a new gas-oil separating platform (GOSP) in the Safaniya offshore field, which, at the time, was producing around 1.5 million barrels a day. This new GOSP, Safaniya GOSP 3, was to be located in the middle of the oilfield, about twenty-three kilometres offshore in water seventeen metres deep. The location was adjacent to a number of existing pipelines, some of which were to be tied in to the new platform. My job was to map and photograph the existing pipelines within a hundred metres of the proposed new GOSP location.

I spent a couple of days in Aramco's offices in Dhahran,

making sure I understood exactly what had to be done and had all the necessary information. The Aramco people, mostly Americans from Texas and Louisiana, were extremely hospitable and I was introduced to Sadiki, their home-brewed firewater, which was vile and extremely potent. Then there was the three-hour drive north to Safaniya to join my diving crew. The contrast between the Irian Jaya jungle and the Saudi Arabian desert could not have been sharper, and it didn't stop there. Our Petromer Trend assignment had had priority over everything else for obvious reasons. Two hundred and fifty kilometres away from Dhahran, my new assignment had no priority at all. I was to learn very quickly the production department is king in the oilfield and new projects run a very poor last. With crude oil at an all-time high of US$53 a barrel, Aramco was under enormous pressure to squeeze every drop from its 140 offshore production platforms. They had two workover rigs, half a dozen general maintenance work boats, and all this was supported by just one diving tender with three divers.

I attached myself to the diving crew and assisted where I could in an effort to embarrass the production superintendent into releasing the divers for my assignment, but it was all in vain. Eventually, another diving tender was dispatched from Ras Tanura. Hope springs eternal but when the tender arrived, its radio could not tune into the Safaniya Field work frequency, so it was not allowed to enter the field. After two weeks of frustration, the Aramco project management department decided to shelve the survey and I flew back to Singapore. Two years later, when I was next in Safaniya, GOSP 3 had been installed and commissioned without me. But the trip hadn't been a complete waste. I had been introduced to the wonders of Europe, the workings of an offshore oilfield and had seen Joe Cocker in *Mad Dogs and Englishmen* in the Safaniya camp cinema. I was being educated.

My next assignment in Singapore was not so much a response to troubles in the Middle East but more to the growing importance of the South-East Asian economy and the mushrooming demand for petroleum products in the region. In 1961, Royal Dutch Shell built a 20 000 barrels a day refinery next to its tank farm on Pulau Bukom. By 1974, after three expansions, the refinery was one of the largest in the world, processing 400 000 barrels of crude oil a day. Berth space around the tiny island was limited. Shell's solution was to install an SPM to accommodate crude oil delivery tankers up to 355 000 DWT displacement. The mooring was to be located five kilometres to the south-east of the refinery, just outside the northern limit of the Malacca Strait, the world's busiest sea lane for tankers carrying crude to the Far East from the Persian Gulf.

Pulau Bukom's strategic location has bestowed it with an interesting past. The 800-kilometre Transcaucasus Railway, between Baku on the Caspian Sea and Batumi on the Black Sea, was completed by the French Rothschilds in 1883. This opened a worldwide market for the Baku oilfields, which, by 1890, were producing fifteen million barrels a year of refined kerosene. The problem was the European market was saturated. The Rothschilds approached Marcus Samuel, a Londoner of Iraqi-Jewish descent and successful Far-East trader. Could he open markets in the Orient for them? At first, Samuel was indifferent, but he agreed to visit Baku. Perhaps he was intoxicated by the pervasive hydrocarbon odour. Whatever it was, his trader instincts took over. To succeed he had to find a way to ship via the Suez Canal rather than The Cape. Tankers of the day were floating bombs and banned from the canal for safety reasons.

He spent the first six months of 1891 selling and developing his ideas with his trusted agents in the Far East. This included identifying potential bulk storage sites from which kerosene could be unloaded from tanker ships via pipeline. By the time Marcus left Kobe for London in June 1891, he and his 'tanker syndicate' had firm plans for terminals in Bangkok, Calcutta, Madras and Singapore (Pulau Bukom) and outline plans for Burma, Java and Japan. Back in London, he commissioned James Fortescue Flannery, the country's leading naval architect, to design a tanker ship to a standard the Suez Canal Authority could not reasonably refuse. By summer's end, Flannery had developed a design that was to be the template for tanker design for the next seventy years. Named *Murex*, after a predatory sea snail, it boasted the following groundbreaking features.

- A 349-foot-long by forty-three-foot-wide hull with nine transverse bulkheads and a segmented double bottom, facilitating integrity and ballast control in the event of grounding
- 4000 tonnes of kerosene in ten tanks, set amidships between the transverse bulkheads, each with its own summer tank

- A tank steam-cleaning system for return cargos
- Coal-fired triple-expansion steam engines
- Two pumps set amidships, capable of unloading in twelve hours
- A fan-driven ventilation system designed to evacuate all gasses from the hull once every twenty minutes
- Steam heating and electric lighting in manned areas, avoiding naked flames.

Flannery secured Lloyd's 1A.100 safety rating for his design. This was Lloyd's gold standard and, despite protests from Rockefeller's Standard Oil, the Canal Authority gave the design its approval. No doubt the Rothschilds's role in financing the canal had been influential. Marcus Samuel's wife, Fanny, launched *Murex* in May 1892, and on 23 August 1892, loaded with 4000 tonnes of Rothschilds's kerosene, *Murex* was the first tanker to navigate the Suez Canal.

The ultimate destination was Pulau Bukom, where Mr Samuel had arranged for the construction of a tank farm. Samuel had conceived and executed his incredibly audacious coup in twenty-one months. Within eighteen months, Samuel & Co had launched ten more ships, all named after seashells, including *Conch*, *Clam*, *Elax*, *Bullmouth* and *Cowrie*. Their grip on the trade was such that ten years later, of all the oil to pass though Suez, ninety per cent belonged to Samuel and his tanker syndicate. In 1897, he formed a new company to manage his petroleum trading interests and called it Shell Transport and Trading, after his painted seashell business.

Meanwhile, in 1880, Aeilko Jans Zijklert, a Dutch tobacco

farmer searching for new farmland on the east coast of Sumatra north of Medan, found traces of oil near Pangkalan Branden. Money was raised to drill wells and ten years later, after crude oil had been found in commercial quantities, Zijklert incorporated the Royal Dutch Company for the Working of Petroleum Wells in the Dutch Indies. Work began on the construction of a refinery and shipping terminal at Pangkalan Susu. This was completed in 1898 and the major elements of that refinery stand to this day. In 1897, Shell Transport and Trading discovered oil in East Kalimantan and built a small refinery at Balikpapan. Five years later, Royal Dutch and Shell Transport and Trading formed a joint venture (JV) to handle shipping and marketing for both companies, and in 1907 the companies merged to form Royal Dutch Shell, still Europe's largest company.

Fast forward to 1974. Compared to the Botany Bay SPM, Pulau Bukom's was a monster. With its forty-eight-inch diameter submarine pipeline connecting it to the tank farm, it would unload a 355 000 DWT supertanker in just over thirty-six hours. The key to the project was the design and installation of the five-kilometre pipeline in an area where 3.3-metre spring tides generate currents up to three knots. The customary installation method for a pipeline of this size and length is from a lay barge starting from the shore end and progressing offshore. Shell awarded the installation contract to American contractor J Ray McDermott, who proposed undertaking the work with one of the latest additions to its offshore construction fleet, *Lay barge 25* (*LB 25*). This behemoth appeared off Singapore in January, having made the journey from the Bass Strait, where she had been working for Esso.

A lay barge is in effect an enormous floating sausage machine, but instead of sausages the result is a string of welded pipes suspended from the stern of the barge to the seabed. Each pipe (known as a pipe joint) is twelve metres long, and as each new joint is welded to the front end of the pipe string, the barge moves forward twelve metres, thus laying a further twelve metres of completed pipeline on the seabed. In between moves, the barge is secured by between eight and twelve anchors attached by steel-wire ropes to winches coordinated to ensure that, on command, the barge moves the required twelve metres along the planned pipeline alignment.

LB 25 was a state-of-the-art flat-top barge, 125 metres long, thirty-nine metres wide and eight metres deep, with a work deck on top and a hotel below for the 250 men required to keep it working twenty-four-seven. The pipeline assembly line, known as the firing line, ran above deck along the centre line on ten height-adjustable V-shaped roller pairs. The starboard side of the barge was generally kept clear of materials and stores. This allowed two one-hundred-tonne Manitowoc crawler cranes to move freely from bow to stern, transferring the twenty-one-tonne pipe joints from supply barges to the line-up station, the first of nine workstations along the firing line. For this project, the first five stations, including the line-up station, were welding stations. These were followed by the X-ray station to confirm weld integrity, a repair station, a prime and coat station, and a dope station, where the gap between the concrete coatings on successive joints was filled with hot mastic known as dope. From the dope station the pipe string would begin its transition off the barge to a touch-down point on the seabed, some two to three hundred metres astern, depending on water depth. The first one hundred metres of this transition were supported by a buoyancy raft hinged to the barge stern and known as the stinger.

A forty-eight-inch-diameter pipe string is anything but a string. With a four-inch-concrete weight coating to ensure the pipe sank and was stable in three knot currents, the assembled pipeline was extremely stiff. It had to be installed on an even grade to avoid creating spans that would tend to promote scouring, causing even longer spans and potential pipe crimping. My first task was to survey the intended pipeline route and to design a vertical profile that would minimise the dredging required to remove seabed features likely to create spans. Having surveyed the intended route and plotted the vertical profile, we calculated the minimum allowable pipeline radius and attempted to optimise the profile by hand using traditional railroad track curve templates. The results were unsatisfactory and then came the eureka moment. Highway engineering had hardly been my forte at university. However, I did remember a clever computer programme used to optimise cut and fill for road and rail projects. We bought a licence, modified the programme to allow cut only and came up with a simple profile that eliminated unnecessary dredging.

With our fancy new computer-generated profile, we had significantly reduced the anticipated dredging quantities so foresaw no problem smoothing the route well in advance of

March 15th, when *LB 25* was scheduled to start work. As far as I know, the poet, Robbie Burns, never did work on a construction site, and if he had it would never have been attempting to dredge rock in an area exposed to strong winds and even stronger tides. But if he had, the line from *To a Mouse*[5] might have been, *The best laid schemes o' engineers / Gang aft agley*. Time after time, over the next three months, that haunting poem came to mind. Engineers should never forget it.

We started work in early December with one bucket dredge. It struggled. Soon enough it was obvious the high spots were not sand but either stiff clay or rock. Time was lost replacing dredging bucket teeth and fighting strong tidal currents. The answer was a heavier dredging bucket, heavier anchors, and a heavier tug. But not even these remedies stemmed the bleeding, so in mid-January a second dredger was mobilised.

We weren't the only ones making a mess of things on Pulau Bukom. On January 31st, a gang of four terrorists—two PLO and two Japanese Red Army—hired a fishing boat, landed on the island, attached limpet mines to three storage tanks and detonated them. There was a small fire but fortunately no substantial damage. They had picked the wrong tanks. The gang escaped by hijacking the island ferry and holding the crew to ransom. They were eventually flown to Kuwait in exchange for the release of the ferry crew unharmed.

There was an upheaval in the RJBA office too. I was disappointed to discover my latest mentor, Art van Lent, had decided to return to Holland and take up a new position in the RJBA head office in The Hague. His replacement, Jack Hill, an urbane Texan of amiable disposition, was from a contracting rather than engineering background, but whatever he may have lacked in technical ability he made up with a wide range of contacts in the oil and gas industry.

Meanwhile, the dredgers were making better progress, but in mid-March, as *LB 25* took up position to commence laying pipe, our surveys were showing a ridge across the route only 800 metres from the island. Shell convened a crisis meeting. We resolved to persevere with the dredging but the cunning contingency plan was to lay explosives across the ridge and blast it away if the dredging failed. We had less than a week if there was to be no delaying the lay barge. Procuring the gelignite and detonators was not so difficult. However, in the post-Konfrontasi era, securing a Singapore Government permit for an explosion near the Indonesian border would be extremely difficult. There were some not-so-old wounds.

In May 1961, the Malayan and British governments had proposed incorporating Singapore, Sarawak and Sabah into what would become the Malaysian Federation. At first the Indonesians had no objections, but President Sukarno soon saw an opportunity to promote his own territorial ambitions and early in 1963 announced his opposition to the plan. Three months later, Indonesia launched Konfrontasi with an attack on a police station in southern Sarawak. Despite the hostilities, the Malaysian Federation was consummated in September of that year. Although the main fighting in the conflict was confined to Borneo, there was a sustained Indonesian bombing campaign in Singapore from 1963 to 1966. The worst of these killed three people in MacDonald House on Orchard Road in March 1965. Two Indonesian marines were arrested, tried for murder and sentenced to hang. Sukarno was deposed six months later. The new Indonesian President, Suharto, suspended Konfrontasi and formally recognised the Malaysian Federation. However, his pleas for clemency for the soldiers were ignored and they were executed in 1968.

Since it was a Shell project and Shell was a senior corporate citizen, it was left to its top brass to approach the Singaporean Government to secure the blasting permit. The standby rate for *LB 25* in those days was close to US$100,000 a day. That must have caught their attention. We had the permit five days later. The authorities were advised the charges would be detonated on the low tide on March 21st. This would ensure minimal tidal currents and better visibility for the divers placing the charges. The survey crew came out for a final survey to identify the ridge and drop marker buoys. The ridge was gone. We checked again and, sure enough, the concentrated dredging effort through the week had achieved the desired effect. There was no way we were going back to Shell to explain we hadn't needed that permit after all. We placed and detonated the charges twenty metres off the route. Unfortunately, the detonation wire was not quite long enough and the plume from the explosion nearly sank our tender. Jack Hill had asked me to film the event with his pride and joy, his brand-new Beaulieu Super 8 movie camera. When we viewed the film afterwards, Jack was rather crestfallen to see the spray from the explosion, initially a few drops but soon after a deluge, landing on his precious lens.

The Pulau Bukom end of the pipeline was pulled ashore from the lay barge on March 16th, at which point the barge started heading south-east towards the SPM location. Once a lay barge gets going it's an exciting beast. Initially, progress was relatively slow, at about a joint an hour, but as the crew warmed to the task this improved to forty-five minutes. The focus was on a hundred per cent weld integrity for each joint. This was confirmed by a 360-degree X-ray of each weld, certified or not, by independent technicians. Immediately, a weld was accepted the barge superintendent would be notified and would sound a klaxon warning that the barge was about to move forward twelve metres. Everybody on the firing line would then clear the pipe string of all tools and stand back until the all-clear had been sounded. A new pipe joint would then be placed in the line-up station and the process would be repeated. If there was a weld defect, the barge would have to wait until it had been repaired or cut out all together and done again. This would take hours in the repair station.

Twelve days later, we were sixty joints short of the SPM location and making plans to attach the pipeline end manifold and install the SPM. It may have been the mounting end-of-term euphoria that spawned the wind that defied the best efforts of the tug captains and winch operators to keep the barge on course. That enormous pipe was no better than a piece of spaghetti under those conditions and buckled on the seabed. The following day when the weather had settled, an attempt was made to recover the buckled joint by reversing the barge and pulling up the pipeline, joint by joint. This only served to rupture the buckled joint, which allowed water into the pipe, making it so heavy it broke the stinger. Now there was a serious mess that would take months to fix.

I remained on the project for long enough to prepare a report on the buckle. McDermott was faced with repairing the stinger and dewatering and recovering the pipe. As this would take months I went into the RJBA office to assist with the preparation of a study for an insulated loading line for a new crude oil export line from the Sangatta field on the north-east coast of Kalimantan.

My brother Chris had arrived in Singapore a month earlier. He and his friend, Chris Piggott, who had been a classmate of mine at university, were hitchhiking to London. They achieved the 3000-kilometre Dalby-Darwin leg without too much trouble. Then, a week before Cyclone Tracy smashed Darwin, they flew to Denpasar, Bali, where they hitched another 2000 kilometres through Java and Sumatra to catch a ferry to Singapore. In those days, no trip to Singapore was complete without a trip to Bugis Street for the late evening ladyboy show and, if you were lucky, a performance of the dance of the flaming arseholes. We weren't disappointed. The traditional stage for this hallowed ritual was the roof of the public dunny where liquored-up sailors undressed and made asses of themselves dancing with burning editions of the *Straits Times* stuck up their backsides. Singapore is too genteel for that nowadays—and probably too crowded for what came next. As we were driving home along Bukit Timah Road, we managed to stop before running over an enormous python stretched over at least two traffic lanes. That's seven metres. It was late and there was no other traffic so Chris insisted on getting out and encouraging it to cross the road. It gave him a menacing stare and refused to move, so we bid it goodnight, gave it a wide berth and continued home.

A few nights later, we joined Philip Conn for dinner at the Marco Polo Hotel on Grange Road. When I first met Philip, he was a final year architecture student working part-time for renowned architect, Jim Birrell, during the construction of the first stage of the Union College building. He was also involved in Willy Young's *Architecture Reviews* at the Avalon Theatre. Whether you are a rugby player, a plumber, an opera buff or a bishop, no visit to Singapore is complete without a walk along Asia's most famous shopping street, Orchard Road. Within days of arriving in Singapore, as I was doing just this, I ran into Philip. I had no idea he was there and working for a company called International Project Consultants (Ipco) with offices in Orchard Road. Twenty years later, Ipco, then Ipco Marine, saved me from the jaws of penury by giving me a job.

Before our dinner at the Marco Polo, Philip called to ask if he could bring two Indonesian girls to the party. We were not to know it at the time, but Rani Suwarto and Inong Satibi were truly daughters of the 'New Order' that came into being with the murder of six high-ranking generals on the night of 30 September 1965 and the eventual overthrow of President Sukarno. The real story of the events of that fateful night is still unclear, but many believe President Suharto, a lowly colonel at the time who rose to prominence rounding up the 'perpetrators', was in it up to his neck. Rani's father was commander of the influential Indonesian Army Command and General Staff College at Bandung when he died in 1967. Many members of the new government, including President

Suharto, had been his students, and now Rani's mother, Ibu Yanti, was a well-connected businesswoman—very possibly because she knew where the bodies were buried. She was helping Philip with a project in Jakarta and had asked him to keep an eye on her daughter who had gone to Singapore to keep her friend, Inong, company.

Inong Satibi had been sent to Singapore by her father-in-law, Ali Sadikin, to recover from a marriage breakdown with one of his sons. General Sadikin was the influential governor of Jakarta with close ties to another Indonesian mover and shaker, General Ibnu Sutowo, president director of Pertamina, Indonesia's national oil company. Sadikin carved a thirty-acre site from a sports complex in the centre of Jakarta to provide Pertamina with a site for what was to become for years, the premier hotel in Jakarta, the Jakarta Hilton. So, when General Sadikin needed a residence in Singapore for his exiled daughter-in-law, General Sutowo was only too happy to ask his Singaporean business partner, Tong Djoe, to come to the party. Tong Djoe owned the shipping company Tunas, which carried much of Pertamina's oil. Indonesia was certainly in a state of 'you scratch my back and I'll scratch yours' in those days. To be fair, following his retirement as Jakarta's governor, Ali Sadikin became a leading member of 'Petition of Fifty', a group of prominent soldiers, politicians, businessmen, academics and journalists that bravely campaigned against the worst excesses of the Suharto family.

Rani and Inong were charming, well-groomed and well-educated, with more than passable English. If Inong was slightly subdued, Rani made up for it with her bubbly vivacity.

The dinner was a great success and days later the two Chrises packed their gear, made their way to Bukit Timah Road and hitched north to Malaysia. They eventually made the 1500 kilometres to Bangkok, but after 7000 kilometres of hitchhiking, they had had enough and caught an Aeroflot flight to London via every stop in the book. I had been mesmerised by Inong and was delighted days later when she agreed to a dinner *à deux sans duenna*.

Our meeting couldn't have come at a better time as I was to have two months in Singapore uninterrupted by travel. I had just moved into a nice house off the Upper Thomson Road and had been fortunate enough to buy a beautifully preserved pillar-box-red TR4 from a departing expat. Inong was a princess, a Sundanese princess, a Siamese cat. Of course, we enjoyed dancing at the Marco Polo and the Hyatt, but more than anything else in the three months before she and Rani returned to Jakarta, she enjoyed introducing me to Asian cuisine—laksa in the Orchard Road carpark, satay in Newton Circus and, best of all, chilli crab in the old Beach Hotel on Pasir Panjang.

Coincidentally, with Inong's departure a new project came up in East Kalimantan. In 1972, three years after the Maui field was discovered, Roy M Huffington's exploration company, Huffco, was looking for oil in the Mahakam Delta and was disappointed when all they found was a seven Tcf gas field, twice the size of Maui. If Maui was a monster, this was a mammoth and named accordingly—Badak, meaning 'rhino'. Their disappointment soon dissipated when potential Japanese customers queued to sign binding contracts to purchase the gas in liquefied form (LNG). Two years later, they were even happier when the Yom Kippur War worked its magic and doubled oil and gas prices. US construction giant, Bechtel, was commissioned to build a 3.3 million tonnes a year plant at Santan, thirty kilometres to the north of Badak. A construction camp was built but it was soon apparent Santan was an unsuitable site. Ground conditions were poor and suitable tanker moorings were remote. *The best laid schemes o' mice an' men / Gang aft agley.*[5]

This was a problem because by now there were binding delivery contracts in place and penalties for non-performance. A new site would have to be found quickly. Bob Brown had resigned from Bechtel to form RJBA, and it may have been this connection that prompted Bechtel to contact us in Singapore with a request for a proposal to find a new site. Fortunately, we were able to move immediately. Joe Moll and I packed a portable fathometer, gathered all the admiralty charts and tide tables for the east coast of Kalimantan we could find in Singapore, and on 3 May 1974 flew to Jakarta for meetings with Bechtel and Shell. Joe was a rare Dutchman who could charm birds out of trees, so we had no problem getting in to talk to Shell who, as related earlier, had been operating in East Kalimantan since 1897. It had undertaken the original geodetic control surveys in East Kalimantan and was happy to provide us with the location, description and coordinates of numerous established survey control marks along the coast. This was incredibly helpful since in the pre-GPS era establishing an accurate survey grid in virgin territory was time consuming and difficult. It was also able to provide guidance for the tidal lag between Bontang and Balikpapan, for which we had reasonably accurate tables.

Pertamina had a substantial interest in this project, so when Joe and I arrived in Balikpapan the next morning there were Pertamina as well as Bechtel people to meet us. Joe spoke fluent Bahasa Indonesia so went into town with the Pertamina representative, Ir Gatot Soenoto, to search for any other useful data in the Pertamina offices. Pak Gatot was to spend a lot of time with us during the next three months and was particularly helpful during the latter stages of the project when Joe had to be in Singapore on other business. Like most educated Indonesians of that era, he spoke fluent Dutch and his English was pretty good too. On one occasion, when we had become friends, I asked him if he was Muslim. 'No,' he replied, 'Chrislam,' and noting my bemused expression, said, 'Christian from the waist up and Muslim from the waist down'. In those days, Indonesians could take four wives if they could afford them and Bintang beer was the national drink.

If I hadn't appreciated the urgency of our mission hitherto it certainly sank in when I found there was a Bell Jet Ranger helicopter waiting to take me to Santan. I was now in the big league. Bechtel's project superintendent, Red McGee, met me off the helicopter and arranged accommodation for Joe and me in their camp. Bechtel was world champion of mega projects and knew the first thing to do on any job was to keep the workforce well fed and in reasonable living quarters. No expense had been spared on this camp. It was a shame it was now in the wrong place.

I spent the afternoon with Red McGee fine tuning our

plans for the reconnaissance survey. Before leaving Singapore, we had selected three potential new sites—Bontang South, Bontang North and Sangatta, using admiralty charts and other information in the public domain. Red had already selected Bontang in his own mind so was happy to go along with our plan. Joe and Soenoto arrived in the morning and we took a helicopter up to Sangatta and back. Sangatta was already an established Pertamina oil production site, but more than a hundred kilometres from Badak and with no deep water close to shore, it was easy to eliminate as an option. Bontang was a tiny fishing and logging village but had two potential plant sites near relatively deep water, one to the north, the other to the south. Our next step would be to rig the fathometer in a small boat and run sounding lines in the approaches to the two sites.

The following morning Joe, Soenoto and I took a chopper to Bontang where we hired a small boat and rigged the portable fathometer. The boat driver knew the area well and showed us the approaches used by cargo vessels loading logs at both sites. By day's end, we had covered them with multiple longitudinal and transverse depth-sounding lines albeit with no more than rudimentary horizontal control. That night we plotted the results using the Balikpapan tide table to reduce the soundings to chart datum. Our preliminary results indicated both options provided viable sea approaches to a potential LNG plant. Four days later, after meetings in Balikpapan and Jakarta, which provided further meteorological and environmental data, we returned to Singapore.

Within a week we had produced a report with recommendations for detailed hydrographic, geotechnical and environmental surveys at each site. Jack Hill delivered it to Bechtel in San Francisco and four days later we had a telex asking us to start the work. My job was to coordinate site activities. A week later, our five-man team—two surveyors, two technicians and I—were lodged in Santan and commuting the thirty kilometres each way to Bontang by helicopter pending the arrival of our survey vessel, which would also provide onsite accommodation. Our first task was to establish enough tellurometer stations to enable us to accurately fix the position of our survey vessels anywhere in the survey area. We did this work with motorboats hired in Bontang.

Joe Moll's job was to make sure I got the necessary equipment and a survey vessel. The equipment included tellurometers for electronic distance measurement, theodolites, fathometers, a sub-bottom profiler, a side scan sonar, a seabed piston corer, recording tide gauges, recording current meters and rechargeable batteries. The only vessel he could hire on short notice to rig for the survey and provide our accommodation was *MV Garuda Mariner*. This was anything but the exotic bird its name conveyed. It was a thirty-four-metre-long landing craft with basic accommodation for its own crew who were happy to leave it to us and sleep on the deck. No wonder—we killed one rat that would have been a match for King Kong, so we all ended up on deck at night, which was fine if it was fine. Then there was the problem with the loo, which was a squatter.

Not long after *Garuda Mariner* had finally arrived, I upset one of Bechtel's liaison engineers by buying all the Bintang in Bontang and issuing it to my team to wash down the nasi goreng served at every meal. The story must have got back to Jack Hill. Not long afterwards, when I was in Singapore renewing my visa, he told me he had arranged to send a more senior engineer from head office in The Hague to run the site operations. Of course, I had done a great job and it was essential I remain to assist the new man who was a Texan and would know how to handle Bechtel. Sure enough, our man arrived by helicopter a few days later. He was in his late forties and more than a little overweight. Overnight, I became aware of moaning in the squatter. Nasi goreng revenge. He had dysentery and the effort of squatting and vomiting at the same time was killing him. The next morning, he returned to Singapore, and we didn't see him again. But we did get a much nicer accommodation vessel, so were able to use the *GM* exclusively for survey operations.

The number one priority was to deploy the recording tide gauges and current meters at both sites. Tide gauge data are used to reduce seabed depths recorded by fathometer to chart datum. It can also be used to generate ongoing tide charts for the specific location and so the data were also sent for processing to the hydraulic laboratory at Wallingford in the UK, an acknowledged authority in the field. The current data would be an important parameter in the selection of the site, approaches to the site and design of the LNG tanker berths. LNG tankers in the early seventies typically carried around 60 000 tonnes of LNG (say, 500 000 barrels of oil equivalent), were 280 metres long and drew 11.5 metres.

While this work was being done from *Garuda Mariner*, we used a local shallow draught boat to accurately map the coastline and the various small islands that formed the approaches to the potential sites. I took this data to Singapore and used it to draw lattice charts for the main survey lines to be run with fathometer, side scan sonar and sub-bottom profiler combined. We commenced these lines with the *GM* in mid-June and covered almost 300 kilometres in five days. The only remaining work after that was soil and coral sampling and underwater reef photography. One afternoon towards the end of June, there was a rare radio call from Santan advising me they were sending a chopper as my visa was expiring and could only be renewed in Singapore.

The helicopter took me from Bontang to Santan. A Skyvan had been arranged to then take me to Balikpapan via Sangatta the same day. A tyre blew out as we landed at Sangatta and we performed a clean 360-degree pirouette before grinding to a halt. But not to worry, Pertamina had a comfortable guesthouse and another Skyvan would run us down to Balikpapan in the morning. And so it did, but having landed, the pilot attempted to turn off the runway too quickly and upended us in a drainage ditch. I was relieved and in the mood for a party when I arrived in Singapore in one piece later that night.

Saturday night was party night in the Mezzanine Bar in the Hyatt Hotel on Scotts Road. Nearly everybody and his dog from the oil industry would be there. Everything was going well until I took a one-hundred-dollar bet that I couldn't walk the length of the balustrade separating the mezzanine floor from the hotel reception eight metres below. I was halfway along when the bouncers arrived, but they couldn't risk pushing me over the edge so did nothing. I won the bet and shouted the bar, but the winnings were not nearly enough. And the following week I was banned. Good lesson.

Not surprisingly, I was feeling poorly when I got home but thought nothing of it and went to bed. Hours later, I woke with a dreadful pain in the stomach. I thought it was constipation and sat forlornly on the loo, getting nowhere. It got worse. Philip Conn's was the only home number I had. He was at home and Ipco had a company doctor. He called back in five minutes to say the doctor was on his way. By now it was about 4 am. Much to his credit, the doctor arrived about fifteen minute later. He prodded around in my stomach for about two minutes, manhandled me into his car and took me straight to the Mount Alvernia Hospital where I had an emergency appendectomy. The night before I had been in a remote camp in East Kalimantan.

I was discharged from the hospital a day later. Philip's boss, Sandy Sandford, and his wife, Jill, who had heard what happened from the doctor, insisted I move into their house to recuperate. It had been some time since I had enjoyed real home comforts, so I responded well.

Sandy had retired as Singapore's chief engineer two or three years earlier. He had then established Ipco, specialising in infrastructure development. It had been a struggle, but in 1976 a Saudi Arabian decision to build pipelines from their oilfields in the east to Yanbu on the Red Sea changed everything. The Saudis were in a hurry, but Yanbu had no facilities at all—certainly not a deep-water port. Just like Bob Brown, Sandy was a real engineer with an inventive mind. He came up with the idea of a prefabricated jack-up pier and sold it to the Royal Commission for Jubail and Yanbu. He designed the pier as five jack-up barges and had them built in four different fabrication yards in Singapore. All the gear and materials required for the project were stacked on the barges and towed 8000 kilometres to Yanbu. There, each barge was floated into place and jacked to the required level on its own piles. When the 35 000 DWT *MV Garden Venus* berthed there on 1 November 1977, to unload 9000 tonnes of forty-eigtht-inch line pipe for the Trans Saudi Petroline, it was just six and a half months since Ipco had signed the contract. Shortly afterwards, Sandy built a similar facility in Malaysia and retired again.

The Bontang survey report was completed mid-August. Bontang South appeared to be the better prospect from a marine perspective, and this was the option Pertamina eventually adopted. Bechtel went on to complete what became known as Bontang Train A, with a capacity of 2.3 million tonnes of LNG a year, in 1977. It had been eight years from discovery to the first LNG shipment. Tanker *LNG Aquarius*, drawing 9.8 metres, left Bontang for Japan with the first cargo on August 9th. Since 1977, there have been eight expansions and the capacity is now twenty-two million tonnes per annum (MTPA).

Not long after my messy departure from Bontang, my father was in Tokyo on business and staying at the Imperial Hotel, a Frank Lloyd Wright masterpiece. Dad was having a drink in the famous Old Imperial Bar when he got into a conversation with an American who was working on a project in Indonesia. It turned out to be Red McGee. He must have made some kind remarks about me because Dad couldn't wait to tell the story. He may have even felt his sacrifices on my behalf hadn't been in vain after all.

The Fasht al Arab

There was a lull in the RJBA Singapore office following the dispatch of the Bontang report, and lulls provide fertile ground for change. Jack Hill had been a stopgap replacement for Art van Lent until a permanent appointment could be made, and that turned out to be Saeed Khan. Saeed had been with RJBA almost from the start but had taken time off to complete a master's degree. The Singapore office was no more than about ten people when Saeed took control. When I went back there twenty years later, it was close to one hundred people. But the tide for change swept me along as well. A month after finishing the Bontang site work, Saeed asked me if I would like to join the RJBA head office in Rijswijk. What's more, I could take a month's holiday and travel to the Netherlands via Australia and RJBA's office in Houston. I was settling nicely into life in Singapore, but this seemed too good to be true. Working one's way around Europe as a young adult is hardwired into the Australian psyche. I would be paid for it. I accepted before he changed his mind, not forgetting ...[1]

There is a tide in the affairs of men.
Which, taken at the flood, leads on to fortune;

Omitted, all the voyage of their life
Is bound in shallows and in miseries.
On such a full sea are we now afloat,
And we must take the current when it serves,
Or lose our ventures.

It wasn't difficult to sell the TR4 and early in September I was on a flight to Jakarta. I saw Inong briefly, then Rani Suwarto took me for a weekend to her family home in Bandung. It's a spectacular train journey from Jakarta to Bandung but not nearly as memorable as the confrontation looming at our destination. Stepping from the carriage I was approached by a man with his face covered by a cloth. Two paces away he removed it to reveal a gaping hole where there should have been a nose, a bit like the mouth in *The Scream*. I gagged but somehow managed to find money for his outstretched hand. Rani hustled me away. The trouble with poverty is people in countries like 1970s Indonesia are inured to it.

A few days later I was back in sunny Queensland. I managed to spring my sister Sarah from her boarding school, St Hilda's, Southport, for a race meeting in Brisbane. Years later, she told me she had hated boarding but there were no signs that weekend. Then, it was home to Dalby for a week. Dad was at his best. He was sending so many containers to Japan, South Korea and Taiwan he was becoming one of the Australian National Line's biggest customers. Trade is a wonderful tonic. He even chartered a plane to fly me back to Brisbane to catch my flight to Amsterdam. He sat in the front seat next to the pilot. As we flared to make the landing in Brisbane, buffeted by crosswinds, I noticed Dad's feet move instinctively towards the rudder pedals. Flying must be like riding a bike.

Bob Brown was always aware of the precise number of nationalities employed by RJBA and took pride in its diversity. Naturally, there were many Americans but with an office in The Hague there were more than a handful of locals. That was never a problem because the Dutch speak English fluently and often many other languages besides. More importantly, engineers are a revered species in Holland. But even by 1974, when RJBA was barely five years old, there was a wide spectrum of South Americans, Europeans and Asians. I was the first Australian and Bob made a big fuss of this as he introduced me around the office. The Maui project office had been closed and Paul Dantz, Tony Brass and Jose Gonzalez were familiar faces back from New Plymouth, so I was not to be a stranger in a strange land. Unfortunately, Art van Lent was no longer with the company. He had resigned to join Protech International BV, a Rotterdam-based process engineering company ambitious for an entree to the offshore oil and gas industry.

There was no particular project in mind for me when I arrived in Rijswijk, so I became an extra hand for anyone in the office who needed help. All the projects were interesting. There were the finishing touches for the design of a modular lay barge to be built in Holland and shipped via the Baltic Sea and the River Volga to the Caspian Sea, where it would lay pipelines in the Baku oilfields—the very oilfields that produced the kerosene Marcus Samuel shipped to Pulau Bukom eighty years earlier. The most interesting, however, was the stinger design for *Viking Piper*. This semisubmersible giant was a Bob Brown concept and when it commenced laying the Ninian pipeline into the Shetlands six months later, at 167 metres long, it was the biggest submarine pipeline installation barge by far—thirty-three per cent longer than *LB 25*. The Ninian pipeline was thirty-six inches in diameter and 136 metres deep at the offshore end.

I was taken in hand by a hard-bitten crew from the office who had lunch in a bar across the street in the Boogaard Centre. After a month on *Garuda Mariner*, I was a stripling at forty-five kilograms. Six weeks later, I was pushing sixty kilograms. So it was a good thing when I joined a Qatar-bound survey team to map a pipeline route from the Idd El-Shargi field to a landfall just to the south of Doha. There was also a twenty-kilometre section of cross-country pipeline. The client was Shell. Nick Kanakis, an old Bechtel hand, was our team leader, and John Burns, one of my new lunchtime beer-drinking friends, who had been with RJBA since its inception, had come to run the offshore survey.

Once we had established our control stations, running the 400 kilometres of survey lines required for the offshore portion of the survey was straightforward. While this was under way, it was my job to select a route for the cross-country section from Wakrah to Umm Said. Cross-country pipelines are buried to a depth such that the top of the buried pipe is one metre below grade. Accordingly, a 600-millimetre diameter pipe is installed in a trench 1.6 metres deep. Part of my route selection process was to dig a 1.6 metre test pit every 500 metres along the pipeline route, and for this I hired a backhoe and operator. Although it was approaching winter, standing in the Qatari desert while the operator dug each pit was hot work, so I persuaded him to teach me how to operate the machine and I dug the pits. But I was still sixty kilograms when I left Qatar a month later.

Not so a senior Shell executive who had gone to Doha to renegotiate Shell's concessions years earlier. To eliminate the risk of Delhi belly he had packed his own primus and tinned foods and only ventured forth from his suite in the Gulf Hotel when absolutely necessary. The concessions had been renewed and all was going well until the emir invited him to a celebratory feast. A sheep's eyeball and a falafel or two later he was as sick as a dog and went home on a stretcher. The moral of the story: when in Doha, do what the Qataris do.

I went back to The Hague for long enough to pack my bags for Christmas in London with my brother Chris. He had been there nine months and was enjoying life in the great metropolis. Five years earlier, the Sydney manager of Bunge & Born, international grain and oilseed traders, had called my father for help. Mark de Bertodano, a Bunge scion, had arrived in Sydney looking for outback adventure. Dad suggested he join Chris, whose university vacation job was mustering on a cattle station 120 kilometres west of Rockhampton. Another hand would be welcome. Mark couldn't ride a horse when he arrived at Junee, but a year later he could.

Chris's arrival in London was not that of the regular backpacker. He was offered a traineeship with Bunge & Born and temporary accommodation in a house with a maid in Ennismore Garden Mews SW1. Six months later, he was a Bunge chartering clerk on the Baltic Exchange and driving around in a red MGB roadster. At about that time, I asked Dad how big Bunge was. He thought for a moment and replied, 'They have a terminal in Chicago that exports more wheat than the entire Australian crop.' In the meantime, Mark de Bertodano, now back in London, introduced Chris to a friend of his, John Langdon. John had a comfortable flat in Ranelagh Gardens with a spare bedroom and suggested Chris move in. He did, and so I had a base for my next two weeks.

Christmas is a wonderful time to be in England. It is celebrated with great warmth, perhaps in preparation for the gruelling months of January and February. Chris was adamant we visit Harrods on my first morning in London. Four days before Christmas it was heaving. The decorations were magnificent. We went into the stationery department to buy a 1975 diary. Edward Heath was doing the same thing. I was flabbergasted the man who had been Britain's prime minister only a year ago was out shopping, apparently alone. But this is England. John Langdon invited us out to his parents' house near Godalming for the traditional Boxing Day beagling meet. To the uninitiated this is a truly barmy pursuit. In the middle of the English winter country people, rich and poor, chase hares on foot with beagle hounds. The ground is inevitably boggy, even if it isn't raining. The traditional way to keep warm and beat the mud is to drink as much sloe gin as possible. Generally, the hares are pretty safe.

A few days later, John asked me if I would like to accompany him to a pheasant shoot in the New Forest. As he explained the drill, I realised it was completely different to the duck shoots my father took part in when we lived at Mt Oscar. Basically, the shooters, known as 'guns', line one side of a suspected pheasant habitat, known as a 'cover'. When they are in position, beaters, generally recruited by the gamekeeper from the local village, walk slowly through the cover making a lot of noise to encourage pheasants unfortunate enough to be there to take off and fly towards the guns. The guns shoot the pheasants without shooting the beaters or neighbouring guns.

We arrived at the Master Builder's at Bucklers Hard in time for a traditional English breakfast, that staple of English catering that can be relied on for quality and quantity. Soon after, we were joined by David Anderson, John's host. One of the guns couldn't make it. Could I shoot? I had done some clay pigeon shooting but that was some time ago and I didn't have a gun. Don't worry, the gamekeeper will look after you and you can use one of mine. And with that, he opened his gun case to reveal a priceless pair of matched Purdeys. The prospect of using one of these jewels was frightening.

Years earlier, I had been duck shooting on a dam with my friend John McDonald who lived on a property near Mt Oscar. Scrambling around the dam surround John had stumbled and plugged one of his gun barrels with mud. Soon after, he took a shot at a duck and transformed the barrel into a stringy trumpet. Fortunately, John and the duck survived. His father wasn't happy.

Breakfast over, we headed through the fields to the first drive less than a mile away. The guns gathered to draw lots for shooting positions that would rotate drive to drive. The gamekeeper introduced himself and showed me to my peg where he made sure I knew how to load the gun, engage the safety catch and keep the gun broken until the birds started flying. He explained the difference between cock and hen pheasants, asking me not to shoot hens. Soon enough, we could hear the beaters approaching and eventually the nervous wait was over as the odd bird broke from cover. I learned to recognise the distinctive call of the cock bird and when one flew my way, I managed to shoot it, drawing warm applause from my coach.

Needless to say, a sunny mid winter's day in the New Forest is a far cry from the steamy mangroves of East Kalimantan. For me, it was like stepping through the wardrobe into another world. We were shooting on the Beaulieu estate and Lord Montague, who was taking part, had arranged lunch at Palace House, his thirteenth-century stately home—smoked salmon, shepherd's pie, ham, pork pie, wholemeal bread, cheddar, stilton, real beer and red wine. The sun would be down by 4 pm, but there was time for two more drives after lunch. We shot forty brace. I was pleased to have contributed and was delighted when John and I were given a brace each to take home. The generosity and camaraderie had been wonderful, and as far as I was concerned, could never be repaid, but it was extended with such style and warmth that it was not awkward. I didn't know it yet, but England was to be my home for the next seventeen years. It was the traditions, the history, the countryside and the people that made those years so happy.

Back in London, Chris had organised a farewell drinks

party in John's flat. The irrepressible June Langdon, John's mother, prepared the food and drove in from Godalming to deliver it. It was more a reunion for the crew, including Chris, who had sailed in the Mediterranean with John on his uncle's Chinese junk for two weeks during the summer. It was based in Port Grimaud. The party of a dozen or so must have been a success since they were still talking to each other. Two of them, Peter and Claire Stratton, were about to leave for Lausanne where Peter was to spend a year at the IMEDE management school. When they returned, we became close friends, and years later I was persuaded to revisit a church to be their eldest son's godfather.

On the following day, I packed my bag to return to The Hague—but driving not flying. Although the MGB was Chris's prize possession, it was a problem. It was impossible to park in the city during the day and difficult to park overnight in the vicinity of the Ranelagh Gardens mansion blocks. So I acquired another red sports car. On the Sunday night after New Year, I made my way down to Dover to catch a ferry to Calais. I was unaware 1974/1975 was yet another winter of industrial discontent in England and holiday makers are soft targets. There was an almighty queue at the port, so it was midnight before I reached Calais with a four-hour drive to The Hague. But at that time of night the roads were empty so I was able to push the new car and it went well.

Not long before leaving for Qatar, I had moved into a small flat in the Kramsvogellan in Vogelwijk, a genteel district on the North Sea coast. The milkman delivered milk and Grolsch, Dutch lager in a bottle with a glass stopper. This was The Hague; it was fun, and I was settling into my new life there with enthusiasm. I registered at the police station, city hall and the Australian Embassy. I gave up my plans to learn Dutch because there wasn't a person in the office or in the shops and bars that didn't speak English. I joined the Friday night excursion from the office to tenpin bowling. There I met Gisa Ehrlich, a bright girl from Hamburg, who worked in a client's office. We found the Concertgebouw in Amsterdam and went to a Renata Tebaldi recital.

I was busy working on the Idd El-Shargi to Umm Said pipeline survey report. Then my domestic bliss was shattered by a call from Art van Lent. Eighteen months earlier, he had offered me a job with RJBA in Singapore as a junior engineer. Now he was asking if I would be interested in setting up an offshore engineering department for Protech in London.

It was a dilemma. RJBA had been a good and generous employer. In the 1970s 'innovation' was a word rarely used, but Bob Brown was an innovator and his enthusiasm permeated the company. RJBA was a family and the notion of abandoning it was distressing. What's more, the company had gone to the considerable expense of relocating me to The Hague and I had been there less than three months. On the other hand, this was an opportunity to move to London and, following my recent holiday there, that was appealing. Art sensed my hesitation and assured me there was no need for an immediate decision but asked if I would meet Stuart Garner, Protech's London managing director, who would be visiting Rotterdam later in the week. Marcus Brutus's tide was turning again. I agreed.

Stuart Garner was an engaging cockney ergo a consummate salesman. Protech's business in London was predominantly oil and gas process engineering. Shell and BP were important clients and their main work was associated with onshore oil and gas process plants in the Middle East. Recently, however, they had won Aramco projects in the Safaniya and Zuluf offshore fields, which included substantial platform structures and pipelines—all interesting, but not nearly as interesting as the fifty per cent increase in salary offered. A letter confirming their offer of a one-year contract at £8000 a year arrived soon after. This was a generous salary in 1975, and since I would be spending most of my time abroad it would be tax free. I knew I would accept but took days to sideline my misgivings. I gave a month's notice on the first day of February. George Hinkle, Bob Brown's business partner, was ropeable and insisted I finish what I was doing and leave the next day. Most likely he had guessed Art van Lent was involved. I rang Stuart Garner, who asked me to start as soon as I got to London. I cleared my desk and left the next day. That night there was a farewell party at my flat. I was not a total outcast. I had made good friends at RJBA and at a day's notice there were almost twenty people from the office to say goodbye, including Paul and Netty Dantz and Jose and Ludi Jauregui Gonzalez, who had been in New Plymouth. Jose and Ludi had introduced me to *The Magic Flute* and gave me a complete box set of the 1964 Karl Bohm Berlin Philharmonic recording as a farewell present. Fortunately, I was to run into many of these people afterwards. I was learning this was the nature of the oil and gas industry.

Two days later, I was on the Hook to Harwich ferry, disembarking on a frosty Friday morning. I drove the eighty miles into London on black ice—scary for the beginner, but I managed to find Protech's office in Southall mid-morning. There was a warm welcome from Stuart Garner and his deputy, Mike Wood. They briefed me on the new Aramco contracts. Aramco was taking advantage of US$50 a barrel oil and boosting production in the Safaniya and Zuluf offshore fields by 400 000 barrels a day.

The plan for Safaniya was to install eleven new six-well platforms and two new multi-phase trunklines, TL7 and TL8, to bring the crude ashore for degassing in Safaniya GOSP1. Multi-phase pipelines were to transport unprocessed crude, associated gas and sometimes water, directly from the wellhead. Each trunkline was to be around twenty-one kilometres long, increasing in size incrementally from twelve to thirty-six-inch diameter, as successive new six-well platforms increased flow in the line.

The Zuluf field is sixty-eight kilometres north-east of Safaniya, fifteen kilometres south of the Geneva Line separating Saudi Arabian and Iranian waters in the Persian Gulf. The reservoir extended into Iranian territory, so Aramco was keen to ensure it produced its fair share by developing Zuluf to its fullest potential as soon as possible. In early 1975, production from the field was processed in Zuluf GOSP1 and transferred via a short pipeline and an SPM to a permanently moored 450 000-DWT storage tanker. From week to week, this would be transferred to export tankers. The plan for Zuluf was to increase production capacity by 200

000 barrels a day by installing three new six-well platforms and a new GOSP, Zuluf GOSP2, some three kilometres to the east of Zuluf GOSP1. Production from GOSP1 would flow to GOSP2 via a twenty-four-inch-diameter pipeline and production from the entire field would be taken to Safaniya via a new forty-eight-inch-diameter submarine pipeline. The storage tanker would be retired and all crude from the Safaniya and Zuluf fields would be piped to Ras Tanura for export worldwide.

My job would be to manage the design of the three new offshore trunklines and the associated flowline connections to the new six-well platforms. Aramco's project manager, Ken Foss, would be visiting London in about two weeks and we would commence the work following his briefing. I used the time to get to know my new colleagues and settle into London life.

Dick McMahon, my old landlord from the Captain Cook Hotel in Sydney, had been out of London during my Christmas and New Year visit. Since leaving Sydney, he and a school friend, John Brauer, had set up Bligh Appointments, a temporary employment agency for Australian backpackers. It was thriving and Dick had rented a flat in St John's Wood with a spare bedroom. He suggested I move in. It was ideal. It was a two-bedroom ground-floor flat with separate dining and living rooms and a garden. Parking was plentiful. It was a twenty-five-minute drive to my office in Southall and a ten-minute drive to Dick's office in Conduit Street. Otherwise, it was a fifteen-minute walk down Abbey Road past the Beatles' recording studio to the St John's Wood Tube station. It was to be my home for the next seven years and, having become used to an *amah* in Singapore, my first domestic priority was to employ a charlady. I found one via a noticeboard in the local newsagent. She washed, ironed and kept 104C Clifton Hill tidy and was probably the reason Dick and I were able to live together in relative harmony.

Back in Southall, Protech was gradually assembling its team for the Aramco project. One of the senior members, Tony Cruddas, was a process engineer. It was the first time I had worked with this discipline, and it was an education. The art of the process engineer is to outline a complete project on one sheet of paper, called a process flow diagram (PFD). This illustrates the relationship between major items of equipment needed for the project and the nature of the related process flows. This sheet is then converted to a process and instrument diagram (P&ID), defining the size and specification of the piping connecting the process equipment and the instrumentation required to monitor and control that equipment. Having been issued, the P&ID is only changed under extreme duress as it ensures all the engineering disciplines, such as mechanical, electrical, instrumentation, structural and civil, working on a project are working from the same page.

Tony had produced draft P&IDs for each of the trunklines by the time Ken Foss arrived for his project briefing. This work had confirmed we understood the basic elements of the project, however, Ken's main concern was the proposed alignment of the new forty-eight-inch-diameter pipeline from Zuluf to Safaniya. The direct, and therefore shortest, route for the pipeline took it through a blank area to the north-east of Safaniya, labelled on the latest British Admiralty chart as the 'Fasht al Arab'. *Fasht* means reef in Arabic, so the preliminary route selected for the pipeline avoided this area by heading west-south-west from Zuluf GOSP2 towards Safaniya GOSP3, and from there heading south along the eastern flank of the Safaniya field into Safaniya. The problem with this route was multiple crossings of existing flowlines in the Safaniya field and extremely expensive shutdowns for the month the lay barge would need to traverse the field. And it would also be approximately seven kilometres longer than the direct route of sixty-eight kilometres.

I had spent three weeks in Safaniya just over a year before and was well acquainted with the restrictions placed on any activity in the field not considered a routine operation. A lay barge using an eight-point anchor spread to move itself through a field crisscrossed by hot flowlines would test the mettle of the most experienced production superintendent. I asked Ken if there had been any attempt to find a route through the Fasht. No. I suggested the survey would be a small price to pay even if it was unsuccessful. He was slightly irritated by this and, thinking I would shut up, challenged me to do it. Aramco's offshore survey department was already scheduled to survey the proposed pipeline route through the Safaniya field, so I readily agreed to manage a reconnaissance survey across the Fasht if Aramco's survey department agreed. Ken assured me of its cooperation and in the ensuing years I was to learn Aramco project managers usually got what they wanted.

A week or so later, we were advised a survey vessel equipped with Raydist receivers for horizontal control, echo sounder, side scan sonar and sub-bottom profiler would be ready to start work towards the end of March. There were three weeks to prepare. I went on a fact-finding mission to Aramco's engineering and procurement support office in The Hague. Paul Markenstein, Aramco's chief engineer, couldn't have been more helpful. There would be no need to undertake a ground survey to set up base stations for Raydist transmitters. Aramco had wisely established a network of permanent Raydist base stations from Ras Tanura to Khafji, including a solar-powered station on Arabiyah Island, approximately one hundred kilometres north-east of Jubail, so coverage in the Zuluf and Safaniya areas was excellent. It had established permanent recording tide gauges at Ras Tanura and Safaniya and had developed tidal predictions for years into the future. Paul provided as-built drawings for existing pipelines and platforms in Safaniya and Zuluf, which enabled us to fine tune our preliminary alignments, and hence lattice charts, for the pipeline surveys.

I took QF2 from London to Bahrain on Friday 21 March 1975. The flares were still there to illuminate our descent through the night. It was a ten-minute flight from Bahrain to Dhahran. From there, it was up to Safaniya on a DC3, my first flight in one of those classics since prep school days. From Safaniya, I was taken by helicopter out to McDermott's *LB 26*. It was laying flowlines and I was to wait there for *Decca Pilot*, the survey vessel assigned to the TL7 and TL8 surveys. They had four days' work to do before starting on the Fasht survey. When Toby Thorpe, *LB 26's* superintendent, heard this he offered me a cabin on the lay barge.

It would have been silly to refuse a real bed, first class food and the opportunity to talk to Toby about *LB 26's* capabilities. He was reputedly McDermott's most experienced lay barge superintendent. My most important questions related to the ability of *LB 26* to install a forty-eight-inch-diameter riser on the Zuluf Platform in 110-foot water depth and the minimum depth required by the barge to lay the pipeline across the Fasht al Arab. He had no qualms about the Zuluf riser but alarmed me when he explained the minimum depth required across the Fasht would not be determined by the lay barge but by the anchor handling tugs, which drew at least ten feet. I had been thinking all along about a route forty metres wide. This was clearly not enough. It would need to be more like a 600-metre swathe to accommodate not just the barge but its anchor pattern as well, and it would have to be at least ten feet deep, although there could be isolated shallow patches given the neap tide range was five feet.

We eventually commenced the Fasht survey on April 2nd. To start our first line, we went out into deeper water to the north-east of Safaniya via the navigable waters of the Safaniya field. We checked all the gear, waited for low tide and commenced a very slow run along the direct line from Zuluf across the Fasht into Safaniya. It was almost an anticlimax. There were some high spots but nothing above the magic ten feet deep. Over the next three days, we ran parallel lines 300 metres to the north and south of the first line and numerous transverse lines. There were some tight spots, but despite the generally shallow water, the limited side scan sonar coverage indicated a detailed survey would confirm a direct route from Zuluf into Safaniya. On April 5th, I flew down to Dhahran with the preliminary results. Ken Foss was delighted and a week later I was back in London with sufficient survey data to design a sixty-eight-kilometre, forty-eight-inch-diameter pipeline from Zuluf directly into Safaniya.

I was back in time to see my oldest friend, John McDonald, the one who had plugged and shredded his father's shotgun, in the role of Ferdinand in the Leeds Theatre production of *The Tempest*, which had moved to Wyndham's Theatre in the West End—not so much due to John's commendable performance but more likely because the legendry Paul Schofield was Prospero.

John was from a neighbouring property, Highland Plains, outside Clermont. We had been friends before we went to Toowoomba Prep together in 1957. We would board the Queensland Airlines DC3 in Clermont and fly to Rockhampton where we would spend the night with his grandmother. The following day we would fly down to Brisbane in another DC3 and catch a bus to Toowoomba. In 1960, John had gone on to his father's old school, Geelong Grammar, and I went on to my father's old school, Churchie. We met up again four years later at the University of Queensland, where he had embarked on a law degree and was representing Queensland in Australian Rules football. A friend from the Dramatic Society, Willy Young, who was staging a production of *Electra*, was having trouble finding an 'Orestes'. John had the perfect look but just laughed when I suggested he audition for the part. I introduced him to Willy, who persuaded John to give it a go. He must have appealed to John's ego because he eventually took the part and, in the event, gave a creditable performance. He got the bug, gave up the law and in 1968 went to London to study at RADA (formerly known as the Royal Academy of Dramatic Art). The only problem was the theatre doesn't provide a living for many and *The Tempest* was probably the apex of John's acting career.

Back in the Protech offices, we were moving on with the pipeline designs. In addition to the three trunklines, there were a dozen twelve-inch-diameter flowlines, each with a riser connection to a six-well platform and seabed tie-in to one of the trunklines. Each riser and each tie-in was unique, requiring its own stress analysis. One of the new Protech recruits, Mahdi Hassan, was a no-nonsense structural engineer from India, and having worked on the Bombay High field from its early stages, had the experience that enabled him to formulate practical models for each situation. Some of the riser assemblies were complicated, however, I was able to discuss them with Toby Thorpe during an otherwise fruitless trip to Safaniya in mid-May. He had a few suggestions we were able to incorporate, and having done so, we knew we had practical designs a competent contractor could install.

The main purpose of my May trip to Safaniya was to manage a soil-boring programme for shore approach trenches for the new trunklines. To ensure the pipelines would not be a hazard to navigation in the shore approaches, they were to be installed in trenches sufficiently deep to prevent their protrusion above the seabed within a kilometre of the shoreline. Unfortunately, the survey vessel chartered to undertake the drilling was unable to obtain clearance into the Safaniya field. It was one of those ridiculous clashes with bureaucracy known all too well by outsiders in foreign lands. The harder one tries, the more they resist. Not even an Aramco project manager could solve this one. The nutmeg of consolation was I was able to spend a couple of days on *LB 26* with Toby Thorpe again, and he was able to reassure me our trunkline designs looked sensible from an installation viewpoint. After two weeks of frustration, I flew back to a warm reception in London from none other than Mum, who had arrived a few days earlier.

Business had boomed for Dad in the wake of the 1974 flood. By law, he was prevented from competing with the cooperatives that marketed the traditional Darling Downs crops, such as wheat and sorghum. He often complained Australia could teach Russia a thing or two about communism. So, over the years he and my grandfather had persuaded local farmers to plant exotic crops, such as canary seed, mung beans, Poona peas and linseed. The flood rains had resulted in bumper crops, and they were attracting premium prices in Japan, Taiwan and South Korea. As Wilson & Wilson was one of Australian National Line's biggest customers at the time, the prize was centre court seats for Wimbledon—not just for a day but for the entire two weeks. He wasn't going to leave home while business was going so well but didn't have any trouble persuading Mum to go. She loved tennis and was keen to visit her boys in London, so off she went.

She moved into my bedroom in Clifton Hill, and I bought a sofa bed and moved into the living room. It was cosy, but Dick in his inimitable way, made Mum feel at home. We had a lot of roast dinners and a lot of fun. In the lead-up to Wimbledon, we played social tennis in the long evenings at Camden Hill where Mum met a few people who were only too pleased to accompany her to Wimbledon on days when Chris and I couldn't meet her there after work. I was lucky enough to be able to escort her to the final so saw the famous Arthur Ashe victory. At the time, I was travelling backwards and forwards to The Hague for meetings with Aramco. She accompanied me on one of those trips and Art van Lent's wife, Haneke, showed her the sights while I attended my meetings. We were back in London for dinner. On another weekend towards the end of her stay we flew up to the Shetlands to visit Grut Wick where the mighty *Viking Piper* was preparing to initiate the Ninian thirty-six-inch-diameter pipeline installation.

The inspiration for the trip was Joe Williamson, the Texan, who, a year earlier, had come out to Kalimantan to oversee the Bontang LNG Plant survey and left a day later with Delhi belly. We had become friends during my brief sojourn in The Hague, and around the time of my departure, Joe had been seconded to BP as a client's representative on the Ninian project. We had kept in touch, and he had suggested I come up for a weekend to see *Viking Piper* and the northern lights. Unfortunately, the new lay barge had teething problems (literally—the gear boxes on its enormous winches were playing up) and the best we could do was view it at anchor off Grut Wick. We didn't see the northern lights either but enjoyed the pursuit. Mum and I checked into the Scalloway Hotel where Joe and his wife, Carol, were in long-term residence. It was a Saturday night only a week after the summer solstice, the sky was clear and there was no wind. The hotel organised a picnic basket and we drove to a grassy knoll overlooking a cove a mile or two south-west of the town. We built a campfire and waited in vain for the northern fireworks. Fortunately, there was a pod of seals to amuse us, but midnight came and went and we returned to the hotel in soft twilight.

We had experienced the Shetlands, albeit on a rare perfect evening, as they had been for hundreds of years before North Sea Oil transformed them and the entire British economy. Joe Williamson was just one of the thousands of workers who gathered there in 1975 to build the Sullom Voe terminal and its feeder pipelines from the Shell Brent and BP Ninian North Sea oilfields. First, oil was shipped in November 1978. This was Brent crude, and in the ensuing years, Brent crude became a major benchmark for world oil prices. West Texas Intermediate (WTI) is the other major benchmark and although both are light, sweet crude oils, WTI is slightly sweeter than Brent, meaning it has a lower sulphur content.

Building the Brent pipeline was a tremendous challenge, made even more so by poor route selection. Earlier chapters have noted the prime objective of pipeline route selection is to minimise cost and this usually means minimising length. Brent was the exception and the experience revolutionised offshore pipeline design and construction. To reduce length, Shell elected to bring the Brent pipeline ashore at Firth rather than at Grut Wick, BP's landfall choice for the Ninian pipeline. This meant the Brent line had to cross Yell Sound through a ten-kilometre zone of rocky outcrops, pinnacles and cliffs in water up to one hundred metres deep and with cross currents up to six knots. The savings made by length reduction, also around ten kilometres, could never have paid for the subsea civil works required to smooth a twenty-metre-wide corridor across Yell Sound. But they did it, and by September 1975 the section had been installed, although post installation surveys identified substantial spans.

Arrangements were made to support the spans with grout-filled mattresses and rock dumping, however, before this could be done, a 120-metre section was stripped of its concrete weight coating and floated to the surface. In the same way that a thirty-five-knot gale destroyed the Tacoma Narrows Bridge by inducing harmonic oscillations in its deck, so the six-knot cross currents in Yell Sound instigated damaging vibrations in the Brent pipeline spans and their concrete weight coating was effectively hammered off by incessant collisions against a rock-hard seabed. The Loch Ness monster had moved to the Shetlands. Fortunately, concrete weight coating aside, the pipeline was undamaged. The floating section was flooded, submerged and stabilised with concrete saddles. Easily said, but it was a long, complex and expensive task, providing priceless lessons for future offshore pipeline projects in the North Sea and beyond.

For a farewell extravagance I was keen to take Mum to Covent Garden. The summer opera offering was *Peter Grimes*, so I booked Prokofiev's ballet, *Romeo and Juliet*.

Dick McMahon had taken to ballet and earlier in the year had invited me to a performance of *Swan Lake*. There were inspiring moments, but it didn't turn me into a devotee. *Romeo and Juliet* did. Chris came as well and we were in the balcony box immediately above the royal box. From there we looked down on the Russian Israeli conductor, the orchestra and across the stage. I was mesmerised from the moment the curtain opened on the skirmishing Montagues and Capulets to tears for the doomed couple at the end. I wonder what Shakespeare would have made of this sublime music and the way it told his powerful story. Perhaps ... *If music be the food of love, play on.*[7]

And so I did. Mum's visit had kept me in London for almost two months and there was much to be done in Saudi Arabia. Shortly after her departure, the Aramco project management department asked me to go to Dubai to brief J Ray McDermott on the three new trunklines to be installed off Safaniya: TL7, TL8 and the Zuluf forty-eight-inch-diameter trunkline.

On arrival in Dubai, I was delighted to discover McDermott's Aramco liaison engineer was an old friend from Singapore, Ross Quick. Ross was a Victorian who had joined McDermott when *LB 25* was laying pipelines for Esso in Bass Strait. When the lay barge moved to Singapore for the Pulau Bukom project, he followed as project engineer. We became friends. At the time I was living in a hotel, so when his wife returned to Australia for a few months, Ross suggested I move into his house. It was an extremely comfortable colonial bungalow off Thomson Road. More importantly, we were looked after by an *amah* who kept the house and our clothes spotlessly clean. I have never been without an *amah*, a charlady, *pembantu* or daily since.

As Aramco liaison engineer, Ross had a Beechcraft King Air at his disposal for trips to Saudi Arabia. We decided it would make more sense to hold our briefing in Safaniya on *LB 26*. It took us just over an hour to fly there from Dubai and Aramco arranged a Jet Ranger to take us out to join Toby Thorpe on his barge. It was more Toby briefing Ross and me and it didn't take long. Ross dropped me back in Dhahran where I spent three days reprogramming the soils investigation for the new Safaniya trunkline shore approaches. Three months on from my last visit to Dhahran, there had been no progress, so we decided to start again. A new tender was issued with a view to undertaking the work towards year end in cooler and more settled weather—and with a contractor who knew how to get his vessel into the Safaniya field.

Meanwhile, Protech Schiedam had landed a thirty-three-kilometre pipeline route survey contract between blocks K8 and K14 in an extension of the Groningen field in the Dutch sector of the North Sea. They had completed the field work early in August. This included a recording of current measurements over a complete lunar cycle. A draft of the report had been prepared and Art van Lent asked me to come to Schiedam to check it. Apart from a shipwreck requiring a minor detour, there wasn't much to check. Unlike Yell Sound, the sandy seabed off Groningen is as smooth as a baby's bottom. I spent a week turning Dutch English into Australian English and taking an interest in the Groningen gas field, which had played such an important part in Holland's post-war revival.

I have described the 3.8 Tcf Maui gas field as a monster and the 7 Tcf Badak gas field as mammoth so am lost for words to describe the 100 Tcf Groningen field. It was discovered in 1959 and, being an onshore gas field in close proximity to a ready market, the field and its sales gas network were developed quickly. Within ten years, eighty per cent of Dutch households were connected to Groningen gas. The substantial export revenues that ballooned after the Yom Kippur War funded post-war reconstruction, a generous welfare state and Holland's amazing sea defences. Paradoxically, there were economic penalties. By 1974, fifty thousand coal miners had lost their jobs and by 1980 the strength of the Dutch guilder had reduced manufacturing competitiveness with the loss of even more jobs. This sad phenomenon became known as 'Dutch disease'. It was largely resolved by 1990 when Holland joined the European Economic and Monetary Union, however, just as this problem was receding, the Groningen area began to experience earthquakes. It soon became clear that gas extraction was the cause, even though the reservoir is three kilometres deep. Since 1990, there have been more than 250 tremors measuring in excess of 1.5 on the Richter scale. The operator, Nederlandse Aardolie Maatschappij, a fifty/fifty joint venture between Royal Dutch Shell and ExxonMobil, continued to extract gas from the field and pay compensation to affected locals. However, in 2018 the government announced the field would be shut down in 2030 for safety reasons.

But the Groningen problems were way into the future as we wrapped up the K8 to K14 submarine pipeline report and I headed back to London to arrange a visa to return to Saudi Arabia. Earlier in February, in the wake of the Yom Kippur oil price shock, King Faisal had unveiled a plan to gather and treat all the natural gas being wastefully flared as part of the crude oil production process. The estimated reserves of associated gas were around 200 Tcf. The plan provided for the gas to be used mainly as feedstock for a petrochemical complex to be built at Jubail. The Fasht survey had been considered a success and Gordon Moore, one of Ken Foss's colleagues, had requested my services to manage site investigations for a new pipeline delivering gas to Jubail from offshore.

A few days before my departure, Dick McMahon and I were on the town and talking about Saudi Arabia. Out of the blue he suggested we start a consulting engineering company—Marcus Brutus again and, like all the others, it came as a surprise. Even though my father's advice on self-reliance was never far from my mind, I didn't consider myself ready to run an engineering company. To that end, I had applied to enter the MBA programme at the Cranfield Institute of Technology, a leading UK business studies school. But Dick hadn't been a Philip Morris salesman for nothing. Bligh Appointments was thriving and had an office in Conduit Street with the capacity to house and support the new company while it got off the ground. The cost would be trifling, there were no families to feed and I could learn on the job. When we talked it over with Dick's partner, John Brauer, he was all for it and being an accountant was quick to come up with a new corporate structure for the 'Bligh Group'. He suggested we form two new companies, Bligh Engineering (BE) and Bligh Technical Recruitment (BTR), of which I would be a fifty per cent owner, with Dick and John taking twenty-five per cent each. I would run Bligh Engineering and become a paid director of Bligh Appointments. Dick would run Bligh Technical Recruitment and John would continue to run Bligh Appointments. It was agreed all this would be put into effect when my contract with Protech expired in February 1976.

I went back to Saudi Arabia with much to think about. I spent the first month core drilling in the Berri field immediately to the north of Jubail. In 1975, it was a tiny fishing village. Forty years later, it was one of the largest industrial complexes in the world. The Berri field produces light sour crude oil, meaning it has a low viscosity and a high hydrogen sulphide (H_2S) content. One well in the field was producing a massive 82 000 barrels a day. Its wellhead was supported by a platform only three metres square. I boarded it one day to make theodolite observations—not easy with the wellhead piping whistling, the platform vibrating and the heat making the space unbearable. Knowing H_2S is not only corrosive but deadly poisonous, I was pleased to finish my work there.

The drilling contractor was Oceaneering International, better known then as a global diving contractor. It had mobilised a novel diver-operated rig invented by a company from Perth. Basically, the rig was lowered from a small barge to the seabed where it was operated by a diver/driller. The barge was manoeuvred between drill sites by *Lamnalco Hawk*, a supply boat doubling as an accommodation vessel. When the rig was working, it recovered good cores to a depth of five metres, far in excess of anything needed for pipeline route dredging, but breakdowns were frequent and progress patchy. Years later, Oceaneering's expertise in developing the robotics used to make work possible in deep water took it into other industries, such as space and healthcare.

I was the only member of the team with a Saudi visa, and it was often necessary for me to go into Al Khobar to buy spare parts. As it was two hours steaming to the nearest jetty where there was little or no passing traffic, by far the fastest way into Al Khobar was to pack clothing and money in a waterproof plastic bag, swim ashore some 300 metres, walk to the nearest road and hitch a ride. On one such occasion, as I came ashore, I was observed by an old Bedouin squatting alone on the beach. As far as he knew, I was a merman emerging from the sea as by that time *Hawk* had disappeared into the haze. He offered a nonchalant '*Marhaba*' and was completely disinterested as I dressed and headed down the road, hitchhiking.

The Berri field drilling concluded mid-November and the rig headed up to Safaniya. I followed a week later and went aboard *Hawk* to lay buoys for the drilling required for the TL7, TL8 and the Zuluf forty-eight-inch-diameter TL shore approaches. We finished the work in deteriorating weather and anchored for the night off Safaniya Point. By the time we had finished dinner and the cook had secured the crockery, the wind was approaching gale-force. There wasn't much to do but bunk down. I was away with the fairies when the captain raised the alarm. The anchor wasn't holding, and he couldn't start the engines. We rigged another anchor, but this didn't hold either. Fortunately, we were heading for a sandy beach but there was no telling what would happen when *Hawk* went aground, so the captain had little option but to call a mayday and abandon ship. Those who couldn't swim made the beach around a hundred metres off on a life raft. The remainder swam. We spent the rest of the night drying out in Safaniya camp mess.

Come morning, the wind had passed and *Hawk* was very much aground, albeit in one piece. But it would be a long wait for a spring tide of sufficient magnitude to float her. We salvaged our personal gear and I took the Aramco company plane to Dhahran. The inshore drilling for the Safaniya trunklines had been thwarted again. Regardless, Ken Foss and his team continued with the preparation of the necessary tender documentation. I spent the next two weeks in Dhahran working with them. They were a great team. Ken was a softly spoken Canadian who had moved to Aramco from Santa Fe International, a drilling and construction conglomerate. He was without doubt the best project manager I ever met. I didn't understand why then but did in later years. He knew what had to be done and wasted no effort getting there. Bruce Bailey, Ken's senior project engineer, was a born-and-bred Cajun who had previously worked in the Gulf of Mexico for Chevron, an Aramco shareholder at the time. When the chance came to transfer to Saudi Arabia, he grabbed it with both hands. Erhard Voss, a project engineer, could remember his days as an orphan scrounging for food in post-war Berlin before he was rescued by the Americans who placed him in foster care in San Francisco. He took great delight in nicknaming me 'Wallaby', much to the amusement of the team.

A meeting was convened in early December to acquaint major offshore pipeline contractors with the project and its major milestones. The work scope included more than a hundred kilometres of large-diameter trunklines together with eleven flowlines, so it would be a substantial contract by any standard. The usual suspects—J Ray McDermott, Brown & Root and Italian offshore contractor Saipem were there, but much to their surprise the meeting was also attended by representatives from Hyundai Heavy Industries (HHI). HHI didn't own a lay barge and everybody knew it, but it did have a large derrick barge that could be converted to lay pipe. This was a typical Ken Foss manoeuvre. He knew that throwing a new spanner in the works would keep the bidding keen.

The following day, I flew all the contractor representatives, including Ross Quick, up to Safaniya in an Aramco DC3. Although I had taken Ross Quick up to Safaniya in August, he was keen to go again. I suspect his motive was to persuade his competitors that J Ray McDermott would win the bid hands down because *LB 26* was in the field already. In the event, he was correct, but that didn't seem to worry HHI's senior vice president, YD Kim. He was playing a long game.

YD Kim's boss, Chairman Chung Ju-Yung, founded Hyundai as a construction company during the Korean War. Twenty years later, in 1972, he formed HHI to build ships.

He funded Korea's first shipbuilding dry dock on the back of an order for a tanker from prominent Greek shipowner, George Livanos. Chairman Chung soon realised the facilities required for shipbuilding were the same as those required for the fabrication of offshore oil and gas production facilities. So, the US-educated YD Kim was lured from his cosy job in America to build a world-class offshore construction company from scratch. He found a strong supporter in Ken Foss. Ken was not one to make life easy by handing contracts at inflated prices to the usual suspects and the solution was to encourage competition.

To that end, Ken sent Erhard Voss and me to Paris and Baltimore to deliver tender documents and make presentations to contractors who had been unable to attend the meeting in Dhahran. I flew to London for winter clothes and met Erhard three days later at the Intercontinental in Paris. It was a Friday night and the hotel was humming with *Joyeux Noel* celebrations. One party was dancing to a boogie woogie band. I thought I was pretty good at it but was not in their league.

The following day, we took a taxi out to the Entreprise Travaux Publics Maritimes (ETPM) offices in Montmartre. ETPM was a prominent French offshore contractor with a base in Bandar Bushire in Iran on the opposite side of the Persian Gulf to Safaniya. Francis Guerin, its chief executive, and two colleagues were there to meet us. I gave a short presentation on the scope of the technical work and Erhard answered a few commercial questions. Later that evening, Francis and his wife took us to a restaurant where he encouraged me to try oysters from Brittany. This might have been one of the occasions I began eating for pleasure rather than fuel. The following day Erhard and I flew to Baltimore via New York where we went through the same process with Standard Dredging. Erhard's sideline was rental houses and flats in San Francisco, so after the meeting he headed west. I returned to New York.

Bligh Appointments had a New Yorker on its books. Brad Garnett wore glasses, so on his tour of duty in Vietnam was assigned to the typing pool. He now funded his annual summer vacation in London working as a part-time secretary through Bligh Appointments. Theoretically, Bligh could only employ British and Commonwealth citizens, so while in London, Brad pretended to be Canadian and had been primed to respond 'Ottawa' if asked the capital of Canada. I had met him on his last visit and, as people do without really meaning it, he suggested I look him up if ever I was in New York. So, I did. In New York he was a struggling actor living in the basement of 'The Little Church Around the Corner', an Episcopal parish church on East 29th Street. In return for accommodation Brad played acolyte on Sundays. Ever since 1870, when the rector had agreed to hold a burial service for another impoverished actor, the church had enjoyed a close association with that profession and Sarah Bernhardt had worshipped there. Although I wasn't an actor, the rector very kindly took me in, so in the run up to Christmas, I had five days to explore New York from a base smack in the middle of town.

What Brad lacked in funds he made up for in connections,

so it was an extremely sociable five days. In late January / early February each year the Germanistic Society holds (still to this day) its annual Quadrille Ball in the Plaza Hotel. The centrepiece of the occasion is the quadrille, an elaborate French square dance performed by twenty couples. The secret of its enduring success is the social network developed in the months leading up to it when the participants attend weekly parties in various houses throughout New York to rehearse the choreography. Brad took me to one of these 'rehearsal' parties on my second night in town. I surely met all the people I needed to know for a gold-plated entree into New York society, had I decided to stay on. Who wouldn't be tempted to stay in that fabulous city with such generosity? I spent the next three days wallowing in it. But I did make time to visit the Frick Collection where my eyes were opened to the pleasure and otherworldliness of being in the presence of masterpieces. But the Bligh Engineering adventure beckoned, so with three days left for Christmas shopping I flew back to London.

Apart from the Christmas shopping, there was data from almost three months' work in Saudi Arabia to annotate and file. There was three months' salary to collect as well—£2000. John Brauer was quick to swoop and prevailed on me to put £500 towards establishment costs for the new company. Dick McMahon's throwaway suggestion was becoming a reality. But it was still two months off. Meanwhile, my brother was walking out with a new girlfriend, Cherry Kisch. She had invited Chris to her parents' country house in Surrey for Christmas. When Cherry learned Chris had a brother who might be at a loose end, she insisted I come as well. I was soon to learn this generosity and style was typical of the entire Kisch family.

We drove down the A3 to Hatchford Corner early on Christmas Eve. The house was a whirl of decorations and comings and goings, with Cherry's father John at the centre keeping everybody, well almost everybody, amused. The exception may have been Cherry's unflappable mother, Gillian, who kept the show on the road. Cherry had a twin, Nicky, and two younger sisters, Maggie and Woni (Antonia). They had guests as well and John and Gillian's guests were Ansell and Wendy Eggerton, Australians. Ansell was director of strategic planning at Rothmans International. A year or so later, Ansell introduced me to eel farming.

It was a full house but somehow or other we were all assembled and shepherded down the road to Ockham where we were invited for supper and to sing Christmas carols. John Cooper, our host, apart from being an excellent cook and pianist, was an Oxford graduate with a first-class degree in philosophy, politics and economics and managing director of a merchant bank. For his antipodean guests he gave a brief history of William of Ockham, the village's most famous son. This Franciscan friar is credited with the philosophical tenet known as 'Ockham's Razor', the KISS principal in modern parlance. For example, if it looks like a duck, swims like a duck, and quacks like a duck, then it probably is.

It didn't snow for Christmas, but it was perfect without it. In the morning there were stockings full of brilliant small presents at the foot of every bed; there was a beautifully decorated tree; John Kisch was a textbook Santa Claus; Gillian stage managed a wonderful lunch; and everyone was merry. Later in the day, I told John about our plans for Bligh Engineering whereupon he immediately dubbed it Jockstrap Inc.

To mark the arrival of the year of Jockstrap Inc, on New Year's Eve, Dick McMahon and I drove to Paris in the MGB to attend his brother's wedding. As midnight struck, we were caught in an almighty traffic jam on the Champs Élysées, exchanging pleasantries with nearby locals who couldn't move either. Nobody seemed to mind. It was a relatively mild evening and not such a bad place to celebrate the arrival of 1976—that's if you weren't lost and terribly late for a party Peter McMahon's fiancée's family was throwing to welcome the opposition. We eventually escaped to the Avenue Winston Churchill, parked under a streetlamp and were trying to read a map when the car with which we had earlier exchanged a jolly *bonne année'*, stopped. Carmine red MGBs are rare in Paris. A charming woman got out and asked us in English if we were lost. Yes. And when she told her driver we were looking for an address in St Cloud she simply said, 'you will never find it, follow us.' When we arrived at the party some fifteen minutes later, we did all we could to persuade them to come in for a drink, but they just gave us another cheerful 'Happy New Year' and drove off. So, don't believe all the stories you hear about rude Parisians. They weren't the only hospitable locals we met. Peter's soon to be brother-in-law and his twin brother were at the party and in the days and nights that followed left no stone unturned introducing us to the not so well-known delights of Paris. The wedding was, as is customary with weddings, a happy occasion, made more so because Australians occupy a special place in the French soul, and this was plain to see. More than that, the bride's mother had been a prominent *Maquisard,* so it was an honour to meet a member of that brave brotherhood.

Jockstrap Inc

My contract with Protech was up on the February 10th. On my first day back in the office after the Christmas/New Year break, I advised Stuart Garner I would not be seeking to renew it. When I told him about the plan to start a submarine pipeline engineering company he was amused and wished me well. I was pleased we had parted on good terms, and indeed we cooperated on various Aramco projects afterwards.

Stuart was amused because he had a good idea how tough it would be to start an engineering company from scratch. It is difficult enough keeping an established company run by professionals busy, let alone a start-up company run by a twenty-eight-year-old. But we were setting up Bligh Technical Recruitment as well and following the success of Bligh Appointments were hopeful BTR would provide sufficient income to support the new companies in the early stages. It would run along similar lines to Bligh Appointments, but instead of hiring out short-term secretarial staff it would hire out short-term technical staff, such as engineers, draftsmen, construction inspectors and specialist technicians to the oil and gas industry. Dick McMahon's primary role was to set up and run BTR, and in time its extensive personnel database allowed Bligh Engineering to ramp up quickly on new projects. For Bligh Engineering, the initial focus was to make a two-man company look bigger than it was. Dick wasn't an engineer but eventually he would become the company anchorman, allowing me the freedom to spend long periods out of the office either working or chasing work.

BE and BTR commenced operations in Bligh Appointments's offices on the fourth floor of 19 Conduit Street W1, on 16 February 1976, with two dedicated phone lines, a telex machine and bespoke stationery. To announce our presence, I started writing to people in the industry I had met in the last year. This included people from the rapidly developing North Sea. Forties Field Crude Oil, the first from the North Sea, had come ashore near Aberdeen just three months earlier. Few if any of my letters were acknowledged. The exception was a letter from my grandfather, dated February 21st.

Dear Dave

Thanks for your letter from London of the 11th inst. I got it several days ago, your dad sent it on to me from Dalby. You will see from this the postal service is good. In times past I have read letters in Dalby posted 4 days previously in London.

It is good to have your news & I hope in future, you do not have to spend much time in Saudi Arabia. Does the formation of your new company mean you will spend more time in London? The quick changes of climate you have endured lately can't be too good for your health!

I have been here with Mary & Marjorie since last

Thursday week. Marjorie purchased a nice house yesterday in the locality. It is in an elevated area only about 600 yards from Mary's home. Actually it is off Hart's Road and opposite St Peter's School. The homes adjoining & opposite are all nice with tidy gardens. Marjorie's house has a nice area too & has been well kept. As soon as Marjorie takes possession I shall move in with her and help her to get settled. She & Mary are out together now, shopping for suitable furniture I guess.

This city life may not suit me for too long periods & in case the monotony becomes too strained I shall have my Dalby flat to return to for occasional visits. I am becoming very deaf which is most embarrassing, so I suppose living alone saves irritating other people and has its compensations in this way.

Old age is something we must consider and my wish is I don't become a burden to anyone. I must be thankful that my health is a lot better than a few I know who are a lot younger than I.

The girls have just returned so I shall join them.

With best wishes to you & Chris and thanks again for your letter.

Love Dave

If I knew what I know now, I would have been able to read between the lines of this desperately sad letter in its immaculate handwriting. Six months later, he was dead. The gentleman warrior who had overrun the German lines at Pozières was gone. I was in Saudi Arabia at the time, but a month later when I was back in London Mum rang to tell me. She was still distraught. She loved her father-in-law and following the death of Dad's mother was more than happy for old Dave's house to be uprooted and transplanted to our backyard in Myall Street. The move was a great success and I fondly remember university vacations in Dalby when he would join us for morning tea before setting off for his day at the office where he reluctantly became a part-timer after his eightieth birthday.

For a while it looked as if I were to be no more than a part-timer as well, but the Yom Kippur War came to the rescue. In 1967, following the Six Day War, Israel occupied the Sinai Peninsula, including the Abu Rudeis oilfield in the Gulf of Suez. It had annexed enough oil production to supply almost half the country's needs. This predominantly offshore field had been owned and operated by Compagnie Orientale Petroles des Egypte (COPE) in partnership with the Italian petroleum company, Agip. The Israelis kicked COPE out of Abu Rudeis and replaced it with their own newly formed operating company, Netivei Nepht. As the new company had no oil production experience a deal was struck whereby Agip maintained its fifty per cent share in the field in return for technical services. All went well until October 1973, when the Yom Kippur War raged over the Suez Canal. In the fog of battle, an Egyptian heat-seeking missile locked on to the flare stack on the field's central processing platform (CPP). A week or two later, when the fighting had finished, a hastily assembled team of firefighters managed to shut in the CPP wells and extinguish the fire, but there was nothing left above the waterline. Production from remote wells was maintained by bypassing the CPP. In the aftermath of the ceasefire, the return of the field to Egypt became one of the major issues in the peace negotiations. Knowing that they were likely to lose the field at any moment the Israelis were reluctant to rehabilitate the CPP, and indeed in November 1975 Abu Rudeis was returned to the Egyptians. Netivei Nepht marched out and COPE marched back in.

The CPP wasn't COPE's only problem. The entire field was in a sad state of repair above and below the waterline. First priority was a comprehensive audit to assess and prioritise the rehabilitation and maintenance activities required to return the field to full production. COPE's engineers were perfectly capable of looking after the above-water assets but had appointed Oceaneering International, who had a team of divers based near Abu Rudeis, to inspect and report on the state of the facilities below the waterline. These facilities included the remains of the CPP, five wellhead platforms and some forty kilometres of submarine pipelines.

I had maintained contact with Oceaneering following my spell with its drilling crew in Saudi Arabia in November. It was working with Hydrotech, an American oilfield tool manufacturer that had developed a suite of coupling tools designed to obviate the need for welded underwater pipeline connections. I had thought these tools might be useful when making the flowline-to-trunkline connections required in the Safaniya field, but Toby Thorpe had explained how in relatively shallow water where diver time was not at a premium these connections could be made with simple lap joint flanges. But the oil price was pushing the industry into deeper water, so there would be other opportunities. In the meantime, Oceaneering needed an engineer/diver to accompany their diving inspection team in Abu Rudeis. Mike Barry, its Middle East marketing manager, asked me if I would be interested. Certainly. Within a week of opening the doors, Bligh Engineering had secured its first job, £300 a day and expenses. John Brauer was delighted. We all were.

My job would be to record the divers' observations and measurements, make a comprehensive photographic record and compile a report. Mike Barry and I left for Cairo on February 23rd, flying via Geneva and Athens. John Brumby, the company's country manager, met us at the airport and took us to the company's guesthouse in Heliopolis where we spent the night. Cairo was sad and looking as if a good puff of wind would blow it away. But that didn't slow the traffic trying to kill any pedestrian with the gall to cross a road—*Ozymandias, look on my works and despair.*[8]

Our meeting next morning with COPE's operations manager was straightforward, but when we were asked to return later in the afternoon to meet his chairman, we began to appreciate the political dimension of our mission. The return of Abu Rudeis to the Egyptians had been a non-negotiable issue in the latest phase of Henry Kissinger's Sinai withdrawal agreement and the COPE management was clearly under pressure to perform.

John Brumby and I flew to Abu Rudeis the next morning. Huddled in the Sinai sands on the featureless eastern shore of the Gulf of Suez, 240 kilometres south-east of Cairo, the base was no more than a collection of workshops, portable cabin offices and accommodation surrounded by a security fence. It had a small jetty unsuitable for the workboats that took us out to the field. These plied from Nazzazat jetty, some fifteen kilometres to the south. Unfortunately, the road between Abu Rudeis and Nazzazat was shared by Egyptian and Israeli patrols on a three-hours-on, three-hours-off basis, so if you missed a slot, you had a three-hour wait until the next one and there was no way known to persuade the Egyptian drivers to test the limits. This meant we had to be at Nazzazat by 6 am, and if the weather deteriorated, and it did often, then there was a long wait. Weather conditions in the Gulf of Suez were markedly different from those in the Persian Gulf. Winds were generally from the north, frequently in excess of twenty knots and cold at night. Under these conditions it was difficult to lay alongside an offshore platform for prolonged periods, so there was weather downtime aplenty.

In the event, the survey took a month. Apart from weather delays, there were times when we found oil leaks that couldn't be left to bleed, so time was lost making emergency repairs. One of these repairs required the removal of a substantial amount of debris caught in the CPP jacket in the aftermath of the fire caused by the heat-seeking missile. The diving team was able to do much of this with a thermal lance, which works as well underwater as above. I had taken a Nikonos II thirty-five-millimetre underwater film camera with me and was able to take some great photographs of this operation on a day when we had perfect visibility. Fortunately, the weather downtime wasn't completely wasted because it provided time for me to write the report as we gathered the data. So when I returned to London it was ready for typing and on completion formed the basis for a work programme that kept Oceaneering's divers busy in Abu Rudeis well into the future. Mike Barry was happy, but there was no follow up for Bligh Engineering.

It was back to the drawing board. We put an enormous effort into preparing two proposals. One was for a market survey in Russia for Hydrotech's submarine pipeline installation and repair tools. The other was to prepare a lay barge stinger design for Singapore-based Jardine Offshore. Fortunately, we had help from Paul Enemark. Paul, Dick McMahon and John Brauer were old school friends and I had stayed with Paul in his house in Annandale for my last six months in Sydney. Having attended Peter McMahon's wedding as best man, he had taken extended leave from his father's Sydney-based advertising agency to catch up with his old friends in London. His marketing expertise gave the proposals some pizazz, but neither was accepted. In retrospect it's easy to see why. We simply lacked the necessary resources and it showed.

Work prospects may have been dim, but life in London for expatriate Australians with some money to spend was anything but. On my return from Abu Rudeis, I had been in London for just over a year and, even though much of that time had been spent abroad, life in London had developed to the point where there was no time for TV. My brother Chris introduced me to the Camden Hill Lawn Tennis Club where he had met Cherry Kisch. This was a popular after-work destination for summer evenings. A rule limiting doubles games to one set, after which the losers made way for anybody waiting, encouraged members to mix and socialise. Camden Hill, barely a stone's throw from Notting Hill Gate, was also a hive of cheap and cheerful restaurants and popular pubs, such as the Windsor Castle. So evenings at the tennis club inevitably ended up moving on.

Then there was the opera. By early May, when I left for another Saudi Arabian sojourn, I had been to *The Magic Flute*, *Tosca* and *Rigoletto* at the Coliseum and *Fidelio*, *Die Frau Ohne Schatten*, *Il Tabarro* and *Gianni Schicchi* at the Royal Opera House. One of my favourite opera companions was Jenny Locke, a friend with whom I had maintained contact since Sydney days. Jenny enjoyed the opera but worked for a company providing stage lighting for rock and roll concerts. So, she would often reciprocate with seats to one of her gigs. The most memorable were an Elton John and Ray Cooper two-man show somewhere up the Edgware Road and a Bruce Springsteen spectacular at the Wembley Arena. I thought I could work hard in those days, but Bruce Springsteen went non-stop for three hours and shattered the sell-out crowd.

Then there were dinner parties. Dick McMahon and I would have at least two a month and there would be at least half a dozen away. The dining room at Clifton Hill could seat eight comfortably and ten at a pinch. The food didn't matter as the parties were no more than an excuse for a soiree, but typically there would be smoked salmon starters, a stew or a roast for main course, vanilla ice-cream and chocolate sauce for dessert, aperitifs, wine, port and coffee—no salads in those days. We rarely called home because it was so expensive, but it was okay for emergencies. So, I did call Mum on one occasion for instructions on how to roast a leg of lamb. There were ashtrays on the table, everybody smoked and there were Montecristo No. 4s after dinner. Not long after my return from Egypt, Dick moved out of Clifton Hill into a house he bought in West Kensington, but dinner parties continued at Clifton Hill until I moved to Holland Park Avenue in 1982.

Country weekends were popular too. For Australians this was a new institution. We were familiar with weekends at the beach and even beach shacks, but English country houses were quite different. I'm not talking about weekenders, cold and dark on arrival Friday night with lawn to be mowed Saturday morning, raining or not. I'm talking about country houses where people lived and enjoyed the beauty of the English countryside and its traditions—cricket, tennis, school fetes and kitchen gardens in the summer, fox hunting and Christmas in the winter—readymade meaning for the lives that inhabit them. Siegfried Sassoon captured the notion best in *Memoirs of a Fox-Hunting Man*.

My first country house, as mentioned earlier, was Richard and June Langdon's Rough Hill House, Godalming, Surrey. It was a grand two-storey manor house with more bedrooms and bathrooms than the Ritz, a swimming pool, a tennis court and a paddock for Mrs Langdon's donkeys. I can still see the dining room table set for the lavish lunch we enjoyed that day and many Sundays thereafter. Richard was the senior partner of Spicer & Pegler, chartered accountants, so commuted to the City daily. One day when the lunchtime conversation turned to the pleasures of British Rail, he explained how every morning he took the same train from Godalming and sat in the same seat, in the same compartment, in the same carriage, with the same five companions. And so they returned from Waterloo each evening. Conversation was usually sparse as there was more interest in the newspapers. That was until the day one of the brotherhood was missing from the return trip. Following an enquiry, the conductor advised the absentee had died during the day and was returning freight to Godalming. The dismayed silence was eventually broken when one of the company asked, 'why freight, when he had a first-class return?'

As related earlier, my brother Chris and I spent Christmas, 1975, with the Kisch family at Hatchford Corner, Cobham, Surrey, also down the A3 and not far from Rough Hill House. It too became a regular weekend retreat, not just because the Kisch girls attracted queues of amusing admirers from Oxford and Cambridge, but also because John and Gillian were such enjoyable company. Hatchford had a tennis court and swimming pool and, most importantly, a croquet lawn where John took delight in roqueting opponents' balls into the boundary hedge—his metaphor for life. John's father, Sir Cecil Kisch, had been a distinguished public servant who rose to be deputy undersecretary, India, from 1943 to 1946. John had followed in his father's footsteps and joined the Colonial Office. He was in Kenya during the Mau Mau rebellion where he was secretary to the governor's emergency committee. So he had more than a passing interest in my excursions to the Middle East and its turmoil.

Not long after my return from Egypt, I was invited for Sunday lunch. It didn't occur to me anybody would have heard of Abu Rudeis, let alone know something about it, but the moment I mentioned it John almost exploded. It transpired that his cousin, Michael Kisch, had been the site manager there for Netivei Nepht. He was determined I should meet Michael next time he came to London, and I did, but that meeting would have to wait for a pivotal trip back to Saudi Arabia.

Shortly after the weekend at Hatchford, I was surprised and delighted to receive a call from Erhard Voss, temporarily stationed in Aramco's offices in The Hague. I had quietly advised Aramco contacts that Dick and I had started Bligh Engineering but hadn't pushed too hard as I was queasy about upsetting Protech and not confident the world's biggest oil company would want anything to do with its smallest engineering company. Erhard asked me if I would come over to discuss some work. It doesn't take long to fly from London to Rotterdam if you are in a hurry. I was there the next day. Erhard was his usual bustling self—'Any work yet Wallaby?'—and lots more to that effect. Aramco was installing more of its standard six-well platforms in the Zuluf field. The design contract had been awarded to Protech but Ken Foss, Erhard's boss, wanted me to manage the route selection surveys. In the wake of the Fasht survey, I had become the Aramco Offshore Projects's go-to man for pipeline route selection, and the Zuluf GOSP area would be complicated due to the proliferation of existing pipelines. I readily agreed to manage the survey and suggested to Erhard that on completion of the field work, rather than hand the raw data to Protech, who had no expertise to handle it without me, I prepare the pipeline route selection layouts, pipeline design calculations and alignment sheets. It would relieve Protech of an irritant and provide Bligh Engineering with its first real engineering assignment. 'Good idea, Wallaby. Leave it to me.' I spent the rest of the day in the contracts department where a friendly Englishman, Peter Pease, took all the details necessary to prepare a standard Aramco Overseas Company (AOC) call-off contract for Bligh Engineering Pty Ltd. The centrepiece of this contract was a table of man-hour rates to be charged for work carried out for Aramco by Bligh in London, and it was between AOC, a Dutch Company, and a British Company. Bligh Engineering had taken off.

A week later, I was aboard the *Grayquest* heading north from Dammam to the Zuluf field. May is the start of the hot season in the Persian Gulf and with the heat comes the winds. Not long after leaving the West Pier, there was a storm warning, so we weathered the night in the lee of the Abu Ali Peninsula where I had spent so much time with the Oceaneering drilling crew a year ago. We then spent an uncomfortable day pushing through the northerly swell up to Safaniya where we hove to, taking care to avoid being blown ashore in the middle of the night as we had six months earlier. A week later, there were two days of reasonable weather when we were able to run 260 kilometres of survey lines. We then had to wait another two days for the winds to settle sufficiently to complete the last 150 kilometres. In the meantime, I was able to prepare preliminary layouts, which I took to Dhahran to discuss with Bruce Bailey.

Platform-to-platform pipelines initiate with an export riser and a dogleg and terminate with a dogleg and an import riser. The risers connect the platform topsides piping to the pipeline on the seabed and are supported by the platform structure. The risers are connected to the pipeline via doglegs, which are sections of pipe installed at right angles to the main pipeline and sized to absorb thermal expansion in the pipeline. The primary concern for route selection and riser/dogleg assembly design in congested areas around a GOSP is the installation methodology. Ideally, the assemblies are installed with all welds made above water and one hundred per cent radiographed to confirm weld integrity. In some cases, a seabed flange connection may be permitted when the assembly cannot be installed in one piece, in which case the flange is usually the lap joint type.

Three weeks after leaving London, I was back with the unprocessed survey data and preliminary layouts. Dick had arranged interviews with several cartographers, so within days BTR had made its first sale and Bligh Engineering had its first employee, albeit temporary. There was no space for a drawing board in the office in Conduit Street, so we rearranged the furniture in the living room at Clifton Hill to make room for a drawing board and the dining room table, which became a layout table. There was a lot of pressure from Protech to produce the report and drawings quickly as they were relying on information, such as water depth and riser location coordinates, to complete the design of the riser supports on the wellhead platforms. So, having returned to London, my main focus was to work with the cartographer to plot the seabed contours and turn the preliminary pipeline layouts hatched in Dhahran into formal drawings. Erhard Voss approved them and issued them to Protech, who were happy. I was then able to move on with the preparation of the survey report, including interpretation of the geotechnical data gathered by the sub-bottom profiler deployed during the survey. The cartographer continued with the preparation of individual pipeline alignment sheets, which included a contoured plan and profile, route coordinates, line pipe diameter, wall thickness and specification, concrete coating thickness and specification, corrosion protection details and the location and description of any obstruction in the vicinity of the route. The work was finished early in July. The Clifton Hill drawing office was closed and restored to a living room. There was no further work on the horizon, but at least the days of rising early, often feeling shabby, to make the place presentable for the cartographer were gone.

Often feeling shabby because by early June, when I returned from Saudi Arabia, the summer of 1976 was in full swing. It was the sunniest summer of the century and could easily have inspired *Four Weddings and a Funeral*. There were garden parties, tennis parties, cocktail parties, dinner parties, bridge parties, engagement parties, theatre parties and sailing parties, and every party served smoked salmon. Early in July, John Langdon borrowed a comfortable sailing boat and organised a crew to sail it from Bosham to Yarmouth and back. Dick and I were invited and joined the boat late Friday night in preparation for an early morning departure on the high tide. Apart from Dick and I, the other guests were new acquaintances, Stuart and Julia Wood, Bill

Higgins and two more Julias, who were remarkably tolerant of Bill's Julia jokes.

John was a good sailor and, having weighed anchor on the early morning tide, he easily negotiated our passage down the Chichester Channel and into the Solent. Sailing there can be miserable even at the height of summer, but this was a day to make you want more—glorious sunshine, enough wind to keep the boat moving comfortably and bonhomie. We had a picnic lunch at Cowes and were alongside in Yarmouth in time for a pub dinner. That's where we met a few other crews who proposed after-dinner dinghy races around the marina. These went well until we succeeded in uniting nonparticipants in opposition. No matter how much one has imbibed, sleeping damp to wet through on a crowded sailing boat is unpleasant and rising early to make a leisurely return to Bosham was an easy option. Despite being a short voyage, it fostered long friendships. By a strange coincidence, we all ended up in offices in Mayfair, so it was inevitable we would join up on future skiing and fox hunting expeditions.

From Bosham we repaired en masse to Rough Hill House, Godalming. It was 4 July 1976. John's parents, Richard and June Langdon, warm Americanophiles, were giving a party to mark the two-hundredth anniversary of Independence Day. We had all been invited, together with the great and good of the Godalming parish. Mrs Langdon and her half-American daughter-in-law in waiting, Claudia Luscher, hadn't left a stone unturned in giving the party an American flavour. Her donkeys were draped in red, white and blue; there was a great bonfire; we ate hot dogs and hamburgers and drank lots of beer. It was a wonderful party, but I doubt any of the younger guests thought to reflect on the significance of the special relationship between Britain and the US over the last 200 years.

About relationships, Gisa Ehrlich, who had moved back to Hamburg from The Hague, visited in early July. She was just in time to attend Chris Wilson's garden party in the gardens of his Wetherby Gardens flat. Chris had pulled out all the stops and it carried on late into the night until the complaints from the neighbours couldn't be ignored. Gisa spoke faultless English and enjoyed the party, but a couple of days later when we went to the Old Vic to see Glenda Jackson in *The White Devils*, she struggled to understand the language in Webster's bloodthirsty Elizabethan tragedy.

Gisa went home in time for Chris and me to fly to Brittany with the French contingent from the Camden Hill Lawn Tennis Club. The club was popular with French expatriates, including Michel Cornudet, whose family had a French château near Rennes. The torrid summer had nurtured at least two French/English betrothals, and the party included Yves Tailleur and Mary Shaw, one of the happy couples. The *vacances d'été* is a sacred French institution, so by the time we arrived at the Château du Verger au Coq, Michel's entire family, including three brothers and two sisters, were well and truly in residence, with Madame Dorothy, Michel's mother, firmly in control. This was a real château with its own chapel dating back to the seventeenth century, but it had kept up with the times, so there were more than enough bathrooms with more than enough hot water. We were welcomed with a magnificent dinner on our first night. Everybody spoke English. The French really do make a fuss over Australians, and Michel's father, Gilbert, was no exception. In the years to come, I was to learn how the heroism of the Diggers fighting in France during WW1 hasn't been forgotten.

Not long after my return from France, Brad Garnett arrived in London for his annual visit. This provided new impetus for the summer parties, one of which was the opening of Sandy Goudie's summer exhibition in his Tite Street, Chelsea, studio. Sandy told us Christine Keeler lived in the flat opposite, but I never did see the woman who was responsible for the prohibition of *The Courier Mail* for a week at Churchie in 1963. This mid-summer madness was fun but didn't pay the bills. Towards the end of July, John Brauer, Dick and I took Erhard Voss to dinner at Pontevecchio in Old Brompton Road. We had a table on the footpath. You couldn't fail to notice the scene in the pub opposite, The Colehearne, full of Freddy Mercury lookalikes. By now, Erhard had moved his family into a country house outside Battle in East Sussex and was commuting daily to Protech's office in Southall. The cooperation with Protech on the Zuluf infield pipelines had worked well and Erhard was keen to find a new project for us. He called a few days later, asking me to get to Dhahran as soon as possible. Ken Foss had a job for me and would brief me on my arrival. I flew down to Bahrain on July 29th on QF002. In those days, it wasn't unusual to run into people you knew on flights between London and Australia. Don Batchelor, an old UQ Dramsoc luminary, who had recently retired as stage manager for Harry Miller's Sydney production of *Hair*, was on his way home after a holiday in London. Christine McMahon, the senior stewardess on the flight, had joined me for dinner at the Chelsea Arts Club the evening before. We had maintained contact since our first meeting during a Bahrain-London flight months earlier.

It was now fifteen months since the completion of the sixty-eight-kilometre pipeline route survey from Zuluf to Safaniya across the Fasht al Arab. As expected, J Ray McDermott had won the forty-eight-inch-diameter pipeline installation contract with *LB 26*. The barge and its veteran superintendent, Toby Thorpe, were already working in the Safaniya field, so it was the obvious choice. Some 5300 lengths of forty-eight-inch-diameter pipe, each approximately twelve metres long and referred to as joints, had been manufactured in Japan and delivered to the Al Qatahni pipe-coating yard in Dammam. The one-hundred-millimetre-thick concrete weight coating applied to each joint would ensure the pipe string formed by welding successive joints on the lay barge would sink to the seabed as the barge moved forward. Everything was going smoothly until it was realised there wasn't a jetty in Dammam with the capacity to load out concrete-coated forty-eight-inch-diameter pipe joints. The concrete increased the weight of each joint from six to twenty-one tonnes. Hitherto, the heaviest pipes loaded out from the Al Qahtani yard were thirty-six-inch-diameter joints weighing just twelve tonnes each. This meant the load-out crane footprint on the jetty had increased from around eighty to 140 tonnes. A new jetty was required pronto, otherwise there would be project delays and possibly liquidated damages. This was to be Bligh

Engineering's new project. However, building a new jetty in Dammam was to be easier said than done.

In 1976, Saudi Arabia's Eastern Province was at the peak of a construction boom fuelled by nine million barrels of oil a day at US$50 a barrel. On any day, there were more than 150 ships at anchor waiting to discharge construction materials in Dammam Port. The wait was in excess of two months. In response, the Saudi Ports Authority embarked on a programme to build sixteen new piers. It took six years, during which time annual throughput went from 2.5 to 14.5 million tonnes. The project assembled the largest dredging fleet ever seen, including *HAM 211* and its Australian crew, which had finished their work in Botany Bay. The area inside the port was supposed to be organised chaos but was just chaos. Construction equipment and trucks delivering construction materials jostled with trucks attempting to collect imported freight on the crowded and broken port roads. Fortunately, Aramco and Al Qahtani had influence and had secured a site in the port precinct. My job was to find and buy suitable material for the jetty, design it and build it within two months.

Bruce Bailey met me at the airport and thirty minutes later we were in the heat, dust and glare of Dammam Port. The site had navigable access to the Arabian Gulf, as it is known in Saudi Arabia, and was mere metres away from the road running through the port. My first task, therefore, was to prepare a design brief. The barges used to transport concrete-coated pipe offshore to the lay barge were typically seventy metres long by twenty-four metres wide and 3.5 metres deep.

Fully loaded, they carried 155 twelve-metre joints stacked two deep for a load of 3200 tonnes. They drew 0.5 metres unloaded and 2.5 metres loaded, so the jetty had to provide a minimum depth of 2.5 metres at low tide. The spring tide range in the port is 1.8 metres, so the jetty deck had to be at least 1.9 metres above sea level at low tide. This meant the jetty face had to be a minimum of 4.4 metres from seabed to deck level.

Having established these parameters, it was necessary to determine the loads to be expected from the crane. The biggest available mobile crane was a P&H 9125. With a thirty-metre boom and twenty-eight-tonne counterweight, it could just swing a joint out to the centre of a barge moored alongside, so turning the barge during loading would be necessary. Fully loaded with a twenty-one-tonne pipe joint, the crane weighed 140 tonnes. When queried about the minimum jetty face length required for the cargo barges, J Ray McDermott advised fifteen metres.

With these fundamentals in mind and with help from Roman Namacek, a draftsman/designer working for Aramco who later joined Bligh Engineering, I prepared preliminary designs for two options: a pile-and-beam structure and a sheet-pile-with-rubble-backfill structure. I had written a sheet-pile structural analysis programme during my time in the MSB design office in Sydney so was familiar with the basics. The next step was to trawl the Aramco Material System (AMS), looking for steel piles and beams vaguely resembling the requirements for both options. In 1976, Aramco was building and operating the world's largest crude oil production, processing and transportation complex in the middle of nowhere. It could take months to source a torch battery let alone a high-spec component for a high-pressure pump station. If it had to come via ship, there was another two months delay at Dammam Port as well. The solution was an attempt to carry spare parts for anything and everything, and it was all stored outside Dhahran in a vast array of storage yards and warehouses. But this was to be a heavy-duty jetty and there was nothing even close to the piles or steel sections required. We would have to find the material elsewhere. Inquiries were communicated to every supplier and agent in the Gulf region.

Within days, we had a call from Middle East Equipment Company (MEECO) in Bahrain advising it had 170 lengths of Z section sheet piles, each about eight metres long and 350 millimetres wide. It took Roman Namacek and me a few days to revise the calculations and drawings to ensure they provided a solution. Having done so, I flew over to Bahrain to inspect them. There was no need to hurry. The rust flakes indicated they had been there for ages, but they had been stacked properly and suffered no deformation so were clearly still fit for the job. I renewed my Saudi visa and returned to Dhahran where I spent the next week finalising a cost estimate for Aramco Budget Committee approval, drafting a purchase order and arranging a barge to collect them from Bahrain.

This is where Mike Khouri came into the picture and changed my view of the Palestinians. During the two months I was to spend in Dammam working on the Zuluf pipeline loadout jetty, Mike had been my fix-it man. We became friends. In doing so, I came to appreciate, yet again, how fortunate I was to have been born in Australia. He was one of the unfortunates born in Palestine. Hitherto, I had thought they were the people who hijacked airliners, bombed cafes and murdered athletes. This perception changed as he related how his family had been wrecked, as stone by stone and stick by stick their land was taken away. He had found a Saudi sponsor who helped him to come to Saudi Arabia. His wife and children were parked in Beirut, but his extended family had been scattered to the four corners. Nevertheless, he was irrepressible. With his sponsor's help, he had started a general contracting company, had negotiated a call-off contract with Aramco Offshore Projects and was reliably and successfully undertaking relatively small jobs, such as the jetty. J Ray McDermott offered to build the jetty for US$1,000,000. Mike did it for $200,000 and did it well.

Towards the end of August, a letter arrived from the Port Authority confirming the site location and approving the sheet-pile jetty design. Mike Khouri went to work clearing the site and sent a barge, *Jubail III*, to Bahrain to collect the piles. I went to make sure there were no hiccups. Ken Foss came too. He was itching for a break from Dhahran. In the mid-seventies, a weekend in the Gulf Hotel was as close as you could get to civilisation in that part of the world. There was even a discotheque, Juliana's, run by Claire Stratton's adventurous cousin, Sally Mossop, otherwise known as Big Sal. Incredibly, friends from Singapore days, Tim and Camilla Whittle and Stephanie Smith, had moved to Bahrain and become friends with Sally, so Bahrain was a nice break for me as well.

Of course, there were hiccups. The purchase price of the piles didn't include loading, and Customs wouldn't allow *Jubail III* to come alongside without an in-transit shipping bill. Having Ken Foss along saved the day. Brown & Root, J Ray McDermott's main competitors in the Gulf, were based in Bahrain and would do anything to keep him happy so sent a man who miraculously sorted everything out. They also arranged another Saudi visa for me but for two weeks only.

Back in Dhahran, Ken invited me to his office to talk about a new project he had in mind for Bligh Engineering. At that time, Aramco was operating four offshore GOSPs, sixteen gathering platforms and 142 well platforms in the Safaniya, Zuluf and Marjan fields. All but the GOSPs were unmanned, and significant production losses were being sustained during poor weather when crew boats could not come alongside the ramshackle boat landings. The situation came to a head in June '75 when an inspection team drawn from representatives of various Aramco departments went up to Safaniya to review offshore platform access safety. The weather was uncooperative. The only way to board a platform that day was by helicopter.

A project to upgrade platform boat landings was hatched. It came to be known as the 'boat landing project', involved upgrading 162 platforms in the Safaniya, Zuluf and Marjan fields and would transform Bligh Engineering from a tiny pipeline engineering company to a full-service offshore facility engineering company. The work would include a survey of all the platforms and the design of replacement boat landings for twenty different platform types. This was the perfect job for a new design office. The survey would provide the time needed to set it up and recruit the necessary personnel. I assured Ken we could do it and over the following weeks spent my evenings preparing a proposal and estimate. This was a good enough excuse for a rare call to London. Dick McMahon was delighted. What size office would we need? About 2000 square feet.

But there was still a jetty to build, and six weeks into the project there was a great sense of achievement as the first pile was driven. That sense should have been reserved for the last pile. As the pile hammer was being positioned on the second pile, the rigging gave way and the hammer toppled into the harbour. Fortunately, nobody was injured. It was a serious blow just when it looked like we might meet our target schedule. We looked everywhere for a replacement but even in the Gulf, which was a giant construction site, idle pile hammers were few and far between. The solution was to recover the one we had and send it to a workshop to be stripped and rebuilt. A week later, the visa I had secured in Bahrain was due to expire. I flew over to Bahrain for an extension, but not even Brown & Root and the Aramco Government Liaison Department could save me this time. Ken Foss said Mike Khouri could do the rest and suggested I go back to London and prepare for the boat landing survey.

QF001 arrived in London, as usual, just before 6 am. It was the autumnal equinox and in the days before we frightened children with global warming there was still no sign the long hot summer had run its course. Dick was in the Bligh Appointments offices in Conduit Street when I arrived. He had found an office in Bourdon Street, off Berkeley Square, only five minutes' walk away. The agent from Savills would be there to meet us at 10 am. Number 8 Bourdon Street had been a convent. It would provide nearly 3000 square feet of office space on two floors, not counting the consecrated chapel on the ground floor. Bond Street Tube was about six minutes' walk and Green Park eight minutes. It was fifty metres from Berkeley Square and a hundred metres from Bond Street. Then there was the best part. The lease on offer was the four-year remains of an existing long lease and the lessee didn't require personal guarantees for the rent, a whisker under £6000 a year. It was perfect. The agents sent the lease to David Lloyd Jones, our solicitor. He gave us the all-clear to sign it. Bligh Engineering had its own offices smack in the middle of Mayfair.

Meanwhile, Dick had arranged interviews with four structural engineers. Bligh Technical Recruitment was going according to plan. It wasn't making a lot of money—barely a salary for Dick—but it was gradually collating details for a wide range of technical personnel, enabling ready responses to third-party recruitment enquiries as well as those from Bligh Engineering. The standout candidate was a twenty-nine-year-old Kiwi with an honours degree from the University of Canterbury. Ken Barret had then joined New Zealand's Ministry of Works, where he worked in design and construction before moving to London, where he spent three years on North Sea projects with household names, such as Ove Arup, Sir William Halcrow and Brown & Root. I couldn't understand why he would want to leave the security of his current job with Crest Engineering, but a week later he accepted my offer to join us as a senior structural engineer. We found a secretary/receptionist as well. With an MA from Dundee and a Dip Comm from Strathclyde, Marty Dunning joined us, having spent six years as a research officer with the Ministry of Defence. With her cultured Scottish brogue, she was a model Miss Moneypenny, and as much as we teased her about being an ex-spy, she never denied it. Marty was a wonderful organiser and within weeks had Bourdon Street up and running. Having a real office in a location attractive to clients gave us a tremendous boost and we soon had a regular stream of Aramco visitors, including Ken Foss, who was visiting London mid-October.

Erhard Voss alerted me to Ken's stopover and suggested I arrange a limousine to meet him at Heathrow. Ken Barrett and I would be leaving for Saudi Arabia for the boat landing survey the following week, so it seemed like a good opportunity to discuss our plans and to make sure there were no changes. Shortly after lunch on the appointed day, the gleaming black limo, complete with peak-hatted chauffeur, rolled up to the front door at Bourdon Street, and off I went. Finding Ken was no problem and as we pulled away from the terminal, I took a sly look at my watch and was confident we would be at the Park Tower Hotel comfortably inside the minimum two-hour charge for the limo. As I did, Ken had a brainwave and suggested that as Protech's office was on the way into town we divert to Southall and say hello to Stuart

Garner. Would that be a problem? No, not at all Ken. It would be great to see him.

Ten minutes later, we were in Stuart's grand office—if an office overlooking the main street of Southall can be described in those terms. Mike Wood, Stuart's deputy, and Mahdi Hassan, Protech's project manager for Aramco work, joined us. There was well-deserved amusement at my expense when it emerged there was a limo and chauffeur waiting downstairs. Stuart Garner went into overdrive and left no stone unturned, including drinks all round, to ensure the bill was one I wouldn't forget. There was nothing to do but grin and bear it, but it turned out for the best since before long we were doing the pipeline portion of another Aramco project for Protech. And on the way into town, Ken told me Mike Khouri had completed the Zuluf pipeline loadout jetty and it was doing its job.

A week later, Ken Barrett and I were in Safaniya surveying the 162 platforms to be upgraded by the boat landing project. It was hard work. We left Safaniya jetty on a workboat every morning at daybreak, armed with as-built drawings, a Polaroid SX-70 folding single-lens reflex camera, a fifty-foot tape measure, a notebook and a packed lunch from the Safaniya camp mess. The objective each day was to photograph and confirm key boat landing measurements on as many platforms as we could, weather permitting. If we were still offshore at lunchtime, we took our lunch tied up alongside the platform we happened to be working on. By this time, the boat crew, who would have spent the entire morning fishing, cooked their catch together with fried rice on a makeshift gas-fired barbeque. Their lunch looked delicious; ours tasted like cardboard. One day, they took pity on us and invited us to join them. Having spent a fair amount of time in Indonesia, where cutlery is a foreign concept, I was quite happy to eat with my right hand as the crew did. Ken struggled, but not wishing to offend, did his best. The reckoning came later. In the middle of the night, I woke to the unmistakable sounds of retching from the bathroom separating our rooms. There was nothing to be done. He had dysentery and was glued to the loo with his head in a plastic bucket. Back to the sandwiches.

Ken recovered and the weather was kind so by mid-November we had been to every platform. We spent weather-affected afternoons and evenings compiling our data and photographs and by the end of the survey had categorised the platforms into eleven types. Having done so, we arranged a tour of an example of each platform type with representatives of Aramco's production department to ensure our design ideas captured their concerns. We then spent three days in Dhahran, reviewing the data and photographs with the relevant members of Ken Foss's team. One of these, Ken Herbert, mentioned in passing that he had resigned and was returning to London for family reasons. He didn't have a job to go to and was a competent engineer with tonnes of Aramco experience, so I made him an offer and again was surprised when he accepted. We now had the engineering manpower we needed for the platform modification project. All that was missing was draftsmen, and Dick had shortlisted candidates for interview on our return.

Bourdon Street had been transformed. Dick had employed a recruitment specialist to work with him in BTR and Marty Dunning had arranged everything needed for a working office, such as typewriters, telephones, telex and photocopier. Within days, we had employed an Australian draftsman so were ready to start the work—work that was outside my sphere of competence and would be the first step in transforming the company from specialist offshore pipeline engineer to general offshore production facility designer. Our initial brief for the platform modification project was survey and preliminary design but, following approval of a budget for the project, we were awarded the detailed engineering design contract as well. Combined, the three phases amounted to 10 000 man-hours, billed out in the vicinity of £160,000, providing a base load for 1977 unimaginable three months earlier.

But that was not all. Aramco was producing more crude oil offshore than any other company anywhere and its offshore facilities development agenda was staggering. There was a programme to gather all the associated gas currently being flared offshore. This would require substantial modifications to the company's four offshore GOSPs and new pipelines to take the gas ashore.

Then there was the problem of acid-water production. This is a phenomenon well known to Texan oilmen and in those days there were plenty in Aramco, all nourished on the Spindletop legend. The fabled gusher erupted on 10 January 1901 at an estimated 75 000 barrels a day, doubling the entire American output. Twelve months later, the well started producing water and two years after that production was down to 10 000 barrels a day. Seventy years on, the problem was well understood and managed by limiting well production rates, but even so, by 1976 some Safaniya wells were beginning to produce water. When combined with CO_2 or H_2S, this water became acidic and hence corrosive. This hadn't been foreseen so none of the pipelines installed to date had been fitted with facilities to enable regular 'pigging' operations to remove water accumulations in low spots. A pipeline fitted with pigging facilities has a pig launcher and receiver fitted on the upstream and downstream ends, respectively. The pipeline is pigged during normal operations by launching a pig from the upstream end and recovering it after it has travelled the entire length of the pipeline. Pigs come in a variety of shapes and configurations, depending on the mission. There are spherical pigs, scraper pigs, batching pigs and even smart pigs. Retrofitting pigging facilities on the Safaniya telescoping trunklines was a substantial undertaking. For example, one of the trunklines initiated as a twelve-diameter line and terminating as a thirty-six-inch line had gone through four intermediate size increases. Lines like this were impossible to pig so extensive modifications were required.

Then there was the need for new facilities to maintain output. In 1976, the combined output from Safaniya, Zuluf and Marjan was about three million barrels a day. Maintaining production at this level required around three new six-well platforms a year.

The Aramco departments responsible for this work, such as Exploration, Drilling, Production and Offshore Projects in Dhahran and Petroleum Engineering in The Hague were mostly working with their own information sources, and there were conflicts. I had spent the last eighteen months doing surveys for projects, which in many cases could have been avoided. The platform modification survey had given me time to think. Bligh Engineering was becoming Aramco's preferred offshore pipeline engineer. Our entree had been finding a route across the Fasht al Arab for the Zuluf forty-eight-inch-diameter pipeline. This had saved the client money and headaches. We needed to consolidate our position, and it occurred to me we could achieve this by persuading Aramco to commission us to assemble and unify all its offshore survey data, so that all departments would be working with the same information.

While Ken Barrett and Ken Herbert went to work on the preliminary design for the platform modifications, I went to work on a proposal to establish an offshore data development team (ODDT). The ODDT would assemble all existing Aramco Offshore survey data, produce an offshore pipeline data book and offshore platform data book, consult on the work scope and specifications for future facility surveys, manage those surveys, and finally, ensure the data books were updated with data from future surveys. As the man-hour estimate took shape, I began to worry we might have been over ambitious. For a start, we didn't have the people, and if we did, there was no way we could accommodate them in Bourdon Street. Dick McMahon insisted we would cross that hurdle when we got there. In the meantime, winter was coming, and it was time for some opera.

Dick had organised a box at Covent Garden for *Cosi Fan Tutti* and *La Boheme*. In later years *Cosi* became one of my favourites. However, I found this performance stodgy despite Kiri Te Kanawa's presence and voice. The Glyndebourne Touring Company's production at the Hippodrome in Birmingham in 1987 brought it alive for me, especially John Shirley-Quirk's performance as Don Alfonso. Three weeks later, also at Covent Garden, all was forgiven as Jose Carreras had us all blubbing as the tide went out for his beautiful Mimi.

A busy year was drawing to a close. Jockstrap Inc was on the map. Ken Barrett and Ken Herbert had the Platform Modification project under control. The ODDT proposal, amounting to another 10 000 man-hours, had been sent to Aramco. I had time for Christmas in Australia with a stopover in Florence for Michael Langdon and Claudia Luscher's wedding.

I had met Claudia in Harrods on my first day in London. Michael Langdon, John's brother and Claudia's fiancé, said there was nothing unusual about this because Claudia was always in Harrods. Unusual or not, Chris and I had just entered from Hans Crescent and were taking the escalator up to menswear when I couldn't help noticing a most attractive and beautifully dressed woman descending on the other side. This casual interest soon turned to alarm. As she was about to pass us, my brother vaulted the moving balustrade and embraced her. It startled Claudia too, but it was soon clear they were acquainted. Indeed, the following day Mike and Claudia were both at Rough Hill House for Sunday lunch and for the next two years I saw as much of them as I did of John.

Claudia's mother was American and her father Swiss, so naturally, she was born and bred in the beautiful villa in Florence that effortlessly accommodated the ceremony and reception planned for December 22nd. To make sure the English guests turned up on time, Richard and June Langdon gave a dinner for at least sixty the night before. John Langdon was Michael's best man and delivered his speech that night. It was a side of John I had not seen. He was witty and warm and, I suspect, exceeded even his own expectations. The other nice thing about this dinner was it gave us a day to explore Florence—just enough to appreciate doing it properly might take a lifetime. Having done the Piazza del Duomo and taken a stroll through the Uffizi Gallery our group was overcome by cultural overload so succumbed to lunch. The Chianti put a stop to any further exploration. So, there is unfinished business in Florence.

A wedding adds extra fizz to a party and this was a good one. If there had been a team competition for the tailor and cutter award, the Italians would have won handsomely. Of course they would; they had the bride on their side. I was reminded of my visit to the Via Condotti years earlier but was not quite the greenhorn I had been then. I enjoyed meeting Chris and Vicky Holloway, who were wedding guests that I subsequently became friends with. They had driven from Paris in a Porsche—impressive, but not as impressive as Michael's friend Bing, who arrived from the west country in a Ferrari. Later, I joined Chris in his Porsche as we raced Bing through Florence looking for a night club. That wasn't a great success but I was back at the hotel in time to pack and catch my flight to Brisbane via Pisa, Rome and Sydney.

Bourdon Street

Back at London, Heathrow, Chris Wilson and Cherry Kisch were also Brisbane bound for the summer holidays. But Qantas wouldn't allow Cherry on the flight. Remember Enoch Powell's 'rivers of blood' speech. Nearly ten years on, immigration restrictions for Commonwealth citizens had mushroomed. Australia, still mostly white at the time, was not excluded and retaliated. Cherry needed a visa. Who would have thought this applied to nice people too? Fortunately, Chris had the wit to call Mum and Dad's old friend, Sir Wallace Rae, the Queensland agent general.

The Queensland agent general is based in London to promote Queensland trade, tourism and inward investment. He is also there to look after the children of Queensland Government ministers and their friends who happen to be in London. In the days before Labor governments borrowed heavily to employ thousands of Labor voters as redundant civil servants, everybody knew where to find the Queensland agent general. He was in Queensland House in the Strand, just across the street from The Savoy, where Sir Wallace had a permanent reservation for lunch in the River Room. If you were clever and arranged to see him around midday, you might even be invited to join him there. Now that's a lunch. But for all that, Wally Rae was effective. His outback charm was popular at all levels so he knew everybody in London who mattered, including the Queen Mother and the Australian high commissioner.

Fortunately, Wally was in when Chris phoned. Half an hour later, Chris was called back to the Qantas desk and advised Miss Kisch would be allowed to board the plane and her visa would be waiting for her on arrival in Brisbane. Queensland House was sold in 2015 to facilitate the employment of more redundant civil servants. Wyaralong Dam, initiated by the Liberal Government and completed in 2010, was the last dam built in Queensland. Labor governments in Queensland haven't built any dams, presumably to allow the employment of more unnecessary civil servants. Does Queensland still have an agent general in London? Who knows?

Everybody was in Mooloolaba for the January '77 holiday—Lock and his wife, Mary, with their children, Ben and Sam; Chris and Cherry; Sarah and of course Mum and Dad. Christine McMahon came up from Sydney for a few days as well. Dad had taken an extra apartment in Shemara Court for the overspill. We enjoyed the usual delights of raking over the ups and downs of the past year with friends and relatives. One of the sobering revelations was that seven years on from my graduation, new graduates were finding it much more difficult to find a job. Here was a reminder that *we few, we happy few*,[9] born hard on the heel of WW2, were the luckiest generation ever. We graduated in time for the great post-war boom, we could buy a modest house for less than three years' salary, few have been called to military service and we enjoyed the world and its great cities ahead of mass immigration and tourism.

Refreshed, I returned to London mid-January. The office was going well and I sensed an effort had been made to show the company could function without me. I would have been delighted if this were so. I had often wondered how nice it would be to make money in your sleep. But that was not going to happen. There was always something needing attention, particularly in The Hague. One of Protech's competitors there, Project Engineering Services (PES), had two projects in the Berri field off Jubail, each with a substantial offshore pipeline component. Their Aramco project manager suggested subcontracting the pipeline work, including the surveys, to Bligh Engineering, and they were happy to do so. Mechanical and electrical engineers don't like being offshore in small boats. The work couldn't have come at a better time as the preliminary engineering for the platform modification project was petering out. It would ramp up with a vengeance following approval of the preliminary engineering and budget, but in the meantime we were fortunate to have the pipeline work from PES. In the months following my return from Australia, I was a regular visitor to The Hague. Day trips were not unusual or difficult. I could leave Clifton Hill at 6.45 am, drive to Heathrow, park and catch an early flight to Rotterdam for a meeting in The Hague, in just over two hours.

It was a busy time and looking very much like becoming busier. Mid-February, I stopped in The Hague on my way to Dhahran to discuss our offshore data development team proposal with Aramco's chief engineer, Paul Markenstein, and his deputy, Paul Brand. Sure enough, they were interested but suggested changes, including renaming the project to 'offshore facilities manual'. Would that be possible? Certainly, Dr Markenstein. They didn't hand me a contract there and then. However, they left me in no doubt they were extremely interested but would need time to gather support from other departments. I called Dick McMahon to remind him of his 'Don't you worry about that' remark following my wild prediction two months earlier we might have concurrent projects in 1977 peaking at around fifty people. At the time, we were eight people in Bourdon Street, with room for a dozen or so more.

The prime reason for my trip to Dhahran was to attend the budget approval meeting for the platform modification project. Aramco had bound fifty copies of our preliminary design drawings, long-lead materials list and report into books, which I took on the flight. Excess baggage fifty-four kilograms. Ken Foss met me at the airport and because there was no accommodation available in Dammam suggested I stay with him at his house in Aramco's compound in Dhahran.

I had been in the compound before but not to stay. The gated township could have blown in from rural California and, like Mr Bojangles, *lightly touched down*,[10] but the reality is more interesting. Many of us have seen David Lean's *Lawrence of Arabia* and can be forgiven for thinking Lawrence's comrade in arms, Feisal, founded Saudi Arabia following the downfall of the Ottoman Empire and WW1. Not so. In the post-WW1 Middle East carve-up between

France and Britain, pursuant to the Sykes-Picot Agreement, Feisal went on to become the first King of Syria and following that, Iraq. With Feisal occupied elsewhere, the field was left open for Ibn Saud, then sultan of Nejd, to unify the disparate kingdoms of the Arabian Peninsula and proclaim the Kingdom of Saudi Arabia, which he did in 1932. This was done with the blessing of the British, but a year later, it was the Americans who secured the exclusive concession to prospect for oil in the Eastern Province of the new kingdom. We will never know why for sure, but it's a fair bet Ibn Saud had not forgotten the Sykes-Picot Agreement, which crudely ignored Lawrence's promise of a united Arab nation in return for Arab support in defeating the Ottoman Empire.

In September 1933, the California Arabian Standard Oil Company's (CASOC) geological mapping party landed on an uninhabited coastline at Jubail, now the site of the world's largest petrochemical complex. They explored and mapped the barren hinterland north to Kuwait, west to Riyadh and south to Doha using camels, cars and a single-engine plane equipped for aerial photography. The first drilling target identified by the geologists and named the Dammam Dome was about a hundred kilometres south of Jubail and just across the water from Bahrain, where oil had been discovered a few years earlier. A new camp was established to support the drilling crews. At the suggestion of local Arabs, it was named Jebel (hill) Dhahran. Drilling started in 1935. Six dry holes and three years later, CASOC's parent company, SOCAL (Standard Oil of California, formed in 1911 when John D Rockefeller was forced to break up Standard

Oil), was losing patience—no surprise given one of their palaeontologists, having concluded a tour of the prospects, declared he would drink all the oil found in Saudi Arabia. By early 1938, the company's board was poised to abandon the concession. The chief geologist in Saudi, Max Steineke, flew to San Francisco and persuaded them to hold off pending completion of the seventh well, which at the time was making very slow progress towards a deeper formation. Well No. 7 started producing oil in the first week of April and by the end of the month was producing 3000 barrels a day. A year later, Ibn Saud came to Ras Tanura and opened a valve to transfer Saudi Arabia's first crude oil cargo to the tanker, *DG Schofield*, bound for SOCAL's refinery in Bahrain, fifty miles away. His dependence on the Mecca pilgrimage, previously his only income, was over.

By 1948, Texaco, Exxon and Mobil had farmed into CASOC, and the name had been changed to the Arabian American Oil Company, or Aramco for short. Jebel Dhahran became Dhahran, Aramco's primary base in Saudi Arabia and the nerve centre for the oilfields that have made Saudi Arabia rich and funded the movements that have destabilised the Middle East ever since. By 1977, the Aramco compound at Dhahran was, for all but the most observant visitor, a town just like any other in the drier regions of the American heartland. The citizens were all 'Aramcons', mostly white Americans from the Deep South, with a few Canadians thrown in. The cars were American, the street signs were in English, and there was a golf course, a bowling alley, baseball fields and tennis courts. But there was no church, no bacon in the commissary and no saloon bar. In 1951, an intoxicated Saudi prince murdered a British diplomat. Ibn Saud imposed a ban on alcohol in the kingdom in all but a few places, where a blind eye was turned on discrete use. One of these places was the Aramco compound in Dhahran. New arrivals were issued with a still and the latest issue of *The Blue Flame*, a handy guide to moonshining. A few Dhahran enthusiasts produced great alcoholic beverages, or 'Sadiki' as it was referred to locally. Occasionally a careless amateur would get it wrong and blow himself up, in which case, if he survived, he was quickly and quietly sent home.

The budget approval meeting for the platform modification project was scheduled for early March, so I had two weeks to kill while Aramco's project planning and budget coordination department prepared a budget. I spent much of the time up at Safaniya, including a day out at Zuluf GOSP2, where Toby Thorpe was setting up *LB 26* to install the forty-eight-inch-diameter Zuluf Safaniya trunkline riser. This is a near-vertical section of pipe supported against the platform substructure connecting the pipeline on the seabed to the topside's piping. Ideally, all the joints are welded above water, so installing a forty-eight-inch-diameter riser assembly coated with four inches of concrete in water just over thirty metres deep would test the most experienced barge superintendents. Not Toby Thorpe. A week later, the job was done and the entire line was ready for hydro testing. Ross Quick was nearby on the *DB 19* installing a new standard six-well platform. I took a chopper over to see him. It was now over three years since we had worked together on the Shell Pulau Bukom pipeline and

SPM in Singapore. These invaluable excursions gave me the opportunity to talk directly with operators and constructors in their own backyards to ensure our engineering and design addressed their specific needs, wherever possible. There was certainly not one engineer from Offshore Projects in Dhahran who had spent as much time in Aramco's offshore fields as I had, and I think this may have given them the confidence to award significant projects to a fledgling engineering contractor.

The Platform Modification Project budget was approved but not without additions. I spent the following week writing up the minutes to reflect the changes and the week after that chasing attendees to sign off on them. With the last signature, the project was approved. Ken Foss suggested I get back to London ASAP to get on with the detailed design. I didn't tell him Ken Herbert had an advance copy of the minutes and had started already. I was planning to celebrate with a long weekend in Paris.

Weekends in Dhahran were observed on Thursdays and Fridays. I booked a seat on an Air France flight leaving Dhahran late Wednesday night and arriving in Paris first thing next morning. Three months previously, at Mike and Claudia Langdon's wedding in Florence, Chris and Vicky Holloway had given me their address in Paris, insisting I come to stay if I was there. I called from the airport and woke Chris, who was at first bemused but once he had all the pieces in place suggested I catch a taxi to their flat in Rue du Cherche-Midi.

You know you are in Paris when you exit the Périphérique

at Porte Maillot and drive up the avenue leading to Étoile. And if you ask the taxi driver to cross the river on the Pont de l'Alma, you can be enchanted even further by the Eiffel Tower—one of the great city landmarks, along with the Acropolis, St Peter's and even the Sydney Opera House (understandable prejudice from an Australian opera tragic). It was still early when I arrived at the Holloways, so I walked down to Boulevard Raspail where a street vendor was selling nothing but ham in baguette sandwiches and Côtes du Rhône by the glass—the perfect antidote to a month in Saudi Arabia.

Chris and Vicky were ready to receive their surprise guest by the time I returned. But there was a problem. On Friday morning they were driving to Courcheval in the French Alps to join a party in the chalet of Chris's partner, Mike Hawkes. The solution was for me to go as well, never mind there was no room in Chris's Porsche for three of us or that I had never seen a snowflake. What about the gear? Don't worry, you can rent what you need when you get there. So it was settled. On Friday night I would take the overnight train to Courcheval. With two days in hand before then I had time to catch up with Peter McMahon's in-laws who had been so hospitable during the wedding fifteen months earlier. There was also time for a visit to the Impressionists in the *Jeu de Paume*. This collection was moved to the Musee d'Orsay ten years later when its brilliant conversion from railway station to museum had been completed.

By now I was beginning to learn a journey is as much about the getting there as it is about the destination. A mundane trip from Dhahran to London was being transformed by a detour into the French Alps, and what a process! You start with a good dinner and plenty to drink in Le Train Bleu in Gare de Lyon. You give yourself time to find your *couchette* on the midnight train to Moûtiers. You then fall into it and pass out but not before making arrangements to ensure you don't miss your stop at Moûtiers. From there, you take a shuttle bus up to Courcheval 1850, not 1600 or 1350.

I followed the script and indeed slept from Paris to Moûtiers. A maiden foray into the Alps for a Darling Downs native is a memorable event. Our house on the banks of Myall Creek, which drains 1800 kilometres to the Southern Ocean, was around 345 metres above sea level. That's a fall of one in 5000—imperceptible. Quite the opposite in the Alps. I had seen them from the air. On my trip back to London from Cairo a year earlier, as the plane passed by Mont Blanc, I felt I could reach out and touch them. I saw snow wafting from the peak in an updraught. But being on the ground gave you everything—the fresh air, the scent, the crunch of snow and the panorama—a sure-fire tonic for a hangover. Not that I had one. Like the Man from Snowy River's stock horse, I was *sniffing the battle with delight.*[4]

Chris was at the bus terminal to meet me, and we walked up to Chalet Eboulis, where I met the various members of the party as they emerged from their bunks. There were fourteen, not counting two chalet girls, who kept the place tidy and produced delicious breakfasts and dinners. Apart from Chris and Vicky, the only other guest I knew was Bill Higgins, who had been on John Langdon's Bosham-to-Yarmouth voyage nine months earlier. I met the others over breakfast.

Afterwards, Chris took me to the ski-hire shop, where I was fitted with skis, boots, a pair of salopettes and a ski jacket.

We took a chairlift to Verdons, at the top of the nursery slopes, where my introduction to the art of skiing began—first a snow plough, then a side slip and then, praise the lord, a green slope back to the lift station at the bottom of the mountain. This sounds easy, and it is when you get the hang of it, but it takes time and more than a few falls. After shepherding me down the hill a couple of times, Chris headed for more testing slopes off the top of the mountain, leaving me to practise on the nursery slopes, where, from time to time, other members of the party would swoop by to lend encouragement or offer advice.

The plan for the day was to rendezvous for lunch on top of La Loze. As I was not sure where the restaurant was, I was there with time to spare so was able to observe the style with which most members of our team arrived *en scène*. Pom Hawkes, Mike Hawkes's wife, skied beautifully, and like all the women in the party, looked the part. With my new best friends I queued for lunch. The English are fanatical about being in the sun, so a table had been booked on the south-facing sundeck, despite the fact that even in the sun the hot food eventually takes on a frozen glaze in such cold climes. However, it was soon overcast and threatening snow. Fortunately, we were able to retreat to an inside table but by the time we had finished our coffee/cognacs it was quite white outside. The beginner's slope back to 1850 from La Loze is difficult enough to follow at the best of times, let alone in a whiteout. Fanny Johnstone and Suzy Hoddle, other members of our party, insisted on accompanying me, and thank goodness they did otherwise I would probably be pushing up the Edelweiss somewhere along that track.

Thus was my introduction to the French Alps and skiing and to a group I count as friends more than forty years on. That is, all except dear Fanny, who proved only the good die young by doing so tragically less than twenty years later. On Sunday night, I took the train back to Paris and was in Bourdon Street before lunch on Monday.

Work was well under way on the platform modification project detailed engineering. It was basic structural engineering, the major element being a sixty-metre-long single-span footbridge between adjacent platforms. Otherwise, it involved the design of improved safety features, including boat landings on more than a hundred platforms in the Safaniya, Zuluf and Marjan fields. It was a project heaven sent for a fledgling engineering company. Ken Barrett and Ken Herbert had established a working design office with drawing boards and desks for a team of a dozen engineers, structural designers and draftsmen, and the work was going well. I was delighted with the quality of the drawings, which, as a company standard, were produced in ink using lettering templates. This gave them a uniform appearance regardless of the draftsmen. And in the pre-personal-computer age, all calculations were performed using handheld electronic calculators.

Programmable Hewlett Packards were the calculators of choice and the engineers were compiling a catalogue of the programmes that were improving accuracy and saving time. The Kens were a good team. The former, a graduate structural engineer, had learned his trade working for household offshore engineering names, such as Halcrow and Brown & Root. The latter had tonnes of practical offshore experience and knew the Aramco system backwards.

Bligh Technical Recruitment was going well too. Dick had a nose for the people who would fit in well at Bligh Engineering, so even when searching for candidates for external clients, he had an eye out for potential high performers for our own use. One such recruit was Murray Chancellor, who came to us as an Australian graduate civil engineer with no relevant work experience but an appetite for anything. Initially, we had him working on North Sea submarine pipeline calculations, which he did quickly and accurately. As he was keen to get to the field before long, we had him working on offshore surveys for Aramco. Another source of valuable recruits was the large pool of English engineers and designers commuting weekly to Holland due to the lack of work in London. As we grew, they came knocking on our door and we were soon to grow exponentially.

We were awarded the offshore facilities manual contract early in April. The project would eventually encompass the assembly of all available records, including hydrographic survey maps, soil reports, diver reports and as-built information associated with Aramco's 260 platforms and 1000 kilometres of submarine pipelines. These records would be incorporated into a manual of more than 400 facility maps covering Aramco's entire 6000 square kilometre offshore area. This manual would then be issued to all departments for maintenance planning and for positioning drilling rigs and construction equipment around existing platforms as well as for use in planning new facilities. And, it would have our name on it. The budget was 10 000 man-hours. At an average £11 per man-hour, it was a big engineering contract by any measure.

The award precipitated a flurry of activity. Ken Herbert took off to Saudi Arabia to gather all the records he could lay his hands on. He knew everybody in Dhahran so was the ideal man for the job. We estimated the project would peak at around twenty-five people. There was no way we could accommodate this team in Bourdon Street alongside our current commitments, so rather than move into a larger space we opted to look for a temporary project office. The property market in London leading up to Mrs Thatcher's glorious reign was struggling, so we had no trouble finding a suitable mews house on a short lease just a stone's throw from Bourdon Street, in Bruton Place. It was even closer to one of our favourite bars, the Guinea Grill.

This momentous award required a special celebration and Marty Dunning found tickets for the Royal Opera's *La Traviata* with Sylvia Sass. Prior to this, I had seen the Lanfranchi film with Anna Moffo in the Eldorado Cinema, Indooroopilly. As an engineering student, one went to the Eldorado more for spaghetti westerns than Verdi opera. But *La Traviata* remains and *A Few Dollars More* has gone. I will always remember the pathos of the overture as Violetta's ghost wanders through her abandoned villa. At Covent Garden I took a greater interest in the detail of this desperate tragedy where the only villain is love. I'm often asked for my favourite opera. Sometimes it's *Rigoletto*, other times *The Magic Flute*, and from time to time it's the last one I have been to, but no matter what, *La Traviata* is hard to beat, and a month later I was back at Covent Garden wiping the tears away as Violetta died in Alfredo's arms once again.

Ken Herbert returned from Dhahran in mid-May with so much data I had to go out to Heathrow to help him get it back to Bruton Place. By then we had transformed the mews house into a fully furnished drawing office and had employed enough people to get the project under way. Ramping up at this pace was a strain on the finances, but John Brauer wasn't too concerned as long as we got the invoices out the door promptly at the end of the month. At the end of June, these amounted to £54,804.73, a far cry from the £600 I had put in as capital eighteen months earlier.

But just as everything was going so well, there was a setback. Marty Dunning advised us she intended to return to Scotland. It was a setback because in the short time she had been with us she had become the company major-domo. She knew how to handle Dick and me and we both knew the office was in safe hands when we were away. Apart from that, we could rely on her to deal with administrative matters in The Hague if necessary. We did everything we could to change her mind but, like Mrs Thatcher, the lady was not for turning. Months later, the real reason for her departure became clear when she married Ken Barrett and they lived happily ever after. There was no way Marty was going to allow anybody to tease her for an office romance. But typical of her sense of duty, before leaving she found a replacement and Barbara Mitchell was up to the challenge.

Meanwhile, on the back of good rain in March, Mum and Dad planned a trip to London for the summer. Wally Rae organised Royal Ascot and Jimmy O'Sullivan conjured up tickets for Wimbledon. Jimmy was one of Dad's contract bridge partners and proprietor of Jackson and O'Sullivan, the printers in Queen Street. On my twentieth birthday I was arrested in the RE (Royal Exchange Hotel, Toowong) for underage drinking. I called Jimmy and he came to the Roma Street police station and bailed me out. He promised not to tell Dad, but I think he did. I booked the only tickets left for Glyndebourne, sight unseen. And finally, Michel Cornudet invited Mum and Dad to his wedding in Normandy in July. So, an outline plan for an English summer was in place.

They arrived a week before Ascot, in good time to make sure they had everything they needed for the big day. There were a few showers around, but all was forgiven when Sagaro, with Lester Piggott at the helm, won the Gold Cup for the third time. I joined them afterwards for a garden party that went on well after dark. Long evenings were still a novelty for me, let alone Mum and Dad, who were intoxicated by the occasion as much as anything else.

We spent the next weekend with the Langdons at Rough Hill House, Godalming. The highlight was Mrs Langdon's Sunday lunch extravaganza, sure to send even a giraffe into a deep sleep if not followed by a brisk walk around Rough Hill. Then it was back to St John's Wood to prepare for Wimbledon. Dad was not an avid tennis spectator but Mum had no trouble finding walkers, so this left Dad with time to visit his London customers. He lost his way a few times and swore being in the northern hemisphere had scrambled his sense of direction. He bought a compass and I still have it. Of course, he visited Bligh Engineering as well. Both offices were up and running and work on both projects had begun, so the timing couldn't have been better. I think he was impressed. More importantly, we had a telex, so he didn't feel quite so out of touch with his own office as he might have otherwise.

The next week, they were to be driving around Scotland but not before lunch on Saturday with the Kisches at Hatchford Cottage, Cobham. Dick McMahon and Margaret Armstrong, one of the Bligh Appointments originals, came as well. There was no end to Kisch family hospitality. After lunch there was croquet. I suspect this was Dad's introduction to the game, and years later when spinal injuries sustained ditching his Kittyhawk near Merauke in 1945 prevented him playing golf, he took up croquet and excelled. He had a good eye but more than that loved the strategies involved in a game akin to an amalgamation of billiards and chess.

With his new compass Dad had no trouble finding his way to Scotland and back to Ludlow, where we rendezvoused at the Unicorn Inn in time to watch Bjorn Borg beat Jimmy Connors in a five-set Wimbledon final. But we weren't in Ludlow for Wimbledon. There was a festival and John MacDonald was playing 'chorus' in an outdoor production of *Henry V* set in the ruins of Ludlow Castle. *A kingdom for a stage, princes to act and monarchs to behold the swelling scene!*[11] This was the same John MacDonald from a neighbouring station at Clermont, who was my best friend at Toowoomba Prep twenty years earlier. Mum couldn't believe it and didn't care who she embarrassed when she applauded nearly every time John opened his mouth.

Back in London, Camden Hill Lawn Tennis Club remained a popular gathering place during the long summer months and, with Wimbledon over, Mum loved going there either to play or just enjoy the company. This included many of the group preparing to invade Normandy for Michel Cornudet's wedding later in July. But more immediately another member, David Crossley, had kindly invited us, *en famille*, to his family's country house near Tiverton in Devon. Apart from anything else, this took Dad through Daphne du Maurier country. Twenty years on from reading *The King's General*, *Rebecca* and *Jamaica Inn* etc., and as we drove west along the A303, Dad would see a road sign and say something like 'The Roundheads thrashed the Cavaliers out there at the Battle of Alton in 1643' and similar remarks for Roundaway Down and Langport. He had an extraordinary memory. He knew the telephone number of every farmer in the Dalby district and I still remember contract bridge evenings when, discussing a particular hand with his partner, he could recall every card in every hand.

Years later, Patrick O'Brien replaced Daphne du Maurier in Dad's affections. Who could resist Jack Aubrey? Dad read each of the twenty novels at least twice. So, it was appropriate our next event was not so far from Aubrey country. Our party of ten, including Mum and Dad, John, Gillian and Cherry Kisch, my brother Chris, Dick McMahon and Suzon Stenhouse (a friend from Scotland), set off for Glyndebourne from London in perfect weather. *Die Schweigsame Frau* was Richard Strauss's first opera following the death of his librettist, Hugo van Hofmannsthal. Van Hofmannsthal was not only a fine librettist but also a poet, novelist and philosopher. So, for his next libretto, Strauss approached Stefan Zweig, another Austrian with a similar CV. In his chilling autobiography, *The World of Yesterday*, Zweig described how this encounter blossomed into a friendship with the man he considered to be the *last of the great line of thoroughbred musicians that reaches from Handel and Bach by way of Beethoven and Brahms to our day*.[12] Unfortunately the great man, by his own admission, was past his best, and *Die Schweigsame Frau* is more for aficionados than a party that would have been more comfortable with *A Chorus Line*. It is sung in German and the plot is complicated, so by the interval we were gasping for champagne. And that was that. At the bells for the second act, there was no way we were going to interrupt a wonderful picnic on a beautiful day in the glorious gardens of Glyndebourne.

One could be forgiven for thinking the summer had been an endless weekend, but between the socials progress on our main Aramco contracts was sustained. We even managed to win a small North Sea pipeline study through Paul Dantz who had moved from RJ Brown and Associates to BODL (Burmah Oil Development Ltd). The study was a basic cost exercise examining the feasibility of linking the Brent and Ninian pipeline systems. We had high hopes it would lead to something substantial but during 1977 oil prices softened and North Sea projects were the first to suffer because they were expensive. The mighty *Viking Piper*, the world's largest pipeline installation barge, having installed the Ninian pipeline, suffered the ignominy of demotion to a floating hotel for offshore hook-up work.

No such problems in the shipping world. At the end of his traineeship with Bunge & Born, my brother Chris opted to join its shipbroking department as an intern broker on the Baltic Exchange. The Baltic provided a floor in an imposing building in St Mary Axe in the City, where brokers gathered to match ships looking for cargoes with cargoes looking for ships. A successful match became a fixture from which the brokers earned a commission. It was a gentleman's club, so naturally there was a dining room. As Mum and Dad's London visit was drawing to a close, Chris invited Dad and me to lunch there. We were joined by some of his colleagues and another father, and after a tour of the building, including a visit to the trading floor, we had an enjoyable lunch. Fifteen years later, the IRA detonated a lorry loaded with a tonne of fertiliser parked on the street outside. Three people were killed and the building was wrecked. The Baltic was never the same again. It wasn't the bomb though; it was the internet, and by the time the institution had found a new home much of its business had gone.

Fortunately many of the photographs taken during the summer of 1977 remain. At Glyndebourne, Dad looks pensive, almost distant, in some shots. Who could say why? Possibly because he wasn't allowed to pay for anything. The following week in France he was clearly enjoying himself and, sad but true, if Dad was happy Mum was over the moon. They set off for Michel and Hedwige's wedding in advance of the rest of us and spent two days in the Trianon Palace Hotel in Versailles. Mum was stunned by the gardens and couldn't stop talking about them as we drove down to our hotel near Alencon on the eve of the wedding.

Weddings are supposed to be happy occasions and this one succeeded in spades. Perfect weather helps, but the rest must be attributed to the joy people feel to be part of a day that means so much to the betrothed and their families. Again, the photographs tell the story—father of the bride and father of the groom arm in arm in morning suits and beaming as the newlyweds drive away, mother of the bride rounding up over-excited page boys and flower girls, best-dressed guests milling around outside the tiny Norman church at Vimarcé enjoying each other's company. And so the day went on as we moved to a warm reception at Hedwige's family estate, Château de la Lucaziére, at Mont St Jean. Mum and Dad were received as old family friends and could not have come to the end of their visit on a happier note. They left for Tokyo three days later.

There was a sad footnote. I spent May 2019 in an apartment in the market town of Sainte-Foy-la-Grande on the Dordogne. My brother Chris came to stay for a week so we thought we should try to catch up with Michel and Hedwige. None of the old numbers worked, so I tried looking for them via the internet. Not a nice way to discover an old friend had died three years earlier. Via the funeral notice we were able to contact Hedwige who was still living in Château du Verger au Coq. She insisted we come to visit, so we did. It was a sad return—the demise of a great family that had abandoned its survivors, particularly Hedwige, to a hopeless struggle to save a château, full of life and laughter when we knew it, from turning into a Thornfield Hall.[13]

Ken Barrett left for Saudi Arabia. Early in July, my thinking behind the offshore facilities manual began to bear fruit. The Aramco project management department had plans to install thirty-two new platforms and 280 kilometres of new submarine pipelines in the Safaniya, Marjan, Maharah, Lawhah, Berri and Jana offshore fields. Rather than conduct the surveys piecemeal they bundled them all into an omnibus survey and asked Bligh Engineering to manage it. Providing a man to run a survey is no big deal, but it was the fallout that was important. Having done the survey, we were the automatic choice to undertake the engineering that followed, and this would keep us busy into the following year.

Ken had finished the surveys by the end of August. At the same time, the combined manpower in Bourdon Street and Bruton Place peaked at over forty. Dick McMahon and I did our best to find more work to keep everybody busy, but towards the end of October, as the Offshore Facilities Manual neared completion, we had to progressively lay off the draftsmen and advise the landlord we would not be renewing the Bruton Place lease. The draftsmen were on short-term hourly-rate contracts but that didn't make sacking them any easier. Fortunately, just as things were looking bleak for Bourdon Street as well, we received the first dividend from Ken Barrett's survey.

The bulk of his pipeline survey work had been in the Berri

field and Aramco ranked Berri number one in its campaign to manage acid-water production. Berri field crude has a high hydrogen sulphide content, thereby raising the corrosion risk even further. The acid formed by water combining with H_2S or hydrochlorides in the crude emulsion tends to drop out in low spots and, if not removed, gives rise to corrosion which, in extremis, can lead to a rupture. The remedy is to install corrosion-monitoring and inhibitor-injection systems and to ensure all piping slopes to an installed drain. Pipelines must be installed or retrofitted with pigging systems. Given our familiarity with the problem and the field, we were awarded a contract to prepare preliminary designs and cost estimates for three new tie-in platforms, a new water-intake platform, cantilevered extensions to support pigging and chemical injection facilities on seven existing platforms. This was a substantial contract requiring the addition of mechanical and electrical engineers to our team. Fortunately, word travels fast in the industry and shortly following the award of the contract we were approached by an experienced project/mechanical engineer, Trevor Freund, who wanted to move back to London, having spent four years on Aramco projects in The Hague. So we had an ideal project manager for the job that would keep us busy well into 1978.

The oil and gas industry was a mystery to most people I met socially in London. However, Andrew Salvesen, a member of the Chalet Eboulis skiing party I had met in Courcheval in March, was a Scot and had an interest in an Aberdeen-based company providing well-workover services in the North Sea. Towards the end of September, he hosted a grouse shoot at Kinloch, his uncle's Perthshire estate. Dick and I were invited. Andrew had assured us we didn't need to worry about taking guns but it was clearly an occasion requiring something slightly more formal than a pair of jeans. The answer was Cordings at 19 Piccadilly, a stone's throw from Bourdon Street. Once again, the journey was as enjoyable as the destination. Cordings is still a wonderful shop and by the time we had finished there, apart from looking a little too shiny, Dick and I might have passed as country gents.

The sport for the day was walked-up grouse, meaning the guns formed a line and walked at a measured pace across the grouse moor, shooting any bird disturbed into flight. They are easier targets than driven grouse and I managed to kill a few but couldn't help wondering about the ones I missed or thought I missed. Years later, I was happy to forgo shooting for fox hunting. A hunted fox is either dead or alive after a hunt, but mostly alive. And you don't have to eat it. Grouse is an acquired taste, stringy at best.

Towards the end of October, Dick and I went to The Hague for a coordination meeting with Aramco's Hague-based engineering contractors. It was an opportunity for Dick to promote Bligh Technical Recruitment's services and he made the most of it. Erhard Voss suggested he join us on our trip to Dhahran a week later. It was a great opportunity for Dick to familiarise himself with our work in Saudi Arabia and he accompanied Erhard and me to Berri and Safaniya for briefing meetings with senior field personnel who would be operating the new facilities we were designing. The trip immeasurably improved Dick's understanding of our work in Saudi Arabia and encouraged Aramco managers to deal with him if I was out of town. Indeed, in the years to come, Aramco people came to London to spend a night out with Dick, who took them to pubs and parties they would never have found in Louisiana. And in the coming months I was to be away from the office frequently.

Mid-December, I left for Australia via The Hague, Jeddah and Abu Dhabi. The meetings in The Hague with Aramco's contracts department were constructive, however, the Jeddah and Abu Dhabi meetings were a waste of time and effort. You have to kiss a lot of toads to find the handsome prince of oil and gas. We were lucky to have found Aramco.

Sydney was my first stop in Australia. I had lunch with Frits de Wit. It was almost five years since my fateful motorcycle accident in Ryde. The Botany Bay port development project was nearing completion and Frits was contemplating retirement in New Zealand. The Darling Downs had received good rain in November so Christmas at home in Dalby was upbeat. This extended to Alexandra Headlands, where Dad persuaded me to buy a house block on a canal just south of Point Cartwright for $20,000. I returned to London mid-January a landowner but not for long. Six months later an agent approached Dad with an offer of $40,000. Being a trader, he couldn't resist and begged me to accept, so I did.

For the Chinese, 1978 was the year of the horse. For Bligh Engineering, it was the year of the pig. We launched into the new year full steam ahead, preparing preliminary designs for pigging facilities in the Berri field, but it soon became clear Aramco wanted pigging facilities on all six trunklines in the Safaniya field as well. This would be an enormous undertaking involving complexity, disruption and risk. Complex, because two of the trunklines initiated as twelve-inch-diameter pipelines and telescoped up to thirty-six-inch-diameter pipelines via five changes in diameter. Disruptive, because retrofitting the new facilities would require lengthy shutdowns, reducing production and tending to exacerbate corrosion. Risky, because there was no way of telling how much sediment had settled in a pipeline that hadn't been pigged and in an extreme situation this sediment could trap a pig and block the pipeline.

Aramco decided to initiate the Safaniya campaign with a pilot project. We were invited to submit a proposal for preliminary engineering to install pigging and chemical facilities on Safaniya Tie-In Platform P3. This would facilitate pigging operations on the inshore section of TL1 (sixteen-inch diameter), the oldest offshore trunkline in the field and the entire length of TL6 (thirty-inch diameter). The project would encompass substantial structural modifications on P3 to provide the space necessary to install pumps, chemical storage tanks, diesel generators and pig launchers and the installation of facilities onshore to wash 450 million barrels of crude oil a day. Fortunately, our work on the Berri pigging facilities had provided most of the estimating data needed for the proposal, so with the outline agreed and various chapters allocated to the respective lead discipline engineers, I was able to take a week off to join the Holloways in Meribel.

Like Courcheval, Meribel is a ski resort in France's Trois Vallées region. Chris and Vicky had assembled a great party for the week, including Stuart Wood, without Julia since she had found out about his affair with his secretary, Nicky. Woody was a good no-holds-barred skier and, although feeling low, was happy to take me under his wing to ensure I didn't get into too much trouble. As a result, by the end of the week my skiing had improved to the extent I could test some of the more difficult slopes. But the main result was Woody and I became good friends and years later when I was struggling with the eel farm he proved to be much more than an amateur ski instructor.

In the era of infinite communication, it's difficult to imagine how wonderful holidays were pre mobile phones. Back in Bourdon Street a week later, it was deeply satisfying to find the P3 pigging facilities proposal was ready to go. It was barely out the door when Art van Lent called. He was now Protech's general manager in Houston and needed help with the structural analysis of long spans developing in an operating crude oil pipeline in the northern sector of the Persian Gulf. It had to be completed in three weeks and was I available? It sounded interesting, and in the wake of the P3 pigging facilities proposal there would be a lull. Art had also offered a generous fee, so I agreed.

Société Irano-Italienne des Pétroles (SIRIP) had installed the eighteen-inch-diameter line in 1969 and it was taking around 18 000 barrels a day of sour crude from the Nowruz field to the Bahrgan Oil Terminal. The original designers, Bechtel, had been aware of sporadic seabed currents up to five knots along the pipeline route and had installed it with a 150-millimetre-thick concrete weight coating to make sure it didn't move. These currents had failed to move the pipeline but had scoured much of the sand from underneath leaving it as a series of spans supported by hard outcrops. Some of these spans were as much as fifty metres long. Our analysis had to determine the risk of structural failure in the longer spans and, if needed, remedies.

So off I went to America. Art checked me in to the Oaks Hotel in The Galleria, an upmarket mall on Houston's Post Oak Road, a short walk from his offices. It was comfortable and liar dice was popular in the lobby bar. Apart from Saks Fifth Avenue and Nieman Marcus, The Galleria also had an ice rink and by the end of my stay I had mastered the basics. There was also time one Sunday morning to visit the NASA space centre. Six years on from *Apollo 17*, NASA was still three years away from space shuttle *Columbia's* maiden voyage. But by far my most interesting experience in Houston was stumbling on a Ronald Reagan election rally in The Galleria. With more than two years to run to the Republicans' 1980 National Convention, it was a low-key affair and would have gone unnoticed save for the antics of a band of pro-choice campaigners vehemently opposed to Reagan' s pro-life stance on abortion. They put on a show and at times poor Mr Reagan had a job making himself heard. But in the end it made no difference. Six months later the Shah of Iran was deposed and admitted to the US for medical treatment. Iranian students retaliated by overrunning the US Embassy in Tehran. It was a no-win situation for President Carter and Reagan trounced him in the 1980 presidential election. The pro-choice campaigners need not have worried.

As president, Reagan had bigger fish to fry and the turmoil in Iran was one of them.

We completed the Nowruz pipeline study mid-April. The analysis confirmed the longer spans in the SIRIP pipeline were in danger of buckling and recommended remedies. These were never implemented. In September 1980, Iraq's Saddam Hussein thought he could take advantage of the situation in Iran and invaded. The conflict soon went offshore with the belligerents attacking each other's crude oil tankers. In February 1983, a damaged tanker collided with the Nowruz platform, all but upending it. It was then set on fire by an Iraqi airstrike causing a million-barrel oil spill. Seven Iranian oilfield workers were killed capping the wells.

Bligh Engineering was awarded the P3 Pigging Facilities preliminary engineering project a day or two before I returned from Houston. I was nominated as project manager but this role was effectively assumed by the nominated project engineer, Trevor Freund, who had far more experience at running projects like this than I did. My job was to be more the specialist pipeline engineer and in this role I was invited to return to America to tour Aramco's parent company facilities in Texas and Louisiana.

My first port of call was New Orleans, Chevron's (formerly SOCAL) operations base for the Gulf of Mexico. They were extremely hospitable and there is nothing like a night out in Basin Street, but their biggest crude oil pipeline in the Gulf was a twenty-four-inch-diameter export pipeline so there wasn't much to gain there except, by comparison, an appreciation of the scale of Aramco's activities. The next stop was the operations control centre for the Mobil Pipeline Company in Dallas. Located downtown in a high-rise with a jogging track on the roof, this centre managed the movement of parcels of refined product from refinery to depot via a sophisticated pipeline system using batch pigs. This was instructive but again irrelevant.

Undaunted by these disappointments, I soldiered on to the headquarters of EG&G (formerly Edgerton, Germeshausen, and Grier, Inc.) in Boston. This company emerged from the Manhattan Project and had gone on to develop a number of instruments widely used in subsea survey work, such as side scan sonar and the high-resolution boomer. As a result, it had been an RJBA subcontractor on the Maui and Bontang projects and I had got to know some of their technicians well. But Boston was more than a social call. EG&G had invited me to take a look at one of their newest developments. The basic 'smart' pig carried instrumentation that could measure and record pipeline wall thickness as it travelled through a pipeline. It was an interesting concept and would figure prominently in the future, but again, was not something that would influence our designs for Saudi Arabia. The final leg of my pigging technology odyssey was Paris, where Total had offered to demonstrate its 'gel' pig, currently in development. The main purpose of a gel pig was to safely remove accumulated sediment from a pipeline, and it could change shape to conform to variations in diameter, so it did have a potential application in Safaniya.

The P3 Desalting project, as it became known, surely transformed Bligh Engineering into a truly multi-disciplined engineering organisation and this couldn't have been achieved without Bligh Technical Recruitment, who efficiently produced appropriately qualified and experienced engineers, designers and draftsmen as and when needed. The key was BTR's external clients, the who's who of London engineering, including Bechtel, Brown & Root, Crest Engineering, Foster Wheeler, Kellogg International and Matthew Hall. Job seekers were beating a path to the BTR door, particularly those tired of commuting to The Hague.

By end August, it was clear the P3 project would be ineffective in isolation. Aramco asked us to reset and undertake studies to determine the best way to protect all six Safaniya trunklines, considering multi-diameter, multi-shot and instrumented pigging, chemical supply and delivery options, power supply and monitoring options and, finally, in the Persian Gulf in 1978, environmental impact. This study and the detailed engineering that would follow meant Bligh Engineering's near-term future was secure. There was time to smell the roses.

John Kisch, Cherry's father, was as good as his word and at the first opportunity following my return from Egypt in March 1976 had introduced me to his cousin, who was a regular visitor to London from Tel Aviv. Michael had been Netivei Nepht's general manager in the Abu Rudeis oilfield following the Yom Kippur War in October 1973 until November 1975, when it was returned to the Egyptians. He was astonished to meet somebody in London who had actually been to Abu Rudeis and his first question was, how is Snr Ricci? Ricci was Agip's representative and had been in

Abu Rudeis throughout my entire stay there and had always been helpful and considerate. I didn't know he had been there before the Yom Kippur War and had remained throughout the war. Michael was pleased to hear Ricci was alive and well and was interested to hear my stories about the current state of the field. He was particularly amused to hear that I had occasionally used COPE's helicopter to visit a Micoperi crane barge operating in the field. If I had known the Israelis had stripped it of its original gearbox before handing it back to the Egyptians, I would probably have swum out to the barge.

Michael came to London regularly and, as an engineer, enjoyed coming into Bourdon Street. He often took me to lunch at the Naval and Military Club in Piccadilly, better known as the 'In and Out'. It was no more than a five-minute walk from the office, and we frequently played squash there. Eventually he suggested I join. My application was refused on the basis I had never achieved officer status in the military. The club secretary was clearly suffering acute embarrassment as he explained this to Michael but suggested he could arrange for me to become an honorary non-voting member. I did and thereafter enjoyed all the benefits of the club, including the squash courts and snuff after lunch in the dining room.

Afterwards I would wonder why Michael had been so influential. Years later I found a possible answer in Chaim Weizmann's memoir *Trial and Error*. Weizmann, a Russian Jew who immigrated to Manchester in 1904, was one of Israel's founding fathers and largely responsible for persuading Arthur Balfour to issue the fateful Balfour

Declaration in November 1917.[14] Deceptively simple, it paved the way for the birth of Israel:

His Majesty's government view with favour the establishment in Palestine of a national home for the Jewish people, and will use their best endeavours to facilitate the achievement of this object, it being clearly understood that nothing shall be done which may prejudice the civil and religious rights of existing non-Jewish communities in Palestine, or the rights and political status enjoyed by Jews in any other country.

In 1919, following the Treaty of Versailles, the Balfour Declaration became the essence of Great Britain's Palestine mandate, by which, following World War I, it remained in Palestine to keep the peace as Jews from all over the world settled there. From 1921 to 1931, Weizmann was chairman of the Palestine Zionist Executive, coordinating this exodus. Relations between the settlers and their colonial minders were strained but improved when Weizmann appointed Colonel Fred Kisch, an English Jew with a distinguished WW1 service record, to liaise between the Palestine Zionist Executive (PZE) and the British administration. Much of this success stemmed from his ability to get on well with the Arabs as well as the British.

Kisch resigned from the PZE in 1931 but remained in Haifa to start a business. When WW2 broke out, he returned to active service in Egypt as General Montgomery's chief engineer and a brigadier. As such, he was the senior-ranking Jew in the British Army when he was killed by a German landmine in Tunisia in 1943, but not before fathering Michael who, as a colonel in the Army Corps of Engineers, served with distinction during the Yom Kippur War and ended up managing the Abu Rudeis oilfield. The Kisches are indeed a prominent family of the military and I had a great time in the 'In and Out'.

Then there was bridge at Boodles. I had remained in touch with John Kisch's friend, Ansell Eggerton, since meeting him during Christmas at Hatchford in 1975. Ansell's full-time job was as director of strategic planning at Rothmans International, but he was also director of a small trading company, MacPherson Train & Co, and board meetings were held on the second Friday of the month when the House of Lords was in session. The company's owner, Gordon Macpherson, Second Baron Macpherson of Drumochter, would take the overnight train from Inverness to St Pancras, attend the company board meeting in the morning, the House of Lords in the afternoon and, having qualified for reimbursement of his rail fare and attendance allowance, would retire to Boodles to play bridge. Ansell Eggerton organised the game and, if one of the regulars was indisposed, I would be invited to join. Dress was black tie. We would convene at 5.30 pm, play until dinner, hosted by Lord Macpherson, and having finished the port, play on 'til late. The stakes were not at the James Bond level, but we did play for a pound a hundred, which could be lucrative or costly depending on the cards and partner.

Then there was Emmanuel Tassin de Montaigu. Emmanuel was a French aristocrat born in an inconvenient age but not without the looks, charm and style, which had propelled him into a dazzling marriage. His wife, Francoise Gallimard, had looks, charm and style but, more than that, she had money and influence. Not only an heiress to the Gallimard publishing fortune, she was a senior figure in the company as well. As a young man, Emmanuel had worked for Bouygues Offshore, a well-known French offshore contractor. This had acquainted him with the industry and he was now using his contacts to become the Lemon Drop Kid of offshore oil and gas. Emmanuel would be appalled by the Bob Hope comparison but he did have the ability to laugh at himself. He and his equally feckless aristocratic friend, Gunther Andre, used to joke about setting up a club for husbands with rich wives. The club would have a secretariat whose job would be to make the members look like captains of industry by setting up sham business meetings, lunches, conferences and travel.

Gunther's rich wife was the Countess Christina Beck-Friis of Börringekloster, Svedala, Sweden. Gunther and Kina had decided to move to London, so Emmanuel had invited Dick and me to a dinner to meet them. The moment our eyes met we fell for each other. We talked about it afterwards. It was instantaneous and it was mutual, although neither of us realised how the other felt at the time. Kina was beautiful in every sense. I never did understand what she saw in me. No doubt she was heartily sick of Gunther and his daffy get-rich-quick schemes but that explains nothing. Of course, in this civilised world we enjoyed our dinner, went home and life with its secrets went on.

The Safaniya trunkline pigging studies were well under

way in September when Bill Clune from Aramco Offshore Projects called to say the Saudi Royal Commission for Jubail and Yanbu wanted to build Jubail's new petrochemical port on top of the Berri trunkline. This was no ten-inch-diameter flowline, it was the thirty-four-inch-diameter trunkline transferring around 600 000 barrels a day from Berri GOSP on the northern tip of the Abu Ali Peninsula to Aramco's tanker terminal at Ras Tanura. It would have to be moved and would I come down to Saudi as soon as possible to manage a survey and suggest a solution. Bligh Engineering was now around twenty-five strong and well organised, so it was not only possible for me to leave the office but it was also desirable. A trip like this would probably lead to more work and we would be paid for it.

It would take two weeks to secure a vessel and the necessary gear, but I went as soon as I had the visa. This gave me time to fly around the area and to visit my guru, Toby Thorpe, who I had hoped would be up in Safaniya on *LB 26*. Toby was away on leave but his sidekick, Robert Huvall, was just as helpful. With a name like Huvall, Robert couldn't have been anything but a Cajun. Cajuns cut their teeth installing pipelines in the Louisiana swamps and from my aerial reconnaissance I knew the revised route would have to be through shallow water. The issue would be to find the route requiring the least dredging to provide access for a shallow water lay barge. Robert gave me all the parameters I would need to calculate the quantities.

The survey took six days but might have taken longer had I not impetuously acted to save the gear one night. I have since realised looking before leaping is not my strong suit. We spent the first two days of the survey running reconnaissance lines in a small boat rigged with the echo sounder and Raydist position-fixing equipment. Having completed this work and selected three possible routes for the new pipeline, we were heading from Abu Ali to Jubail in the main survey vessel *Greyquest* for an early morning start. October is one of the best months for weather in the Persian Gulf but on this particular night it was blowing hard. I was on the bridge with the captain when a crewman clambered up from the main deck to announce the line towing the small boat had parted. The captain did his best to stop *Greyquest* as I went to the stern to see what was happening. The small boat, with much of the survey gear aboard, was disappearing downwind into the night and towards a beach and we were heading in the other direction. Replacing the gear would take months, so I went in after it. I was wheezing by the time I caught and boarded the runaway but managed to start the engine and get back to *Greyquest* with all the gear intact. We finished the survey four days later.

By now I was a dab hand with the magnetic card programmable HP 65 hand calculator, and as we ran the survey lines I developed a programme to calculate the dredging quantities. Within three days of finishing the field work, we had prepared drawings, calculated the quantities, selected the optimum route and written a preliminary report Bill Clune and I presented to the Royal Commission in Jubail.

The studies undertaken to inform the preliminary design for the Safaniya trunkline pigging project were more or less complete by the time I got back to London. The issues included dual-diameter pigging, multi-shot pigging, multi-phase pigging, pigging frequency and procedures for safely removing past accumulations of sand from trunklines already in operation. Our proposal for the preliminary engineering was submitted at the end of October and the work started immediately for completion in January. Safaniya was producing 1.5 million barrels a day so we were in the firing line, but our team understood the job and Aramco, so the mood in the office was buoyant if not a little congested. Bourdon Street's 3000 square feet of office space, that looked very empty two years ago, had wall-to-wall drafting boards and work desks.

When it rains, it pours. Shortly after completing the Nowruz Pipeline Study, Art van Lent was offered a senior position with SBM in Monaco. The single-point mooring IHC Holland had commissioned in Botany Bay in 1972 had been designed by SBM and my work on that project had landed me the job with RJ Brown and Associates and Art van Lent in Singapore in 1973. Five years on, SBM had become a household name in the industry, with its mooring and offloading systems an integral part of many offshore oil developments, particularly as exploration drilling moved into deeper water. The Americans were drilling in depths up to 2000 feet in the Gulf of Mexico, but subsea production systems were in their infancy so there was no realistic option for development at that depth in 1978. The most ambitious project under way at the time was BP's Magnus field development in 600 feet in the North Sea. The basic concept was a steel jacket with separate export pipelines to shore for the crude oil and associated gas.

SBM could see the trend and knew future developments in deeper water would rely on the ability to make pipeline connections without divers. Diverless connections had already been performed in full-scale field tests and real operating systems but not below 600 feet. Manufacturers such as Hughes, Vetco, Cameron, FMC (formerly Food Machinery & Chemical Corporation) and Coflexip had anticipated the trend and launched products that were in the market. Art called and asked if we could review the current technology and prepare a report. SBM knew it had to go deeper.

We were flat out with the Safaniya project and this study would have been a distraction, but it was the sort of exercise that could improve our ability to win work in the deeper waters of the North Sea. As luck would have it, two of RJ Brown's brightest and most highly qualified engineers, John Kenny and Paul Davies, had resigned with a view to setting up a specialist pipeline and deep-water consultancy, JP Kenny and Partners, in London. A day or two after the call from Art, they dropped into Bourdon Street for a chat. I asked them if they could write a proposal and, if accepted, do the study, and they agreed. All we had to do was the typing and binding. One of the key elements of the proposal was deciding what constituted deep water. We agonised over this and eventually opted for a cut-off of 1200 feet, twice the depth of the Magnus project. SBM accepted the proposal and our new associates went to work. Forty years on, oil and gas developments had reached water depths of 8000 feet.

A month or so after the lightning strike dinner with Gunther and Kina Andre, Dick and I received invitations to join them for an extended weekend at Kina's family estate, Börringekloster, in the south of Sweden. First, it was a regular BA flight to Copenhagen and then a Twin Otter for a fifteen-minute hop across the Øresund to Sturup Airport, now Malmö International Airport. Gunther was there to meet us. It was less than a five-minute journey to the big house because the airport had been built on the estate. We arrived in darkness but a scattering of lights in several front-facing windows were sufficient to convey the dignity and beauty of this glorious house. No wonder Kina was what she was. The cobbled reception hall was decorated by an imposing collection of mounted stag heads and its double doors were built to accommodate arrivals on horseback. Having shown us where we would be assembling for pre-dinner drinks, Gunther showed us to our rooms. They were comfortable.

Our pre-dinner drink was aquavit served from an ice-encrusted bottle—a foolproof way to get a party started. Dick and I weren't the only guests. Emmanuel de Montaigu's brother, Foulques, and his wife Isabelle, were there together with Francois and Celliane, another elegant couple also from Paris. With only eight, we were all but lost when we moved to the enormous formal dining room. I was still mesmerised by Kina but did my best not to gawp, and she certainly gave no indication of any special regard she may have had for me.

It was not a late evening because Gunther was keen for the men to rise early to man the miradors. These shooting towers stood in cultivated fields around fifty metres from the forest fringe. The idea was to walk to a mirador and climb it as quietly as possible in darkness. Then you sat there with your rifle on safe, waiting for the dawn and the game to break cover to graze on the cultivation. Those wily animals stayed put and if they hadn't it would have made no difference. My new Barbour from Cordings was no match for that cold. I was shivering so much I would have missed a barn. Bacon and eggs in the breakfast room off the cavernous kitchen restored spirits. Gunther was a tireless host and his dedication to field sports took us all over that wonderful estate. We walked up red deer, fallow deer and pheasants, waited impatiently in hides for ducks that stayed away and even had an afternoon trout fishing in the magnificent lake a short walk to the south of the house. We didn't kill much but I did come to enjoy the cold black-and-white landscapes so reminiscent of Bergman films that I didn't enjoy at all.

But I *was* enjoying the English National Opera (ENO) winter season. Barbara Mitchell had arranged a box and first cab off the rank was *La Boheme.* This offering struggled to compete with the brilliant Royal Opera production from two years earlier with José Carreras, but being a favourite, it didn't matter. And if one wasn't enjoying an opera at the Coliseum, there was always dinner at Sheekey's in Covent Garden. Next in line was my first taste of *Il Seraglio.* It's not one of Mozart's big four but is charming if not a little long. Perhaps that's what Joseph II meant after the 1782 debut when he remarked, 'Too many notes'.[15] Mozart didn't take a backward step in his response: 'There are just as many notes, Majesty, as are required, neither more nor less'.[15]

A regular guest in our box was ENO stage manager, Rachel Richardson. She knew the people and the stories, the main one being a changing of the guard. Mark Elder was soon to be music director and coincidentally there would be a raft of new productions. The first of these was *The Marriage of Figaro*, Jonathan Miller's first creation for the ENO. It was one of many Jonathan Miller successes, which went on to threaten the Royal Opera's supremacy in London. The second was Janáček's *The Adventures of Mr Brouček* with Charles Mackerras conducting. It's a fantastic story and the staging was clever, but in the end we go to the opera for the music, and in this respect Mr Brouček failed.

The year was racing away. I was in Houston early in December for more piggery, this time to attend the launch and recovery of a Linalog pig through a twenty-inch-diameter pipeline. This was a so-called 'intelligent' pig designed to measure any wall thickness reduction either from corrosion or erosion. The recovered data indicated areas in the pipeline where there may have been metal loss, but further runs would be required to assess the tool's reliability. This was important because if they were to be used offshore they would require a substantial amount of platform space.

Shortly after my return, Art Van Lent called from Monaco to ask us to start work on the study we called 'Present State of the Art in Diverless Underwater Connections'. John Kenny and Paul Davies were ready and in no time at all were bombarding us with content. Our report-publishing process was to nominate a project secretary whose job was to progressively maintain a lever arch file with the latest version, no matter how premature. The first document into the file was the draft table of contents noting the responsible person for each line item in that table. As draft content became available, a copy would be slotted into the appropriate place in the file. This enabled me to regularly review the progress and quality of each project regardless of who was in charge. The prose from otherwise grown Englishmen was often appalling, but that apart, we couldn't have been in a better position as we closed for the Christmas long weekend with both projects in good shape.

My invitation to spend Christmas with Peter and Claire Stratton included detailed instructions on how to find the Stratton Family seat, Manor Farm, in Wiltshire. Basically, you take the A303 west—but don't leave before nine on Christmas Eve. I couldn't anyway because almost everybody in the office was heading for The Audley, a pub in Mount Street, as we did most Friday nights. On these occasions, Dick McMahon was in his element and could make even the most junior draftsmen feel part of the team. My drive west was tolerable and Stratty was up to show me to my bed when I eventually arrived.

The Salisbury Plain has been farmed since Roman times and the Stratton family have farmed it for generations. Even so, Stratty's father, Richard, was no ordinary West Country farmer. He studied agriculture at Cambridge University and, having graduated, transformed Manor Farm into a modern agricultural enterprise that supported his work in the community and the South & West Wilts Hunt, of which he was a Joint Master. Unfortunately, we didn't get to ride any of Richard's beautiful horses because Stratty was allergic to them. But after the traditional Christmas morning activities of opening presents followed by lunch, we did take a drive around the farm and surrounding countryside, including the White Horse memorial, marking the site where King Alfred defeated the Vikings in the Battle of Ethandun in AD 878.

We had a quiet evening in anticipation of the pheasant shoot Mr Stratton had organised for Boxing Day. Then, after breakfast, I committed the grand faux pas. Claire Stratton was expecting her first baby in a month or so. Stratty's sisters, with their husbands and babies, were also home for Christmas. One of the babies was making an awful fuss and I turned to Claire and quipped that if her baby were to behave like that it might be the end of a beautiful friendship. The remark was overheard by the baby's mother, who erupted in fury and complained to her mother about 'Peter's friend'. Happy families. Fortunately, the shoot provided an escape. But then I made matters worse by shooting Mr Stratton's tractor. Dinner that night was frosty. Stratty did everything he could to mollify his mother and soothe my embarrassment but in the end, retreat was the best option, and we did. Emily Stratton was born a month later and has always behaved impeccably.

Bourdon Street was open between Christmas and New Year. It was an imperative; we were up against deadlines. Not so anywhere else. It was the 'Winter of Discontent', a cascade of calamity. First, it was cold—the coldest since the Great Freeze of 1962/1963, when the Thames froze over. Then, it was inflation. Inflation, largely precipitated by skyrocketing oil prices following the Yom Kippur War, ballooned from eight per cent in 1978 to thirteen per cent in 1979. The event responsible for transforming my fortunes was causing misery for millions of others. Naturally, wages couldn't keep up. The first to strike were the lorry drivers, causing heating oil and food shortages. Pensioners died and schools closed. Garbage collectors and grave diggers went on strike. Garbage piled up in streets and parks and corpses were stored in warehouses, windows open wide. Bligh Engineering didn't escape. There were rail strikes too and key people, including Andy Cooper, our engineering manager, who lived out of town, often struggled to get to the office. Sunny Jim Callaghan, the prime minister, threw in the towel in March and called the general election that Mrs Thatcher won with a forty-three-seat majority. We all know what happened after that.

We managed to keep the heating running in Bourdon Street, but the office was so crowded it might have been better without. The SBM study was finalised, bound and dispatched to Monaco towards the end of January. That was good because the Safaniya pigging project was growing like a weed. There were regular reviews and as the enormity and complexity of the project grew, so did the requests for change. The first big review meeting was convened in Aramco's offices in The Hague for late January. It was attended by a senior Aramco vice president who hoped to demonstrate his technical mastery by asking what the effect of bird shit would be on the solar panels providing power for the chemical injection pumps. But the emerging fear was historical sand accumulation in the pipelines.

John Kenny, who had just co-authored a book entitled *Solid-Liquid Flow Slurry Pipeline Transportation*, reviewed the data and we prepared a draft procedure for removing any such sand from the pipelines. While this was progressing, I was able to spend a week in Courcheval with the Holloways in Chalet Eboulis. It was a welcome break from London's gloomy winter and, as usual, Chris and Vicky had assembled a jovial party. It included James and Harriet Tuckey who I knew from the Camden Hill Lawn Tennis Club, and Henry Lazarski, a flamboyant Parisian lawyer of Polish extraction who arrived in a full-length mink coat and matching ushanka hat. Many years later, Harriet would write a wonderful biography of her father, Griffith Pugh, a physiologist. As the scientific advisor attached to Sir Edmund Hillary's 1953 Everest expedition, he made an enormous contribution to its success by ensuring members paid strict attention to the scientific imperatives, such as hygiene, diet, clothing, tents and most importantly, the gas mixture they inhaled at high altitude. My skiing was improving to the extent I was venturing on to some of the easier black slopes but it was the bonhomie of these occasions that made them so enjoyable—particularly dinners in a chalet warmed by a real wood fire.

Towards the end of February John Kenny accompanied me to The Hague for the next Safaniya Pigging review. Assessing the extent of historical sand accumulations in the pipelines was the main item on the agenda and John did a good job explaining the work we had done in this regard. Ultimately it was agreed that having installed pig launchers, a series of pig runs, starting with foam, graduating to spheres and eventually to full-size scrapers, would dislodge most of the sand present and carry it through the pipelines to the separators onshore. There was also a discussion about manhours. When we started in October, the estimate was 4500 manhours, valued at £47,700. Four months later, it had ballooned to 14 000 manhours, and this was not the only job we were busy with at the time. We had commenced work on an Aramco platform data book and managing more pipeline surveys in the Berri field. Less than three years after moving into Bourdon Street, we were outgrowing it.

There were options, such as the annexe at Bruton Place. But that had been a temporary solution, splitting the company and reducing our ability to work people on multiple projects. It was much better to show a prospective client into a large well-organised and busy office. But we would never find what we were looking for in the heart of Mayfair and certainly not on the terms we enjoyed in Bourdon Street. We approached agents and advertised but weren't offered anything remotely suitable that wasn't on a long lease with the rent secured by directors' personal guarantees—unacceptable to us and David Lloyd Jones, our solicitor.

The issue was unresolved when I went to Saudi Arabia for the final preliminary design review for the Safaniya project in late April. Bruce Bailey was now the project manager and wanted key people from the drilling and production departments to review the draft report before setting a date for the formal technical and budget approval meeting. There were a few changes and we agreed to hold the meeting in Ras Tanura on June 12th. There were two other items. He asked me if I thought we were ready to tackle the detailed engineering for the Safaniya pigging project. 'Certainly, and we are moving into bigger offices to accommodate it and any Aramco personnel you would like to sit with us.' He was happy with that and without writing a blank cheque assured me the contract was ours to lose. I was delighted. Bruce had been Ken Foss's understudy, but the two couldn't have been more different—one an urbane Canadian always in immaculately polished black lace-up shoes, the other a Cajun with a mane of shoulder-length brown hair and crocodile-skin boots to match. But they were both gifted managers and Bruce's word was as good as Ken's.

The second item should not have come as a surprise. Local content was the latest mantra and Saudi employees were achieving senior positions in Aramco. The rising star was Ali Naimi, who was elected to the board in 1980 and became president in 1983. If Saudi engineers were to make an even greater contribution to Aramco's development and operation, why not encourage engineering service providers, such as Bligh Engineering, to establish themselves in the Kingdom? Bechtel led the charge by establishing a substantial presence in Jubail, where it was working for the Royal Commission. But it caught me unprepared. We were about to be awarded a substantial contract in London and to accommodate it were looking for a bigger office. We were being advised to set up in Saudi Arabia as well. Without more North Sea work, the London office might become redundant. We would also need a local partner. Aziz Omran, one of Bruce Bailey's brighter Saudi project engineers, offered to introduce me to

HRH Turki Bin Nasser Bin Abdul Aziz. Prince Turki was the commander of the Saudi Air Force Base at Dhahran Airport. In theory, he was the ideal partner. Not only was he powerful, but he was also British Aerospace's partner in Saudi Arabia. I thanked Aziz but for once was reluctant to rush my fences without consulting Dick McMahon and John Brauer. Not only that, but I also needed to spend time in Safaniya checking measurements and other details on the platforms associated with the Safaniya pigging project.

Dick and John were warm to the idea of an office in Saudi Arabia. They saw it as a golden opportunity for Bligh Technical Recruitment, already providing manpower for clients there. Indeed, the more we thought about it the more sense it made to initiate there as a manpower service supplier, with engineering bringing up the rear. This didn't resolve our office problem in London. We were at the stage we thought we might have to lease an annexe when John Brauer called, asking if we had any work for an American student looking for vacation employment. We couldn't legally employ an American and were strapped for space, but I suggested she come for a chat anyway. She was a bright girl and clearly loved being in London. As I was about to thank her for coming round and apologise for wasting her time, it occurred to me she might be the perfect person to wander the streets of London looking for our new office.

Carolyn was nonplussed at first but quickly caught on as I explained our predicament. Most offices for let in London were long leases advertised in newspapers, agents' offices or on billboards attached to the premises and were of no interest to us. We were looking for around 5000 square feet of open-plan office space on a short lease, somewhere between Mayfair and the City of London and no more than 500 metres from a Tube station. I explained a short-term lease was usually the remains of a long-term lease and was rarely advertised because agents couldn't charge much for finding a short-term tenant. Such an office would normally be above a ground-floor shop front. Her job would be to walk around looking for upper floors with the lights out and therefore vacant. Having found something like this, she was to make enquiries and if it looked remotely suitable call either Dick or me, otherwise come in regularly to report. She accepted my offer of a secretarial salary paid weekly in cash. Within weeks, she had the hang of it and was soon identifying possibilities, and as we assessed these her understanding of the brief grew. By the time I returned to Saudi Arabia for the Safaniya Pigging technical and budget approval meeting, I was quietly confident our roving property scout would come up with the goods.

Dick Larkin, one of our senior piping designers, accompanied me to Dhahran. We were accommodated within the Dhahran compound in Steineke Hall. This was preferable to a hotel in Al Khobar since it was so much easier to accept the numerous dinner invitations extended to visitors by Aramcons eager for news from the outside world. Having arrived a week in advance of the project approval meeting, we were able to arrange preliminary presentations in Safaniya and Ras Tanura. As a result, the main event went smoothly. All that was needed then was to prepare the minutes and persuade the attendees to sign off. This took about two weeks, but the effort was not without reward. With all the signatures in place, the project would be funded and we could start work on the detailed engineering in London.

Meanwhile, Murray Chancellor arrived to manage a survey in the Berri field. I took him to Ras Tanura to meet Bill Planck, Aramco Survey Department head. Murray was a quick learner and keen to spend time in the field. The direct income from these jobs was not so important but they had been the pathway to the larger jobs Bligh Engineering was now enjoying. I was no longer willing or able to spend extended periods in the field, so it was important to encourage a bright young engineer who was. It was also important considering our plans for the local office. One obvious objective was to ensure this office was the go-to office for any new offshore project. The key to that was up-to-date survey and soils data and records of all Aramco's offshore facilities. If anybody had it, we did.

With the local office in mind, I also sought a meeting with Prince Turki bin Nasser, our putative joint venture partner. Unfortunately, he was in London, but Fouad Zatar, the general manager of the prince's holding company, Lama Establishment, was familiar with our ideas, so I met him in Al Khobar and took him through our plans for the Arabian Bligh Corporation (ABC). Fouad was obliging and constructive, offering support with office space for the initial stage of the venture and the recruitment of local staff. Afterwards, he agreed to join me for the meeting I had arranged with local lawyer, Ahmed Audhali.

The first thing I noticed as we walked into Audhali's office reception was J Bright's eighteenth-century cartoon depicting a plaintiff pulling a cow by its horns, against a defendant pulling it by the tail as lawyers feverishly milk it. Later on, I was to discover Ahmed had acquired more than a legal degree during his sojourn at Oxford (or was it Cambridge?). He took us through the steps required to establish a Saudi Arabian joint venture corporation, assuring us it would be painless and inexpensive. In the event, painless and inexpensive turned out to be £7,000, but he was the only lawyer in the Eastern Province who spoke English.

After five weeks in Saudi Arabia, I was beginning to feel like an Aramcon, eager for news of the outside world, even though in the six years since my first visit communications had improved to the extent it was possible to make an international phone call. Dick Larkin had returned to London with all the information required to prepare the detailed engineering estimate for the Safaniya pigging project, so there was no hurry in that regard, but I was keen to be back in England in time to qualify for the Fastnet Race.

Not long after Michel Cornudet's wedding in Normandy, Chris Wilson accepted an offer to join EA Gibson Shipbrokers in London. His boss, John Vening, an experienced sailor, had soon pressed Chris into his crew on *Paper Moon*, a Nautor Swan 39. Shortly thereafter I joined as well. It meant Friday nights in the summer were often spent driving down to the Royal Southern Yacht Club on the Hamble for dinner, spending the night on *Paper Moon* and rising to catch the tide for the Solent. Early in the '79 season, John announced his intention to give it focus by entering the Fastnet Race. It didn't mean much to Chris or me, except five days seemed a long time to spend in a sailing boat. To qualify we had to complete two races, so we did the Round the Island Race and the Cross Channel Race to Le Havre. We were ready to go when a week before the start the boat snagged a wire and bent the propeller shaft. It couldn't be repaired in time for the race, so John had to withdraw. We were disappointed but not for long. The forecast wasn't good, but the race started on Saturday in fair weather. Early Monday morning, much of the fleet was becalmed in fog off the Cornish coast, but everybody knew there was a low to the west of the Fastnet Rock, heading straight for them. On Monday night, those that hadn't withdrawn sailed into a hurricane that capsized seventy-five boats and drowned sixteen crew. The rescue campaign launched by the Royal Navy, the RAF and the Royal National Lifeboat Institution brought out the best of Britain. They risked appalling conditions and saved hundreds of lives. Miraculously, none of the rescuers died.

On the day I wasn't as sick as a dog in a yacht fighting a hurricane in the Western Approaches, Bligh Engineering received a letter from Aramco requesting a bid to prepare a detailed engineering package for the Safaniya pigging project. Three weeks later, we submitted our estimate of 17 000 manhours at a cost of £190,000 over a duration of ten months. We were thirty strong in Bourdon Street and in the process of recruiting ten more, but there wasn't enough space. Just as it looked as if we would have to take drastic action, there was a call from Carolyn, our property scout. 'I think I have found the office Mr Wilson, but the landlord is difficult.'

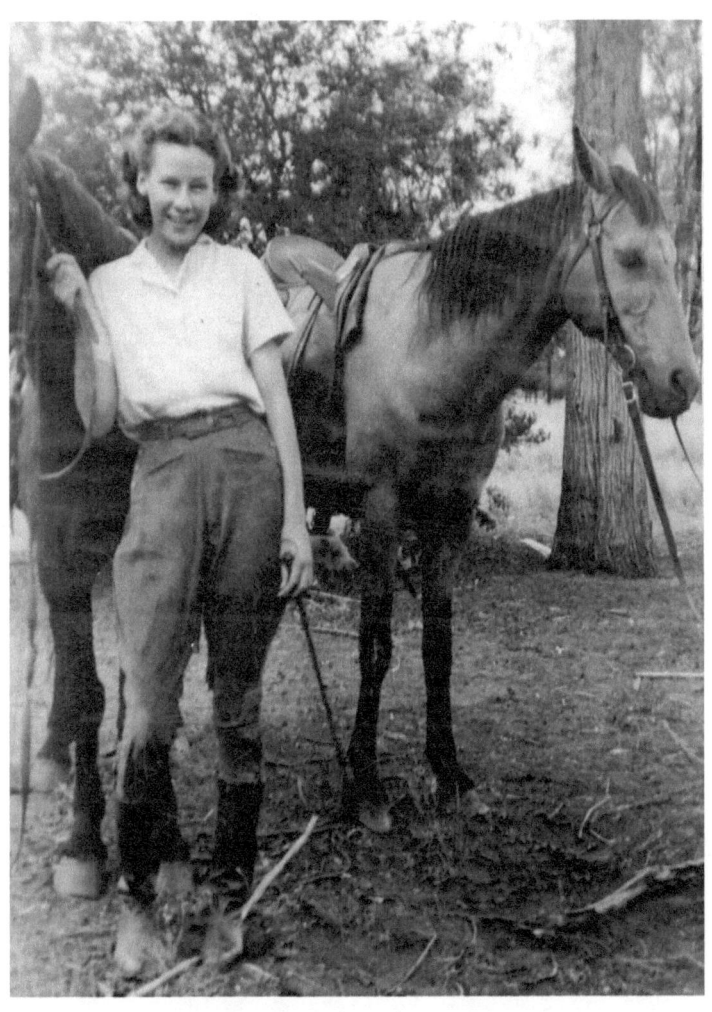

1941   Mum on Billi Station just before enlisting in 1942

1946 Mum and Dad in Townsville 1946

1953   With my brothers Christopher and Lockwood at the house by Dalby Aerodrome

1956   Grandfather Dave, Lock, Dad, Chris and I at the new stockyards at Mount Oscar

1959   With Dal Skirving, Ian Russell and John MacDonald at Toowoomba Prep

1972   Initiating the Botany Bay Port revetment

1973   Petromer Trend's Jaya Number One Well in Irian Jaya that initially produced 63,000 barrels per day

The author

1974   With Inong Satibi in Singapore

1974   Trappings of Flash Harry days in Singapore, a Honda Four and a TR4

1975 Laybarge 26 at work in Aramco's Safaniya Field in the Persian Gulf

1977 With Dad at Michel and Hedwige Cornudet's wedding in France

1980   Aramco's Zuluf GOSP1 in the Persian Gulf

1983   The indefatigable Ginger

1985   Sitting for Sandy Goudie in Glasgow

1987   Dispatching eels from Ratcliffe-on-Soar power station in Nottinghamshire

1992   Installation of the Bontang Train F gas trunkline in East Kalimantan

1997   Guests including Johnny Morris, Peter and Claire Stratton and, Mark and Sarah Beaumont at a dinner at Brooks's

1999   The Bakrie Engineering office in Jakarta

2000   A Tunu Field manifold platform designed by Bakrie Engineering

2001   DW in the Bakrie Engineering offices shortly before returning to Australia

Paul Street

The difficult landlord, Mr Cowan, was not there when Dick and I arrived to meet Carolyn and view the office. Vera, his friendly secretary, showed us around. It was on the second floor of a two-storey building a hundred feet long and fifty feet wide, running east-west with the entrance at the western end on Paul Street. There was a small office suite at the front occupied by Mr Cowan's company, British Merchants (Sales) Ltd. Later we heard how Mr Cowan had acquired British Merchants as an asset-stripping exercise. The office lease was all that remained. The available space to the rear was around 4700 square feet of open plan, save for around ten partitioned offices lining the southern and eastern walls. The open-plan space was well illuminated by skylights and had been occupied by an architectural firm that had been unable to hang on for Mrs Thatcher's economic revival. Most importantly, it was within 800 metres of Liverpool Street Main Line Station and the Moorgate and Old Street Tube stations. Liverpool Street Station was perfect since most of our designers and draftsmen lived in Essex.

The asking price was £4.30 per square foot, or £20,210 per annum, paid quarterly in advance. We were already paying £18,000 per annum in Bourdon Street, so this was a good deal, but given Mr Cowan's situation and the prevailing economic climate, we offered £4.00 per square foot. The response was swift and abrupt. Take it or leave it. Mr Cowan left us in no doubt he wasn't going to be jigged around by a pair of jumped-up colonials. So we took it and shortly thereafter the contract arrived. The agreed start date for the tenancy was September 21st. There was a lot to do, not to mention distractions.

My other brother, Lockwood, and his wife Mary arrived late September for a four-week visit during which, apart from a week in France, they would be staying with me in Clifton Hill. Any excuse for a party—three actually. Doug Justins, Lock's friend from Medical School and Union College, threw the first. His journey to London started in outback Quilpie where, as a medical intern indentured to the Queensland Health Department, Doug must have realised he was on the road to nowhere. He decided to run for it and responded to a newspaper advertisement for a ship's doctor. At the interview he was baffled when questioned about his sailing experience— none. He was soon to discover the 'ship' happened to be *Anaconda II*, a participant in the Sydney to London leg of the 1975 *Financial Times* Clipper Race. He was offered the job and accepted without wondering why no one else had. The voyage was a nightmare. Leaking diesel contaminated much of the food; the skipper all but drove the crew to mutiny; and when the yacht capsized in a South Atlantic gale the ship's doctor had to set his own fractured wrist. But they made it to London where Doug went on to publish learned papers on pain management and first aid at sea. More importantly, he joined the Royal Ocean Racing Club where he took us for a grand dinner.

There were more cocktail parties at Clifton Hill and at Chris's flat in Wetherby Gardens and a succession of theatre evenings—*Love's Labour's Lost* at the Aldwych, *Evita* at the Prince Edward, *Aida* at the Coliseum, and *Once a Catholic* at Wyndhams. These confirmed there's no business like show business. England may have been at a low ebb but the lights were still on in the West End. Notwithstanding the above, the event Lock and Mary were talking about years later was their visit to Buckingham Palace. To welcome them to London on the day of their arrival I had arranged to take them to lunch at my favourite restaurant, the Connaught Grill, and had invited Caroline Kelly as well. In the months leading up to the visit, Caroline, sister of one of the three Julias on the voyage to Yarmouth three years earlier, had been a regular companion at the opera. What's more, she worked at Buckingham Palace for the Keeper of the Privy Purse, the Queen's treasurer. One of the perks was tickets for the Royal Boxes at Covent Garden and Albert Hall. They were rarely used by the Royal Family so my introduction to the Proms was from the comfort of the Royal Box rather than the scrum in the stalls.

The plan was to meet Lock and Mary at Heathrow at 7.30 am, take them to Clifton Hill for a shower and a rest, go into the office for the morning and send a taxi to take them to the Connaught at midday. Not long after arriving in the office, Caroline called. The 'Family' is up at Balmoral. Would your brother and his wife like to visit the Palace? I called Lock to see how they were going. Wide awake. Then get dressed and we will go for a drive around Mayfair. I got back to Caroline, who said the guards would be waiting for us. I picked them up from Clifton Hill and drove to Admiralty Arch via Park Lane, Hyde Park Corner and Piccadilly. From there we cruised slowly down the Mall, towards the Palace. As we got closer, I asked Mary if she would like to visit the Palace. Don't be silly David. And as I pulled into the Palace gates, she was verging on apoplectic until a soldier leant over and said, 'Good morning, Mr Wilson, you can park by the front door.' As we did, Caroline came out to meet us. We spent an hour or so wandering around the glorious state rooms, the royal apartments and the gardens. What better way to work up an appetite for lunch at the Connaught Grill?

Bligh Engineering moved from Bourdon Street to Paul Street over the weekend of the 22 September 1979. Bligh Technical Recruitment stayed on in Bourdon Street as it would be easier to sublet while still occupied. The move to Paul Street occasioned a revision of our call-off contract with Aramco in The Hague. The key to the contract was the manhour billing rate based on a profit margin of twenty per cent applied to the employee salary plus a fixed rate to cover overheads. To determine the overhead component, we undertook a detailed analysis of anticipated costs for the next year, during which we expected to grow to thirty-six, including contract draftsmen and designers. The numbers confirmed cash flow management would be crucial: engineering staff, £249,000; overhead staff, £50,000; contractors, designers and draftsmen, £150,000; office expenses, £73,000; total costs, £522,000; projected income, £740,000. It looked good on paper but as Robbie Burns sagely said, *The best laid schemes o' mice an' men / Gang aft agley.*[5]

Nevertheless, things were going well and since the pigging project was seen as vital to the enduring wellbeing of the Safaniya field, Bruce Bailey requested we accommodate one of his team as a liaison engineer. This would have been difficult in Bourdon Street but we had no problem allocating an office for Chuck Schwieder in Paul Street, and he became a valuable member of the team. Most importantly, he made life easier for us by dealing with the never-ending stream of questions raised by the various Aramco departments. Then, in October, he told me Bruce Bailey was considering Bligh Engineering for another major project.

Bruce was considering Bligh Engineering because we were Aramco's go-to pipeline engineers. This project also included two platforms, each with 3000-tonne topsides, as large as anything installed at that time in the Persian Gulf. The project was the upshot of Aramco's rush to beat the Iranians to the oil in the Zuluf reservoir, which extended into Iranian waters. In the two and a half years since, Zuluf GOSP2 and the forty-eight-inch-diameter pipeline to Safaniya had been commissioned with production from three existing and three new six-well platforms. Four more six-well platforms had been installed, each connected to a GOSP by a twenty-inch flowline and a ten-inch test line. The result was a spaghetti junction of pipelines choking the area around each GOSP, virtually precluding the installation of the new well platforms required to maintain production. The remedy was to install bridge connected tie-in platforms next to each GOSP and reroute all pipelines to and from each GOSP via the relevant tie-in platform. We didn't have the space or people for a big new project in the office right then, but Chuck indicated it was still months away.

Around this time I received a visit from Mr Cowan's secretary, Vera, who conscientiously maintained a daily solitary presence in the British Merchant Sales office, because as far as I could tell, Mr Cowan was never there. Would Dick and I like to join him for lunch at the Eccentric Club the following day? If so, he would send his car to collect us at noon. It was a strange invitation given Mr Cowan had been quite short with us at the time of the transaction. But that was now done and dusted, and the Eccentric Club sounded interesting, so we accepted and sure enough a limousine arrived at noon the next day and off we went.

The Club was in Ryder Street, Mayfair, immediately behind Christie's. Mr Cowan, *call me Eddie*, was there to meet us and took us through to the bar for an aperitif. He was no longer our landlord; he had become a generous and charming host. And, when we eventually got to it, it was no ordinary lunch—smoked salmon followed by generous cuts from the roast beef trolley. Generous, because, as the maître d' was honing his blade, Eddie subtly interrupted the ritual with a pound note. There was the mellow claret, then the cheese, the port, the coffee, the petit fours, the cognac, and finally, the Montcristos. Eddie was keen to hear the Bligh Engineering story but was equally forthcoming with his own. He started life in the meat trade and at an early age had gone to Cairo where he made his fortune. There was no point going back to the office afterwards.

Early the following week, Vera caught my eye as she made her way through the office in my direction. *What now?* I wondered. *Mr Cowan would like you and Mr McMahon to join him for lunch tomorrow.* I explained to her what had happened the previous week but not wanting to sound churlish said I would ask Dick. He was of the same view, so we accepted the invitation, but Vera must have said something because instead of the Eccentric, Eddie suggested the Charterhouse Grill by Smithfield Market, five minutes by cab from Paul Street. We met at the bar but before ordering anything Eddie suggested a tour of Smithfield. It has been a livestock market for more than 900 years and a popular spot for butchering people as well. William Wallace was hung, drawn and quartered there in 1305. It was still a bloody, muddy place in the 1830s when Dickens described Bill Sikes and Oliver Twist's journey from Bethnal Green to the bungled burglary at Shepperton. These days it's more genteel, but the opening hours, from 2 am to 10 am, are still unsociable. Nevertheless, the place was still a hive of activity as Eddie showed us around, occasionally greeting an acquaintance of old.

The steaks should have been good at the Charterhouse Grill, and they were. But in the wake of my hangover from The Eccentric, I refused the cigars and cognac. Who needed them when you could listen to Eddie's stories of life in Cairo leading up to the Suez Crisis? In those days, the most lavish gentlemen's club was a bordello, where you could arrange to meet the mayor, the chief of police or any other official who could help with a regulation or two. Lunches with Eddie became regular events and from time to time we were even allowed to pay. Then, six months after moving into Paul Street, we found a tenant for Bourdon Street, meaning we could relocate Bligh Technical Recruitment into Paul Street. It was a move that was good for both companies but we needed Eddie's office space. We found ourselves in the unenviable position of having to evict our landlord.

When we approached him with our dilemma, he explained he needed his office as an excuse to get out of the house each day, despite the fact he was rarely there. The 'house' happened to be the penthouse and sub-penthouse above Scotch House in Knightsbridge. He had installed a connecting staircase, Mrs Eddie lived upstairs, and he lived downstairs. We offered to provide an office for Vera but after a bit of a grumble he assured us he would work it out, so we revised the lease and BTR moved into Paul Street. We didn't hear from Eddie for around two months, when out of the blue Vera called and arranged for Dick and me to join him for lunch at the Charterhouse Grill on the following Thursday. As we arrived on the appointed day, we were surprised to be met by Vera, who apologised for Mr Cowan, saying he was upstairs taking a call and would like us to order a drink from the bar. Eddie didn't take long to appear and couldn't wait to tell us it had been impossible at home so he had bought the Charterhouse Grill Restaurant and installed Vera in the office upstairs to keep the books.

Six months later, Eddie was dead. In the summer leading up to the despairing call from Vera, we had met for lunch at the Grill regularly and he was never anything but his avuncular self—always interested in what we were doing and where we had been. In just one short year, Dick, Eddie and I had built a friendship that is an abiding memory of my life in London. The family arranged a private funeral. We couldn't even say goodbye. As oldies lose their friends, they need someone else to talk to. Dick and I were fortunate the irrepressible Eddie Cowan picked us.

The move to Paul Street coincided with the onset of the winter opera season. *La Traviata*, *Aida* and *Die Fledermaus* at the Coliseum; *Norma*, *The Magic Flute* and *Cosi Fan Tutti* at the Royal Opera House; and *Eugene Onegin* in Glasgow. Opera is a great way to entertain people, whether they are aficionados or not. It's a great occasion and they don't have to worry about making conversation. Conversation can wait for dinner. The standout opera-land restaurant is J Sheekey, albeit much closer to the Coliseum than the Royal Opera House. The Savoy Grill is closer to the ROH but lacks the bohemian flair of Sheekey. And, for something slightly less indulgent, there is Joe Allen, an upmarket subterranean hamburger joint. Wonie Kisch and I went there one night in 1982 after a performance of Jonathan Miller's *Rigoletto* at the ENO. As we babbled our way down the stairwell, the man in front of us turned, face beaming, and asked if we had really enjoyed it. It was Jonathan Miller, and he was delighted with our reaction to his famous creation—famous because instead of setting the action in sixteenth century Mantua, as in Piave's original libretto, Miller moved it forward to 1950s New York and transformed the shameless Duke into an equally shameless mafia Don.

Management accounts confirmed Dick and I were riding high in the autumn of 1979. And our wily accountant, Barney

Cue, had significantly reduced our company and personal tax liability by creating a corporate structure that took advantage of our non-domiciled status. As a prudential professional adviser he then suggested a further effective tax mitigation strategy might be for Bligh Engineering to buy an expensive motor car, perhaps a Bentley, to underscore our thirst for engineering excellence. It so happened his royal blue 1970 Model T was for sale. His North London house did not have a garage and there was no end to the procession of nobodies keen to run a key or a coin across the paintwork. We could have it for the once-in-a-lifetime price of £8860, with all the scratches removed. For a pair of jumped-up colonials this was impossible to resist. We became the proud owners of a Bentley that was much grander than Eddie Cowan's limousine.

That changed when my sister, Sarah, then nineteen years old, arrived for her long summer university vacation. My father had never considered it necessary for his sons to have cars at university, but it was an imperative for his daughter—not a tiddly girl's car but, because he didn't want her to come off second best in an accident, a beefy Ford utility. So she was used to driving big cars and jumped at the opportunity to drive Dick or me around London in the Bentley. This meant she could also use it to move between Chris's flat in Wetherby Gardens and mine in Clifton Hill. There are endless things to do for any visitor to London but the lead-up to Christmas is special with the razzamatazz in the great department stores, the Christmas parties and, in addition to the opera mentioned earlier, ballet and pantomimes. Sarah's first big event was *Swan Lake* at Covent Garden. Peter Ikert, an Aramco project manager at that time, and his wife, came too. Years later I was to see a lot of them in Indonesia where Pete worked for the IIAPCO oil company. Sadly, they lived in a posh district of Jakarta subsequently identified as a Creutzfeldt-Jakob disease cluster. In 2007, having returned to America, Pete died from it.

In the year following our first meeting, Gunther and Kina had moved into a flat in Belgravia and settled into London life. Dick and I saw them often and in November were invited to another bracing long weekend at Börringekloster. It was nice to be able to respond with an invitation to *The Magic Flute* at Covent Garden. Sarah came as well. I was still no less an admirer of Kina than I had been from the moment we met, but for me she was a mirage. And she certainly showed no sign she was anything but happily married. A week or so later they came to a cocktail party at Clifton Hill, so it was a good opportunity for them to meet a few locals, including the Strattons and the Langdons. They also joined us for a rowdy Christmas lunch for 'orphans' at Dick's place in Irving Road W14. This might have been the first time I met their daughter, Alex, by that time, a three- or four-year-old.

Christmas or not, we still had work to do. We were three months into the detailed engineering for the Safaniya pigging project with five months to go, so it was approaching its peak. We were also preparing proposals for two North Sea pipeline projects, one for Shell Cormorant and the other for Marathon Brae. So, the office was open for the two working days between Christmas and New Year. Preparations and planning were also well underway for the formation of the

Arabian Bligh Corporation in Saudi Arabia. Barney Cue suggested we keep our bank, The Clydesdale, briefed. Our local branch was in Buckingham Palace Road but our original manager there, Ian Cook, had recently been promoted to head office in Glasgow, so I made an appointment to see him there. It was a good excuse to take Sarah to Scotland to meet the Stenhouses, Scots who had been friends in London but had since returned to Glasgow.

We caught the Glasgow Shuttle on Friday afternoon, arriving in time to settle into Paul and Suzon's stylish townhouse with its beautiful stained glass in Kew Terrace. Paul explained how, at the end of the nineteenth century, Glasgow was the world's richest city on the back of cotton, shipbuilding and whiskey. Rich merchants imported the Italian artisans who were the masters of stained glass and who in turn must have inspired Glasgow's most famous architect, Charles Rennie Mackintosh. That night Paul and Suzon took us to the Scottish National Opera's production of *Eugene Onegin*, the story of a rake who kills his friend in a duel. *And all men kill the thing they love, The coward does it with a kiss, The brave man with a sword.*[16]

On Saturday we drove to the Stenhouse family estate, Maxwelton House, near Moniaive. The house had been the birthplace of Annie Laurie, subject of the famous Scottish ballad. When Paul's mother and father bought the historic relic in 1968, they embarked on a three-year restoration, creating a magnificent mansion with at least a dozen lavish guest bedrooms. With the restoration barely complete, Paul's father, a leading Scottish industrialist in his prime, was killed in a car accident on his way there for a weekend. Paul's mother soldiered on, albeit with a fierce demeanour covering for her grief. She had an eye for fine art and the wherewithal to collect it, and there wasn't a wall in Maxwelton unadorned by an original painting. Many of them were contemporary, and she was a great patron of our mutual friend, Sandy Goudie, whose superb family portraits graced many of the public rooms. With all that, Rosamunde was a generous host and particularly kind to Sarah, who had shown a great interest in her beautiful gardens.

We were back in Glasgow for my Monday meeting at the Clydesdale Bank. I provided an overview of our current situation and plans for Saudi Arabia and asked them for introductions to customers active in the North Sea who might have work for us. If future Aramco work was to be done in Saudi Arabia, we needed local work to keep London busy. Predictably, they did nothing, but I didn't follow up either. Virtually all our resources were concentrated on Aramco work, not just Safaniya Pigging but several smaller offshore pipeline-related projects as well. We had reached the stage where we had people in Saudi Arabia all the time so the momentum for a local presence was growing. So was the Arabian Bligh Corporation file. Early in February, Barney Cue and I flew to St Helier, Jersey, to instruct lawyers, Michael Voisin & Co, to form a Jersey-based holding company. Barney was keen to ensure any investment in Saudi Arabia was thoroughly insulated from the Bligh Group, including Bligh Appointments, and its directors in the UK.

Before going to Jersey, Barney asked us to suggest a name

for the new company. He didn't want us to use 'Bligh', so we had to come up with something new. Earlier in August I had attended a performance of Wagner's *The Valkyrie* at the ENO and had become fascinated with the 'Ring of the Nibelungen' legend. Wotan, the chief god, employed two giants, Fafner and Fasolt, to build his palace. So, why not use the name of one of those legendary builders for our new company? And that's how our Jersey company became Fafner Ltd. Alexander Pope said, *'A little learning is a dangerous thing, Drink deep or taste not the Pierian spring'*.[17] Later in the legend, Fafner turns out to be a greedy villain who kills his brother and is in turn killed by Siegfried, the ultimate hero of the story.

At an impromptu dinner party one evening in San Frediano in the Fulham Road, the conversation turned to frustrated ambitions, such as never having braved a parachute jump, completed the Fastnet Race or crossed Russia on the Trans-Siberian Railway. It was an easy one for me. As a student I had seen Albert Finney's *Tom Jones* at the Eldorado, Indooroopilly, and had been mesmerised by the stag hunting scene. At thirty-two years old, an age I then considered nigh on senility, my burning ambition to ride to hounds was fast becoming a frustrated ambition. This declaration had barely escaped my lips when one of the girls in the party, Suzy Colton, confessed to being a fox hunter and offered to take me along one day. *Can you ride a horse? I am a boy from the bush, of course I can.* So, arrangements were made and a date set for a day out with the Surrey Union towards the end of February.

By the appointed day I had assembled the kit and learned how to put it on—hunting shirt (Parkers), long warm socks, breeches, top boots, garter straps, spurs, stock, stock pin, waistcoat, black hunting coat, hunting gloves and top hat. Suzy's parents lived just outside Leigh in Surrey, and I was invited to spend the night before the meet. Suzy's father suggested it might be an idea for me to try out my horse for the next day over a few practice jumps. No problem. I was in a pair of jeans, so off we went to the stables. I hadn't been on a horse since leaving Mount Oscar twenty years earlier and certainly not with a saddle, so I was a little nervous. But not for long. Riding a horse is just like riding a bicycle, and with a saddle it's a lot easier. The horse was easy to handle and I had no problem coaxing it over a couple of pony club style jumps. Mr Colton was content and at eleven o'clock the next morning Suzy and I joined the Surrey Union for my first day out with foxhounds. Fortunately for me there was nothing approaching the action in Squire Allworthy's hunt, but it was a wonderful day and I wanted more. Unfortunately, it was the end of the season and I would have to wait.

It was also more than two years since I had been home and further information was required in Saudi Arabia to prepare a development plan for the office in Al Khobar. So I made plans to leave for Australia mid-March with a week in Saudi Arabia on the way back. These plans were under discussion at a waifs and strays Sunday lunch at Irving Road a week or so before the tentative departure date. Gunther and Kina were there and, without any ado, Kina chimed in and said she was coming too. There was a pause. So, for good measure, she said it again and that was that. Gunther was silent. We didn't know it at the time, but he had a girlfriend on the side so there wasn't much he could say. I was delighted but not ready to entertain the idea Kina was interested in anything but visiting Australia.

A plan was hatched and it was decided Kina would leave for Brisbane at the end of the month, spend two weeks in Queensland, after which I could take her to Sydney. Understandably, she didn't want to go all the way to Australia to miss out on our great metropolis. And that's what happened. I took QF2 to Brisbane on March 19th, arriving two days later. I spent the first week in Dalby and then we decamped to Mooloolaba. In the two years since my last visit, Mum and Dad had found a new coastal bolthole. They had swapped Shemara Court's panoramic sea views for 'The Gunyah,' a two-storey Queenslander looking out over a wide expanse of the Mooloolah River. It had a never-ending procession of pelicans looking for scraps from fishing boats coming into the nearby marina and was a five-minute walk to their favourite beach. Later, I was to discover our landlord was the pioneering vascular surgeon, Sam Mellick.

Kina arrived a day or so later and the stage was set for the blossoming of a most unlikely liaison. We had fallen for each other eighteen months earlier but neither had realised it was mutual at the time, and good manners had kept us apart anyway. Kina had seized the moment and broken the impasse at Dick's lunch in London three weeks earlier. A full moon over the beach at Mooloolaba did the rest. The Gunyah was a world away from Börringekloster, but Kina took it in her stride. Lock and Mary came down from Rockhampton and Sarah joined us from her university in Brisbane. They had all been in London within the preceding six months so there were familiar faces for Kina. Not that it would have mattered. Despite Kina's apparent reserve, she was good at making friends and was soon very much a part of the morning social on the beach at Mooloolaba.

We finished the holiday in Rockhampton, where we spent a couple of days with Lock and Mary. Kina then flew to Sydney for a week or so and for me it was another trip to Saudi Arabia. Dick, John and I had agreed on the broad principles for the establishment of the Arabian Bligh Corporation but we needed a detailed plan, and for that we needed current data. I spent a week researching the cost and availability of everything we would need to set up an office, including rent, accommodation, transport, living expenses and local office staff. By the time I was back in London, I had drafted the plan we eventually issued in June. The basic objective was to develop a fifty-man engineering consultancy and design office over a two-year period. The Arabian Bligh Corporation was to be a joint venture corporation formed between Bligh Engineering and Lama Establishment, representing the interests of HRH Turki Bin Nasser Bin Abdul Aziz. It was contingent on securing formal approval for commercial registration from the Saudi Government. Our formal application was filed in late April and we had paid the first twenty per cent of the agreed £7000 fee to Ahmed Audhali.

Kina arrived back in London from Sydney within days of my return from Saudi Arabia. Gunther had looked after Alex, their daughter, while Kina was away, and now she was back she had some catching up to do. She had decided to move out of their flat but that would take some time. We continued to see as much of each other as possible but that was not always easy because neither Kina nor Gunther was keen to leave Alex with a strange babysitter. But we managed, and apart from a few short trips abroad, we had a great summer in London.

One of the short trips was to Pamplona for the festival of San Fermin, also known as The Running of the Bulls. My brother Chris had a colleague, David Hamilton, who had a commercial pilot's licence and was more than happy to charter a four-seater Piper Arrow on our behalf and fly us there. We took off from Fairoaks Airport late morning on the day of the Borg/McEnroe Wimbledon Final and, after clearing Customs and immigration at Bournemouth, headed south. The weather couldn't have been better so from our relatively low flight level there were wonderful views of Saint-Malo and Biarritz en route to San Sebastian, where we cleared Spanish Customs and immigration. From there, it was a short hop to Pamplona airport, where the obliging and, as it turned out, attractive, air traffic controller arranged a taxi for us.

As we arrived at our hotel, we noticed an animated gathering glued to a communal TV set. The Wimbledon final was far from over. It was around 6 pm local time and after three hours of play, with Borg leading two sets to one, there was a tie break for the fourth set. The next hour was one of the finest ever in grand slam tennis, with Borg the popular winner through sheer tenacity. It was exhausting for spectators as well, but afterwards there was plenty of time to settle into the hotel, explore the town and find a restaurant, because dinner never starts until late in Spain.

The story of Saint Fermin and why he is venerated by an intoxicated religious festival in Pamplona in July every year, is baffling. We know he was born in Pamplona of noble Roman parents circa AD 270. He was converted to Christianity and baptised by St Saturninus. Then, as a seventeen-year-old, he was ordained priest. At twenty-four he became the first bishop of Pamplona. The rest is conjecture. It is said he then embarked on a crusade through France, culminating in his election as bishop of Amiens, more than 800 kilometres to the north. It was a poisoned chalice. The French authorities were hostile to Christianity, so they cut off his head. His mentor, St Saturninus, met a similar fate in Pamplona, but rather than cutting off his head, the authorities tied him to a bull that dragged him through the cobbled streets until he was dead. Somehow this tragedy was linked to Saint Fermin and commemorated by a bull-running festival that may have remained a local curiosity had it not been made famous by Ernest Hemingway in his 1926 novel, *The Sun Also Rises*.

It was still light when our taxi dropped us in the Plaza del Castillo, a square slightly larger than a football field, surrounded by bars and cafes. And that's where we ran into Nicky Knowland. Nicky lived in Paris and was a friend of Chris Holloway. He was with a group of San Fermin veterans and by the end of the night we were thoroughly versed in the tradition and purpose of the Bull Run. There is a *Corrida*, consisting of six bullfights each evening during the festival. The bulls are assembled in holding pens about 700 metres from the Plaza de Toros. A series of narrow cobbled streets is barricaded to provide an inescapable pathway to the bullring.

At eight o'clock each morning, a flare is launched and the bulls selected for the evening programme are released. The flare is the signal for the bull runners assembled in the street outside the pen (and there are many hundreds) to attempt to beat the bulls to the bullring. The bulls are mean, have long sharp horns and weigh up to 700 kilograms. The fun starts when they catch up to and mow down the runners that can't get out of the way. At best, it's a few cuts and bruises. Quite often it's fatal.

Nicky, who I think had decided to steer us clear of trouble, met us outside the bull pen. Chris and I had decided to run and were wearing the obligatory red berets, sashes and neckerchiefs procured from a street stall. Dick and David sensibly volunteered to take the photos. As the clock ran down there was no shortage of braggadocio from the runner pack, many sporting rolled-up editions of *Diario de Navarra*—of doubtful use in an encounter with a raging bull. Just as we were about to go, there was a Shakespearian moment. A marshal spotted a woman dressed as a man mingling with the runners and quite rightly arrested her. Franco was in his grave but in Spain women's liberation was still for the pathetic gringos.

Up went the flare and six fighting bulls and six steers, sensing freedom, surged from their pen into the Calle Santo Domingo. The runner pack, including Chris, Nicky and I, took off as well, the anxious rear hard up against the curious front. The bulls were soon making mincemeat of the tail end and as they turned into the narrow confines of the Calle Estafeta I sensed they were not far behind. I had been in cattle yards before and bush instincts took over. *Find an escape route.* It turned out to be a sturdy downpipe I climbed like a rat up a rope. When I was sure the danger had passed, I followed and eventually entered the Plaza de Toros via a tunnel, which was closed shortly afterwards. Chris and Nicky made it unscathed as well. After three or four summers mustering scrubbers on Junee Station, Chris knew how to dodge angry bulls. It had all taken less than five minutes.

There was a brief lull as the bulls were corralled under the stadium to await the afternoon events. Then the fighting cows entered the bullring. These were smaller than the bulls and their horns were padded but they were dangerous nevertheless, so we spent the next twenty minutes pretending to be as cool as the matadors who would be performing later in the afternoon. According to Nicky's friends, the veterans we had met the night before, the not-to-be-missed star turn would be local hero, Luis Francisco Esplá. So, after some lunch, a siesta and a tour of the town, we made our way back to the Plaza de Toros for the first *Corrida* of the fiesta. Esplá lived up to his reputation and killed his bull with grace and dispatch and we as uninitiated foreigners, instinctively opposed to bullfighting, might have left Spain with a dim appreciation of its place in Spanish culture. But that possibility was immediately extinguished by the appalling spectacle that followed.

The trouble with bullfights is the bulls are bred to fight and only those that are true fighters make the *Corrida*. They erupt into the ring as proud, angry combatants with heads held high. The matadors don't stand a chance against them in this mode so the fight is a process designed to exhaust the bull and lower his head for the kill. Initially, the matadors use a cape to entice him into a series of tiring passes and pirouettes. Then the picadors go to work. They are mounted on heavily padded and blindfolded horses and armed with sharp lances. Their job is to lower the bull's head by severing his upper neck muscle. This is best done by encouraging him to T-bone the horse and using the moment of impact to go to work on his neck with the lance at close quarters. This doesn't always go well for the horse and that's what happened. The badly injured mount was retired, no doubt to the knacker's yard, and the show went on. Slowly. Gore was welling from our hero's neck and he was frothing at the mouth, but his head was held high. The banderillas took over. The matadors drove barbed skewers into his neck and shoulders, seemingly to no effect. There was no more grace, just a grisly farce. I was faint. My tough rugby-playing brother's face was ash-white when he turned to Nicky, announced he was about to pass out, and did.

It was clearly not the first time the locals had seen a gringo swoon at a bullfight. Two kind women helped us move Chris to an external balcony and fresh air. I'm not sure about Nicky, but it was the first and last time Chris, Dick or I went near a bullfight. We spent another day in Pamplona, but two days of drinking is enough, so Tuesday morning we flew to Madrid. Chris's shipbroking counterparts there had booked us into a hotel on the Gran Via. Having settled in, we were able to view a rowdy parade by supporters of one of the more conservative elements of Adolfo Suarez's Union of the Democratic Centre alliance (UDC). Spain was in its fifth year of transition to democracy from Franco's authoritarian dictatorship. The UDC was nominally right wing, but it had a slippery grip and in the election of 1982 the Spanish Socialist Workers Party, led by Felipe González, took over.

Madrid, like all great cities, is great for walking—blue skies, wide boulevards and bustling squares, and since the Spanish are night owls, it never stops. But my abiding memory, having just witnessed the cruel slaughter of a horse and a bull in Pamplona, is of one picture in the Prado Museum—Picasso's *Guernica*. At the time, it was a copy (the original arrived a year later), but I was unaware of that and it didn't matter. What mattered was the image's success in conveying Picasso's 'loathing for the military caste',[18] and here we were in Spain, forty-three years on, and these warm and friendly people were still struggling to put Franco, fascism and the worst features of Catholicism behind them.

For the next stage of our journey, we had arranged to join Michel and Hedwige Cornudet in Brittany. It was now three years since their wedding, so Chris and I were delighted to be able to catch up with them on our way home. They were spending the summer with Hedwige's sister and her husband in a rented farmhouse. It was close to the airfield at Dinard and more or less on the way back from Spain to England so it made sense to drop in for the weekend, even though there were four of us. We needn't have worried about the accommodation. There was tonnes of it and an enormous kitchen. We played tennis, David Hamilton took the children for a joy ride in the plane and there was an excursion into

Saint-Malo, during which I bought a framed picture that wouldn't fit in the plane's luggage compartment for the flight home. We shoehorned it into the cabin by supporting it against the roof, but it was a squeeze for Dick and me in the rear seats, so there was more than one reason to be pleased when we eventually landed safely at Fairoaks following a descent through thick cloud.

It was around this time we were approached by a major American contractor, Brown & Root International (BAR), who were tendering for the construction of a 500-kilometre thirty-four-inch-diameter gas pipeline from Brega to Misurata in Libya. Four years earlier, BAR's Bahrain office had been instrumental in arranging a shipping clearance for the sheet piling purchased to build Aramco's temporary pipe load-out jetty in Dammam. They had one of the world's largest offshore construction fleets and so were J Ray McDermott's principal competitor. Their office in Colliers Wood, South London, had spent the last two years completing the conceptual engineering for a gigantic scheme in Libya that became known as the 'great man-made river project'. This landmark project would eventually transport water in four-metre-diameter concrete pipelines from giant aquifers in the south-east of Libya to its population centres in the north. Bligh Technical Recruitment had been supplying contract engineers and designers to BAR for this project for the past two years. We must have done something right because as part of their tender for the construction of the gas pipeline, Bob Brown (not the Bob Brown of RJBA), the company's business development manager in London, called and asked Bligh Engineering for a proposal for a circa sixty-man construction management team for the project for two years.

This would be an enormous undertaking requiring the funds to service a £90,000 a month payroll, but we agreed to do it. Our formal proposal went to BAR a week later. It included the résumés of nearly one hundred construction specialists, including construction managers, planners, quantity surveyors, material controllers, welding supervisors, instrument technicians and commissioning engineers. It could not have been done without a well-organised Bligh Technical Recruitment. Certainly, our decision four years ago to establish and run Bligh Engineering and BTR together had been vindicated. Brown & Root was impressed. Just two weeks after submitting the Libya proposal, I was in Houston on Aramco business. Tommy Knight, a BAR Group vice president, invited me to lunch in their Houston head office. I assumed it was to talk about the Brega Misurata pipeline, and indeed there was preliminary chat about that and what I was doing for Aramco in Houston, but the real business of the lunch was an offer to join BAR and run its Australian operations. Certainly, I was flattered, but Bligh Engineering had more on its plate in London than BAR did in Australia so it was not difficult to refuse there and then.

The nominal kick-off date for Brega Misurata was early September 1980 but following the closure of the US Embassy in Tripoli in December 1979 relations with Colonel Qaddafi went downhill and the project was shelved. But relations with BAR and Bob Brown remained cordial as we explored other avenues for cooperation. In early August, Bligh Engineering was invited to submit a proposal for conceptual engineering for the tie-in platforms in the Zuluf field that Chuck Schwieder had alerted us to ten months earlier. I had discussed the project at length with Bruce Bailey during my visits to Dhahran in February and April, and Murray Chancellor had already managed associated pipeline surveys, so we were familiar with the scope and able to submit an execution plan and estimate within days. Having done so, I went down to Saudi Arabia to locate all drawings and data associated with the existing facilities and plan the hydrographic and soil surveys that would be required, not just in the Zuluf field, but Marjan and Manifa as well. Additionally, it would be necessary to undertake topside surveys of ZGOSP1 and ZGOSP2 in the areas that would eventually connect to the new tie-in platforms. We were awarded the £187,866 contract three days before I got back to London. The timing couldn't have been better as we were coming to the end of the Safaniya pigging project and the new job would feed the beast for another nine months.

It seemed like the ideal moment to buy a flat. I paid £48,650 for a ninety-one-year lease on the ground-floor flat at 155 Holland Park Avenue. With a living room, kitchen-dining room, bedroom and bathroom under 900 square feet of high ceilings, it had a nice sense of space and light. The living room looked out across tree-lined Holland Park Avenue to the Norland Place School, where the yummy mummies deposited their little darlings each morning. The rear view was over the Holland Park Lawn Tennis Club where, just before Wimbledon, you might have caught a glimpse of Chris Evert practicing on the grass—and all this only 400 metres west of the Holland Park Tube and a twenty-minute ride to Liverpool Street. It needed a coat of paint. I asked Kina about a colour scheme. White. That, and improvements to the bathroom and kitchen, were all done and at the end of October I moved from Clifton Hill to my first home, magnolia white from top to bottom.

Meanwhile, momentum for the Arabian Bligh Corporation was growing, but Lama was shying away from putting up its share of the money. Mid-October I was back in Saudi Arabia and was able to discuss this problem with Ahmed Audhali. He resolved it to Fouad Zatar's satisfaction by devising a corporate structure for ABC that would satisfy the Saudi authorities and give Fafner complete control of the Lama shareholding in return for an agency fee of five per cent on sales. Fouad Zatar agreed and reaffirmed his offer of office space at a reasonable rent to get us started. I kept Bruce Bailey abreast of these developments and our new romance with Brown & Root. J Ray McDermott was winning the lion's share of Aramco's offshore construction work and Bruce was keen to inject some competition into the tendering process. He even suggested we team up with Brown & Root for the Safaniya pigging project, particularly if we were establishing an office in Al Khobar.

The preliminary studies associated with the Zuluf and Marjan tie-in platforms design were well underway when I returned to London mid-October. The most important of these was the evacuation and relocation of the forty-eight-inch-diameter Zuluf trunkline and its riser from ZGOSP2 to the ZGOSP2 tie-in platform. This included the relocation of the massive pig launcher and associated pig-handling gear. Andy Cooper had also employed specialist draftsmen to draw three-dimensional perspectives of the new platforms. Each new platform consisted of a six-leg substructure supporting four decks. The illustrations were invaluable tools for the studies as well as ensuring there were no clashes between structural and piping elements. Another innovation introduced during this period was the Wang word processor. We bought two and they transformed our report-publishing processes. The defining event was successfully pairing with another Wang word processor in Houston via a telephone connection and sending our first report in electronic form. The world would have to wait another fifteen years or so for email.

Towards the end of November, Ahmed Audhali advised us the Arabian Bligh Corporation had been registered (CR 6839) and suggested we prepare stationery. He also drew up a sublease agreement for the temporary offices to be provided by Lama. Momentum was building. Brown & Root was taking a keen interest and when I stopped over in Dhahran for a few days on my way to Australia for Christmas, I stayed in its local guest house. The main purpose of the visit was to check in on the survey management team we had working in the Manifa field. They had suffered delays waiting for equipment to arrive, so it was important to reschedule and advise the Aramco project management team.

Christmas 1980 was my first in Dalby for three years and the last we spent there as a complete family. Chris had left London for good two weeks earlier. Lock and Mary drove down from Rockhampton and Sarah was home from Griffith University. It's hot and dry in Dalby in December so we played tennis and generally caught up with old friends. Then it was off to the coast for the impromptu parties that mark year's end. We were in The Gunyah again and enjoying it, but it occurred to me it might be nice to have our own holiday house, so I started looking around. The Mooloolaba beach bush telegraph did the trick. Within days, an old school friend, George Lewis, who had a house between Alexandra Headland and Mooloolaba, said he wanted to sell. So, that was that. I bought 24 Douglas Street, Mooloolaba, for $55,000. With three bedrooms and two bathrooms, it was ideal, and although inconvenient for somebody living in London, it was secure—perhaps because the next-door neighbour was Joh Bjelke-Petersen's handpicked police commissioner, Terry Lewis. Nine years later, following the Fitzgerald Inquiry, he was locked up for ten years for perjury and corruption.

On the way back to London, I stopped briefly in Singapore and Dhahran. The main objective in Singapore was to chase a long-overdue debt to Bligh Technical Recruitment. The miscreant was an old colleague from RJBA Singapore days so I felt personally responsible. In the event, we never did collect this debt. It left a bad taste in my mouth, but its impact on the company was negligible compared with the shock we were to receive three months later. There was much better news in Dhahran. I reviewed the current concepts for the proposed new Zuluf tie-in platforms with Aramco's project engineers, Lee Miller and Graham Briar. There were a half a dozen comments related to details, but the feedback was positive and afterwards Bruce Bailey asked me if I had thought about doing the detailed engineering. Of course I had. Our rough estimate was 30 000 manhours over nine months, peaking at forty people and requiring a bigger office than Paul Street.

It was business as usual in London. The conceptual design for the Zuluf tie-in platforms was by far the biggest job, employing a team of twenty. Andy Cooper was planning to finish by the end of March and it was anticipated the detailed engineering would kick off early May. More space was required but not until July, so we had time to assess options. Having been in Paul Street for less than eighteen months, we were reluctant to go through the administrative hassle of a complete move so the preferred option was to find a similar-sized short lease in the neighbourhood. Unfortunately, Carolyn, our erstwhile property scout, had returned to the USA, so we advertised. A relatively new 10 000-square-foot, single-floor, open-plan space came to light in the Barbican Centre only 800 metres from Paul Street. It was a viable option but not quite what we were looking for, so we continued the search.

In the meantime, Kina was able to get away from London for two weeks, so we joined the Holloways in Courcheval. I had assumed that being Swedish, she would be at home in the snow but I soon learned people from cold climates just want to be in the sun, which is why she had enjoyed Australia so much. An abiding memory of the holiday was a parachute jump. Chris Holloway and I were enjoying coffee cognacs in a café just above the Courcheval Altiport following an early morning ski run when we noticed a girl manning an indoor kiosk selling parachute jumps. Within minutes we had talked ourselves into having a go, so Chris went to enquire. He came back with two tickets. The plane would be landing in minutes and an instructor would meet us in the hangar. Sure enough, the plane landed and as we strapped on our parachutes the instructor highlighted the dos and don'ts in French, and Chris paraphrased in English. Parachutes on and still in our skiing gear, we boarded the plane and took off. For me, winning the toss to jump first was a pyrrhic victory. The moment came. The instructor clipped on my static line and as I hesitated, legs dangling in the slipstream, there was a push. After the excitement of waiting for the parachute to open, there was little more than an undignified flop into a snow drift. But it was nothing like the slow-motion fall to earth I was to experience over the next nine months.

The Aramco Affair

The call that signalled the end of our dream run came on 10 March 1981. Joop Veltman was the Aramco Overseas Company's project manager in the office recently established in Wembley to monitor Aramco design contractors in London. Bligh Engineering had been assessed for tax by the Saudi Arabian Government for 612,000 Saudi Riyals, around £80,000. What's more, the senior management of AOC was concerned that in applying for registration of the Arabian Bligh Corporation we had overstated the value of AOC projects. On hearing this, I went cold. I knew there must have been a mistake that could be rectified, but the timing, with the award of the detailed engineering design contract for the Zuluf tie-in platforms imminent, could not have been worse. Joop asked for a copy of our application for the commercial registration of ABC.

Dick McMahon was as shocked as I was and quick to identify another issue. It was March and we were contemplating doubling our office space by July. We couldn't make any commitments while this issue was unresolved. A three-page letter with appendices went to Joop Veltman the following day. The appendices included copies of our development plan, letter of appointment of Ahmed Audhali as our local attorney and an English translation of our application to the Saudi Government for the commercial registration of ABC. This last document included a list of significant works performed by Bligh Engineering, including six 'Aramco' projects. This had suggested to the Saudi Tax Authority the work had been performed in Saudi Arabia. The problem may never have arisen if we had listed the client as 'Aramco Overseas Company'. In the Veltman letter I suggested this had been our mistake and when we eventually received a copy of the Saudi DZIT (Department of Zakah and Income Tax) demand dated October 1980, it was clearly so. To ensure Bruce Bailey was in possession of all the facts rather than rumours, I sent him a similar letter direct.

Perhaps I was still hoping for the best a few days later when I soldiered on with a housewarming party for 155 Holland Park Avenue. The kitchen and bathroom had been transformed, the magnolia white made the pictures look good and Kina had arranged magnificent curtains for the bay windows looking onto Holland Park Road. Salad days—Claire Stratton, looking wonderful just a month on from her second baby, Edward, and Stratty looking pleased—Delia Higgins, still laughing at Bill's jokes after a year of marriage—Cherry nee Kisch, with her new American husband, Chip (Cherry and my brother had broken up some time earlier)—Dick McMahon, only betraying the pickle we were in by smoking more Gauloises than usual—Bridget Jennings (from a neighbouring office in Bourdon Street days), glamourous as ever without her fiancé, Roger. Gisa Ehrlich loves a party even if it means coming from

Hamburg. But it was no more than a brief diversion from the business at hand.

Joop Veltman called the next day to report his management were still concerned and suggested I go to The Hague. A meeting was arranged with Finance vice president (VP), Bill Tammes, accompanied by a legal advisor. My main objective was to dispel any notion we had misrepresented the value of AOC contracts in our application to the Saudi Government for commercial registration of ABC. We had a good case. The value of the 'Aramco' projects listed in the sheet accompanying the application was 5,450,000 Saudi Riyals. The invoices paid by AOC for those projects amounted to £729,830 or 5,400,742 Saudi Riyals at the prevailing exchange rate when the application was submitted. Tammes seemed mollified but insisted the problem was ours not theirs. This was fair enough, but I swallowed my pride and asked them to help. They agreed to do what they could and asked me to keep Ahmed Audhali informed but to do nothing myself.

Towards the end of March it became apparent that even with help of the AOC we needed Audhali to plead our case with the DZIT. There were a number of issues related to the tie-in platforms surveys we were managing in Zuluf and Marjan, so I made plans to leave for Dhahran on April 11th. In the week prior to my departure, there was blood-curdling news of a Briton imprisoned in Saudi Arabia for tax evasion. It suggested the prisoner's only source of food was from friends or colleagues on the outside. On the eve of my departure, I called Tammes to enquire whether AOC had made any progress. He was quite cool and in effect said we were on our own. So much for friends when you need them. That night, Kina and I went to *L'Elisir d'Amore* at Covent Garden. My heart wasn't in it and the next day I would have used the flimsiest of excuses not to board the British Airways flight to Dhahran. My only consolation was that, in extremis, Dick and John would be able to raise enough to cover the claim.

The Saudi police weren't waiting for me at the airport so instead of Dammam Central Jail, I spent the night in the Al Khobar Marriott. Life in the conurbation of Dhahran, Al Khobar and Dammam had changed dramatically in the seven years since my first visit when I stayed in an austere company guest house. In 1981, the Marriott wasn't the only hotel, there was a KFC for lost Americans and an Arirang franchise for homesick Koreans. Korean food is an acquired taste, but without rice wine, acquiring the taste takes longer. KFC is the same no matter what you drink with it. Fortunately, I didn't have to resort to any of these as there was still a warm welcome for me in Dhahran, if not in The Hague. I spent the next four weeks in Saudi Arabia and spent most evenings in Dhahran with Aramcon friends.

My first day in Dhahran was spent with Bruce Bailey's team, arranging technical review meetings for the Zuluf tie-in platforms project. My first meeting with Ahmed Audhali was the following day. The cartoon of the cow stretched between plaintiff and defendant was still there, alerting clients to their likely fate. Being a good lawyer, Ahmed was keen to start from the beginning so asked me to ask Aramco for a copy of the DZIT demand. He was on first name terms with Aramco lawyer, Jim Rappaport, and arranged for me to meet him at 8 am the next day.

It was a strange meeting. I told Rappaport why and how we had set up the Arabian Bligh Corporation and how that had presumably given rise to the DZIT assessment. He asked how we knew about it and I recounted the conversation with Veltman and the meeting with Tammes. He denied knowledge of any letter but requested an assistant to bring a file, which he went through and asked me to return later in the day. I did, and a month after first hearing of the demand I had copies of not just one but three letters. The first, dated 26 October 1980, was the DZIT tax assessment addressed to Bligh Engineering, % Manager, Aramco Affairs, Riyadh. The second, dated the same day, was addressed to Manager, Aramco Affairs, Riyadh, admonishing Aramco for not reporting Bligh Engineering's activities to the DZIT. The reply, dated 13 January 1981, from DD Bosch, Manager, Aramco Affairs Riyadh, to the Director General DZIT, Ministry of Finance and National Economy, Riyadh, advised 'an exhaustive search of our contract files and inquiries to various departments dealing with pipeline contracts have evidenced no contractual relationship between Bligh Engineering and Aramco'—legally correct, but even a Philadelphia lawyer might have tried to be more helpful.

Audhali now had everything he needed to make his case, had a friend high in the DZIT and was confident the claim would be dropped. I was able to turn my attention to the Zuluf tie-in platforms. One of the main issues was the relocation of the forty-eight-inch-diameter trunkline riser from the Zuluf GOSP2 auxiliary platform to the new tie-in platform. This would be a mammoth undertaking, involving the displacement of crude oil from the entire sixty-eight kilometres of the pipeline with chemically treated seawater at least twice and once more for luck, should there be a mishap. These chemicals could not be pumped back to the sea. The pipeline held 500 000 barrels of oil, so we needed a site for a 1.5-million-barrel evaporation pond as close to the pipeline landfall at Safaniya as possible. I spent the next week there looking for a low-lying area around 300 metres square and eventually earmarked a space between Safaniya GOSP1 and its airport.

Then there was a message to call Ken Foss. He was managing a liquids terminal project in Yanbu and would I like to visit over the weekend? Yes, I would. I was in no hurry to leave Saudi Arabia without a clearance from the DZIT. It would be great to visit Ken's project and, as a bonus, Sandy Sandford's revolutionary jack-up pier installed in 1977. Since then, there had been enormous change and this had only been accelerated two years later with the Shah's downfall and the onset of the Iran-Iraq war. The first cargo unloaded at the jack-up pier had been Japanese line pipe for a forty-eight-inch-diameter crude oil pipeline designed to carry 1.85 million barrels a day across Saudi Arabia from Abqaiq in the east to Yanbu in the west. Ken's project was an export terminal for a parallel twenty-eight-inch-diameter pipeline designed to carry 270,000 barrels a day of natural gas liquids from the east. Natural gas liquids (NGL), such as ethane, propane and butane, are the valuable by-products acquired when natural gas is stripped to produce the 'dry' methane used in power stations and for domestic heating.

It's a two-hour flight from Dhahran to Yanbu. TE Lawrence met Crown Prince Faisal near there in 1916 and they launched their campaign against the Ottoman Empire. At the time, it was a run-down port bypassed by the Damascus Medina railway. Lawrence and his merry band blew it up time after time before finally capturing Damascus in 1918. Sixty-five years on, Yanbu's fortunes had changed dramatically. It had become an enormous construction site, not only for crude oil and NGL export terminals, but also a refinery and petrochemical complex. A construction site is always of interest to an engineer, particularly if it's on the scale of Yanbu at that time. World-scale earth-moving scrapers, capable of shifting thirty cubic metres of sand at a time, world-scale crawler cranes capable of upending and placing hydrocracking reactors fifty metres tall. Then there were the floating cranes HHI was using to set and secure the various components of the NGL Pier. A 1200-tonne derrick barge was setting, levelling and piling each of the seventeen four-pile jackets providing the foundations for the trestle and pier. A 1600-tonne shear-leg floating crane was placing deck sections up to forty metres in length on the piled jackets. A gathering of the world's most spectacular construction equipment was transforming a hot and dusty ghost town on the edge of the Red Sea into one of the world's most important ports in the blink of an eye. But that doesn't happen without talented project managers. It's a concert where the conductor takes a musical score, assembles the musicians and their instruments and inspires them to play a symphony.

The pier built at Yanbu to load specialist NGL tankers

is 500 metres long, providing two berths in water twenty-five metres deep. The trestle from shoreline to pier is 2.2 kilometres long and supports fifteen product pipelines and a service road. The US$170 million contract to install the facility was awarded to Hyundai Heavy Industries late in 1979. The company, originally formed as a shipbuilder in 1973, had soon realised its dry dock, related workshops and skilled South Korean workforce could build oil and gas facilities just as well as they could build ships and six years on had won its first major contract in that industry. It was a great achievement for Senior Vice President YD Kim who, with encouragement from Ken Foss, had patiently courted Aramco since the time I first met him at a contractors' briefing in Safaniya three years earlier.

HHI had designed the trestle and pier as a series of four-pile jackets linked by steel deck frames incorporating the pipe supports, service road and utility ducts. These components had been prefabricated in Ulsan in South Korea and shipped to Yanbu on giant cargo barges. The fabrication phase had gone well but by early 1981 installation of the prefabricated elements was way behind schedule and the Saudis were nervous. The Iran-Iraq War had destabilised the Persian Gulf, so Yanbu as an alternative to the Strait of Hormuz for Saudi exports had become even more important. Aramco had to do something to get the project back on schedule. The solution was to replace their original project manager with Ken Foss. Ken's first initiative was to cut his predecessor's fifty-man project management team (PMT) to five: a project engineer, a planner, a logistics specialist and a project secretary. The project was back on schedule within four months. The master project manager had understood why mega projects of the future were destined for massive cost and schedule overruns.

Before the 1980s, owners traditionally executed large projects in three stages: design, procurement and construction. An engineering organisation, such as Bligh Engineering, would design the facilities and assist the owner with procurement of major equipment components. The owner would procure the major equipment, award a construction contract and free issue the major equipment components to the successful contractor, who would normally provide what was known as the bulk materials, such as structural steel, piping, wiring and concrete. Lump sum turnkey (LSTK) project delivery became fashionable in the 1980s. In theory, it delivered a faster, cheaper result, but mostly it was quite the opposite for anything that wasn't a well-understood capital project, such as a power station. The owner would prepare a brief specifying location and duty and invite qualified contractors to provide a lump-sum price to design, procure, build and commission the required facility. One of the attractions of this approach was it required a much smaller owner team during project development, with the bulk of the project cost occurring after the project had been funded. This included the cost of the larger PMT required to monitor the design procurement and construction phase. Hence the problem. Enlarged PMTs inevitably include freelancers, whose main interest is prolonging rather than completing a project, and many of them, such as 'safety' and 'quality' inspectors are in a prime position to do just that. The other problem inherent in overblown PMTs and government bureaucracies is two people doing the job of one take twice as long. These delays naturally cause project cost overruns, but the knock-on financial and lost production costs are usually far more substantial.

It had been more than three years since I had last stayed with Ken in Dhahran so there was plenty to talk about, but mostly he wanted to talk about Hyundai Heavy Industries. His crusade to promote a viable competitor to the large American contractors in the offshore construction market, such as J Ray McDermott and Brown & Root, had been successful. But to be genuinely competitive offshore HHI needed a pipeline installation barge and he thought Bligh Engineering could help them. It was a tremendous compliment and at the same time a challenge. I returned to Dhahran excited about the prospect of a new client and venturing into the world of naval architecture.

My main focus back in Dhahran was pushing Ahmed Audhali, but even though he was confident the DZIT claim would be dropped he was equally concerned we would end up in court if we pushed too hard, and that would end badly. His influential friend in the DZIT was still in America and we would just have to wait for his return. So I spent the next two weeks shuttling between Dhahran and Safaniya, fine-tuning interface issues between the Zuluf tie-in platforms project and the wide-ranging gas-gathering project being engineered in Houston. This was encouraging and only happened because, as far as Bruce Bailey and his team in Dhahran were concerned, Bligh Engineering would be awarded the detailed design engineering contract for that project. By way of confirmation, I was given an advance copy of Aramco's project execution plan, specifically naming Bligh Engineering as final design contractor.

Having spent five weeks in Saudi Arabia, I returned to London mid-May. I called our *bête noire* in The Hague, Bill Tammes, to let him know where we were with Audhali and the DZIT. He was non-committal but advised AOC was auditing our account. It was amazing how everybody in Aramco, except Bill Tammes, wanted to help us with our problem. But that meant nothing because he was AOC's vice president finance, and it didn't pass unnoticed that AOC payments were not arriving with their customary regularity. Alarm bells were ringing and at a board meeting early in June we resolved to start preparing for the worst: draconian cash-flow management, vacating Paul Street and, unkindest cut of all, selling the Bentley. That car did wonders for our image and my last night out in it was to take Jenny Locke to a Bruce Springsteen concert at Wembley Stadium. Actually, Jenny took me, but I called for her in the Bentley. I may have been on the edge of bankruptcy but we drove up to the main entrance and the parking valet couldn't wait to look after it for us.

By the end of June, we were struggling: creditors £180,000, cash £120,000, debtors £150,000, including £115,000 AOC appeared to be holding on behalf of the DZIT. I called Tammes to ask if there was a problem with our May invoice. He promised to investigate. Hours later, this telex arrived:

JULY 9, 1981
BLIGH ENGINEERING LTD.
U.K.

ARAMCO HAS RECEIVED NOTIFICATION FROM THE SAUDI ARAB GOVERNMENT DEPARTMENT OF ZAKAH AND INCOME TAX (DZIT) THAT BLIGH ENGINEERING LTD. HAS BEEN ASSESSED SR. 612,052 FOR TAXES FOR THE YEARS 1976, 1977 AND 1978.

SAG LAW AND DZIT REGULATIONS, IN THE CASE OF TAX ASSESSMENTS AGAINST AN ARAMCO CONTRACTOR, REQUIRE ARAMCO OR ITS CONTRACTING PARTY AFFILIATE TO WITHHOLD PAYMENTS UNTIL THE TAX ASSESSMENTS ARE SETTLED AND FINAL TAX CLEARANCE CERTIFICATES FOR EACH YEAR'S OPERATIONS ARE SUBMITTED TO ARAMCO. THEREFORE, THIS IS TO NOTIFY YOU THAT EFFECTIVE IMMEDIATELY AOC IS WITHHOLDING PAYMENT OF BLIGH ENGINEERING LTD'S INVOICES UNTIL EVIDENCE IS SUBMITTED BY BLIGH AND OR DZIT TO ARAMCO OR AOC SHOWING CLEARANCE OF THE ABOVE ASSESSMENT AND TAX CLEARANCE CERTIFICATES FOR THE YEARS 1979 AND 1980.

H.W. TAMMES
VICE PRESIDENT FINANCE
ARAMCO OVERSEAS COMPANY
THE HAGUE, THE NETHERLANDS

Now we were insolvent, and the main creditors were the Inland Revenue for PAYE (Pay as You Earn) employee salary deductions and HM Customs and Excise for employee National Insurance salary deductions. We knew that as directors we could be personally liable if these were not paid. But the message was worse than that. It was telling us AOC would hold all our invoices, not just sufficient to cover the DZIT claim (amounting to £95,000), at the prevailing exchange rate. We couldn't continue to work for a client that had declared they wouldn't pay for it. We had no option but to respond with the following:

```
TO:          H.W. TAMMES – VICE PRESIDENT
             FINANCE – A.O.C
FROM:        R.M. MCMAHON – DIRECTOR – BLIGH
             ENGINEERING
DATE:        9 JULY 1981
REFERENCE:   YOUR TELEX 9 JULY 1981
```

AS PER THE LETTER NUMBER 6-122-81 DATED 13 JANUARY 1981 TO THE DZIT FROM D.D. BOSCH MANAGER ARAMCO AFFAIRS, RIYADH. QUOTE – PLEASE BE INFORMED THAT AN EXHAUSTIVE SEARCH OF OUR CONTRACT FILES AND INQUIRIES TO VARIOUS DEPARTMENTS DEALING WITH PIPELINE CONTRACTS, HAVE EVIDENCED NO CONTRACTUAL RELATIONSHIP BETWEEN BLIGH ENGINEERING AND ARAMCO. – UNQUOTE.

THIS CONFIRMS THAT BLIGH HAS NEVER DONE ANY

WORK FOR ARAMCO IN SAUDI ARABIA AND THEREFORE AS YOU WELL KNOW DOES NOT OWE THE DZIT ANY TAX OTHER THAN THAT WHICH IS PAID ANNUALLY THROUGH AOC. THE SUBJECT ASSESSMENT IS INVALID AND BASED ON INCORRECT INFORMATION.

UNDER THE TERMS OF PARAGRAPH 5 (E) ATTACHMENT 'C' SECTION 9 OF THE DESIGN AND DRAFTING SERVICES CONTRACT BETWEEN AOC AND BLIGH ENGINEERING LTD., BLIGH SHALL REIMBURSE AOC FOR DEBTS ARISING OUT OF INCIDENTAL BUSINESS TRIPS UPON RECEIPT OF BILLING AND EVIDENCE OF THE DEBT.

AOC KNOWS THAT BLIGH ENGINEERING HAS DISCHARGED ALL ITS RESPONSIBILITIES TO THE DZIT ARISING FROM INCIDENTAL BUSINESS TRIPS FROM 1976 TO 1980 AND CONSEQUENTLY AOC HAS NO RIGHT TO WITHHOLD MONIES OWING TO BLIGH ON THE ABOVE PRETEXT.

ACCORDINGLY WE WILL NEED TO TAKE THE FOLLOWING ACTION:

INTEREST WILL BE CHARGED ON ALL OUTSTANDING INVOICES AT THE BANK OF ENGLAND'S MINIMUM LENDING RATE PLUS 3.5 PERCENT PER ANNUM.

CURRENT WORK IN PROGRESS FOR AOC WILL BE SUSPENDED PENDING PAYMENT AND THIS INVOLVES THE IMMEDIATE WITHDRAWAL OF PERSONNEL FROM PMT (LONDON) AND THE FIELD.

WE ARE CONTINUING OUR EFFORT THROUGH OUR SAUDI LAWYERS TO HAVE THE DZIT ASSESSMENT

WITHDRAWN DESPITE THE FACT THAT WE HAVE NEVER BEEN SENT IT ALTHOUGH WE BELIEVE IT WAS ISSUED IN 1980.

OUR LAWYERS ARE ADVISING US ON THE ACTION WE SHOULD TAKE ON A NUMBER OF MATTERS INCLUDING BREACH OF CONTRACT.

Dick, John and I knew by pressing 'send' for that telex we had signed the death warrant for Bligh Engineering's relationship with AOC, but by preserving cash there was a chance we could save the company and some jobs. The impact on the office and our people in Saudi Arabia was devastating as we started laying off everybody associated with Aramco work. Our Aramco supporters in Saudi Arabia were astonished but powerless.

A few days later, Tammes called Dick and offered to pay our invoices in return for a bank guarantee payable in the event we failed to secure a clearance from the DZIT. We talked to Bob Cruikshank at the Clydesdale, but he wasn't encouraging. He didn't say it, but I suspect the Clydesdale would have only provided a guarantee on the basis of freezing sufficient funds to cover any claim. Banks are great fair-weather friends. So we declined the AOC offer on the basis it was unlikely to improve our cash position and was likely to incur more cost.

Then, Ahmed Audhali asked how we planned to pay his fees. I told him, 'With great difficulty' if he couldn't persuade the DZIT to drop the claim. He suggested a no-cure-no-pay fee of SR 100,000, which, as far as we were concerned, was encouraging but also excessive but, again, there was no other option so we accepted.

One of the embarrassing aspects of this fiasco was the problems caused for our friends in Aramco, such as Bruce Bailey and his team, who were responsible for delivering the Zuluf tie-in platform project. Our departure from the scene would undoubtedly cause delays. Our formal contact for the project was with Joop Veltman and his Wembley-based PMT, who reported to Bruce Bailey in Dhahran. Three of Joop's team members worked through Bligh Technical Recruitment. If Tammes was determined not to pay us, then he wouldn't pay for them either. Fortunately, we were able to transfer them to another agency and so they kept their jobs. Joop was grateful. He was also embarrassed by the way we were being treated by AOC and suggested I call Tammes's boss, Saad Ashgar, AOC's Saudi president. I didn't think Ashgar would take my call, but he did. He was certainly familiar with the matter and sounded sympathetic as I outlined our case, including the point that Tammes was withholding £115,000 and the DZIT claim was £95,000. Days later, there was a letter from Tammes advising AOC would be paying the difference.

The £20,000 arrived shortly afterwards—a lifeline and a tonic. We were no longer insolvent and had breathing space. It enabled me to travel to Germany with a group from the English National Opera supporting Mark Elder making his debut there, conducting *Die Meistersinger von Nürnberg* on the second night of the Bayreuth Festival. We arrived on the Saturday afternoon of the first night—*Tristan and Isolde* with Daniel Barenboim conducting. We didn't have tickets but went anyway to enjoy the occasion and visit Villa Wahnfried, Wagner's house. What an occasion! I hadn't seen so many people so elegantly dressed since walking through the Via Condotti five years earlier—the pugnacious Franz Josef Strauss, head of the Bavarian Government and ex-Panzer officer, still looking the part; cardinals in crimson; military officers in full ceremonial; and flying nuns inspired by *The Sound of Music*.

Bayreuth performances normally start at 4 pm. For the longer works of around five hours, there are two intervals each of one hour. Afternoon tea is taken during the first interval and dinner during the second. Mark Elder joined us for dinner and afterwards invited me to accompany him to his backstage dressing-room where he was studying his *Meistersinger* score for the following evening. It gave me an opportunity to view the third act of *Tristan and Isolde* from the wings. I love Wagner's early works: *Der fliegende Holländer*, *Rienzi* and *Tannhäuser* but find the rest heavy going, apart from a few passages of sublime beauty. Isolde's final aria, 'Verklärung' (Transfiguration), is one of those passages, as the first night audience's animated applause confirmed. They must have enjoyed Daniel Barenboim as well since he returned to Bayreuth every year for the next eighteen, bar two. As an Israeli, he may not have had an affinity for the virulently anti-Semitic Wagner but he certainly had an affinity for his music and in 2001 courageously conducted the 'Verklärung' in Jerusalem.

Back in London, Bligh Engineering was still in dire need of 'Verklärung'. In the weeks following the rift with AOC there had been ruthless cost cutting and deck clearing, to the extent Bligh Engineering and Bligh Technical Recruitment had been pared to just seven people, including Dick, John Brauer and me. BTR had twenty or so people out on contract with other clients, such as Brown & Root, but the margins were thin, so there was no way that would sustain us. We were in constant contact with Audhali. He was adamant he would secure our clearance but equally adamant we had to be patient—not so easy when you are sacking people who have become family.

Salvation came from an unexpected quarter. Bob Brown called to say he was no longer with Brown & Root but had joined Canadian company, CanOcean Resources Ltd. Did I have time for lunch? Of course. CanOcean had started life as Lockheed Petroleum Services (LPS) and in the early 1970s developed a dry one-atmosphere manifold for the deeper waters of the Gulf of Mexico. But its real claim to fame came in 1974 with the development of the mechanical claw the *Hughes Glomar Explorer* lowered five kilometres to the North Pacific seabed to grapple and lift the wreck of the Russian submarine, *K-129*. By 1981, Lockheed had decided subsea engineering was not a core business so sold LPS to Canadian conglomerate, Nova, on the understanding the name would be changed. Nova changed the name to CanOcean Resources and employed Bob Brown to start a London-based office to pursue opportunities in the North Sea and Middle East. Bob had talked to his new management about buying Bligh Engineering as a readymade launch pad. Would I go to Vancouver to discuss the idea? Yes, of course.

It was a month before a suitable date could be set for the trip. The meetings were arranged for Saturday September 12th. In the meantime, Dick, John and I pressed on with tidying the accounts and winding up the corporate entities associated with Bligh in Saudi Arabia. There was also a determined effort to find more work. At best, it might save us, at worst, it might save us from a fire sale. There were bits and pieces, including a small study for Shell, which Paul Dantz, my old RJBA boss from the Maui project, was running. And then there was Audhali. If he came up trumps, then *Alhamdulillah*, but so far there was nothing but excuses. As I left for Vancouver on the Friday, nothing had changed. We might have to accept an offer from CanOcean, whatever it was.

It felt strange going to Vancouver. It had become the far side of the world for me when, as an undergraduate, I was bewitched by a philosophy student who won a scholarship to the University of British Columbia to continue her studies. We parted vowing eternal love, something like the deportation scene in *Manon Lescaut*. But distance doesn't make the heart grow fonder for long and, despite finding a telephone box where I could call international for free, the affair soon fizzled out.

In the event, Vancouver was nothing like the desolate and dark place I had conjured up fourteen years earlier. It's a ten-hour flight from London, chasing the sun. Leaving at lunchtime gets you there mid-afternoon, with a chance to view the city's magnificent setting between the Rockies and Vancouver Island. The visit didn't allow much time for sightseeing. However, after a long sleep-in on the Sunday morning, I went for a walk in Stanley Park, surely a rival to Regent's Park. It revealed much about the nature of Canada. There, in mid-September on adjacent fields, was a game of rugby, in which one of the teams was almost entirely Asian, a game of baseball in traditional costume and a game of cricket with both teams in whites.

Bob Brown and I spent our first day in Vancouver in CanOcean's impressive offices and workshops on Annacis Island on the Fraser River. Nova, the conglomerate that had recently acquired CanOcean, had started life as the Alberta Gas Trunkline Company (AGTL). Robert Blair joined the company as an executive VP in 1970 with a plan to extend the company's pipeline network north to Prudhoe Bay in Alaska and south to Texas. Like most forward-thinking projects, it was vigorously opposed by the troglodytes, but despite the setbacks later in the year, Blair, aged forty-one, was promoted to president and chief executive of AGTL. Within ten years, the company had acquired household names, such as Husky Oil, Grove Valves, Western Star Trucks, Ledeen Flow Control Systems, Alberta Gas Chemicals and The Alberta Gas Ethylene Company. Western Star Trucks looked like a black sheep in this family, however, AGTL saw compressed natural gas (CNG) as the transport industry's fuel of the future and intended to build trucks to prove it. CanOcean, essentially a research and development organisation, looked out of place as well, but the oil and gas industry was moving into deeper and deeper water and CanOcean was a leader in this field. In 1980, to reflect its diversity, AGTL changed its name to the gob-stopping 'Nova, an Alberta Corporation'. By retaining 'Alberta' in the new name, Blair, the outspoken nationalist, had underlined how parochial Canadians can be despite the variety of sports played in Stanley Park.

Our host for our first day in Vancouver was Steve Hill, VP for sales and contracts. He took us on a tour of the workshops to introduce the company's 'dry one-atmosphere concept'. As outlined in company literature, it was developed to 'provide a method of utilizing proven oil patch technology on the ocean floor in an environment where experienced oil patch technicians could be utilized for service work. Basically, this meant encapsulating the equipment in a steel chamber and providing a breathable one-atmosphere environment inside for service personnel.' The rival concept being developed by standard oilfield hardware manufacturers, such as Cameron Iron Works and the Hughes Tool Company, was known as the 'wet' concept. They developed equipment that could be used underwater without the surrounding chamber, however, before the age of underwater remotely operated vehicles (ROVs) skilled divers were required for interventions. In the early eighties, CanOcean had success with 'dry' developments in deep waters, such as offshore Brazil, but as the power and dexterity of the robotics attached to underwater ROVs improved, the one-atmosphere concept became uncompetitive.

The workshop tour and discussions confirmed Bob Brown's proposal made sense. Bligh Engineering could provide a launching pad in Europe, not only for CanOcean but for other members of the Nova group, such as NovaCorp

Engineering Services, as well. It wasn't long before we started talking money. Of course, this was likely to happen and Dick, John and I had discussed it. Our basic position was that in the event we were unsuccessful in having the Saudi tax claim waived, we wanted enough to ensure we could meet our commitments. We didn't have to waltz around too much because Steve Hill and Bob Brown had done some homework and had the basis of an offer: £184,000 if the Saudi claim was waived and £152,000 if it wasn't. The offer was contingent on my remaining with CanOcean on a salary of £30,000 plus car for two years. The salary was generous, given my flat in Holland Park Avenue had cost £48,000 and it gave us far more than we needed to pay our bills. But it didn't feel like a win. I knew Dick would be bitterly disappointed. Even with the faint prospect of work from Hyundai Heavy Industries courtesy of Ken Foss, we would struggle without the £95,000 held by AOC.

Days before leaving for Vancouver I told my brilliant and loyal secretary, Barbara Mitchell, I had no idea what would happen next and suggested, rather than being left high and dry, she look for another job. I was back in the office on the Tuesday morning and hadn't long gone over the whole story with Dick for the second time when Barbara came to my door and asked if I had a moment. Danger, danger. I could sense she had waited for Dick to leave and that was ominous. Then she closed the door and burst into tears. Eventually, she got it out. She had been in no hurry to find another job but when she mentioned it to her husband, Andrew, he said he knew where there was a perfect position for her in Sloane Street.

There isn't a girl in the world who doesn't want to work round the corner from Harrods. I managed to cheer her up and assured her that even if the CanOcean deal went through, my new position was unlikely to merit a secretary. But I told her, for the meantime, please find and school a replacement. Pam arrived from Bligh Appointments the next day. Barbara spent two weeks introducing her to the Bligh Engineering system and my peculiarities and left. Days later, she wrote to let me know her new office address and telephone number. Her letter concluded with a PS: 'I wouldn't have missed a minute of the last four years. XX'

RIP Bligh Engineering

The CanOcean offer was now in the hands of the lawyers. They can make a mess of anything, so we had to press on. A few days later I flew down to Dhahran to tie up some loose ends on the tie-in platform project and to close the bank account established for the Arabian Bligh Corporation. Naturally, I went to see Ahmed Audhali. I didn't expect any good news and wasn't disappointed. His friend in the DZIT was still in the USA and was expected back in October. He did confirm, however, that he had shut down the ABC.

Next stop, Bahrain, to meet Ken Foss and senior members of YD Kim's HHI offshore team from Seoul. Encouraged by their success with the Yanbu project, they were targeting projects from South Korea to the Nile Delta. But to compete effectively they needed a submarine pipeline lay barge. We met at the Gulf Hotel, where HHI had booked Ken into a suite and where we spent a day discussing the design parameters for the barge they would need. We went through everything down to the life rafts and by the end of the day had agreed on a 125 x 35 metre centre slot barge designed to American Bureau of Shipping Class A1, with a one-hundred-metre-long hinged stinger, accommodation for 250 and capable of laying pipe from six-inch-diameter to forty-two-inch-diameter in water to a hundred metres deep. I spent the next day preparing an estimate for the design of the deck equipment and stinger and writing a proposal telexed to HHI in Seoul. Essentially, it was 2000 manhours valued at £30,000. I gave SK Kim, HHI's team leader, a copy and he agreed to give me a yes or no within two weeks.

SK Kim turned out to be a straight shooter and over the next fifteen years we became firm friends. The start-work order arrived as promised on October 7th. We had survived a near-death experience. The contract in effect guaranteed CanOcean would stand by its offer and put us in a far stronger position for last minute negotiations, should there be any. Ken Foss, our godfather, had done it again and I was determined not to embarrass him. Designing a new lay barge was a new departure for Bligh Engineering and we would get nowhere without an engineer who knew what he was doing. So my top priority on returning to London was to have Bligh Technical Recruitment initiate a search through contacts in Texas and Louisiana. We had some odd responses from the bayous, but the oddest of all came via Paul Dantz, who suggested an ex-U-boat engineer. Walter Adler immigrated to Texas after WW2 and fell into building lay barges. Paul had met him in Rotterdam on the *Viking Piper* project. When I called him, he said he was retired, but old troupers love to work and it didn't take much to persuade him to come. He arrived two weeks later. By then, we had completed all the calculations required to define the barge's operational envelope and had all the information required from the critical equipment vendors for equipment such as winches, crawler cranes, line-up clamps, welding machines, pipe tensioners, X-ray machines and power generators. All Walter had to do was to show us how to put it all together.

HHI was in a hurry and requested a preliminary report, which we issued early in November. By now, the job was fully staffed so I could afford to attend to CanOcean. Bob Brown was delighted with the new contract and doubled his efforts to formalise the sale and purchase agreement, but CanOcean's lawyers were determined to milk the cow and insisted on going through every agreement Bligh Engineering had ever made. This became impossible and we retreated to an asset purchase agreement, meaning Dick, John and I would retain the empty shell of the Bligh Engineering Company together with any trailing liabilities. Even so, there was no way the deal would be finalised before the end of the month when I was due to leave for South Korea to present the preliminary lay barge design report.

November was also the month Kina did what she had been threatening all year and that was to pack up and move to Sydney with her daughter, Alex. I had thought it had been a pipe dream but too late I realised she had been serious—not that I could have changed her mind anyway. There was a spate of farewell parties and they left towards the end of the month. There was no need for a *Manon Lescaut* deportation scene at Heathrow as I would be in Sydney before Christmas.

Fox hunting starts in November too. Weeks earlier, having run into John Langdon, the conversation somehow touched on hunting and we discovered a mutual interest. It had been seven years since he had taken me shooting on the Beaulieu Estate. Since then, he had married and given up shooting for fox hunting. Could there be a moral in that story? He was now a Chiddingfold, Leconfield & Cowdray Hunt subscriber and his friend and fellow subscriber, Johnny Morris, had a spare horse and was looking for someone to lease it to for the season. Why not come out for a day and try it out? I would love to.

Eventually, it was arranged I would join him at the Shillinglee Park Manor meet and he would bring the horses. Being a newcomer, I gave myself plenty of time and having arrived early, was able to observe the ladies and gentlemen as they arrived, some with their horses and others, like me, meeting them from livery. Hunt subscribers come from all walks of life—the city, the law courts, the civil service, the military, universities, hospitals and most important of all, farms. There would be no fox hunting without the goodwill of farmers. Young and old, they came in all shapes and sizes. Thelwell says it all: some ride well, some don't. But that's not the point; they all love the English countryside and its enduring traditions. Enduring no longer. In 2004, a mob of sanctimonious and smelly campaigners, goaded by the prime minister's wife and funded by holier-than-thou pop stars, managed to destroy the sport and with it an important part of English country life.

It wasn't long before John and Clarissa arrived and with them, Ginger, a beefy seventeen-hand chestnut Irish hunter. There was no way I would look like a raw beginner arriving at the meet on such a magnificent horse, but having been warmly welcomed by the Joint Masters, I was swiftly put in my place by Mr Peel, the huntsman, who made a rude remark about Australians and kangaroos. It wasn't long before he blew 'Moving Off', and we were away. We headed south and spent most of the day on the high ground around Balls Cross, but on this perfect day the scent was poor, so there was no spine-tingling 'blowing away', the call to chase a running fox. The only excitement was offered by the hounds, who found and surrounded a hapless terrapin. Nobody was more embarrassed than Mr Peel. After 'blowing for home', he made a point of assuring me there was normally a lot more fun and please come another day.

Despite the lack of sport, I had enjoyed the company and by early December, when I left for South Korea, I had been out on two days with real fox hunts. That's not to say we killed a fox. In the ten seasons that followed, during which I went out on well over 120 days, I saw the hounds kill foxes on less than five occasions. Ginger had been brilliant. In full hunting kit I weighed in at ninety kilograms. As far as he was concerned, I could have been a flea. He had a wonderful temperament, was determined to stay with hounds and, as I was soon to discover, could and would jump anything, including a five-bar gate. Johnny Morris suggested I lease him for the rest of the season. I leased him for three seasons.

As I prepared for the trip to Seoul, it seemed likely the deal with CanOcean would be concluded early in the new year. The HHI lay barge project was coming to an end but Bob Brown thought there were other prospects we could pursue in conjunction with HHI and suggested coming along as well.

He had a good track record in North Africa and might be able to conjure up something of interest to them, so why not? Bob thought it important to travel business class. I didn't. He offered to pay, so I went business class too. Seoul was an eye-opener. Apart from it being bitterly cold, the country's new military leader had imposed martial law. The pretext was North Korean clandestine infiltration. The real reason was pesky political opposition. There was also a curfew. Our flight arrived just after 7 pm, and by the time the man from HHI had found us it was well after lights out. It's an eerie feeling driving through a dark city. I had the same sensation in East Berlin eight years later. On the plus side, however, there was no traffic, so we arrived at the Lotte Hotel in good time for an early night.

Hyundai's head office was not far down the Sejong-daero from the Lotte, so the meetings got off to an early start the next day. It soon became apparent HHI was no longer interested in the standalone pipeline lay barge we had virtually finished designing for them. Their new idea was to build a combination derrick lay barge modelled on *HC-39*, the derrick barge that had set the foundation jackets for the NGL pier in Yanbu six months earlier. Bob could barely disguise his delight. His Bligh Engineering strategy had been vindicated in spades. We spent the day agreeing on an operating envelope for the new barge, to be called *HC-49*. It would be similar to the barge we had already designed except for the minor detail of a 1000-tonne revolving derrick. They were obviously in a hurry because my suggestion to send Walter Adler to Yanbu to inspect *HC-39* was welcomed, immediately accepted, and arrangements were made. Further arrangements were made to retrieve the as-built drawings for *HC-39*, stored in the fabrication yard's engineering offices in Ulsan. We would be there tomorrow and could select and copy the drawings we thought might be useful in London.

As the day drew to a close, Bob and I were invited to dinner. Of all the exotic evenings I remember, this took the cake. Around eight, we were collected from the hotel and taken to what appeared to be a function centre, although it was difficult to tell in the curfew darkness. Everything changed in the bar and reception area. There were our hosts in their grey suits (could they have been company issue?) attended by a coterie of the most elegantly styled women in traditional dress. As we entered, two peeled off, glided towards us and took our coats and scarves. Two more appeared with aperitifs. We joined the suits. The only one I recognised was an 'executive' VP who had appeared briefly at our first meeting of the morning. The others were all senior, and for all I knew, came from the accounts department. Some of them didn't even speak English, and as we made small talk with those who did, our hostesses, who I was soon to discover were known as *kisaeng*, discreetly circled, making sure we didn't run out of the sticky liquor.

We were soon motioned into the banquet hall with its richly decorated ceiling, panelled walls, lavishly spread table and richly upholstered high-backed chairs. A *kisaeng* accompanied each guest to his place and for the remainder of the evening stood discretely behind, pre-empting every need. My Miss Moon, who spoke a little English, helped with the relentless procession of dishes. There was barely enough time in between to accept another down-in-one challenge from one of the Hyundai team, upon which your glass would be filled with more of the sticky liquor to be manfully quaffed again. Bob didn't look like he was enjoying it any more than me. My eyes were glazing over when it went from bad to worse. The contest of drink descended into a contest of song. A three-piece band appeared and started playing what I imagined to be traditional Korean songs. With little encouragement, each of the Hyundai executives, perhaps in order of seniority, rose and sang. No matter how dreary, each dirge concluded to great applause and more rounds of stickiness. It soon became apparent I was expected to contribute. Few do 'Waltzing Matilda' worse than me, but the band knew it, so off I went. More applause, more drink. I vaguely remember Miss Moon helping me to the car. I don't remember getting back to the hotel, but I do know we flew to Ulsan early next morning. Did Adam Smith consider the collateral cost of trade?

Ulsan is where Hyundai's founder, Chung Ju-Yung, built HHI's first shipbuilding dry dock on the back of an order for a tanker from prominent Greek shipowner George Livanos. It was commissioned in 1974. The shipyard, now the world's largest, is spread over 700 hectares, has nine dry docks and workshops covering 150 hectares. Naturally, the yard was nothing like this in 1981 but in nine years had come a long way. My new best friend, SK Kim, was our host and proudly showed us around the works in progress related to offshore oilfield construction. Hyundai's yard was just as capable of fabricating a manifold deck for an offshore drilling platform as a modular bridge structure for a crude-oil tanker. The company had realised the workshop trades required for a shipyard were just those required for an offshore oilfield fabrication yard, such as J Ray McDermott's in Dubai and Brown & Root's in Bahrain. Everything, from the piles to the control panels, that made up the 2.2-kilometre-long NGL loading pier I had visited in Yanbu in April had been fabricated in this yard, stacked on barges, shipped unloaded and installed 12 000 kilometres away. Brown & Root and McDermott, with yards 3000 kilometres away, couldn't compete. In the thirty years since the Korean War, South Korea had become an Asian tiger.

Now, before going further, a geography lesson. Whether we like it or not, in this regressive age of identity politics the world has been explored and dominated by western civilisations from the northern hemisphere since the Phoenicians invented navigation 4000 years ago. As a result, and thanks to Mr Mercator, we natives of the south have grown up with maps of the world depicting us as shrivelled afterthoughts. Indeed, on a Mercator projection the distance from London to Seoul appears twice that from Seoul to Sydney. So, if you are travelling that route you are entitled to believe, having reached Seoul, you are nearly there. Not so, you are merely halfway. I had a practical experience of this on my way to Sydney via Tokyo, a journey that seemed to take forever—perhaps because I was looking forward to seeing Kina.

Eventually, relieved to escape from frosty South Korea, I found myself in the brilliant sunshine of Sydney. It had been eight years since my seminal motorcycle crash on the Pacific Highway so it was nice to have a week to show Kina around old haunts and introduce old friends. We arranged a drinks party—a curious assortment: Jane Harders, a friend from university dramatic society days, now a real actress; Margaret Armstrong, not long back from London where she had been a star recruiter at Bligh Appointments; Paul Enemark, bloodstock guru and landlord from Sydney days; Doug Barry, another university dramatic society friend, now practicing law; Peter McMahon whose wedding Dick, Paul Enemark and I attended in Paris in 1976; and Scott Woolcock, a civil engineering classmate from the University of Queensland, working for consultants Cardno & Davies. We also had a couple of days in the Hunter Valley, but I was feeling uncomfortable about being so close and not being at home.

The last four months had been upsetting for Mum and Dad. Their greatest sadness was Lock and Mary's marriage, which was on the rocks. There was nobody else involved but there was no reconciliation either. News of Bligh Engineering's woes had escaped as well, and in one of her letters Mum had confided 'Father rather concerned'. So as much as I was enjoying Sydney, there was a feeling of relief when, with days to spare before Christmas, I flew up to Oakey, a short drive from home and the best roast dinner in the world. Chris and Sarah were there too, so it was a happy occasion made happier by news from London that all concerned had agreed the Bligh Engineering sale could proceed, with the agreement signed in my absence. So there was no need for Father to be concerned in that regard. We had a quiet family Christmas in Dalby and a day or so later headed for the coast, where we settled into the Gunyah.

Mooloolaba post-Christmas retained its sedate pace, with early mornings on the beach, leisurely breakfasts, more beach and lunch, followed by tennis or golf. There was also plenty to do at 24 Douglas Street, recently vacated by a tenant who had been there since the sale had gone through in April. I had the plumbing, drainage and wiring refurbished, replaced much of the furniture, installed ceiling fans and most importantly, a telephone. So, I had a link to London. It's hard to imagine now, but although it was relatively simple to make telephone calls between Mooloolaba and London in 1982, the ten-hour time difference made business communications difficult. The time to call was between 7 pm and 10 pm Australian Eastern Standard Time, and on January 9th Dick rang to confirm the Bligh Engineering sale had been completed. A notice was placed in the London newspapers.

On Friday January 8th, 1982, Bligh Engineering Ltd was acquired by CanOcean Resources U.K. Ltd. David Wilson has joined CanOcean's board of directors and assumes responsibility for engineering and project management in CanOcean. All other Bligh Engineering personnel are being integrated into CanOcean. Naturally Bligh's current contracts will be continued without interruption.

There was still work to be done—important work. On completion of the sale, we were able to pay our debts but not much else. If we were to make anything, we had to recover the £95,000 plus interest AOC was holding in The Hague pending settlement of the Saudi DZIT claim. On my return to London, I went to work for CanOcean as per the sale agreement, but Bob Brown gave me the latitude I needed to close Bligh Engineering. Initially, it was business as usual at Paul Street as work continued on the Hyundai project and loose ends for Aramco. Some members of Bob's small CanOcean team moved in with us but the plan was to close the Paul Street office and merge the two teams in a new CanOcean office in South London.

In the course of the next six months, I made four trips to Dhahran. Amongst other things, this kept me in close touch with Ahmed Audhali, who was always upbeat. He was delighted on extracting a letter from Aramco confirming Bligh Engineering had not been notified of the DZIT claim raised in October 1980, until April 1981. It must have done something. I was in Dhahran in June when he called to say the deputy director of the Ministry of Finance had invited us to Riyadh to make our case. We took an early flight to make the twelve-noon appointment. Riyadh is hot and dusty in June. As we waited in the reception area for our audience, I wondered how the locals managed to look so cool in their spotless white thobes and colourful headscarves. As we were called to the meeting, Ahmed suggested I wait for a moment to give him time to brief Sheikh Saleh, the aforementioned deputy director of the Ministry of Finance. Ten minutes later, he called me in and introduced me to the urbane sheikh who sat me down and in perfect English asked me to tell my story.

It was an unexpected request and had me off balance for a moment or two, but I had been through the story so many times I didn't need notes.

The sheikh appeared sympathetic and after a few questions undertook to see what he could do and showed us the door. Ahmed seemed happy and thought we could expect a positive response within days. That was until we reached the ground floor entrance to the building, which was in pandemonium. It was 13 June 1982 and earlier that morning King Khalid had died in Taif. The news had just reached Riyadh and there was not so much grief as chaos. For once, Ahmed's optimistic demeanour slipped. Hamlet put it best: *what's Hecuba to him or he to Hecuba?*[19] In Ahmed's case, the answer was nothing, except he knew there would be turmoil in the government and there would be no resolution of our case for the foreseeable future. It was a shambles at Riyadh Airport, where the King's body was landing for burial. We got back to Dhahran that night but only after lengthy delays.

Ahmed was nothing if not persistent and three months later forwarded a letter from the director general of the DZIT, clearing us of all Saudi tax liabilities from 1976 to 1980. I flew to The Hague with the letter, gave a copy to AOC and flew back to London with a cheque for £111,000 (£95,000 plus interest). I never went back. We had not deserved the treatment meted out by a nasty bureaucrat, but they are always on the lookout for a day in the sun. Bligh Engineering's rise and fall had taken just six years. Starting with offshore pipeline surveys, we had finished with the design of two of the largest production platforms in the Persian Gulf—water depth 106 feet, topsides 1500 tonnes, each 250 feet from top to bottom. It had been a soft landing for most. All of us except Dick had jobs. He was bitterly disappointed. He could have continued with Bligh Technical Recruitment but his heart wasn't in it. It couldn't survive without him, so we closed it down and he married my secretary. His continued interest in Bligh Appointments gave him a good income, so he was financially sound, but for him that was cold comfort. I had landed butter side up. I was well paid and given a new BMW, but the escape spawned a hubris that led to an inevitable comeuppance.

CanOcean

As I started my new job, Mrs Thatcher had been in government for three years. In that time, she had sought to implement the monetarist policies that had revived Chile's economy in the eight years since Pinochet had seized power. The architects of those policies had all studied under Milton Friedman at the University of Chicago. Dick Staveley, one of the pioneering tutors at Union College, often spoke of his time at the University of Chicago and of Milton Friedman and I began to understand why. Friedman had become a superstar, not to mention advisor, to Mrs Thatcher and Ronald Reagan. But it wasn't smooth sailing and there were more hard times as she raised interest rates to ten per cent to curb inflation. Unemployment grew, her popularity plunged and, if it hadn't been for the Falklands War, she would have disappeared into obscurity. But there *was* a Falklands War. Sensing weakness in the UK and not expecting retaliation, Argentina invaded and occupied las Malvinas on 2 April 1982. They hadn't reckoned with the Iron Lady. She instructed Britain's armed services chiefs to remove them.

As Mrs Thatcher's armada set sail for the Falklands, I flew to Singapore to meet Kina for Easter. We stayed with Philip

Conn, who was going through a purple patch and living in style in a grand villa on Mount Faber. It had been the Port superintendent's residence in the colonial era. Never had a poohbah lived in a mansion better suited to his station, with polished teak verandahs providing uninterrupted views of the port, its wharves and warehouses no more than a pitching wedge away. The Far East was a novelty for Kina, so it was fun introducing her to its delights—dim sum in the Shangri La, water skiing in the Johor Strait, tennis at the Tanglin Club and dinner in the night market at Newton Circus. But Singapore was neither London nor Sydney and as our return flights approached there was a sense we were drifting apart. I was bound to spend the next eighteen months in London with CanOcean. Kina was falling in love with Sydney.

I returned to a country glued to its TV set. During the three months it took to liberate the Falklands, London stopped every evening as the BBC news went to air—Falklands War Live. Few have forgotten war correspondent Brian Hanrahan's report on the safe return to *HMS Hermes* of a flight of Harrier Jump Jets from an early attack on the invaders—'I counted them all out and I counted them all back'. Rule Britannia was back too and Mrs Thatcher rode the wave to win two more elections and preside over an economic revival that saw her govern for another eight years.

The victory demonstrated beyond doubt that of all the variables constituting an economy, that elusive ingredient, confidence, is the most important. The British economy was transformed. London was swinging again. Cocktail hour buzzed with talk of rising house prices, Notting Hill, renovations, curtains and nannies. It was fun, particularly if you were single, well paid, had a comfortable flat in Holland Park Avenue and were no longer responsible for the bottom line of an organisation employing nearly a hundred people. CanOcean gave me the latitude to enjoy London's evolving social year as it meanders through the seasons.

It kicks off in March with The Boat Race. That's the Oxford versus Cambridge Universities' six-kilometre rowing race on the Thames from Putney to Mortlake. The weather is usually miserable; the boats have sunk on occasions and there is no good place to watch it except on TV. But of far greater importance is the appearance of the daffodils in parks all over London. After seven years there, I was beginning to understand what Bill Milligan, our English English teacher saw in Wordsworth's line, *A host of golden daffodils*.[20] Those ephemeral narcissi wake Londoners from their winter torpor, and just as confidence is so important for an economy, so are daffodils essential to a healthy state of mind in a bustling city.

The hunting season starts early in November and continues through the winter to March, depending on the country and weather. Regardless, it's well and truly finished by the first or second Saturday in April, ensuring everybody is free for the Grand National, the race of legends Red Rum, Bob Champion, Becher's Brook and National Velvet. This is an eye-watering seven-kilometre steeplechase over thirty fences, including 'The Chair', five foot two inches high, with a six-foot-wide ditch on the take-off side. Initially, the race was for gentlemen, but by WW2 most jockeys were professionals. It was around that time that the fictional character Velvet Brown (played by

Elizabeth Taylor) won the race on National Velvet. To enter, she had to cut off her hair and pretend she was a boy. If she had waited until 1975, the Sex Discrimination Act would have made that unnecessary. The other Grand National film was *Champions*, which told the true story of jockey, Bob Champion, beating cancer and winning on Aldaniti in 1981. Aldaniti retired to his owner's estate in the Chiddingfold, Leconfield & Cowdray Hunt country in 1982 and often joined the hunt, particularly if the meet was at Barkfold.

The annual Army-Navy rugby match at Twickenham comes around in early May. To hear the fish heads and the pongos talking about each other and to see them play rugby, you might be forgiven for believing they were bitter enemies, but they worked wonders together in the Falklands. And it's great to see the inter-service camaraderie in the car park before the match, where the picnics are lavish and there are more than a few who miss the kick-off.

If it was sunny towards the end of May, the Chelsea Flower Show was where you would see the first of the summer hats and dresses, not to mention lavish garden designs and flower arrangements and the Queen. The show takes place in the grounds and gardens of the Royal Hospital Chelsea, home to retired soldiers of the British Army. They are known as Chelsea Pensioners and are distinguished by their scarlet frock coats and black shakos. During the year, they can be seen around Sloane Square and the King's Road in ones and twos, but for the flower show they are out in force and add extra colour to a uniquely English occasion.

Thinking about it, these occasions are all uniquely

English, and the Epsom Derby, falling early in June, is no exception. Lester Piggott won it nine times. His last win on the favourite, Teenoso, in 1983, was a career highlight. Michael Langdon had organised a Price Waterhouse clients' day out and I had been invited as a prospective client. As we captains of industry assembled at the Carlton Club, St James's, for breakfast, it was drizzling and the red open-top double-decker London bus Michael had arranged for the trip to Epsom didn't look like a good idea. But even though it had been raining for weeks, as we crossed Wandsworth Bridge there were patches of blue sky and by the time we had parked on the rail inside the track, just short of the finish line, it was a beautiful sunny day, perhaps the first of the year. That's when the champagne came out. The rest is a fuzzy memory, but I remember walking the course, tasting my first jellied eel and consulting a Gypsy fortune teller, who assured me I would recoup all the money I had lost on earlier races by backing Teenoso.

The beauty of the Royal Academy's Summer Exhibition, which opens shortly after Derby Day, is that it's indoors and warm. Unlike the other milestones on the social calendar, it lasts for two months and you can go whenever you like and as often. I love it and am always reminded of the legend of JMW Turner adding a small red buoy to his seascape *Helvoetsluys* as it was on exhibit at the Royal Academy. That simple daub of paint transformed that painting, just as the Chelsea Pensioners add colour to the Flower Show.

The English, like all Europeans, live for the sun. Nevertheless, there is no formal event to mark the summer solstice. A motley bunch dress up as druids and disport themselves at Stonehenge but the mainstream dress as scantily as possible and flock to alfresco parties where they catch a summer cold. If not, they can go to Royal Ascot. This was something with which I was familiar long before arriving in London. My father loved the musicals and even at Mount Oscar in the 1950s we had a gramophone and recordings of *Die Fledermaus, Oklahoma, The King and I, South Pacific, Carousel, The Desert Song* and *My Fair Lady*. Remember the 'Ascot Gavotte'... *Ev'ry duke and earl and peer is here. Ev'ryone who should be here is here. What a smashing, positively dashing spectacle: the Ascot op'ning day.*[21] It conveyed a sense of world-weariness in the lords and ladies of Eliza Doolittle's era. Not so for our Gold Cup days. A picnic in the No.1 car park routinely organised by a friend, Suzy Shepherd, was legendry and only a short walk from the Royal Enclosure. Everybody made an effort. One of the group, Richard Berry, even arrived with his mum in a Roller one year only to find the bailiffs were waiting to repossess it.

Summer officially arrives in July, and with it, Wimbledon. The Queen didn't turn up and the English rarely produce a champion, but it's still the most popular event of the year. I could be wrong, but unlike a rowing race, a horse race, a game of rugby, or for that matter, a game of cricket, it's a contest of individuals playing a game played by many of the spectators and it attracts half a million over two weeks. A tight Ashes series might draw more, but over twice the time and there is only one every four years. For most of the 128 players who qualify, Wimbledon is Mount Everest and for that reason there is rarely a day without interest, although the finals, particularly the ladies, can be disappointing. That's why I prefer to go to the second Wednesday for the men's quarter finals, which inevitably produce fizzing contests. My mother made three trips to London during my eleven years there—ostensibly to visit her sons, but it was really to go to Wimbledon and for the first two occasions she went every day.

She arrived in London for her final Wimbledon trip on 17 June 1982, two days after the surrender of the Argentinian forces in the Falklands and three days after King Khalid's death with its unfortunate consequences for Bligh Engineering. I had arrived back in London from Saudi Arabia a few days earlier so had time to buy a top-of-the-range sofa bed and to convert the 155 Holland Park Avenue living room into a temporary bedroom. Not that it was immediately necessary. We spent the first weekend with the Kisches at Hatchford, and from there drove down to Dover where we caught a ferry to Calais for a week in France. It was a thoroughly unpleasant day with a stiff westerly blowing offshore at Dover making the sea deceptively calm. Thirty minutes later we were in a force seven beam sea, and in no time at all the decks were awash with vomit. Fortunately, Mum was fine and so was I, but we were more than happy to disembark in Calais and head for Paris on the A16.

We were so fine that about an hour later we left the main road for a small auberge where we stopped for lunch. We ordered the *plat du jour* and a carafe of the *vin de maison*. The patron asked if we were English. No, Australian. It didn't appear to draw a reaction but later when I asked for *l'addition* in my fluent French he indicated that, as Australians, we were honoured guests and nothing I could say would change his mind. The worst of it was I didn't understand why. Certainly, we had just driven a section of the A16 that follows the Somme and had passed signs indicating WW1 war graves. And I was aware thousands of Australian soldiers, including my grandfather, had fought on the Somme. Many had died. But so too had hundreds of thousands of English, Canadians, Indians and Americans, and I didn't think they got free lunches.

The answer came over thirty years later. I was planning a trip to Europe and had just read Lieutenant TP Chataway's *History of the 15th Battalion AIF 1914–1918*, with its description of the action during which Grandfather Dave had been wounded in northern France. On a whim, I called The Australian War Memorial in Canberra and told the woman who answered the phone I was travelling to the Somme hoping to visit the place where my grandfather had survived a bullet through his chest. She requested details and invited me to hold while she looked up the unit diary. A minute or two later, she came back asking if I had access to Google Earth. *Yes, I have it open in the area. Zoom in on Mouquet Farm. Do you see a clump of trees about 400 metres east of the farmhouse? Yes. That's where your grandfather was wounded.* A month later, I walked through a now-tranquil landscape, past old Dave's copse and the countless graves of the not so lucky, all the while giving thanks for a fortunate life.

Then there was time to explore and days later, during a visit to the Sir John Monash Centre at Villers Bretonneux,

I learned why Mum and I had been so generously treated in the auberge outside Amiens all those years ago. In early March 1918, following the Russian Revolution, Russia signed a treaty with Germany ending the war on the Eastern Front. This gave Germany an extra fifty divisions with which to mount a 'spring offensive' on the Western Front. The initial attack launched on March 21st targeted the strategic rail hub of Amiens and in no time at all had smashed through established Allied trench lines from Vimy to St Quentin. They took Albert five days later and were less than thirty kilometres from their objective. With the British 5th Army in full retreat, General John Monash was ordered to the area to stem the German advance. He deployed the 4th Division AIF across a twenty-kilometre stretch between Hébuterne and Dernancourt. Four thousand Australians were all that stood between Amiens and 25 000 advancing Germans. The battle of Dernancourt raged from March 28th until April 4th. The diggers withstood unrelenting artillery and infantry attacks until rain intervened and the Germans retreated. That is why, to this day, the words *'N'oublions jamais l'Australie'* appear in classrooms all over the Somme, and if you take your Australian mother to lunch in a tiny auberge in the area you could be in for a pleasant surprise.

Sustained by our surprise lunch, we continued to Paris where we checked into the Hotel Montaigne. Mum and Dad had spent two days in Versailles on the way to Michel and Hedwige Cornudet's wedding five years earlier, but Dad was a reluctant tourist, so Paris was a new adventure for Mum. She made up for lost time with a determined shopping spree.

Avenue Montaigne was a good place to start, with Christian Dior a few doors down to the right. In between shopping, we did the museums. The Musée Rodin is a torrid affair with its collection of tortured souls, but she laughed when I took her to see the mummies in the Louvre. My favourite, however, was the *Jeu de Paume*, with its impressionists whimsically conveying the spirit of the Belle Epoque. Years later, I was alarmed to hear the collection was to be uprooted and rehoused in a converted railway station. I shouldn't have been concerned. There are many fine art collections in the world but the Musée d'Orsay is hard to beat.

In between museums, we caught up with friends. When I called Henry Lazarski (the Parisian lawyer I'd met at the Holloways' in Courcheval and a keen cyclist) to arrange a get together, he was out of town taking part in a Tour de France preliminary event. He insisted Mum and I move into his flat in the Rue de l'Annonciation. So we did. It was a beautiful flat and being just across the Seine from the Eiffel Tower allowed us to explore the world's most beautiful city from a different perspective.

We had a great week but Wimbledon had started, so after five days in Paris we returned to London via Brittany, where Michel Cornudet's parents entertained us in the Château du Verger au Coq. Once again, I felt the warmth of the French-Australian connection without truly understanding it. Back in London, Bob Brown had moved the company from our inexpensive offices in Paul Street (£20,210 a year) to expensive offices in Wimbledon (£227,000 a year). It was convenient for Bob, who lived south of London, but no good for many of the old Bligh Engineering employees, who lived in Essex and now had a two-hour commute. Most of them found another job. Bob had acquired Bligh Engineering for £184,000. It wasn't worth that much without its people. But there was another problem. The crude oil bull market, which had sustained Bligh Engineering's growth, was over. It had fallen from a peak of US$125 a barrel in June 1980 to US$80 in March 1982.

Finding new work for a new company would not be so easy. It was certainly not the time to be throwing money around and, at a management meeting convened shortly after moving in to the gleaming and mostly empty new offices, the management accounts revealed CanOcean Resources UK Ltd had accumulated losses in the vicinity of £1 million in less than a year. The only work of any substance was the tail end of the Hyundai lay barge design contract. North Sea projects were few and far between and it was becoming clear CanOcean's 'one atmosphere' or 'dry' concept for subsea development was losing out to the 'wet' concept pursued by hardware manufacturers, such as Hughes, Vetco, Cameron, FMC and Coflexip.

The 'one atmosphere' concept developed by Lockheed Petroleum Services was based on the idea of completing deep water wells on the seabed, with a conventional Christmas tree enclosed in a dry one-atmosphere chamber accessible by diving bell. Accordingly, any qualified technician in shirt sleeves could be lowered to the chamber to undertake maintenance in a dry environment. Seabed completions with 'wet' trees required specialist divers or unmanned robots for any intervention. Initially, the training and deployment of specialist divers in deep water was horrendously expensive and dangerous, so 'dry' trumped 'wet' and was adopted in the deeper waters off Brazil. But it wasn't long before underwater drone and robot technology improved and 'wet' tree technology took hold. CanOcean lost its unique selling point. It had to compete as a general-purpose engineer, just as Bligh Engineering had.

The silver lining was a new Aramco project. It came by accident. It had been set in motion in September 1981 when I was down in Dhahran tying up loose ends on the Zuluf tie-in platform project. I was walking through the Aramco Offshore Projects offices when Bruce Bailey called me in to his office and introduced me to Tony Blake from Ewbank and Partners. They were a large Brighton-based power, process and telecommunications engineering group and had formed a joint venture with Halcrow to tender for the front-end engineering for a 734 MBOD twin-train process platform in the Safaniya field. The platform would also be sized to accommodate gas compression and power distribution facilities. The preliminary engineering budget was 350 000 manhours. Halcrow and Ewbank were newcomers to Aramco, and Bruce suggested they would have a better chance of winning and executing the project with Bligh Engineering's help. Tony Blake undertook to talk to his management about it and a week later Dick and I were invited to visit Ewbank's grand offices in Brighton where they formally invited us to join the Halcrow Ewbank consortium. By the time Aramco had issued the bid documents in February 1982, Bligh Engineering had been acquired by CanOcean, so we prepared the bid as the Halcrow Ewbank CanOcean consortium. The estimate came out at 405 000 manhours over thirteen months, with a peak manpower load of 140. There was more than enough work in it for everybody.

Our bid was completed towards the end of April but there were delays printing and binding the tender books and the courier deadline for Dhahran passed. Fortunately, I had a passport with a valid Saudi visa, so on the evening of the bid due date I flew to Dhahran with the books packed in three suitcases. As I checked in for the 9.30 am BA flight the visa was valid, but there were delays and when I arrived Dhahran just after midnight, local time, it had expired. The Saudi border police wouldn't turn a blind eye. They insisted I take the return BA flight to London, leaving in two hours. It was a terrible moment. An enormous effort had been put into preparing the tender, not to mention the cost. Fortunately, I was able to call Ken Foss, who once again proved to be a guardian angel. He dressed, drove out to the airport and was permitted to meet me in the transit lounge. I gave him the tender books, boarded the return flight and was back in London in time for lunch. Despite objections to my role in the project from the usual suspects in The Hague, we were awarded the contract in November.

The award gave CanOcean some breathing space. It also gave me time for some opera, ballet and hunting. Dick and Pam were in London through the summer and as Dick preferred ballet we went to Royal Ballet performances of *Romeo and Juliet* and *Manon* in a big top erected in Battersea Park. I would enjoy *Romeo and Juliet* performed in a barn, but the experiment wasn't repeated, so there must have been problems I didn't notice. A memorable opera performance of this period was Jonathan Miller's production of *Rigoletto* at the ENO, mentioned in an earlier chapter. For a time, it became my favourite and a year or so later, after dinner and too much sake in a Japanese workers' restaurant in Abu Dhabi, a colleague and I reinterpreted 'Bella figlia dell'amore'[22] in a taxi on the way back to the hotel. Our Arab driver joined in, sort of, and got so excited he missed a roundabout and we ended up in a flower bed.

It was an interesting time in the engineering world. In 1980, Bligh Engineering had achieved significant productivity gains using Wang word processors. Two years later, CanOcean bought a few IBM PCs and I bagged one. They were standalone units capable of creating and saving a document or spreadsheet on a floppy disc. They were useful but didn't threaten to transform the engineering design office to the extent promised by 'computer-aided design' (CAD). CanOcean's parent company, NovaCorp Engineering, had installed CAD stations in its drawing office in Calgary, so I went for a look. I should have waited for summer. I had skied in a blizzard in Courcheval, danced an eightsome reel in Scotland during Hogmanay and slithered on icy footpaths in Seoul but had never experienced anything like the winter cold in Calgary. It informs the Canadian psyche manifest in ice hockey, where they bludgeon each other to pulp and kiss and make up afterwards. But necessity is indeed the mother of invention and on my second day I discovered the lifeblood of downtown Calgary, a wonderful maze of underground walkways, shops and elevators. I could walk from the Westin Hotel to NovaCorp's fancy corporate HQ without setting a foot outdoors.

For me, the NovaCorp CAD stations were clunky and expensive. In the days before networks, each station was a standalone printer run by a bespoke computer incorporating a large screen. It also required a lot more space than the normal drafting board. Moreover, as far as we were concerned in London, there was no way we could recover the cost given the nature of the Aramco contract with its focus on manhours rather than productivity. It was to be another ten years before AutoCAD transformed engineering offices everywhere.

From Calgary, I continued west to Seoul where I spent two days with HHI. We had completed our design for a new combination derrick/pipe lay barge earlier in the year. But rather than build a new barge they were now considering simply installing submarine pipeline installation equipment on their existing derrick barge, *HC-39*. This was the barge that had installed the trestles for the NGL terminal at Yanbu eighteen months earlier. They promised to call as soon as they had a decision. I headed south for the warmth of a family Christmas in Mooloolaba.

It would be our second summer in Douglas Street and by now it was well and truly a family house. Mum and Dad spent extended weekends there as often as possible and, as a result, it was truly a home away from home for all of us. Everybody was there in time for Christmas, including Lock's boys, Ben and Sam, and Sam the golden retriever, who presented himself at Myall Street and was adopted after the search for the owners was abandoned. Lucky dog. We also had a visit from Mike Vassilopoulos, the other member of the 'Bella figlia dell'amore' duet who had been passing through Singapore and made a detour to say hello. He was devastated when the Customs officer confiscated a can of foie gras he had brought as a present. We assured him it's the thought that counts and that the Customs officer probably didn't take it home because he probably didn't know what it was.

Following two weeks of surf, tennis, golf and fishing, I headed back to London via Singapore and Dhahran. The main event in Singapore was a meeting with Promet, a local construction and fabrication contractor, to discuss the design of a self-propelled jack-up work barge for the Persian Gulf. I had met the Promet people earlier in Dhahran, where Aramco had identified a niche for such a vessel to undertake the wellhead platform modifications designed by Bligh Engineering five years earlier. We discussed the barge parameters and I undertook to send them a proposal for the preparation of a functional specification. I also agreed to pursue the idea in Dhahran where I had been invited to attend a contractor pre-screening meeting for the wellhead platform modification project. The strong presence of contractors with Arab names or associations demonstrated Saudi influence in Aramco management had grown considerably since the fateful decision to form the Arabian Bligh Corporation four years earlier. The usual suspects, such as J Ray McDermott, Brown & Root and ETPM (Entrepose Travaux Petroliers et Maritimes) hadn't even been invited. Not that they should have been worried. Contract award was not expected for another twelve months. This project was not going to provide one extra barrel of oil a day for Aramco, so it was not a high priority. I flew back to London, having been around the world in fifty-two days with little to show for it.

The Safaniya process platform project had kept the office busy in my absence but wasn't bringing in enough to support Bob Brown's grandiose schemes. He had built an organisation suited to an international construction contractor like Brown & Root, not a fledgling engineering office. It couldn't last, and in March Bob was replaced by a Canadian from Nova's head office in Calgary. Murray Feller had no experience or contacts outside North America but he managed to stem the bleeding and had the confidence of Nova's senior management. We carried on prospecting for work in a tough environment. The Falklands effect on the crude oil price was long gone and it had now fallen back to its pre-war level. But there was one place desperate to rehabilitate its oil and gas reserves regardless of price—Iran.

Despite having CanOcean in London, Nova had decided to row its own boat in the Middle East and by way of announcing its intentions had taken a booth at a trade fair in Bahrain in March. I was invited to join the management team appointed to man it. I was sceptical at first but that changed as I learned about Nova and its capabilities, particularly where they related to cross-country gas pipelines. Nova operated one of the world's most extensive gas grids, so its capability in this area was world class and of particular interest to an Iranian delegation who took an interest in the SCADA (Supervisory Control and Data Acquisition) system the company had developed. They asked if we would be interested in coming to Iran to make a presentation to their operations engineers. *Yes, why not?*

There was a big 'why not?' The Canadians had closed their embassy in Tehran following their courageous participation in the escape of six American diplomats from Tehran during the 1979 hostage crisis. Nova management was reluctant to send Canadians to Tehran and may not have had too many volunteers anyway. Australia still had a consulate in Tehran. Would I be prepared to go? I managed to call the Australian Charge d'Affaires in Tehran, John Dauth. He didn't see a problem, suggested I book the Hilton Hotel and advised me to forward my itinerary as soon as the arrangements had been made.

The arrangements took time, and in the interim the Indian Oil and Natural Gas Commission issued a tender request for the development of its South Bassein gas field off Bombay. We had teamed up with a Singapore-based offshore installation contractor for this project but still needed a local platform fabricator. The industry in India was barely crawling, so there were no such things as traditional oil and gas fabrication yards. The answer was to find a shipyard that could be taught to do the work. The obvious candidate was Mazagon Dock in Bombay, given its proximity to the offshore gas field, but its forward commitments ruled out any participation in the tender. This left Hindustan Shipyard Ltd in Visakhapatnam, on the far side of the subcontinent.

Mike Vassilopoulos and I set off for Visak in early May— Air Pakistan to Delhi via Karachi and Air India to Visak via Hyderabad. The last leg was in a turboprop that had seen better days, not unlike Visak, a dusty sleepy place where we were met at the airport and taken to a reception luncheon in the Naval Mess hosted by Admiral Mennen, chairman of HSL. Any excuse for a party. We must have looked out of place surrounded by at least twenty officers, all smartly dressed in their whites. Mike was seated next to the naval surgeon and took the opportunity to enquire about malaria. *Good question, Sir. We have two varieties. After a bite from the first you have a fever for two weeks, then you die. After a bite from the second, you die immediately.* I didn't hear this story until later. The only hotel in town fit for human habitation had a bar decorated by a 360-degree panorama from the *Kama Sutra*. Perhaps that's why we could only book the double room Mike and I had to share. Before dinner, I had been up to the room and opened the windows and turned the fan on to cool it off. Of course, it was humming with mosquitos on our return. Mike went ballistic, recounted the doctor's story and set to work with a tennis racquet to rid the room of the deadly threat. He was at it all night. We didn't die but we didn't win any work in India either. Back in London, I prepared for my trip to Iran.

At that time, Swiss Air was one of the few recognised airlines flying into Tehran from Europe, so my first stop was Zurich. Coincidentally, Ken Foss was holidaying there with his wife, Pauline. The stopover gave me sufficient time to join them for tea in their elegant hotel by the lake. My great mentor and friend was subdued and I sensed he was no longer enjoying Saudi Arabia. We corresponded afterwards but it was the last time I saw him.

On to Tehran. The arrival formalities at Mehrabad only served to make the six-hour flight even more tedious so, having negotiated the maze, I was pleasantly surprised to discover John Dauth had sent a car to meet me—not just any car but his bullet-proof Mercedes. I was relieved there were no signs a bullet-proof car was a necessity, but my south-facing room in the Hilton did have a neat bullet hole in the panoramic double-glazed window, perhaps to remind me not to be complacent.

The meeting with the Iranian Offshore Oil Company (IOOC) was informative and constructive, although, for me, slightly disappointing with its bias towards operations rather than development. IOOC had been formed in 1981 in the aftermath of the revolution to consolidate Iran's oil and gas interests in the Persian Gulf. This consolidation had included the ill-fated Nowruz production platform, destroyed just four months earlier. They were interested to hear I had participated in the 1978 study recommending span remedial measures along the pipeline. The deputy manager of engineering and technical services provided a broad outline of their offshore production facility portfolio. Before the start of the ongoing war with Iraq, they were producing around 600 000 barrels a day. It was no longer anywhere near that level and maintenance activities had been curtailed as well. The war was partly to blame but they were also struggling without American equipment and know-how, no longer available in the aftermath of the 1979 US hostage crisis.

The Iranian engineers were capable, and necessity had been the mother of invention, but they still needed help and

I sensed they considered Canada an acceptable alternative. They weren't interested in new developments. Their priority was to restore and recertify existing facilities: 150 platforms and 1300 kilometres of flowlines and trunklines in water depths up to 280 feet. We identified three areas where Nova/CanOcean could assist: the installation of Nova's SCADA systems on offshore platforms to facilitate remote monitoring and control, running internal offshore pipeline inspections and training field personnel in Canada. To conclude, we agreed to maintain communications and I undertook to provide further information.

The meeting had taken up my first morning in Tehran so there were two days to kill before returning to London via Dubai. I called on John Dauth to thank him for his help. He advised me to allow at least three hours to complete departure formalities the following day. It was good advice and for the benefit of colleagues travelling to Tehran in my wake I made a note of the thirteen steps involved. Much of it was to do with exchange control checks designed to ensure foreign visitors purchased Iranian rials at the official exchange rate and did not succumb to the temptations of the black market.

Shortly after my return to London, I attended a progress review meeting for the Halcrow Ewbank CanOcean JV, which had now been working for seven months on the preliminary design for the Safaniya 734 MBOD twin-train process platform. The work was on schedule for completion in January 1984. CanOcean's thirty-man involvement in the JV team had made a welcome contribution to the company's bottom line but I was painfully aware the time to find follow-up work was running out.

There was another problem. Dad's sixtieth birthday was looming. My sister, Sarah, foreshadowed the considerable organisational skills she was to develop later by not only anticipating the milestone but sending invitations far and wide for a surprise party she would organise at 61 Myall Street. I called her to say there was no way I could come but by the end of the call had capitulated. With days to spare, I flew to Sydney, where I joined my brothers for a long slow drive home via St George and Roma. The plan was to arrive with the other guests in time for the big surprise.

Dad was in for a memorable birthday party, but not even Sarah could have arranged his present—Rain, and lots of it. One of the reasons we had given ourselves abundant time for the trip was the threat of even more. It had been dry for two years when Cyclone Elinor had hit Rockhampton in March. The tropical storm triggered widespread rain throughout eastern Australia. The wet lasted for three months and flooded the Murray-Darling basin. It's never any different. The water forms a great inland swamp as it trickles south. The cattle can take refuge on small islands together with kangaroos, emus, wombats, rabbits and anything else that hasn't drowned.

Moree was our goal for the first day of the drive north. Michael Boyce, an old friend from Union College and agricultural science graduate, had settled there to make his fortune in the fledgling cotton industry, so we arranged to meet for a few beers. We took the Pacific Highway north to Newcastle, where we joined the New England Highway heading north-west. Banjo Patterson[4] put the Mooki River on the map and we crossed it just after noon.

Down along the Mooki River, on the overlanders' camp,
Where the serpents are in millions, all of the most deadly stamp,
   Wanders, daily, William Johnson, down among those poisonous hordes,
   Shooting every stray goanna, calls them `black and yaller frauds'.
   And King Billy, of the Mooki, cadging for the cast-off coat,
   Somehow seems to dodge the subject of the snake-bite antidote.

From Moree, we continued north-west for St George. It wasn't long before we were driving through the first of the floodwater swamplands. The road was mostly above water so we were able to drive without too much trouble and untroubled by other traffic. Years earlier, Dad had given me his shotgun, thinking I might use it in England, but it was becoming increasingly difficult to keep a gun there so I was returning it. There were ducks everywhere and Lock couldn't resist the temptation to shoot one and did. The only problem was we didn't have a retriever. In a pre-PC age a casual passer-by would have been amused at the sight of my brother stripped to his underwear wading back to the car with a dead duck.

We spent the second night in St George, Mum's hometown. We called on Uncle Roden Knights, who showed us around town and took us out to the airport, where volunteers were loading flood relief hay onto an RAAF Caribou cargo aircraft to be dropped to stranded cattle. Working all day at three tonnes a load would never save them all but would save some. Graziers watch their stock die through drought, fight to save the survivors during flood and soldier on with what's left afterwards. Access to reliable water is the solution to this sad cycle but the sweeping plains of the Murray-Darling basin offer few viable dam sites. There was one just outside St George, and in 1972 the Queensland State Government built the Beardmore Dam on the Balonne River. It holds back enough water to irrigate 10 000 hectares of surrounding farmland subdivided into circa 200-hectare farms. We went out to the dam and marvelled as an estimated 5000 tonnes of water per second plunged over the spillway to resume its meander for 1600 kilometres south to the Southern Ocean.

Roden's son, John, had been fortunate enough to win one of the irrigation blocks in the ballot that followed completion of the dam and its water distribution network. We drove out to say hello and meet Jo, his wife, and Drew, their new baby. The proud father was more than happy to show us the workings of his farm growing mostly cotton. Clearly, there was a lot more to it than irrigation, but as an engineer, I was most interested in that aspect of the operation. The key is shaping the land to get the most from the available water. John had adopted the traditional furrow irrigation method requiring careful levelling to set up an even flow of water across each paddock. It had gone well and demonstrated a 500-acre farm with reliable water could support a family, largely free from the drought-flood-drought cycle. A farmer or grazier in the same area relying on rainfall alone would never be free of the cycle and would struggle to support a family on 10 000 acres.

Our next stop was Roma, where we caught up with more of the Knights family, before leaving for Dalby on the morning of the party. We arrived mid-afternoon, checked into a motel and called to confirm Dad was on the golf course. He was, so we were able to sneak home to a warm welcome and lots of tears from Mum. And the master of ceremonies was there as well, orchestrating preparations. Dad was expecting a few people for dinner but wasn't expected home before 7 pm. The fifty or so guests who had been arriving in town from near and far were asked to turn up at 6.30 pm and to park along the side street where they wouldn't be noticed.

If anything, it worked too well. As he walked through the front door and saw the crowd, he was shocked, particularly when he realised all his boys were there. For a moment I was alarmed. But the party animal rallied and after he had done the rounds and changed, he was in his element. It was a warm occasion—not only because of the good cheer radiated by the crackling living room fire, but because Sarah had thought of everything. There had been some gatherings at 61 Myall Street, but nothing like this—relatives, farmers, local notables, contract bridge players, neighbours, racing friends, girls from the office, an old air force friend and the doctor who had delivered all Mum's children. And there she was, stylish as ever, in a skirt, black cashmere jumper and a simple string of pearls. The lioness loved nothing more than having her cubs around but knew future occasions like this would be few and far between.

One of the reasons I baulked at going to Australia in July was an invitation to join Mike Vassilopoulos and his family on a cruise in the Greek Islands in September. He had chartered his friend's fifty-five-foot yacht and had invited my old friend from Singapore, Philip Conn, and his girlfriend, Angie, as well. With Mike's wife, Isobel, and their three children, we would be a party of eight. It would be my first visit to Greece since my first day in Europe ten years earlier and a lot more relaxed. We rendezvoused in Athens and after dinner spent our first night on *Invicta* in the yacht harbour at Vouliagmeni. With five cabins below, including the master cabin in the stern and bunks forward for Captain George and his offsider, the cook, we were more than comfortable.

By the time I surfaced next morning we were heading south-east towards Cape Sounion and the Temple of Poseidon. It's a profoundly spiritual place, witness to the birth of civilisation. It brought to mind the Mary Renault stories I had devoured as a student. *The King Must Die* tells of Theseus, the Athenian King who having spent part of his childhood in the temple as an acolyte, sensed he was related to Poseidon. I was a little disappointed we didn't stop for a closer inspection, but for the next two weeks we were to be immersed in ancient history, so there was no need to worry. Two hours later, we anchored off a secluded picture-postcard beach on the eastern side of Kea, one of the four main islands of the Cyclades. Some of us swam ashore; the others followed in *Invicta's* Zodiac, an apt dinghy for the Aegean Sea. It was then snorkelling, windsurfing, lunch, a snooze, another swim, up anchor and off to Korissia.

It was a Saturday evening, and for a while chaotic, as a wave of arrivals jostled for waterfront berths. Captain George had connections and we were waved into a prime location opposite the tavernas lining the waterfront. By the time we had changed for dinner, the local football fans, gathered to view a local derby on TV, had created a lively atmosphere. We found a table and enjoyed the local seafood and the retsina. We all have our favourite rough red. This is a rough white infused with a pine resin, giving it an unforgettable, almost bitter, taste. But in Greece you get used to it.

And so it went for a week—overnight in a comfortable berth or anchorage with easy access to a local taverna; up anchor early morning and continental breakfast while cruising towards another cove with a sheltered beach for swimming, exploring and lunch; up anchor early afternoon and off to an overnight haven, another taverna, more retsina and gin rummy into the wee hours. Thus, we meandered southward through a tranquil Aegean, exploring Kythnos, Serifos and Sifnos. That all changed as we set out for Mykonos. Bonhomie turned to misery as a *meltemi* blew up from the north. At first, it was seasick children, but as the grownups followed suit we turned back to Serifos for shelter. It was the same the following day when we abandoned that plan and retreated through relatively sheltered waters to Hydra.

It's an ill wind that brings no good. We had retreated to Hydra, not just because of its large and busy harbour but because Philip Conn thought his European-based brother, Wally, who he rarely saw, might be holidaying there. Mid-afternoon we found a berth and Philip set off to find his brother. An hour or so later he was back. Miraculously, he had literally run into him in the town and we were all invited for dinner. Wally's friend and host was Christian Kisum and during the course of the evening it transpired he was the Danish Ambassador in Tehran, so there was plenty to talk about. He knew John Dauth well but was more interested to hear I was working for Nova. When the Canadian Embassy in Tehran was closed the Danes had volunteered to fill the void. So by a strange confluence of events, I had met Canada's de facto ambassador in Tehran on a tiny Mediterranean island. And he made it clear he would do everything he could to help me during my next visit to Iran.

That would not be for another four months. Within days of my return to London, I was at a conference in Istanbul. Déjà vu. Turkey was emerging from six years of military rule. A general election was scheduled for November and major corporations from Europe and North America had been invited to send representatives to the grandly named Turkey Forum designed to showcase the opportunities for inward investment in the fledgling democracy. The keynote speaker for the event was Al Haig, recently retired US secretary of state and former commander of NATO forces in Europe. Few people would better understand the strategic importance of Turkey to NATO. Naturally, Nova, as a major Canadian resources and manufacturing conglomerate, was invited to send a delegate and since I had become their man for strange places I was asked to attend. I jumped at the offer. Who has seen *Topkapi* and not wanted to visit Istanbul?

In the event, Al Haig was a disappointment and he set the tone for the next three days. The remaining speakers were no better. On the sidelines, however, it was possible to meet the locals, including the Turkish Petroleum Corporation's production manager who had an intractable problem with route selection for a pipeline from a gas field in Thrace to fertiliser plants in Anatolia. The obvious route was directly across the northern end of the Bosporus but the weight of traffic in and out of the Black Sea had ruled that out. The alternative was an expensive eighty-six-kilometre submarine pipeline across the Sea of Marmara. I suggested it would be possible to adopt their preferred route by drilling the pipeline across the Bosporus. This technology had been developed in North America and had become the preferred method for installing pipelines across rivers. There was no need to disturb the riverbanks, the riverbed or river traffic. Mr Kantar asked me if I would go to Ankara to explain my proposal to his boss. Of course.

Arrangements were made and the following day, after visiting the Topkapi Palace Museum and viewing the legendary Emerald Dagger, I flew to Ankara where there was an enthusiastic reception for the idea. And so I returned to London ready to prepare a proposal to undertake a study using currently available survey and geotechnical data. The brisk exchange of correspondence that followed lasted for about two weeks then went quiet. It was a while before the story emerged and it was even more fantastic than the

Topkapi Emerald Dagger legend. It seems the Americans had installed an extensive hydrophone array on the Bosporus seabed and were concerned drilling operations would provide cover for Russian submarines attempting to secretly enter the Black Sea. The project was shelved and as far as I know that natural gas resource in Thrace has yet to be developed.

The Turkey trip may have been a disappointment but there was a silver lining. The return to London included a stopover in Paris, so I invited myself for a weekend with Nicky and Dominique Knowland in their house in Boulevard Malesherbes by the Opera House. In the four years since he had taken a trio of naïve Australians under his wing in Pamplona, Nicky and I had become close friends. He had grown up in Belgium, so was a fluent French speaker, which may be why he was appointed *director pour la France* for UK real estate agent, Healey & Baker. Few knew the local retail property sector better and he could charm the birds from the trees. There were a few others in town from London as well, so Nicky organised a table at La Coupole. Everything in this art deco masterpiece combines to create bonhomie, so it's no surprise we had a sparkling evening. I hesitate to name my favourite opera—possibly *Cosi*. I never hesitate to name my favourite restaurant—La Coupole, and there have been countless happy occasions there since.

The door prize for the Hurlingham Club Ball in the autumn of 1983 was a portrait sitting for emerging artist Barbara Kaczmarowska. The result was not an engineer but more a card sharp after a late night. Reserve and intimations of Dorian Gray prevented me from hanging it in 155 Holland

Park Avenue so at the first opportunity I took it back to Australia and gave it to Mum. I'm not so sure she was over the moon about it, but she did hang it. Looking at it now, I wonder if it foreshadowed the next ten years during which I rarely failed to make a bad decision.

The first of those poor choices followed shortly afterwards. My two-year contract with CanOcean was due to expire early in the new year. I hadn't sensed it, but Murray Feller, Bob Brown's successor as managing director, was keen to return to Canada and I was offered the job. In retrospect, I might have been better off accepting, but I knew the company's future was bleak. In its first year of operations, it had lost over a million pounds. I had trawled the world for two years and apart from the Safaniya process platform project had found no new business. Work was scarce, the rent for CanOcean House was over £200,000 a year and there were too many freeloaders on the payroll. I wasn't prepared to preside over another failure. I thanked Murray for the offer and suggested if he wished me to continue with CanOcean that I do so as a part-timer. He agreed and our association lasted another two years.

This gave me time to pursue my latest passion. The '83/'84 fox hunting season kicked off with the opening meet at Shillinglee. In the two years since my first day out with the 'Chid & Lec', our indefatigable huntsman, Nigel Peel, had taken the trouble to acquaint me with the history, traditions and practice of the sport. Farmers have been killing foxes to protect domestic livestock for five hundred years. Hunting with hounds bred specifically for fox hunting emerged in the seventeenth century. Three hundred years later, the pursuit had become an integral part of country life, not to mention that it employed 15 000 people. Many of these were engaged in collecting dead livestock, an important element of foxhounds' diet. While the hunt staff were busy butchering and rendering their grim harvest, the huntsman's main pursuit in summer was fine tuning his dog and bitch packs for the next season. In principle, hounds of the same size, pace and stamina were preferred since this facilitated hunting as a pack rather than a rabble. The other basics were nose, determination and voice. The spine-tingling cry of a hound that has found a fresh line of scent is only bettered by the huntsman blowing 'gone away', the signal releasing the mounted ladies and gentlemen, the field, to follow. There is no greater thrill than the unscripted pursuit of a pack of hounds and that's why, in the good old days, cavalry officers were encouraged to take up hunting to hone their riding skills across country.

On an exceptional day, a hunt might be as much as five miles point to point, eight miles over the fences. This rarely happened in Chid & Lec country due to its proximity to London, so opportunities to hunt in more remote counties were welcome. This included tours to Ireland. Stuart Wood, who was also a Chid & Lec subscriber, arranged the first for late November 1983. We booked into the Dunraven Arms in the pretty village of Adare, County Limerick, where the manager, Bryan Murphy, a retired National Hunt jockey, arranged four days' hunting and the necessary horses. There were two days with the Limericks and a day each with the Scarteen and Galway Blazers. If anybody ever needed a crash course in riding to hounds, this was it, and we were soon to learn hunting in Ireland was completely different to hunting in England. The differences between Banjo Patterson's[4] *long and wiry natives* of *The Geebung Polo Club* and his *Cuff and Collar Team* from the city *distinguished by exclusiveness and dress* come to mind.

For our first day with the Scarteen, we met at Emly, County Tipperary. We arrived in time to see Johnny Fennell, provider of amazing Irish hunters, unload around ten hirelings, including ours, from the back of a lorry—no fancy horse boxes here, nor the grooming lavished on their English cousins. But it doesn't matter. Even though the paddocks are tighter, the banks are higher and the mud is deeper, Irish hunters will chase hounds whenever there's a keen rider on board. That's why Napoleon's horse, Marengo, was an Irish hunter.

There were four days of spectacular sport in cold, sunny autumnal weather and the opportunity to hunt with icons of the sport, who started hunting in the days before motor vehicle traffic was a menace to hunting. Thady Ryan, the Scarteen's Master and huntsman, was nearing retirement after fifty years in the job. The Ryan family had been perfecting their unique Black-and-Tan hounds for three hundred years. The name was adopted by the constables recruited to reinforce the Royal Irish Constabulary during the Irish War of Independence following WW1.

Our second day was with the Limericks. Lord Toby Daresbury, another icon of the sport at eighty-one, was still hunting two days a week. On retiring as chairman of brewer Greenall Whitley in 1947, he moved to Ireland, where, as

Master, he resuscitated this famous pack from its post-war malaise. After a busy day, Woody and I were invited for tea at Alta Villa, his elegant eighteenth-century manor. Tea is a broad term for anything you like following a day's hunting, so we could hardly resist pints of ale drawn straight from a keg labelled 'Lord Toby's Special, brewed by Greenall's Warrington'.

Ireland wasn't the only area remote from London offering great hunting. Early in February, Bridget Jennings called to say she had to attend to some family business in Somerset and was taking the opportunity to go out for a day with the Taunton Vale. Would I like to come? *I would love to but am booked for Covent Garden that night. Don't worry, we can drive down the night before, spend the night with Mummy and Daddy, go out hunting, change and drive back to London in time for the performance. Great! Would you like to come to the opera as well? Would love to.*

And so it was. We spent the night with Bridget's mother and father near Fivehead, had a great day's hunting and were back in London in time to hear, according to John Higgins of *The Times*, Jose Carreras set Andrea Chenier alight. Michael Langdon, our host, added sparkle by arranging dinner in a nearby Bow Street restaurant, with drinks and the menu in the first interval, starters in the second and the rest afterwards.

It was around this time our old friend Brad Garnett married and as part of his honeymoon came to England. Brad was now Bradford, as Melanie came from one of those grand upstate New York enclaves where long names and equestrian pursuits are *de rigueur*. Having learned this, I suggested they might enjoy a day out on foot following the Chid & Lec. The anglophiles were delighted to accept. I collected them from their hotel and we drove down to Coldharbour Farm, Wisborough Green, where Bill and Margaret Murphy took care of Ginger. The meet at Ingram's Farm was nearby, so I hacked directly from the stables. Bill Murphy kindly escorted the visitors to make sure they were there in time for a glass of sloe gin and well placed to view the ensuing sport. Two covers produced running foxes and good hunts by West Sussex standards, so there was plenty to see.

Anticipating we wouldn't be too far away at the end of the day, Margaret had a real afternoon tea ready for our return—a warm fire, scones, clotted cream, strawberry jam, crumpets, boiled-egg sandwiches, pork pies, sausage rolls, tea, port, whiskey and, no show without Punch, Nigel Peel, always full of beans but more so after a good day. The conversation flowed. Before long, Nigel was quizzing Melanie about her equestrian background whereupon it transpired she came from the Catskills. By an extraordinary coincidence, Bill Murphy knew the area well. He had worked there post-WW2 as the stable jockey for local grandee, Ambrose Clark. Of course, Melanie knew of Mr Clark. He and her grandfather had been racing rivals but she didn't know the fantastic story of Bill's last race in New York.

In 1948, Mr Clark, rather than engage an established jockey to ride his great horse, Tea Maker, in a Grade One race at Saratoga Springs, gave the ride to his stable jockey. Bill was over the moon until discretely approached by a sinister character in a pinstripe suit who offered a generous incentive to run dead, or else. He couldn't do it and rode the horse to win, hoping against hope it would be beaten. No such luck. As he powered down the straight miles ahead of the field, and knowing certain death was the prize for a win, he slipped a stirrup and toppled off within lengths of the finish. He survived the fall, but the police had to rescue him from a mob of angry punters. Mr Clark bundled him into his car and as they headed for New York he told Bill he understood what had happened and forgave him. They went straight to the docks and that night Bill was on a steamer for Liverpool, never to return.

My part-time status in the summer of 1984 didn't mean I wasn't busy. In between six trips to Iran, there was a week in Palm Beach with Mike and Isobel Vassilopoulos; a long weekend in the Catskills with friends of Michael Langdon; *Arabella* at Glyndebourne; playing cricket for Bruce Trentham's Sherfield Sloggers; *Aida* with Pavarotti at the Royal Opera House; a fishing trip on the Great Barrier Reef with Dad, Lock and Chris; and a visit to the Tate Gallery, where my eyes were opened to the magic of William Mallord Turner and George Stubbs—so much so that, having been lured to an exhibition at the Paul Mason Gallery in Sloane Street a few days later, I couldn't resist paying £3,700 for a pair of Stubbs original stipple engravings, *Dungannon* and *Sweetbriar*. They were wonderful pictures and transformed the living room in 155 Holland Park Avenue, which also had a sofa bed. Sleepover guests could now count magnificent thoroughbreds instead of sheep.

Nicky Knowland often stayed when he came to London for board meetings. He was the perfect guest because as an insomniac, he barely creased the sheets. On one occasion I woke to find the door from my bedroom to the kitchen closed. I opened it onto what seemed like a scene from *The Divine Comedy*—the quarry-tiled floor crawling with a dozen live lobsters and a worse-for-wear Nicky in a daggy dressing gown sizing up a baron of beef the size of a Gladstone bag. Being unable to sleep, he had spent the early hours at Smithfield and Billingsgate markets where he bought the beef and the lobsters, which he temporarily freed when he got home. *How many can you muster for dinner?* Fortunately, it was a Wednesday and over the course of the day I managed to find six very lucky dinner guests because Nicky was the best cook I ever knew. The lobsters came as an entree with a lobster guts sauce that was delicious. How he managed to roast that enormous piece of beef in my tiddly oven and do delicious vegetables as well, I will never know. Another memorable day in London.

For me, the joy of life in a London revived by the Thatcher revolution was in stark contrast to the misery inflicted in Tehran by Ayatollah Khomeini. I may have become accustomed to the crump of Iraqi Scud missiles landing in the more densely populated areas in East Tehran, but the main source of misery for locals was food shortages and the appalling casualty rates suffered by young Revolutionary Guard conscripts sent into battle against the Iraqis as human waves. Apart from young men, the war effort also needed foreign exchange so the National Iranian Oil

Company (NIOC) was under intense pressure to revive its dilapidated natural gas export pipelines but, although I sensed dealing with a Canadian company would be politically acceptable, I was getting nowhere fast. Red tape and fear of the consequences of making a mistake trumped necessity. There was a minor breakthrough in September when we were asked to provide a two-week training programme for NIOC employees in Calgary. I attended the first week of the programme and although I learned a lot about the latest developments in gas pipeline monitoring and inspection, the highlight of the programme was joining the NIOC team to watch the Canadian and Russian ice hockey teams knock the living daylights out of each other, playing for the Canada Cup. The difference between the two teams was Wayne Gretzky, so Canada won, but only just.

On my way to Calgary, I had flown east via Seoul. It was my first visit there for almost two years. The timing was perfect. After two years of internal debate, Hyundai Heavy Industries had decided to convert the 1200-tonne derrick barge *HC-39* rather than build a new purpose-built pipe-laying barge. It was the sensible decision for a falling market. Would CanOcean give them a proposal to prepare specifications for the necessary pipe-laying equipment and to design a stinger? Of course. They had it just in time for the opening meet of the Chiddingfold and Leconfield's '84/'85 hunting season at Shillinglee.

After a month of limbering up in the West Sussex countryside, a small group, including Johnny Morris and I, called Bryan Murphy and arranged six days of hunting with the packs closest to the Dunraven Arms. There were two days with the Limericks, meeting at Heathfield House and Rathkeale and days with the Galway Blazers, Black and Tans, the Kilkennys and the Tipperarys, meeting at Athenry, Dromkeen, Mullinavat and Killenaule. There wasn't a day without a hunt and hounds in full cry, but the last day with the 'Tips' was unforgettable. At one point, the hounds led the field into a bog crossed by a barbed wire fence. It's impossible to jump anything crossing a bog, let alone a barbed wire fence. There was no way round and the hounds were going away to goodness knows where. That's when one of the hunt servants took his horse back about twenty metres from the fence, charged it down and continued on with strands of barbed wire tearing across his charger's brisket. It was a shocking moment but later it was explained a lacerated horse was a small price to pay to avoid a potentially serious car accident caused by the hounds crossing a nearby road flat out after a fox.

There was a lively gathering in the nearest pub afterwards, including a couple from Wales on their hunting honeymoon. It didn't include Johnny Morris. News arrived he had fallen badly and the ambulance had taken him to Our Lady's Hospital in Cashel. It didn't sound good so I made my farewells and still in muddy boots found my way to Johnny's bedside. His face was wreathed in bandages. He had jumped a fence with a bog on the landing side and his horse had checked. As he lurched forward, the horse's head came back, smacked him in the cheek bone and broke it. It was nasty, but everything that could be done had been. I repaired to the Dunraven Arms to change for dinner. Bryan Murphy noticed me arriving and asked after Johnny: 'He will die if you leave him in that hospital.' There was nothing I could do and I didn't want to miss dinner at Alta Villa.

Once there, I discovered Johnny hadn't been the day's only hunting casualty. Merry Atkinson, who had first worked with Lord Toby as a whipper-in for the Belvoir after the war and had been with him ever since, had twisted an ankle earlier in the day so was absent as well. Nevertheless, it was a convivial evening. One of the guests who had survived the day was Michael Clayton, editor of hunting magazine *Horse and Hound*. Having been a hunting correspondent for more than twenty years and having survived days out with nearly 200 hunts, he had some interesting stories. Years later, he published two books, *Foxhunting in Paradise* and *The Belvoir*, both with chapters devoted to Lord Toby's fifty years as a Master of Foxhounds.

The next day was a long transition from the Elysian Fields of Eire to the killing fields of Iran. The first test was to extract Johnny Morris from Our Lady's in Cashel and get him on the plane home. It all went reasonably well until, having managed to get Johnny and his baggage safely back to Tedworth Square, his wife, who was understandably shocked by his appearance, launched a broadside, not at Johnny but at me. We made up afterwards but at the time I thought Tehran mightn't be so bad after all.

And it wasn't. In the wake of the training session in Calgary, it was clear Nova's reputation as a leading operator of large gas pipeline networks had been well and truly established in Tehran. At our first meeting, NIOC expressed an intent to develop an ongoing training programme in Calgary for their operations engineers. They were also keen for Nova to manage an electronic survey of the northern section of the IGAT 1 (Iran gas trunkline) pipeline. This forty-two-inch-diameter gas trunkline, from Bandar Mahshahr in the south-west to the northern border via Astara, had been built by the Russians in 1970. In addition to supplying gas to the industrial centres of Shiraz, Isfahan, Tehran and Tabriz, it also exported gas to Russia, generating essential foreign exchange for the war effort. It was now showing signs of wear and tear. The team responsible for the management of the pipeline was stationed in Ahwaz, so arrangements were made for me to fly there a week later.

Despite my growing familiarity with Tehran, I made a habit of advising John Dauth and Christian Kisum of my travel plans and this trip was no exception. Christian said it gave him a perfect excuse to arrange a dinner party and he certainly knew how to do that. It seemed impossible that such a sparkling occasion could take place in a city that was being targeted by Saddam Hussein's Scud missiles, but somehow the locals had learned to live with the random attacks. The party was an interesting mix of locals, diplomats and expatriates, and dwindling oil and gas exports was a recurring theme. John Dauth was there, as was Nils Vallo Christiansen, Maersk Line's local manager, with his wife.

They clearly enjoyed a busy social life and invited me to a party they were throwing the following evening. This was a much larger gathering than that of the previous evening and I was amazed to meet so many members of an affluent and urbane Iranian middle class who appeared comfortable in the company of westerners and their decadent habits. This, despite the strictures of the dreaded Islamic Revolutionary Guard, known as the Pasdars, who had come to power with Ayatollah Khomeini and didn't hesitate to throw enemies of the revolution into Evin Prison. But one couldn't help noticing that all the liquor served at this party, in addition to the original label, was labelled 'Specially Imported for Iraq Army Stores'. I asked our host what would happen if he was caught plying his guests with Iraqi army supplies. 'No problem,' he replied, 'I buy it directly from the Pasdars and they make sure we aren't disturbed.' Not that I needed more proof religion was invented to control the masses.

Days later, I flew to Ahwaz. The security screening for this domestic flight into the war zone was intrusive and tiresome, undoubtedly indicative of breeches discovered in the past. At one stage, I was invited to take off my shoes so the examiner could flex the soles to ensure there was no concealed weapon. A NIOC car was at the airport to take me to my first meeting at 11 am. The main subject was internal and external pipeline corrosion monitoring and control along the IGAT-1 pipeline. Corrosion wasn't exactly my cup of tea, but fortunately the issues seemed to be similar to those encountered in Saudi Arabia so I was able to hold my ground. At the end of the meeting, I was presented with a considerable file of information on the pipeline, which was unusual in Iran. I sensed it had gone well.

Later that evening I had dinner with Schlumberger's local manager. His boss had been a guest at the Maersk party in Tehran and had suggested we meet. Schlumberger is a household name in the oil and gas industry. Wherever there is oil or gas, so is this iconic French company with their distinctive red service trucks. These are equipped with a monitor and control cab and a wireline winch to facilitate lowering an electronic logging tool into a well to map the surrounding formation and measure key indicators, such as resistivity, porosity and permeability. This data is used in many ways, but obvious applications are in the determination of the perforation depths in wells and combining the data from existing wells to determine the location of future wells.

In the early sixties, as the development of the Roma gas field in Queensland inspired exploration in the Bowen, Surat, Cooper and Eromanga basins, Schlumberger established a depot in Dalby. The French manager and his wife often came round to 61 Myall Street to play bridge. They certainly brightened up life in the farm belt where hitherto the only hint of anything remotely cosmopolitan was Nearhos's Café Majestic. Predictably, after three or four years, Jacques and Danielle returned to Paris, but Mum was nothing if not a good correspondent so we were able to catch up with them during our June 1982 trip.

My dinner with the man from Schlumberger was not encouraging. Despite having a well-established base in the area, the logistics were horrendous. Moving equipment in and out of Iran was difficult. Recruiting qualified operators was even more difficult and made no easier by the problems associated with rotating them in and out of a war zone. Quite often they would complete a tour, go home on leave and refuse to return despite the financial incentives. Regardless, I returned to Tehran where I received a formal request for a proposal for Nova to undertake a complete review of the corrosion protection system on the IGAT-1 pipeline between Delijan and Astara. It was a pyrrhic victory. I went to the Christmas party at the Australian Consulate and later that night flew back to London. It had been my sixth trip to Iran in eighteen months and even though I had made friends there, I was always relieved when the return flight was well into Turkey.

After a quiet Christmas with Stuart and Nicky Wood in their cottage outside Marlborough and the Boxing Day meet at Petworth, including a six-kilometre point to Lurgashall, I drove up to Maxwelton for Hogmanay with Paul and Suzon Stenhouse. It was business as usual, with dinner for a dozen and a few more, including a piper, arriving afterwards for eights and reels. The Scots possibly invented these lively dances for up to eight couples to bamboozle Sassenachs, but whether you can or can't, they throw a good party.

On New Year's Day I went hunting with the Dumfriesshire hounds as a guest of regular subscribers, Gordon and Charlotte, friends of Paul and Suzon. They had arranged a hireling from the local livery stables and I was assured it was a goer. It was. We met at Shortrigg Wood, seven kilometres to the south of Lockerbie where Pan Am Flight 103 crashed four years later. The days up north are short in January but that didn't matter. It was clear and still and well before the horses got too cold the hounds did their job and flushed a fox into open country to the west of Lochmaben. We chased it across the River Annan where, according to Sir Walter Scott, *Within the bounds of Annandale, The gentle Johnstons ride, They have been there a thousand years, And a thousand more they'll bide.*[23] My maternal grandmother's great grandfather, Andrew Johnston, migrated to New South Wales in 1802 and settled on the Hawkesbury. Almost three hundred years on, I was back in my ancestral land and fulfilling Sir Walter's prophecy. I didn't get a welcome to country but, having lost the fox after a twelve-mile point, those of us still with the hounds were invited to Gordon and Charlotte's for a well-earned afternoon tea.

My primary focus early in the new year was to coordinate the preparation of the IGAT-1 inspection proposal for NIOC—this against a backdrop of a reinvigorated Iraq. With massive financial support from Saudi Arabia and Kuwait and Exocet missiles from France, Saddam renewed his attacks across the Shatt al-Arab and on shipping in the Persian Gulf. The war went from bad to worse. Travel was becoming increasingly difficult and insurance for the specialised equipment Nova had planned to use for the project was becoming prohibitively expensive. By the end of March, it was clear Nova couldn't possibly commit to an inspection of the IGAT-1 pipeline. I advised NIOC's management and rang Christian Kisum and John Dauth. John wasn't surprised and confessed he would be leaving Tehran in the near future anyway.

Iran's wasn't the only economy suffering from diminishing oil and gas revenues. From a peak of US$140 a barrel in June 1980, the price had halved by December 1984. Projects were being shelved everywhere, including in Saudi Arabia. But just as I thought my days with CanOcean had come to an end, there was a surprise telex from HHI accepting the *HC-39* modification design proposal we had sent them almost six months earlier. I had assumed this project had been another victim of the falling market. Not so. It was a 10 000-manhour project and Murray Feller asked me to manage it. I was happy to do so and handed the report to HHI in November. The project had done nothing but prolong the agony. By March 1986, crude oil had fallen to US$26 a barrel and the industry was on its knees.

Oil and gas had given me a great run and now it was over. I was thirty-eight years old, and it was time to try something else.

Trent Eels

My search for the elusive 'something else' canvassed a swag of crazy ideas and the one that wouldn't go away was the craziest. It had emerged in 1975 following the Kisch family Christmas. One of the house guests was Ansell Egerton who subsequently invited me to bridge evenings at Boodles. There was always a dinner break and on one occasion the menu included smoked eel. I hadn't noticed it before and said so, to which Ansell explained it was a scarce delicacy only offered when available. He went on to relate how in his capacity as director of strategic planning at Rothmans International his job was to screen an unrelenting stream of investment proposals unrelated to tobacco. One scheme of interest, but not to Rothmans, was a proposal for an intensive eel farm to be built alongside Drax Power Station on the River Ouse. The optimum water temperature for eel cultivation is 24 °C. The basic idea was to use waste heat from the power generation process to maintain this temperature in the farm waters all year round.

In the months that followed my rough calculations indicated robust returns, but numbers rarely tell the real story when modelling livestock, particularly exotic livestock. I didn't see it that way; I saw it as an engineering problem and for the next five years it was back of my mind, an itch I couldn't scratch. I wasn't the only one. In 1979, RHM (formerly Rank Hovis McDougall), the baker, ran with the idea. It was doubly attractive for them. It gave them a readymade consumer for their waste dough and there was an annual 5000-tonne eel shortfall in the 30 000-tonne-per year European market. They built a 200-tonne per year facility next to the Drax Power Station. It was producing 130 tonnes per year in 1984 when the station was shut down by Arthur Scargill's miners' strike—no more warm water, no more eels.

Hope springs eternal in the fool's breast.[24] Rather than being deterred by RHM's misfortune, I was encouraged—one less competitor. The mind is good at ignoring the obvious fallacies in fantasies. The Drax shut-down coincided with my transition to part-time status with CanOcean. With more time to pursue eel farming, I contacted the UK's Central Electricity Generating Board (CEGB) and was referred to the coordinator for waste heat utilisation, Frank Dunne. The oil price surges following the Yom Kippur War of 1973 rocked the European community so energy conservation reforms were high on the agenda. These included initiatives to gather and harness waste heat. The largest waste-heat emitters were power stations, and schemes to utilise this heat for community heating, greenhouse horticulture and fish farming became politically correct, regardless of economic viability. Frank Dunne had taken a keen interest in the Drax project but strongly advised against another project there because there had been too much sediment in the water from the River Ouse. Research had established a maximum allowable level of thirty-five parts per million (ppm) for eel culture. At Drax it was more like 350 ppm. Why not look at one of the stations along the River Trent, with sediment levels normally below thirty-five ppm? He offered to take me to Rugeley in Staffordshire and Ratcliffe-on-Soar in Nottinghamshire.

And so began my discovery of a new world north of London. I knew what I was looking for—a base load power station operating twenty-four seven, 365 days a year, clean cooling water at 24 °C and a site adjacent to the cooling towers. Ratcliffe-on-Soar Power Station (ROS) was the obvious choice. It had operated nonstop throughout the miners' strike and satisfied the other non-negotiable criteria as well. It generated electricity using four 500-megawatt water-cooled coal-fired steam turbines. The station drew its cooling water from the River Trent, rising near Stoke-on-Trent, a hundred kilometres to the west and continuing on to the Humber Estuary, around 200 kilometres to the north. Having cooled the turbines, the 'warmed' cooling water was then 'cooled' in cooling towers and returned to the river. Water temperatures entering the cooling towers ranged from 24 to 38 °C, winter to summer, while temperatures leaving the cooling towers ranged from 14 to 28 °C. Therefore, the water temperature in an eel farm built adjacent to the power station, blending water from upstream and downstream of the cooling towers, could be maintained at a steady 24 °C year in year out except for a few weeks during the summer.

Another factor in favour of ROS was the constructive attitude of the man in charge, George Leydon. Having met him, it was easy to understand why his station had remained in service throughout the miners' strike. Within a month of my visit, he wrote confirming the CEGB's interest in the idea. It was enough for me. In between my work on the deck layout and stinger design for Hyundai's *HC-39* construction barge, I embarked on the preparation of a business plan for a new company to be called Trent Eels PLC. I contacted Dr Alan Walker, who had been technical manager of the farm at Drax. He was generous with his advice but, more importantly, confirmed his interest in coming on board should the ROS project proceed.

Just before Easter, Sandy Goudie called to say he was painting a field-sports series and needed a fox-hunter sitter. Would I come up to Glasgow for the long weekend and sit for him? Why not? I buffed my top hat, brushed my pink coat, polished my boots and drove north, arriving at Sandy and Mainee's stylish West End apartment late on Maundy Thursday. We went to work in his grand studio the following day. He had prepared for the project by borrowing a saddle, now ingeniously mounted on a tightly packed kit bag supported on a trestle. For the next three days, fully booted and spurred, I sat astride this mock horse while Sandy worked his magic. There was also a lot of whiskey involved, but at the end there was a life-size image of a well-groomed fox hunter, me, looking at home astride a horse. Two years later, Sandy entered the masterpiece in the Royal Society of Portrait Painters' Annual Exhibition in the Mall Galleries in London and sent me an invitation for the opening night. It was a busy affair and when I eventually found the distinctive work, looking even better in its imposing black frame, it was being viewed by a couple in their thirties. I stood discretely behind them. The wife, having finished her examination, turned to the husband and said simply, 'What a shit!'

The Trent Eels business plan called for the three-stage construction of a tank farm immediately to the north of ROS to produce fifty tonnes of eels in 1987, one hundred tonnes in 1988 and 200 tonnes in 1989. The Stage One cost estimate was £350,000, including working capital. Barney Cue incorporated Trent Eels PLC, an unlisted public company, and went to work preparing a prospectus to raise the necessary capital. It gave me the opportunity to join Mike Vassilopoulos for another cruise around the Greek Islands on *Invicta*. The highlight was attending a performance of Euripides's *The Suppliants* in the Ancient Theatre of Epidaurus. This 1400-seat amphitheatre, with its extraordinary acoustics, was built on the side of a hill some 2400 years ago. It was rediscovered in 1879 and having been restored, hosts an annual festival running from June to August. *The Suppliants* is a tragedy and so was the Trent Eels Prospectus. It was issued on 9 October 1985. Two weeks later, Barney reported four intrepid investors had subscribed £10,000. The money was returned, and with the start of the hunting season, I turned my mind from eels to foxes.

Hunting was interrupted in November by a call from Singapore. Chuck Hardeman had succeeded Sandy Sandford as managing director of Ipco Marine following the successful installation of the Yanbu jack-up pier in 1977. Would I accompany a team they were sending to Perth to talk to

Western Mining Corporation about a marginal oilfield development on the North-West Shelf? Funding marginal developments in a falling market is difficult, but if Ipco was prepared to pay, I was prepared to go, so I said yes. There was the additional bonus of being in Australia for Christmas.

The key to developing a marginal offshore field is finding a suitable jack-up drilling rig at a reasonable price. There are plenty around in a collapsing oil market, many laid up in Singapore. A week later, I was clambering over a few anchored to the west of Pulau Bukom, an area I knew well from my days with RJBA in Singapore. Price and availability would not be a problem but as we headed for Perth the crude oil market was in freefall and prospects for the project were dim. So it was no surprise we left empty handed. I continued to Mooloolaba, arriving on Christmas Eve. I could contemplate the future from the relative calm of Douglas Street.

Once again, my mind wandered back to eels. When I had called Frank Dunne of the CEGB to advise him our fundraising for the eel farm had failed, he reiterated the CEGB's enthusiasm for the project and suggested trying something less ambitious. With time on my hands, I went back to the drawing board. I estimated £120,000 to build a fifty-tonne-per-year plant on a site next to the power station cooling towers and £90,000 for working capital, assuming production costs of £1.85 a kilogram and sale costs of £3.80 a kilogram.

These numbers made the project look possible, so, back in London, my first port of call was Barney Cue. Barney thought the project might attract a government-guaranteed loan of £75,000 and an EEC Fisheries grant of £25,000, leaving

£110,000 to come from shareholders. Friends, including Stuart Wood and my brother Lockwood, pledged £40,000. I would have to come up with £70,000. And so came a fateful turning point. I was financially comfortable, had a flat in London, a house in Mooloolaba and a comfortable income from consulting, but I didn't have a spare £70,000. Fiddlesticks, why not just sell the flat? Well, there was one good reason but it wouldn't occur to a master of the universe. If Trent Eels were to fail, just like Bligh Engineering and just like CanOcean, the master of the universe would be back to square one, not to mention losing his shareholders' investments as well. Odysseus ignored the call of the Sirens. I couldn't resist the call of the eels.

Eels have been found in the sea, rivers, creeks and lagoons for thousands of years, but nobody knew how because they didn't appear to have reproductive organs. Aristotle, Darwin and Freud studied the phenomenon and got nowhere. Then, in 1923, after twenty years of sampling the Atlantic for eels and eel larvae, Johannes Schmidt, a driven Danish researcher, made some progress. He demonstrated mature eels from Europe cross the Atlantic to spawn in the Sargasso Sea, whereupon they die. The eggs hatch and produce larvae, which, in the case of European eels, are returned to the coastlines of Western Europe on the Gulf Stream and the North Atlantic Drift. On sensing the presence of estuarine water, they metamorphose into matchstick-sized translucent juveniles known as glass eels. These wriggle their way into the estuaries and in doing so morph into elvers. These swim further upstream into the rivers and creeks, the habitats where they mature and grow for the next ten to fifteen years, preparing for their 5000-kilometre swim back to, as Richard Strauss would have put it, *Death and Transfiguration*[25] in the Sargasso. A mature eel ready for the big journey is a magnificent beast about half a metre long and in prime condition. It has changed colour from a yellowy brown to silver. It has also dissolved its stomach, because it will make the trans-Atlantic journey on its own fat reserves. And as it does, it provides the last piece of the puzzle—it develops the reproductive organs necessary for the climax of its life cycle—spawning and death.

Researchers have never been able to replicate the Sargasso Sea climax in a laboratory so the starting point for an eel farm must be a reliable source of elvers. The most prolific elver fishery in England is the Bristol Channel, most active in the spring. For Trent Eels to be operational in 1986, it would be necessary to build and commission elver-rearing tanks by the end of April. It was possible if everything fell into place, and it did. By the end of January, I had revised the business plan and Barney Cue submitted it with an application for a government-guaranteed loan. Another copy went to the CEGB with a request for a site in the ROS precinct. They offered a strip of flat land 150 metres long and 30 metres wide immediately to the west of the cooling towers. They also offered the use of a lockable 200-square-metre shed for construction materials and food storage. The site could hardly have been better. It was less than 400 metres from valves providing access to warm water upstream and cooled water downstream of the cooling towers.

On March 7th, the CEGB approved our plan. On March 10th, the Department of Trade and Industry approved the £75,000 loan. All the pieces were in place. I put 155 Holland Park Avenue on the market and employed four labourers. The basic plan was to build the tank farm on a rectangular pad 110 metres long and twenty metres wide, surrounded by a retaining wall on three sides and a rail embankment on the other. The pad supported the tanks one metre above ground level to facilitate natural drainage back to the cooling tower ponds. We poured the retaining wall footings on March 26th and the wall itself days later. Then the earthmoving subcontractor came in with a scraper, a dozer and a roller and within days had filled, compacted and levelled the pad with power station ash. We started building the tanks and pipelines on April 4th. The plan was for ten elver, twelve fingerling and nine grow-out tanks, 3 metres, 4.5 metres and 11 metres in diameter, respectively. The tank walls were formed by bolting curved corrugated galvanised iron sections together. These 'rims' were then carefully levelled and concrete was poured and 'dished' to form a base, draining to the centre. Tank construction continued throughout the summer. However, the pipelines and elver tanks were completed by the end of April, when we introduced our first batch of elvers.

Meanwhile, 155 Holland Park Avenue sold for £88,500. No wonder; it was an elegant flat and I would miss it, but I was excited about progress at the power station and was busy, so there was no time for regrets. As a temporary measure, I leased a cottage minutes away from the power station. Yew Tree Cottage, Thrumpton, had two bedrooms, a bathroom, a living room, a kitchen/dining room and a large garden. George Fitzroy Seymour, squire of Thrumpton Hall and the grandest man in England never to have had a title, was my new landlord. Twenty years later, his daughter published a poignant memoir revealing how he had gaily moved a rent boy into the house, expecting his wife and grown-up children to extend a warm welcome.

My neighbour immediately to the west and just across the Midland Main Line from the power station, was a different story all together. I had advertised in the *Nottingham Post* for housing for Alan Walker and within days Richard Morley called offering a cottage on his farm, known as Redhill Marina—so-called because in 1963 when 200 acres of the farm were resumed for the construction of the Ratcliffe-on-Soar Power Station, it was no longer a viable farming unit. Fortunately, it had a two-kilometre frontage along the River Soar, a popular recreational waterway, so Richard had channelled his considerable energies into developing a thriving marina and boat chandlery. As a result, he had a farm cottage available as a casual let. A week or so after agreeing terms, Richard called again. *Is that you, Mr Wilson? Yes. It's Richard Morley speaking.* With his bucolic brogue, it could hardly have been anybody else. *Do you have a black tie? Yes. Would you join Shelagh and me at the Quorn Hunt dinner dance tomorrow night? Yes, thank you. I would love to. Good, we will pick you up at 7 pm.*

And so they did, and that evening I stumbled into a seven-year association with the world's most famous hunt. The venue for the occasion was The Durham Ox at Six Hills on the eastern fringe of its country, covering some 500 square miles of undulating farmland roughly centred on the village of Quorn, between Nottingham and Leicester. Richard had no idea I had ever been near a horse and the dinner was well under way when one of the guests, having established I was Australian, asked if I had any interest in foxhunting? *Yes*, I said, *I spent the last three seasons with the Chiddingfold and Leconfield. So, you will be coming out with us then?* At that time, there was only one thought in my mind and that was building an eel farm. I hadn't appreciated I was living in Quorn country; hunting had not crossed my mind and I told him so. *You can't come to live in our country and not come out hunting with us.* Richard agreed, and after dinner I was introduced to the joint master, Jim Bealby, who warmly welcomed me to the occasion and asked me to be sure to come to the first cub hunting day, probably late September. And you can't hunt without a horse, so I was next introduced to Barbara Rich, horse dealer to the gentry, including the Prince of Wales. What did I weigh? Just over fourteen stone. She promised to bring a horse to the first meet for me to trial, and four months later she did.

In the meantime, Alan Walker arrived towards the end of April in time for the first intake of elvers. He took over the management of day-to-day eel farming, and I concentrated on construction of the remaining tanks, piping, aeration system and instrumentation. The instrumentation included high and low-level alarms in each tank. Outside normal farm hours, an alarm would ring through to the telephone at Yew Tree Cottage. The other new arrival was my little sister. Mum had rung to say she was at a loose end and would she be able to help at the farm? She had a BSc in biological chemistry (whatever that is), so I thought, why not? She arrived a week or two later, moved into Yew Tree Cottage and went to work straight away. It was one of my better decisions. Sarah had no trouble fitting in with the farm crew and three weeks later, when it became clear Alan Walker was unable to sustain life away from his family in Yorkshire and he resigned, there was a ready substitute.

To his credit, Alan took great pains to brief Sarah before leaving and the farm management system that evolved in his wake owed a lot to his professionalism. Four major activities became the cornerstone of daily farm routine. Each activity, apart from cleaning, required meticulous recording. As eel stocks grew, it became an enormous task to organise, monitor, record and analyse the data coming in from thirty-one tanks. As many as twelve different food combinations had to be delivered to each tank daily, and sometimes twice daily, depending on size. Sarah developed a spreadsheet on an IBM PC to monitor and manage the entire operation. It recorded stock movements, calculated and recorded food requirements on a daily basis, tracked and managed food-stock levels, monitored and recorded food conversion and eel growth rates and, importantly, provided a daily stock valuation. The programme proved its value, not only in achieving demonstrably improved farm efficiency but also in the way it motivated the team, who could see the fruits of their labour in improved stock valuation—or not.

Around this time, Johnny Morris, Ginger's owner, invited

me to lunch at Brooks's, his club in St James's Street. In 1986, the drive from Thrumpton to St James's via the M1 took just under two hours. It was marginally faster than the train from Loughborough to St Pancras and Tube to Green Park, but you had to park. So I let the train take the strain. These days, the M1 is not much better than a car park, so the train is the only option. Piccadilly on a sunny day is a wonderful place to be, with the glitz from the Ritz and the brilliant displays in the shop windows round the corner in St James's, so I was more than ready for a gin and tonic as I arrived at my illustrious destination with its discreet Palladian façade. Of course, Johnny was there to welcome his guest, his office being no more than a short walk away in Cleveland Row. Johnny's firm, Roberts Morris Bray, was the insurance broker specialising in fish farms, so Johnny was keen to hear his latest client's news. Construction was on schedule and below budget, we had elvers in our nursery tanks and had developed a food paste they were keen to eat, so they were growing. We were off to an encouraging start.

It was the perfect lunch—smoked eel, calves' liver and onions, a carafe of the house claret and summer pudding to finish—enough to put anybody in an expansive mood. As we finished with a glass of port, Johnny suggested, since I was no longer a London resident, I should join the club because it offered excellent accommodation and breakfast for out-of-towners. It sounded like a good idea and he undertook to have the club secretary forward a form. Weeks later, after I had returned it and Johnny had rounded up the necessary seconders, he called, clearly upset. The chairman of the membership committee was struggling with my application. I had declared attending Church of England Grammar School, Brisbane. Brooks's had never had a member from a grammar school. Don't worry, Johnny, it's not the end of the world. I was amused but could tell he, an old Etonian, wasn't. He had gone to a lot of trouble to line up the necessary seconders, half dozen or so, and a black ball would be embarrassing. Look, I said, when The Prince of Wales went to school in Australia in 1966, he attended Geelong Grammar. There was palpable relief. Leave it with me, he said. A week later, my membership was confirmed and Brooks's soon became my home away from home in London and I became its first member from a grammar school.

A month after stocking the farm with an estimated 1.2 million elvers weighing in at 366 kilograms, it was time for a stocktake. The results were disappointing. We had lost three per cent and the survivors had grown just two per cent. The problem was getting them to eat. This improved when we changed from a commercial fishmeal formula to cod's roe, but there was another problem. Background sediment levels in the Trent were comfortably below the recommended thirty-five ppm limit, but this was well and truly breached during periods of heavy rain. Not only did the elvers go off their food but, worse still, the spates caused infections. We tried various remedies, but the cures were often worse than the disease. We were nowhere near our targeted growth rates and were losing elvers in large numbers. By August, when we had completed construction of all thirty-one tanks, we had a few fingerlings in the fingerling tanks and nothing in the larger grow-out tanks. Prospects for any income in 1987 were bleak unless we could find an alternative use for our empty tanks.

The answer was carp. Our market research had indicated, in addition to the live-eel markets in Holland and Billingsgate, Chinese restaurants in London and Manchester were desperate for live carp. The margins were not as attractive but faster growth rates and greater demand volumes might keep the farm going while we found a way with eels. Mid-August, we bought 5000 one-inch carp fingerlings from a nursery in Yorkshire. They took to their new environment with promising growth rates and minimal losses. In another encouraging development, prices were on the rise and in some cases matched the eel price. So, with the onset of the hunting season and winter, there was good reason to be optimistic about Trent Eels's prospects.

My first day out with the Quorn was an early morning cub hunt near Old Dalby in late September. Barbara Rich was as good as her word and turned up with a nicely turned-out chestnut gelding. As I mounted, there was a warm welcome from Jim Bealby, the Joint Master I had met four months earlier at the Durham Ox dinner dance. Jim then introduced me to each of the twenty or so assembled followers. It was typical of the warmth and hospitality my sister and I were to experience during our five-year sojourn in Quorn country. My trial horse was too small but that didn't matter as we spent the morning watching hounds drawing blanks. Barbara persisted and arranged a procession of prospective mounts at both Quorn and Belvoir meets. Finally, six weeks later, she came up with Rory, a seven-year-old seventeen-hand bay gelding born and bred in Ireland. He sold himself. From the moment he heard the cry of hounds on a fresh scent his ears were cocked fast forward and he wanted to go no matter what was in the way. Like Ginger, he could and did jump five-bar gates, he had a big heart and was still rearing to go at the end of the day. At £4,000, he was expensive but he was still going strong five years later and never pulled up lame after a big day. As soon as Shelagh Morley heard I had bought Rory she offered to take him into livery. She had a girl groom who fed, exercised and groomed him for hunting days and he was less than five minutes away from Yew Tree Cottage, so it couldn't have been better. My hunting season was off to a good start.

The farm was finding its rhythm as well. Although we had lost more than half our elvers from what was diagnosed as a *Flexibacter* outbreak, caused by the summer sediment spikes in the Trent, the survivors were going well. Their average size had grown from a third of a gram to a gram and a small number of outliers had reached forty grams. The carp trial had gone well, and we had tanks to spare, so by the end of November we had introduced 90 000 carp juveniles, weighing in at 470 kilograms. Six weeks later, they were a staggering 1175 kilograms, an average growth rate of 2.2 per cent a day. At this rate, our carp biomass would double every month—an exciting prospect. To add icing to the cake, on completion of our construction works in August, we had received the government-guaranteed loan of £75,000 and the EEC Fisheries grant of £25,000. So, when our local MP, the Right Honourable Kenneth Clarke QC, paymaster general and minister of state for employment, paid an official visit at the end of September our finances were in reasonable shape and we could see a way forward.

In a sad footnote, thirty years later, as last man standing from the Thatcher era, Ken Clarke rose in the Commons to deliver an impassioned speech opposing Brexit. In a parliamentary masterpiece invoking the ghosts of Edmund Burke, Lewis Carroll and Enoch Powell, Clarke ridiculed the arguments made for economic nirvana post-Brexit and the notion parliament was bound by the referendum. His sweetness was wasted on the desert air and he retired from the Commons two years later.

By September, it was also clear that my best decision with respect to the eel farm was offering Sarah a job. She was the little sister I barely knew. When she was born I was at boarding school so we became acquainted during school holidays. When I graduated and effectively went to Sydney, she was nine. By the time I left for New Zealand she had barely turned thirteen. Following her graduation she was in and out of a number of jobs but as she turned twenty-six she was at a loose end. There are plenty of reasons not to employ your sister and even more reasons not to share a modest cottage, but I couldn't think of them at the time and fortunately didn't. In five months, she had done a great job. From a standing start she had become an expert on raising juvenile eels and treating their infections. She had also moulded a motley gang of farm hands into a motivated team running a seven-day-a-week operation.

There was more. She brought Yew Tree Cottage to life and, despite its size, Sarah could produce dinner for eight seemingly without effort. So, when the hunting season came around we were able to take part in and enjoy the associated hunt teas, dinner parties, Sunday lunches, contract bridge and balls that pass winter away in Leicestershire. There were visitors too, including one of Sarah's friends, Julia Whatley, a talented illustrator whose whimsical rhyme and amusing cartoons brilliantly captured life at Yew Tree Cottage:

> Twas in October's merry month
> I went to stay at Yew Tree Cott.
> A seemly homestead, bright and free
> In all of England there is not
> A more delightful place to be.
>
> The happy pair who dwell within
> Are David and his sister, Sal.
> He, a fellow kind and true,
> She, Australia's finest gal.
>
> The scene is one of bliss domestic
> Gentle sound of bubbling jam
> And only too few bands elastic
> Hinders such the bottling plan.
>
> The faithful hound who follows Sarah
> To and fro and near and far
> Lies near the stove in dreaming state,
> Her paws rest neatly on the grate
> Tis sweet Belle of Mooloolaba.

Not far away, in stable warm
Lives handsome Rory, bold and strong
Who fearlessly pursues the fox,
With stamina, the whole day long.

What lucky chance, was it
You ask, which brought the ink-stained Julia here?
With bag of paper, pens and paint~
(She'd try the patience of a saint)
Nothing save the kind request
To visit, of her friends so dear
Accordingly she made her way~
And stayed for nigh on half a year!

But it wasn't all beer and skittles. On a darkening evening in the middle of January, we set out for a dinner party at Harby, about forty minutes from Thrumpton. Our hostess was one of the finest riders in the Quorn but, more importantly, a professional cook. Dinner lived up to expectations but as the coffee went its rounds the curtains were doing little to muffle the sounds of a developing storm. Driving home in strengthening winds and cold scudding rain took a lot longer than forty minutes. So later, when the phone rang, I was in a deep sleep, and having picked up, there was a moment or two before I understood the mechanical voice at the other end: 'DANGER DANGER DANGER. HIGH LEVEL ALARM'.

This was a call I didn't expect and certainly didn't want. Each tank in the farm was fitted with high and low level limit switches, which, if triggered, raised an alarm in the farm office during working hours. Outside working hours, the alarm diverted to Yew Tree Cottage. I dressed in as much clothing as possible as quickly as possible and made the five-minute drive to the power station through what was by then a full-scale blizzard. It was 2.30 am when I checked in at the main gate. I asked the guard to come looking for me if I hadn't reappeared in an hour. Down at the farm the dim lighting illuminated a chaotic scene, as the cooling towers were roiling the gale into giant vortices, throwing snow back into the sky. Long, sharp wind-deflected icicles forming on the tower supports were as daggers drawn in a gothic melodrama. *Childe Roland to the dark tower came.*[26] But unlike Roland, who had to find his way through a corpse-strewn landscape, my problem was a dozen overflowing tanks with eels slithering around on the ground beside.

Each farm tank received a continuous supply of water extracted from upstream of the cooling towers regulated to 24 °C. Open-ended standpipes secured over the floor drain in each tank maintained the water level at a constant 700 millimetres. The overflow was returned to the Trent via the cooling tower ponds. What was causing the blockage? My first reaction was to run around like a madman in the driving sleet cutting the water supply to each of the overflowing tanks. Then I realised without freshly oxygenated water the remaining stock in the tanks would be decimated. Eventually it dawned on me that return water in the exposed two-inch-diameter pipes connecting the tank drains to the twelve-inch-diameter return line to the cooling tower ponds was freezing. Fortunately, in addition to the small-bore return lines, each tank had a separate underground drain to the roadside. The answer was to open the direct drains from the elver and fingerling tanks. Teeth chattering, I waited until I was sure levels in the affected tanks had stabilised. There was nothing I could do about the errant eels but it was amazing how many were still slithering and recoverable the following morning.

We negotiated the winter without further drama and the growth rates measured in November were sustained. Between January 10th and February 12th the carp biomass increased by 800 kilograms to two tonnes on 2.7 tonnes of food, an implied conversion rate of 3.3, meaning 3.3 tonnes of food produced one tonne of carp. With carp pellets at £288 a tonne, the cost of food to produce one tonne of carp, valued at £3300, would be £950. This was encouraging. However, we were unlikely to be selling any fish before April and cash was running out. At the end of February we were down to £12,000, with expenses of £6,000 a month. We would need sales to stay afloat. We made our first carp delivery to Marr Fish Merchants in Hull on 9 April 1987 and the first shipment of live eels left the farm in August. By year's end, Trent Eels was trading profitably. But that didn't mean everything in the garden was rosy.

In 1982, following Abu Nidal's shocking attack on the Chez Jo Goldenberg restaurant in Paris, the French Government made entry visas mandatory for all visitors apart from those from the EU. Until then, Australians were waved through, and I was a regular visitor. Arranging visas from the embassy in London was so difficult I considered applying for British citizenship, but as a frequent traveller, I couldn't meet the test for uninterrupted residence. Trent Eels changed that, so early 1987 I applied.

Six months later, the application had been forgotten and Yew Tree Cottage had been adopted by a pair of Canada geese. They had become so friendly they regularly came into the kitchen demanding food and were there the morning the postman arrived with a nondescript package requiring a signature. He came into the kitchen too. What followed was a real shit storm. Where it all came from, goodness only knows, but by the time they had escaped, it was everywhere. The package contained my certificate of naturalisation as a British citizen together with an instruction to return my Australian passport to the Australian High Commission in The Strand for cancellation. I was no longer an Australian citizen. I was more shocked than the geese. I had assumed I could have both. Fancy having to get a visa to go home for Christmas. In a panic, I rang Lunar House, source of the offending document. *I don't want it. Don't tear it up Mr Wilson, you will be a stateless person. I suggest you talk to the Australian High Commission.* Fortunately, I had a friend there. After giving me a rocket for being so stupid, she suggested I write to the high commissioner and sent a suggested draft. Two months later, I received a certificate of Australian citizenship. I was a New Australian.

My new passport arrived in time for me to fly home for Christmas. I was pleased I did. Reading between the lines in a letter Mum had written earlier in the year, there was a hint of troubles ahead for Wilson & Wilson. The story emerged later. It had been a poor season and the incorrigible gambler had thrown the dice and shipped a large parcel of mung beans to an untested Indian merchant. Alarm bells rang when he started picking holes in the bill of lading and instead of payment gave a litany of feeble excuses. Come Christmas, Dad had accepted he would never see the money. It wasn't just the financial loss. Aged sixty-four, he had lost his pride and his confidence. Realising he could never trade again, he had decided to retire. So, everything was up for sale—the office building, the grain storage and processing equipment, the stock and the house. In a dry season that wouldn't be easy.

When sorrows come, they come not single spies, but in battalions.[27] Dad's despair wasn't only for his own predicament. His children were in disarray as well. The eel farm was struggling (and with it, both Sarah and me), Lock's marriage had failed and Chris had started a tour company that wasn't going anywhere. He couldn't do anything about it. The father who had spared nothing on his children had nothing left to give. I tried to cheer him but he was bitter and withdrawn. He had lost his *joie de vivre*. Perhaps I was able to make Mum's life a little easier while I was there, but that was it. I hated leaving, but Trent Eels was at the crossroads.

We had found a way to cultivate the larger carp in nets slung in the oxygen-rich waters of the adjacent cooling tower pond, where growth rates were comfortably in excess of three per cent a day. As a result, we had been trading profitably and paying the interest on our government-guaranteed £75,000 loan secured through the Clydesdale Bank. This fell due in April. I thought it would be a good time to talk to them about renegotiating the repayment terms. Silly. I was firmly reminded the repayment due date was non-negotiable. Shortly afterwards, there was a call from a Mr Segal from Woodford Wells in Essex, pretentiously introducing himself as an insolvency practitioner. The game was up for Trent Eels. We furiously sold all the stock we could to ensure there was sufficient money to pay the wages and small creditors.

Could there be anything more soul destroying than watching the company you created fall into a receiver's grasping hands? If I hadn't understood the anguish occasioned by Dad's decision to sell up Wilson & Wilson, piecemeal, I certainly did now. It's the sense of having let so many people down—your employees, shareholders, family, suppliers and, of course, yourself. It's the loss of control and revulsion towards being at the mercy of the smug functionaries, who feign care but couldn't care less.

We delivered our last shipment of eels to Mick's Eels in Billingsgate on April 14th. A week later, there was a creditors' meeting in the Royal Scot Hotel in Nottingham, following which I handed the farm keys to the bailiff. Having said goodbye to George Leydon, I never set foot in the power station again. In the following months, there were rumours the farm eels had escaped to live happily ever after in the Trent where they were playing havoc with coarse fishing contests.

Freefall

Sarah was in Australia when the receivers walked in. She knew there would be no job if she came back but did anyway. I was pleased. Yew Tree Cottage would have been quiet without her. Fortunately we weren't so poor we couldn't enjoy the endless flow of social events associated with life in Quorn country. But this couldn't last without an income. Sarah was a talented seamstress and soon found herself busy as a dressmaker. I needed to find something as well.

Towards the end of June, Mike Vassilopoulos called from Florida. With oil hovering at US$40 a barrel, there wasn't much going on in the Middle East. The incorrigible wheeler dealer had based himself in Palm Beach to pursue opportunities in Chile, where the government had implemented an imaginative programme to reduce its foreign debt burden. Investors were permitted to buy Chilean sovereign debt, currently at a forty per cent discount, redeemable from the Chilean Government at face value less around ten per cent provided the proceeds were invested in Chilean assets. Mike was part of a consortium using the regulation to purchase an iodine mine. He was heading for Santiago in early July and had a spare first-class Miami-Santiago return ticket. Would

I like to join him? *To unpathed waters, undreamed shores.*[28] Why not? I could get to Miami on Sir Freddie Laker's Skytrain for less than £100.

We arrived in Santiago a week later and checked into the Hotel Acacias de Vitacura. Set in a park on the banks of the Río Mapocho, flush with Andean meltwater hurrying west to the Pacific, the hotel was twenty minutes away from the downtown offices that were to be our base for the next three weeks. Our host was Luis Felipe Varela de la Carrera, a local member of the iodine mine acquisition consortium. The iodine mine was a sideline for Felipe. His day-to-day business was exporting fresh seafood and fresh fruit to Brazil, North America and Europe under the name Oceanica Chilena. He and his partner, Gonzalo, shared offices and a secretary with a corporate lawyer and an investor who specialised in developing lawn cemeteries. Now there's a business—otherwise worthless land transformed into an endless cash cow. Mike and I parked in their comfortable boardroom opening onto a balcony with views up and down Estado. Being eleven floors up this was an ideal vantage point from which to observe a regular ritual of contemporary Chilean politics.

Chilean politics was Augusto Pinochet. Having taken over by force in 1973, he had created a veneer of respectability by amending the constitution to preserve his dictatorship until 1988, at which time there would be a national plebiscite to determine whether his mandate would be extended a further eight years. Eligible voters would simply vote 'yes' or 'no'—*si o no*. The seminal event was scheduled for October 5th. For a foreigner arriving in Chile early July, this seemed a long way off but clearly not so for those who were dying to see the end of Don Augusto, and there were many who had—more than 2000, according to the Rettig Report commissioned in 1991.

Despite the real threat to life and limb, crowds of young people would assemble unheralded on the corner of Estado and Huérfanos, both pedestrian zones, to demonstrate in favour of a 'no' vote. *¡Chi chi chi, Le le le! ¡Que se vaya Pinochet!* The Stasi wouldn't be far behind. They started with tear gas. We viewed a number of these protests from the relative safety of our eleventh-floor balcony but immunity from the effects of tear gas was not guaranteed even up there. The faintest whiff was unbearable. Regardless, some protesters with little more than a bandana for a face cover, continued. That's when the police let loose the water cannon. They were effective but not as effective as the cinema. There were at least two nearby in Huérfanos, and with the start of the evening session there wouldn't be a protester in sight. Cinema is as important as football in Latin America and its popularity in Chile, despite political turmoil, brought home the significance of the opening scene from *Evita*.

With three weeks to kill, I cast around for something to do. Becoming familiar with Chile and its history would be a good start. Magellan charted the eponymous Strait in 1520. Pedro de Valdivia arrived from Peru twenty years later. After an eleven-month march south through the Atacama Desert and beyond, he settled in the Mapocho Valley. It was prime farming land and Santiago was formally established on the banks of the river in 1541. Indigenous resistance was restrained at first but when the newcomers began cultivating native land there was a well-organised uprising and Valdivia was brutally murdered following his capture after the Battle of Tucapel in 1553. For the colonists, however, this was no more than a setback and over the next 250 years the locals were reduced to a tiny minority in their own land.

With nothing better to do, the colonials turned their minds to independence. The Americans started the ball rolling in 1776 and before long the Spanish colonies to the south were taking up the cudgels. Chile's turn came in 1818 when Bernardo O'Higgins, the illegitimate son of well-to-do Chilean grandees, defeated the royalists and proclaimed Chile a republic. O'Higgins presided over a junta that lasted five years, until differences with the Catholic Church forced him into exile in Peru. The fallout lasted until the Chilean Constitution of 1833 repealed some of the more liberal aspects of O'Higgins's constitution and restored political stability. The next fifty years saw the construction of nation-building infrastructure, ports and railroads up and down the coast and the addition of further territories to the north and south. With the Boundary Treaty with Argentina ratified in 1881 and victory in the 1883 Saltpetre War with Peru, Chile stretched 4000 kilometres from the Atacama Desert in the north to Puerto Williams in the south, with the Andes to the east and the Pacific to the west.

As the money from the saltpetre mines rolled in, José Manuel Balmaceda, liberal aristocrat and newly elected president, decided to spend it. He embarked on massive public works and defence spending programmes. Chile's fledgling institutions proved incapable of managing them and the corridors of La Moneda Palace reeked of corruption. Congress moved to depose Balmaceda but he refused to go. Civil war ensued. The army supported the president, the navy supported the congress, and the navy won. Balmaceda set a precedent for presidential suicide by shooting himself.

Thanks to mining and agriculture, the Chilean economy managed to absorb the massive cost of the civil war, but as those labour-intensive industries grew so too did the influence of trade unions who managed to elect representatives to congress in ever-increasing numbers. Socialist-leaning governments gained power and as bureaucracy infiltrated every tier of society economic stagnation followed. In 1970, Salvador Allende persuaded the people the answer was not less but more and was elected president with only thirty-six per cent of the vote. As an avowed Marxist, he set about seizing the means of production, fixing prices and raising tariffs. Rural landholdings were expropriated, subdivided and given to farm workers along with the livestock. The utopian dream morphed into an Orwellian nightmare. By 1973, inflation had risen to 280 per cent, the peso was worthless and supermarket shelves were empty. Fresh milk was no longer available in Santiago and parents of newborn babies scoured the countryside for farms selling it on the black market. By September, strikes by doctors, teachers, transport workers and miners had brought the country to a standstill. Another military coup, another presidential suicide, enter General Pinochet.

He may not have been everybody's cup of tea but he had

the power and the courage to adopt and persevere with a novel and radical programme that restored Chile to its place as the most successful economy in Latin America. The roadmap was the brainchild of a group of young Chilean economists nicknamed the Chicago Boys who had studied under Milton Friedman at the University of Chicago. In 1969 they published a report simply entitled *El Ladrillo* (The Brick). It was a blueprint for the economic liberalisation of Chile. The ideas were a distillation of the principals that had created the Asian tigers (South Korea, Taiwan, Singapore and Hong Kong), free trade, open markets, privatisation, deregulation and a lean public sector. It was offered to one of Allende's opponents to use as an economic platform for the 1970 election and was rejected. Following the 1973 coup, career economist, Jorge Cauas, was appointed finance minister. He was not a Chicago Boy but recruited many of them into his Ministry. They persuaded General Pinochet to adopt *El Ladrillo* as their play book, and he agreed.

The main pillars of the plan were tariff reduction, public sector employment reduction and privatisation of state monopolies. It wasn't plain sailing. Chile buys crude oil and sells copper. In 1974, crude oil prices tripled and the copper price halved so the reforms faced severe headwinds from plummeting terms of trade. By 1988, however, the casual observer, as I was, could see Santiago was on the move with a bustling city centre, well stocked shops and supermarkets, tempting restaurants offering local beef, fish and wine, reasonable public transport, clean streets and effective public services, such as clean water, sewerage, power, schools, universities and hospitals. Its newspaper of record, *El Mercurio,* is said to be the oldest Spanish-language daily currently in circulation and rivalled only by *The Times* for longevity. Many claimed it had been instrumental in setting the scene for Pinochet's coup, with CIA funding. Felipe Varela's father, Alex, had been the newspaper's editor in Valparaiso at the time. Felipe suggested his father's day consisted of lunch in his club followed by an hour or so in his office dictating an editorial for the next morning's edition. He didn't sound like a firebrand.

Despite the historical turmoil, it didn't take long to warm to life in Chile. Our new amigos in the Oceanica Chilena office were generous hosts. Santiago was an attractive city and easy to explore with its river running west and white-capped Cordillera de los Andes in the east. Before long I was thinking how nice it would be to have a local interest to warrant a longer-term association. There was no oil or gas but the surrounding seas were teeming with fish. Oceanica Chilena was an experienced seafood trader and I had readymade contacts in that industry in the UK. The obvious answer was a seafood project. But what seafood project? Perhaps eels.

An aquaculture specialist from Fundación Chile, a non-profit organisation established to nurture emerging industries, introduced me to their reference library, including the section covering Chile's commercial fish species. With a 5000-kilometre coastline, it came as no surprise the local industry was one of the world's largest. After a day of pouring through reams of incomprehensible Spanish, the only eel mentioned was the conger eel. This was the 'eel' served in local restaurants. Ugh, not having that again! As for real eels, there was nothing. The focus was salmon. Why not try that? Chile's cold-water coastline south of Puerto Montt (41°S), with over 2000 kilometres of fjords, could be Norway. It was made for fish farming and, although Atlantic salmon are not native to the area, a nascent industry had taken hold. I investigated the idea of setting up a smokehouse, but despite Chile being a low-wage economy the margins were unattractive.

Eventually a visit to the office promoting investment in the Punta Arenas free trade zone crystallised an idea that appealed to the Oceanica Chilena team. The Patagonian region in the cold south was teeming with commercial species but the potential was untapped save for a king crab industry. One prolific local species, merluza, is a cod-like fish which, in the wake of the Cod Wars, sold well in Europe when available. Preliminary enquiries indicated long-line fishing licences were available. With help from Felipe's office, I started gathering the basic information considered necessary to formulate a Punta Arenas fishing project.

With days to go before our return to Miami, Felipe invited Mike and me to a family weekend at their beach house in Zapallar. The beach there was an intimate affair, not unlike Mooloolaba, where everybody knew everybody else. The local delicacy was *erizo de mar* (sea urchin). Who would have believed those spikey critters had a delicious soft centre? But that conversation also revealed the existence of yet another Chilean delicacy, *angulas*. This was indeed a revelation since *angulas* are nothing more than sautéed baby eels, a popular dish along the shores of the Bay of Biscay, traditional homeland of the Basques. Just as the Bristol Channel is England's most prolific elver fishery, the Bay of Biscay is Europe's most prolific elver fishery. The source of this revelation was a Basque *émigré* whose years in Chile had not dulled his craving for *angulas*. Every spring he made his way south to Puyehue Lake where the elusive small fry were a local delicacy. Mike and I were planning a return trip to Chile in September so would have the perfect excuse to include a visit to one of Chile's most beautiful regions, Los Lagos.

Back in England, I continued my research into the Punta Arenas fishing project. In one of those extraordinary coincidences that happen from time to time I met a Hungarian-born Australian, Ludwig Berger, at an Australian Business in Europe lunch in London. As we chatted about Sydney it emerged that he and my uncle (married to my father's sister, Marjorie) had been neighbours in Double Bay. More importantly, he was a director and major shareholder in the Spanish Sol Hotel Group. Naturally, it was a substantial consumer of seafood so I was delighted to accept his invitation to spend a week motoring around Majorca in his grand motor torpedo boat conversion, *Mangusta*. So off I went. It was an enjoyable week and there was ample opportunity to discuss the project in Punta Arenas, but Ludwig was uneasy about dealing with the unrest in Chile, as were many others I approached afterwards. Interestingly, *Mangusta* was moored alongside Robert Maxwell's yacht, *Lady Ghislane*, in the marina at Majorca. Three years later Maxwell drowned when he went overboard one night.

I returned to Yew Tree Cottage empty handed—empty

handed in more ways than one. I was running out of money. By swapping the BMW for a VW Polo worth £1,700, I was able to increase my cash reserves to £12,000. Compared with the average salary of the day of £17,000, this wasn't a lot, but I was better off than Robert Maxwell. Even though the primary objective of my next trip to Chile was to formalise the fishing project in Punta Arenas, it was timed to coincide with what we thought might be the *angula* season in Puyehue Lake.

Felipe and his wife, Ina, had decided to make the most of the expedition by turning it into a family holiday. They had booked into the Hotel Nilque on the southern shore of Puyehue Lake and driven down from Santiago. It was to be our base for the quest for *anguilla chilena*. Mike Vassilopoulos had decided to duck this visit, so having arrived in Santiago I accompanied Felipe's mother, Sylvia, on the 450-kilometre domestic flight south to Osorno, the regional capital. Felipe met us at the airport and as we drove east towards Nilque and the snow-capped Andean peaks beyond, it was easy to understand why Chileans are so enthusiastic about their Region Los Lagos and its delights. Volcan Puyehue, the tallest in the area, is still active and no doubt connected to the hot springs that together with the lakes and snowfields make the area so popular with tourists—so much so that in 1942 construction of the Hotel Termas Puyehue was completed so well-heeled visitors to the area could enjoy the hot springs, the lake and the ski fields in five-star comfort. It was barely a ten-minute drive from Nilque, so we dropped in for a late lunch. Over the pisco sours, Felipe outlined his plan for our search. It was relatively simple. We would drive along the shoreline of the lake and the banks of the Río Pilmaiquén, which drained it, and ask any fishermen we found what they knew about eels. Sylvia could barely contain her amusement.

We got off to an early start next morning, but there was no need, as we soon discovered the traditional trout and salmon season in the lake was December to March, so there weren't many fishermen to talk to. There was, however, one talkative local who reported large numbers of *angulas* making their way from Puyehue Lake up the Río Gol Gol late in the summer. This was encouraging, but there were no corroborative stories of trout or salmon fishermen catching eels by mistake. Another local suggested we might have better luck talking to the locals along the Ríos Tranallaquín and Hueyelhue, which flow directly into the Pacific. We spent a day in the area. One man reported 'eels' up to fifty centimetres in length swimming downstream in the rainy season, but we didn't meet anybody who had seen one out of the water. By the end of the third day we felt we were chasing shadows and I decided to return to Santiago.

On the morning of my departure, as I was checking out of the hotel and having difficulty arranging transport for Osorno, Felipe recognised another guest also preparing to leave. I was introduced to Benjamin Garcia Huidobro, who, with his friend Sergio, the owner of the hotel, was on his way to Osorno for the rodeo. Would I like a lift? Yes, please. Both men were competing so were immaculately groomed in the traditional dress of *huasos*, the Chilean version of an Argentinian *gaucho*.

No sooner were we on our way than the conversation

turned to horses. Don Benjamin managed the largest Chilean Corralero stud in the country for the Edwards family, owners of *El Mercurio*. These stock horses, descendants of the thirty-seven Spanish Andalusians that accompanied Pizarro to Peru in 1531, are the only horses allowed to compete in Chilean rodeos where the main event involves two *huasos* riding to round up a calf and pin it against a cushion. Did I have an interest in horses? Certainly, I hunt with the Quorn foxhounds and during the winter season am normally out twice a week. This precipitated a lively exchange as Don Benjamin explained the estate he managed had a pack of foxhounds used during winter to hunt a species known as Darwin's fox. As they dropped me off at the Ladeco Airlines office in Osorno he had a brainwave. Would it be possible to get some Quorn hounds he could use to improve the stamina in his pack, which was bred from the smaller American hunting hound? I had no idea but promised to find out and let him know.

The platinum blonde behind the counter didn't speak English and I didn't speak Spanish. *'Sprechen sie Deutsch?'* she asked. *'Ein bischen,'* I replied. Shortly afterwards, I was on a flight back to Santiago. The German I had spent four years learning at school hadn't been wasted. Later I was to learn the Osorno/Puerto Montt area was a popular destination for Nazis on the run from post-war Germany.

My first port of call in Santiago was the National Museum of Natural History. This had a much better reference library than Fundación Chile and before long it was apparent the *angulas* our Basque friend went south for every year were not eels but lamprey. The European eel grows to eighty centimetres in length, whereas the Chilean lamprey grows to just fifty centimetres. This was consistent with what Felipe and I had been told the previous week. Disappointing as it was, I took solace from the tale of poor King Henry I, who is rumoured to have died of a 'surfeit of lamprey' in 1135.

With no further distraction from eels, we were able to concentrate on the Punta Arenas fishing project. The idea was to form a Cayman company, acquire the relevant fishing licences for Patagonia and an option over a suitable site for a processing plant. The last part of the plan was to find a suitably experienced partner to operate the boats and plant and to split the remaining equity between Oceanica Chilena, Mike and myself. The Cod Wars and membership of the European Union had gutted the UK fishing industry. I knew companies such as Andrew Marr International and Boyd Line were looking for fisheries in far off places so finding the partner fell to me.

General Pinochet's *si o no plebiscito* was held on October 5th, days before my return to London. I had enjoyed my visits to Chile and its people and knew this was to be a momentous event. In the years and months running up to the plebiscite, political activism, such as the demonstration I had observed from the safety of Felipe's office balcony two months earlier, had been outlawed, but in the month running up to the vote campaigning had been sanctioned. The opposition parties managed to form an alliance and had crafted an effective 'no' campaign focussed on their popular slogan, *¡Chi chi chi, Le le le! ¡Que se vaya Pinochet!* On the day, they won easily, four million 'no' to three million 'yes'. The margin left no wriggle room for *el presidente* who, resplendent in white dress uniform, conceded on TV at 2 am the next day. This was good news, but there had been speculation he might seize the moment and announce his retirement. No way. Instead, the old soldier took the opportunity to remind everybody that, as per the constitution, he would continue as president pending presidential and congressional elections, due in eighteen months. This was bad news and precipitated further demonstrations the day after in which two participants were killed.

The opposition coalition may not have got everything they wanted, but by the time I left for London a week later cooler heads had prevailed and it was business as usual in Santiago. Shortly afterwards, Mike Vassilopoulos confirmed the formation of a new company called Otway Fisheries SA, with a paid-up capital of one million pesos and an account with the Bank of Boston. My job was to find an investor. I kissed a lot of toads but there was no charming prince. A few were interested in the project but all baulked at doing business in what they saw as just another Latin American country. It was galling because Chile was anything but. By Christmas, I knew I was flogging a dead horse and I needed to go home anyway.

The Queen said it best when she described 1992 as an *annus horribilis* for the Windsors. So was 1988 for the Wilsons. I had been home in January shortly after everything in Dalby had been put up for sale. Dad had stopped trading and was at home with nothing to do except worry and wait for buyers. It didn't help that in February and March there were torrential rains and Myall Creek threatened the house again. It inundated the garden but fortunately that was all.

Then came news that Trent Eels had gone broke. Poor Dad. He still felt responsible for all of us and there was nothing he could do. Eventually there was some relief. The Wilson & Wilson business assets were the first to go and 61 Myall Street went shortly afterwards in July. The sales partially revived Dad's spirits. Mum and Dad left Dalby for the coast and moved into Douglas Street. Within weeks, he had bought a block of land on the beach at Warana and engaged a builder to build a three-bedroom retirement home.

To save the princely sum of £350 on my flight to Australia for Christmas, I flew Aeroflot to Singapore via Moscow, Larnaca, Dubai and Bombay. If I hadn't already realised my fortunes were at a low ebb, then that twenty-two hours in economy on an Ilyushin Il-86 would have removed any doubt. I spent the night with Philip Conn and on Christmas Eve after lunch with my old colleague Saeed Khan, caught an overnight Qantas flight to Brisbane. Of course, Dad was at the airport to meet me, and we were back at the new house at 187 Oceanic Drive, Warana, by breakfast time. With the garden being very much a work in progress, it looked bare, but for a retirement home on a beach where Dad could lick his wounds surfing in the morning and fishing in the afternoon it was perfect. That wasn't all. Friends from all over Queensland had retired to the Sunshine Coast and before long Mum and Dad were playing tennis and bridge on a regular basis and enjoying a busy social life. Their *annus horribilis* was over.

Mine wasn't, but shortly after Christmas I ran into Peter Hollingsworth. We first met in 1963 when Dad, as an alderman on the Dalby town council, had been chairman of the works committee overseeing the construction of the town's sewerage system and Peter had been the geotechnical consultant. Twenty years later I would often see him in London where he was a regular visitor as advisor to Bechtel on the Ok Tedi project in New Guinea. He was now director of a company called Neutralysis Industries, pioneering a process producing lightweight aggregate and electricity using municipal solid waste to fire clay in a rotary kiln system. He thought it might be of interest in the UK. The company had built a twenty-five-tonne-a-day pilot plant in a shed in Rocklea. Would I like to see it? Certainly. It was arranged for a day in mid-January when the plant would be fired up to produce aggregate for the testing programme running in conjunction with the University of Queensland.

As it turned out, Neutralysis's founder and process inventor had just retired and a famous Dalby old boy, Peter Thorley, had just been appointed managing director. Peter's father, Harold, had been the Dalby town clerk for forty years and when he retired in 1966, Peter succeeded him. Seven years later, he was appointed town clerk and city administrator of Brisbane, and in 1981, when the Melbourne City Council couldn't lie straight in bed at night and the Victorian Government sacked them he was appointed chairman of the city's governing commission. The Neutralysis board couldn't have found a better man for the job. He was a formidable administrator and could pick up the phone to any mayor in the land and although he was eleven years my senior we were more than nodding acquaintances and both enjoyed the unexpected reunion.

The demonstration was impressive. A truckload of household waste and a truckload of black soil were turned into a neat pile of vitrified aggregate, small drums of recyclables, such as ferrous metals and aluminium, and very little else. It was an elegant solution to a messy problem. The first part of the process involved shredding the waste and recovering the recyclables and glass to produce refuse-derived fuel (RDF). The RDF was then combined with the black soil and water to form a stiff paste that was extruded into pellets. The raw pellets were then dried in a rotary drier at 400 °C and from there introduced to a sealed three-stage kiln process: pyrolysis at 750 °C, oxidation at 910 °C, and finally, vitrification at 1000 °C. Glass removed during RDF preparation was pulverised and injected into the vitrification kiln to glaze the aggregate.

As impressive as the demonstration plant was, its real credibility derived from the work done on the design of a generic 500-tonne-a-day plant by globally renowned process engineers, Davy McKee. They had prepared heat and mass balances for the entire process, prepared performance specifications for the major equipment items, solicited detailed quotations from specialist vendors, prepared drawings and a cost estimate and modelled a budget for Australian conditions. It looked good in Australia, but I was reasonably confident it would look even better in the UK, where they were trying to phase out landfill and a substantial premium was paid for electricity generated from non-fossil fuels. We didn't have the inanity of CO_2-induced global warming in 1989, but acid rain was a real problem and this premium had been introduced to save forests.

To make a success of Neutralysis, Peter Thorley and his team needed to persuade a local authority to commission a plant. The market in Australia was limited to Sydney, Melbourne and Brisbane, possibly Perth. The potential abroad was massive. I volunteered to look for opportunities in the UK and Europe. Neutralysis had worldwide patents for the process so readily agreed. I was happy to do the work, hoping it would lead to an income. Shortly afterwards, having returned to Yew Tree Cottage, I did a cash stocktake. I was down to £3,600. The threat of penury is a huge incentive so I embarked on an urgent investigation of the municipal waste industry in England.

The generic Neutralysis plant had six potential income streams: solid waste disposal; liquid waste, such as sewage disposal; contaminated soils disposal; lightweight aggregate sales; electricity sales; and scrap steel sales. I spent the next two months familiarising myself with these parameters and building a spreadsheet model for a typical 500-tonne-a-day plant. I had been into the Notts County Council offices on numerous occasions on Trent Eels business so had ready access there. Its waste disposal coordination officer was more than helpful. The county council was incinerating 2500 tonnes of municipal solid waste (MSW) a week and sending 5000 tonnes to landfill, all in all, equivalent to two standard 500-tonne-a-day Neutralysis plants. MSW disposal fees ranged from £4 to £20 a tonne, depending on proximity to major centres. That was interesting, but of more interest was his summary of a government green paper issued just weeks earlier requiring local authorities to privatise municipal waste disposal—classic Thatcherism.

By June, I had a good handle on the numbers. Davy McKee had estimated the cost of a UK-based 500-tonne-a-day plant at £34.5 million. The projected revenue from the six income streams amounted to £10.5 million. Annual operating costs came in at £4.6 million, leaving an operating profit of £5.9 million or seventeen per cent.

Thirteen years on from the three Julias cruise from Bosham to Yarmouth, Bill Higgins had married and had moved to Berkshire where he was involved in the transformation of farmland near the M4 into an industrial estate. Richard Morley's Redhill Marina adjacent to J24 on the M1 had similar potential. I mentioned it to Bill and he offered to come up to take a look if Richard was interested. The visit was arranged for late April and Bill spent the night at Yew Tree cottage. Over dinner, I took him through the Neutralysis process and the figures. It didn't take him long to appreciate its potential. Within a week he had sent a formal expression of interest in the technology for a plant in Berkshire.

This was a long way from a rolled-gold contract but the flurry of activity that followed suggested it was a genuine prospect. Bill was nothing if not energetic and in the months that followed sent a proposal to Berkshire County Council, who responded positively, requesting further information. He also formed an alliance with RMC Ready-Mix, who were interested in the aggregate and had a site adjacent to a landfill just outside Reading. Further prospects emerged in Hampshire, Leicestershire and Manchester so by early June, when I went to Sydney for my brother Chris's wedding, there was a warm welcome from the Neutralysis management when I eventually got to Brisbane. More importantly, they were excited about an alliance formed with waste-disposal giant, Brambles Cleanaway, to tender for a fifteen-year garbage-disposal contract with the Brisbane City Council. Perhaps that's why they offered me a £1500-a-month retainer.

Given my straitened circumstances, I was sorely tempted to accept on the spot, but during the months since hitching the ride from Nilque to Osorno with Benjamin Garcia Huidobro, I had been working on the problem of finding and sending foxhounds to Chile. There were times I wish I had never made the offer, but I had. The first hurdle was the hunting season starting hard on the heels of my return from Chile. No huntsman will part with hounds during the season, but at the close there are always hounds to retire (code for put down—code for taken behind the kennels and shot). So when I asked Michael Farrin, the Quorn huntsman, he was not only happy to oblige but took an interest as well. Don Benjamin had requested a dog and a bitch but Michael suggested sending a bitch in whelp with two unrelated dogs. Benjamin readily agreed. Michael set to work waiting for a suitable bitch in heat and finding a suitable sire to do the business.

Eventually, an obliging bitch, Artless, fell pregnant, allowing two fortunate dogs, Dorman and Dalesman, to be selected to accompany her. The Foreign Office certified their vaccination certificates, which were in turn verified by the Chilean Embassy. Two made-to-measure crates, one for the bitch and the other for the two dogs, were ordered and ten months after opening my big mouth I was on my way back to Santiago with 193 kilograms of excess baggage. Fortunately, the Edwards family were paying the bill.

The timing couldn't have been better. Apart from *El Mercurio*, the Edwardses owned Banco Edwards, major creditor of a seafood cannery with global sales in Punta Arenas. Unfortunately, Pesquera y Consevera Cabo De Hornos, whose primary business was catching and canning king crab, had paid too much for a hotel and could no longer service the debt. The bank had taken it into administration. The cannery was still a going concern and the company had deep-water fishing licences, so if it could be purchased at a reasonable cost it would be a far more attractive option than the Otway Fisheries idea.

A member of the Edwards family, Don Maurice Poisson, rear admiral (retd), was installed as company caretaker president pending sale of the business. Felipe called on some of his father's *El Mercurio* connections, and within days we had a meeting with the old salt and one of his new colleagues. At first, 'When I was a Lad' from *HMS Pinafore* came to mind, but he was much more than that. He had a firm grip on his new brief and was keen to get on with the job. He had planned a trip to Punta Arenas for the following Sunday. Would I like to accompany him? *Yes, thank you.*

But first, a day's hunting at Graneros. Felipe and I were invited for a tour of the Edwards estate on Saturday afternoon followed by dinner and an overnight stay for an early morning start. We arrived mid-afternoon, giving Benjamin plenty of time to show us around. The main house, annexes, chapel, stables and kennels, all Spanish colonial and all surrounded by lush lawns and gardens, were secured in a walled compound covering at least ten acres. First stop was the stables and their haughty residents. One didn't have to be an aficionado to recognise the similarities between these and the Lipizzaners of the Spanish Riding School in Vienna. Another interesting exhibit was a beautifully maintained black ceremonial coach, which must have looked fabulous when tacked up with its black shire horses.

From the stables we moved on to the kennels where I was pleased to see the new arrivals from the Quorn were well and settled in their new surroundings. They were nearly twice the size of their new companions, derived from American foxhounds. Benjamin was hoping the bigger English hounds might be better suited to hunting in the rugged mountain terrain, which was where we were next morning, well before the sun began warming the western slopes of la Cordillera. I was foxhunting in Chile. Robert Browning came to mind. *What I love best in all the world is a castle, precipice-encurl'd in a gash of the wind-griev'd Apennine.*[29]

We were a small group, perhaps a dozen, including two boys. All were dressed to the nines: long-sleeve shirt, sweater, riding breeches, high-heel boots and spurs, heavily decorated knee-high leather leggings, all topped off with a bolero hat and a traditional *chamanto*. The hound pack, apart from being physically smaller, was smaller in numbers than an

English pack, perhaps a third of the size. As we climbed, teeth chattering, towards our prey's habitat, I was grateful for the warmth of the heavy wool *chamanto* I had been offered. Alpine riding was a novelty for me, but after an hour or so I sensed my horse knew what it was doing so let him have his head. It was at about that time the hounds started crying and for a while the pace quickened. But the fox knew a thing or two and as the hunt progressed the terrain deteriorated and keeping up became impossible. At one stage, I found myself on a narrow path with a vertical fall into nothing on my right. There was no way to turn—only forward. Drop the reins, hope for the best.

Eventually, Benjamin called a halt and we assembled on a grassy clearing to listen for the hounds. There was nothing but a silence interrupted by the occasional bird. They were gone. Eventually, wine skins were passed around and with time to take in the grandeur of our surroundings, we turned for a lower clearing where a barbeque lunch was in preparation. The fox had won the day but all was not lost. A side of beef and a Chilean claret have remarkable restorative powers and in the ensuing days most of the hounds were recovered. Then, there was even better news; two weeks later, Artless, the pregnant bitch from the Quorn, delivered four male and six female puppies—a good start to rebuilding a pack of foxhounds.

After the lunch Felipe took me back to Santiago to join Don Maurice Poisson for our flight to Punta Arenas. As we were boarding, Don Maurice chanced upon and introduced me to a former colleague who had retired to become a Magellan

Strait pilot. He was on his way south to take a ship through the Strait's 307 miles from Bahía Posesión on the Atlantic coast to Puerto Montt in the west. This sheltered route saved ships the perils and cost of rounding the Horn. But of much greater interest was Don Maurice's story. During the 1973 coup as captain of the navy's flagship, the cruiser *Capitán Prat*, Don Maurice had threatened the Federico Santa María Technical University with annihilation should there be any trouble from the leftist elements of that institution. Four years later, he was in London as Chile's naval attaché. At first, he was snubbed by Harold Wilson's officials, but under Mrs Thatcher things improved—so much so that when he returned to Chile as a rear admiral he played a valuable role in support of Britain's Falklands War effort.

Shortly before the war, the Royal Navy had sold two ships to the Chilean Navy. They were just days away from Talcahuano and a refit when the war was declared. In the spirit of 'your enemy's enemy is your friend', Don Maurice had been instrumental in arranging for the ships to be temporarily returned to the Royal Navy, whereupon they re-joined the British armada in the Falklands theatre.

He was still telling sea stories three hours later as we arrived in Punta Arenas's succinctly named, Presidente Carlos Ibáñez del Campo International Airport. With three cross runways, you know winds in the area can be fierce and fickle—not surprising with Cape Horn only 300 kilometres to the south. It's a fair way into town, so it was late by the time I checked into the Hotel los Navagantes, only slightly better than a flea pit.

Pesquera y Consevera Cabo De Hornos's local manager, Don Alejandro, showed us through the works early next morning. The 1500-square-metre plant and 150-square-metre offices occupied a two-hectare site thirteen kilometres north of town on the western shore of the Strait of Magellan. It was a substantial operation: cannery, warehouse, freezer storage and workshop, with more than thirteen ships and boats fishing, not just for king crab, but snow crab, mussels and scallops as well. The 1988 catch had been 480 tonnes. Most of this was canned and the remainder frozen into two-kilogram caterer's blocks. I asked for the management accounts and Don Alejandro was happy to oblige. More than half the annual income of US$3.7 million came from the king crab catch, but this was in decline. After costs, the annual profit before tax was about US$0.6 million. With a deteriorating king crab catch, this couldn't last. The plan was to supplement the income with merluza. Applications for long-line licences had been lodged with SERNAP (Servicio Nacional de Pesca y Acuicultura). Our next port of call was the local SERNAP office where it was confirmed the applications were under consideration in Valparaiso and likely to be issued later in the month.

There wasn't much more I could do in Punta Arenas so I booked a return flight to Santiago for the following day. Meanwhile, Don Maurice, who was staying at the naval base, invited me to dinner in the officers' mess. Our host was the base commander, Captain Victor Wilson. It was an enjoyable dinner during which the seaman explained how relations between Argentina and Chile were always fragile and hence the vital role Chile's navy and air force bases in Punta Arenas played in securing the border, 2000 kilometres from Santiago. But it wasn't all politics. The evening ended on an exceedingly warm note when Captain Victor and I discovered our respective great great grandfathers were both from County Tyrone, Ireland. Perhaps Gilbert and Sullivan's farce is not so far-fetched after all.

Back in Santiago it was agreed Pesquera y Consevera Cabo De Hornos as a going concern was a far more attractive investment than the Otway Fisheries idea. But we still needed an investor and as this was likely to be Andrew Marr International or Boyd Line it would be up to me to get one of them interested. I went back to England and in early October, after I'd sent Boyd a detailed information memorandum, they sent a representative to Punta Arenas. Their main interest, however, was the fishing licences and although SERNAP had advised these would be issued in September, there was no sign of this happening. Even if the licences came and Boyd decided to proceed with the investment, it would be months before I could hope for any income from the venture and I was fast running out of money.

Fortunately, the Neutralysis offer of a £1500-a-month retainer was still on the table, so my main focus became municipal waste processing. The industry was undergoing a rapid transformation, driven by growing environmental awareness and privatisation. Landfill was on the nose, but so too was waste incineration with its toxic ash residue and flue gas emissions. The Neutralysis process solved the ash problem but the jury was out on the quality of its flue gas emissions. Interesting in retrospect, atmospheric CO_2 concentration growth was becoming an issue, although yet to give young children nightmares.

Another big change of enormous benefit to Neutralysis in the UK was the Non-Fossil Fuel Obligation. In 1989, in one of her landmark reforms, Mrs Thatcher privatised power generation. The legislation included support for those not generating power from coal, natural gas or fuel oil, by placing an obligation on electricity retailers to include a significant proportion of non-fossil fuel power in the supply mix. The initial premium was £75 per megawatt-hour, compared with the £25 per megawatt-hour received for electricity generated from coal. This boosted the annual profitability of a 500-tonne-a-day plant in the UK from £5.9 million to £9.5 million.

This made the UK prime territory for the Neutralysis technology, and the proof lay in the number of projects identified in a relatively short period. In early November, Peter Thorley came to London to see for himself. He was more than familiar with the workings of government and was clearly impressed by the pace of change and the way waste management, like power generation, was being taken over by the private sector. Neutralysis needed to build just one plant and the sky would be the limit. One bright prospect was a forthcoming tender to dispose of Brisbane's municipal waste for the next fifteen years. Brambles, one of Australia's largest waste disposal contractors, had agreed to include a Neutralysis plant as part of its offer.

By the time I got to Brisbane for Christmas, hopes were

high and it was anticipated the Brisbane City Council would be announcing its preferred contractor in April. This didn't happen and rumours emerged of uneasy residents in the neighbourhood of the intended plant site concerned about the toxicity of the flue gas emissions. Air pollution had become a hot topic, and in the wake of the introduction of unleaded petrol in 1985 everybody was an expert. By August, optimism had been replaced by concern. Neutralysis was burning $300,000 a month and would run out of cash by September and the Brisbane contract award wasn't expected until December. My cash position was still precarious as well. After seven seasons, I could no longer afford my great passion, hunting. I asked Shelagh Morley if she would take Rory in return for the outstanding livery fees. She told me not to be silly and promised to look after him until I could afford to hunt him again. I was forced to sell my prized Stubbs engravings to get home for Christmas. I rang Paul Mason, the dealer, and he bought *Dungannon* and *Sweetbriar* back for £5,100.

With my newfound wealth, I was unable to resist an invitation from Gisa Ehrlich to spend a weekend with her cousin in Berlin. The Wall had been down for almost a year so it was an opportunity to visit the city that had symbolised the Cold War, hitherto a constant in our lives. I took a cheap flight from Birmingham to Gisa's new home, Hamburg, and we drove from there in her car via the A24. It had been one of the few links between East and West during the partition and was still a lonely road. A considerable stretch traversed a forest through which a 200-metre-wide strip had been cleared on each side to provide sight lines for the Stasi observation posts situated every kilometre or so. I wondered if George Smiley had been here.

Cuz lived in a magnificent apartment in an art deco building salvaged from the rubble of post-war Berlin, about three stops west of Friedrichstraße on the S-Bahn. It was late when we arrived so my introduction to Berlin didn't start until the Saturday morning—the Brandenburg Gate, the Reichstag, Checkpoint Charlie, the Wall and Kurfürstendamm. That's where I saw a poster for a Komische Oper production of *Die Hochzeit des Figaro*, playing the following night, Sunday. We had no plans so I suggested we all go. They declined but Gisa knew me well enough to insist I go anyway.

We spent the next day in Potsdam, also chopped in half when the iron curtain came down in 1961. A year on from reunification, there were still units of young Russian soldiers parading in the parklands. It was rumoured their government couldn't afford to ship them home or feed them, so the locals were keeping them alive. Potsdam's main attraction is Sanssouci. No wonder; this relatively small palace, with its brilliant terrace gardens, is a masterpiece and might easily have been the location for my evening's opera. The Komische Oper is no more than a ten-minute walk from Friedrichstraße so from Otto and Pia's apartment I walked to the local station and took the S-Bahn. Friedrichstraße was one of the official Berlin Wall crossing points and as far as I could tell, most of the security barriers were still in place. It must have been a frightening place in its day.

The streets of East Berlin between the station and the opera house were deserted, grubby, drab and cold on a Sunday evening in November—no neon lights in this part of town. Fortunately, there were tickets on sale and the auditorium was warm, its lush baroque interior belying a dreary exterior. I had time to peruse the programme—no recognisable names. This was possibly an ensemble performance from the company that had been there before the wall came down. I never found out for sure but I have never had a better night at the opera. What a shame Gisa hadn't come, but she wasn't an opera buff.

By March 1991, the mood in Neutralysis, Brisbane, was tense. They had debts in excess of a million dollars, and bail-out talks with a large public company with quarrying interests and hence an interest in lightweight aggregate, were spluttering. I had carried on regardless in the UK where the prospect in Leicestershire was promising. The county council had identified a site near a quarry at Bardon Hill, and at their request I had given them a proposal for a 140 000-tonne-a-year plant on the site based on the Davy McKee generic design. At a meeting in September, they proposed taking the project to the next level by commissioning an independent £100,000 feasibility study from a top UK engineering consultant, such as WS Atkins or Ove Arup. Leicestershire County Council would contribute £50,000 towards the study, provided Neutralysis made up the difference.

Assembling a consortium willing to fund the study should have been a straightforward exercise, however, in May a story appeared in *The Sunday Telegraph* suggesting Davy McKee's parent company, Davy Corporation, was in dire financial straits. The project would go nowhere without access to the

Davy McKee generic 500-tonne-a-day plant design. The full story emerged in the weeks that followed.

In January 1989 Davy had contracted to convert *Ali Baba*, a semi-submersible drilling rig, into a production platform in eighteen months for the fixed price of £118 million. As one of the largest and oldest engineering contractors in the UK and one of its largest employers, it should have known better. Eighteen months would have been nigh impossible for an experienced offshore oil and gas contractor, and Davy certainly wasn't that. Its forte was onshore petrochemical and mining process plants. The office set up to produce the engineering design wasn't equipped or staffed until three months into the contract. In a foolhardy attempt to meet the schedule, it towed the rig into a dry dock in Dundee and went to work without engineering drawings. That made matters worse. It was a disaster, not just for Davy but for its client, Midland & Scottish Resources. In the event, the schedule overrun was twelve months, and the cost overrun was more than £100 million. The grand old company was forced into a fire sale and the last thing on their minds was a municipal-waste-management project in Leicestershire.

When sorrows come, they come not single spies, but in battalions.[27] Neutralysis went into receivership three months later. Winter was coming and the retainer that had been keeping me alive was no longer. I had to give up chasing rainbows, but with crude still below US$40 a barrel, getting back into the oil and gas industry was not going to be easy. I retreated to Yew Tree Cottage. Thursday was the main day for engineering recruitment advertising in *The Daily Telegraph*.

I polished my resume and sent countless applications for not one reply. Being forty-four didn't help. It was a sad irony. For years I had been the youngest in the room, trying to behave like a grown-up. Now I was trying to do the opposite.

By Christmas, I was struggling to pay the rent and deflecting threats from the landlord. To make matters worse, I was laid low by a chest infection. If nothing else, it meant I was at home when the phone rang a week into the new year. It was Mike Vassilopoulos. *Ipco is looking for a project engineer for a pipeline job in Indonesia. Could you come down to Singapore to talk about it? When? Tomorrow.*

Bontang Train F

Ipco employee numbers ebbed and flowed depending on the state of its projects so was good at mobilising people from anywhere at short notice. When I arrived at the Qantas desk at Heathrow the following evening, I was pleased to find there really was a ticket waiting for me. The thirteen-hour flight provided more than enough time for reflection. In 1972, I had flown to Singapore, sniffing the battle with delight. Eight years later, I was running a successful London-based engineering company employing fifty people. Twenty years later, I was broke and flying back to Singapore hoping for a job as a lowly project engineer. In 1972, I had checked into the Hotel Equatorial and now I was doing it again. Go to jail. Go directly to jail. Do not pass go. Do not collect $200.

On my arrival at Ipco's offices in Jurong next morning I was ushered into a conference room where I was introduced to, among others, Ray Hodgson, director of projects and George Klause, project manager. So far all I had been told was the project was a large pipeline in Indonesia. Ipco Marine was, as its name suggested, a marine engineering and construction company. This was what I knew. I was an offshore pipeline engineer. I had not entertained the idea this project could be anything else. Within minutes it became clear it *was* something else. It was a contract for the design, supply and installation of a fifty-seven kilometre, thirty-six-inch-diameter cross-country gas pipeline from Badak to Bontang in East Kalimantan, to be known as the Bontang Train F trunkline. Cross-country and submarine pipeline projects are chalk and cheese.

I interrupted Ray Hodgson's preliminary remarks and explained there had been a terrible mistake. They had my resume and must have known I had never been associated with a cross-country pipeline in my life. Silence. To Ray's credit, he just said to wait a minute and asked George Klause to leave the room with him. They were out for about ten minutes. I sat there anticipating a miserable return trip to London and the dismal prospects thereafter.

When they came back, Ray simply said, 'We don't have time to find anybody else. Do you want the job?' I didn't even ask what salary was on offer. In the event, it was reasonable—US$5,000 a month plus accommodation. Initially, I would be based in Jakarta. We spent the rest of the day discussing the contract, which was a major element of an expansion of the Bontang LNG plant. Since my first exploratory trip to that tiny fishing village in 1974, Pertamina had built two gas pipelines between the Mahakam Delta and Bontang, where they had built five LNG trains that were now producing and shipping 11.5 million tonnes of LNG a year to Japan. The new project would increase this to 13.8 million tonnes a year by installing a new pipeline and another LNG train. A joint venture between local contractor, PT Inti Karya Persada Tehnik (IKPT), and the Japanese Chiyoda Corporation had won the main contract. They had in turn awarded a US$27 million subcontract for the pipeline to the Kelsri-Ipco Joint Operation. PT Kelsri was another Indonesian contractor confirming the trend towards increased local participation in developments of this nature.

The pipeline subcontract included route survey and selection, design, procurement, construction, cleaning, hydro testing and drying. As project engineer, I would be reporting to the project manager and responsible for the design, including ancillary facilities such as pig launchers and receivers, mainline isolation valves, a pressure relief station, corrosion protection and monitoring and control instrumentation. It would be a steep learning curve, but first I had to return to Yew Tree Cottage to prepare for an extended absence. I did so with mixed feelings. Life in Quorn country had been good but Trent Eels had been a confidence-sapping disappointment. As relieved as I was about the new job, I was equally concerned I might cock it up again.

Sarah marked my last night in Yew Tree Cottage with one of her effortless dinner parties. Fittingly, she had invited Richard and Shelagh Morley and Nick and Helen Connors, two of my favourite Quorn couples. We didn't dwell on my imminent departure as the issue of the day, particularly in rural Leicestershire, was the future of hunting. Mrs Thatcher had resigned two years earlier and a general election was looming. The Labour leader, Neil Kinnock, was favoured to win and many in his party were clamouring for a ban on foxhunting. This wouldn't have been news had it not been for a hunt saboteur who, a month earlier, had successfully passed himself off as a loyal foot follower and filmed Quorn hunt servants digging up and shooting a hunted fox after it had unsportingly taken refuge in a badger burrow. YouTube was yet to be invented but the footage went viral anyway.

In the event, Mr Kinnock lost the unlosable election and hunting secured a temporary reprieve, but the writing was on the wall. *The Hunting Act 2004*, fuelled by political correctness, the evil of the new millennium, eventually emasculated a tradition that did nothing but good for all walks of English rural life. It wasn't apparent at the time but I had been fortunate enough to have enjoyed six years with the Quorn while it was still at its best.

There were more going away parties in London but my most important task before heading to Indonesia was to find out what I could do about the design of cross-country pipelines. I had joined the Institution of Civil Engineers in 1980 as a prerequisite to securing work from BP for Bligh Engineering. Having passed the examination, I hadn't returned despite its reputation for a world-class civil engineering library. I made up for lost time and found everything I needed in the second edition of the *Pipeline Rules of Thumb Handbook*. It is a compilation of expert contributions, including one from Bob Brown (from RJ Brown and Associates) from his time as a senior cross-country pipeline engineer with Bechtel. If my old mentor could transform himself from a cross-country to a submarine pipeliner, I could do the opposite. I borrowed it and, having read it on the flight to Jakarta, arrived an expert.

Inevitably, the Indonesian capital had changed in the eighteen years since my last visit when I was transferring from RJ Brown's Singapore office to the company's head office in The Hague. I had been travelling via Brisbane and Houston so took the opportunity for a Jakarta stopover to visit Inong Satibi and Rani Suwarto. There was now a new airport, tall buildings and more cars than motorcycles—more traffic jams too. The roads couldn't keep pace and that was on days when it wasn't raining. I had taken an early flight from Singapore so was in the Kelsri-Ipco Joint Operation offices in West Jakarta by mid-morning.

George Klause greeted me with a box of name cards adorned with the grand title 'Chief Project Engineer', a label better suited to a Gilbert and Sullivan farce. We spent the day going through the project schedule. As I was soon to find out, building a cross-country pipeline is just like building anything else. The engineering design produces the drawings that tell you what components and materials you need and how it all fits together. The schedule breaks the project into recognisable activities, each with a start and finish date and each identifying the resources required: components, materials, construction plant, manpower and engineering drawings. The most important activities in the schedule are those identified as critical path activities. A delay in a critical path activity is a delay to the overall schedule, almost certainly incurring cost overruns and penalties.

One of these was the pipeline route survey. This was being managed by Worley Engineering, Kelsri-Ipco's design subcontractor, and as it was a critical path activity, George wanted me to go over to Kalimantan on the first flight next day to review methodology and progress. Because the pipeline would be passing through a low swampy area just to the north of Badak, an important survey objective was to determine which sections would require weight coating or anchors to prevent them breaking out of their trenches during the wet season. I had known it would be a steep learning curve but didn't think it would be quite as steep as this. I spent the night in the President Hotel, just off the Hotel Indonesia roundabout. Predictably, route survey was one subject not covered by the *Pipeline Rules of Thumb Handbook*, so it was an early night.

As my flight circled Bontang airfield next morning I had a bird's eye view of the massive transformation that had taken place in that tiny fishing village since 1974. Bechtel had mobilised to build an LNG plant near Santan, twenty-three kilometres to the south. The site was unworkable. RJ Brown and Associates had been commissioned to find an alternative and after the original survey party chief pulled out, I had got the job. My report, completed three months later, identified Bontang as the new site and the rest is history. Bontang had prospered and I had gone broke. As we touched down, Joseph Conrad came to mind. Patusan had done nothing to revive Lord Jim's fortunes.[30] I hoped Bontang would do more for mine.

Ipco's site manager met me at the airport and we drove along the pipeline corridor towards Badak, sixty kilometres to the south. Just past the rusty monument marking the equator we ran into the surveyors. East Kalimantan is nothing if not tropical and you didn't have to be a week away from winter in the East Midlands to appreciate it. That survey crews manage to work in these conditions is a miracle, but they do.

The party chief turned out to be a Queenslander and after a few minutes with Jim Walsh, fluent in Bahasa Indonesia, I knew the survey wouldn't be a problem. He was working from the original Shell survey monuments I had used in 1974, but that's where the similarities ended. He was now using GPS-based equipment and software and, although I could only suspect it at the time, the improvements in accuracy and productivity, both in the field and afterwards in the drawing office, were profound.

The next stop was Marangkayu, a small village by the site secured for Kelsri-Ipco's 120-man construction camp. Marang is traditional Indonesian furniture timber stock. As the village name suggests, it had been a logging camp. According to folklore, the Japanese traders who used the village as a base in the aftermath of WW2 were not renowned for their sympathetic treatment of the locals. The problem went away when the traders were found in their beds in small pieces. It would have been so much easier to treat the natives and their machetes, *parang parang*, with common decency.

With just two months until work started on clearing and grading the pipeline corridor the camp was another critical path activity. In addition to accommodation, it would also provide a workshop with all the gear necessary to service the dozers, scrapers, rollers, graders, cranes and side booms needed for the work. The subcontract had been awarded but there was no sign of any activity, so having toured the swampy sections of the pipeline corridor to the south, I took a flight down to Balikpapan, where Charlie Chong, the subcontractor who was to build the camp, was based.

The photographs from the Battle of Balikpapan that had decorated the lounge bar in the Hotel Benakutai eighteen years earlier were still there. Two hundred and twenty-nine Australians were killed in the attack launched against the Japanese garrison on 1 July 1945. When the atomic bombs smashed Hiroshima and Nagasaki a month later, it seemed they had done so for naught, but Truman didn't take his fateful decision until three weeks after the landings whilst attending the Potsdam Conference. Nor have the locals forgotten the Diggers who put an end to the cruel Japanese occupation.

Not long after checking into the Benakutai and calling Charlie Chong, he arrived at the hotel to take me to dinner. We went to one of the many *rumah makan nasi padang* restaurants in Balikpapan. What could be a greater treat after eighteen years without the Indonesian answer to smorgasbord, only infinitely better? Charlie was an engaging character and after visiting his yard the following day I could see he was assembling all the materials and equipment needed for the camp and had a clear plan to complete its construction by the end of March. I was able to return to Jakarta reasonably confident we had no serious snags in Kalimantan.

It wasn't quite so rosy in Jakarta. Manufacture of the line pipe was and always will be the main concern for a pipeline project, and not just because it is always on the critical path. At US$15 million out of US$27 million, it was our largest item of expenditure by far. Ensuring the quality of each and every one of the 4750 twelve-metre-long joints was mandatory. One defect in one joint would compromise the entire line. To add a further degree of difficulty, burgeoning national pride had demanded the pipe and steel for the pipe be manufactured locally. It was a first and there were teething problems. It wasn't long before these problems became my problems.

A week after my return from Kalimantan, George Klause went back to the UK on home leave. It's never easy for families with a husband/father working abroad. Some manage it, others don't. Within days of leaving, George rang Ray Hodgson in Singapore to resign. It was a bolt from out of the blue. His departure from Jakarta had appeared routine, and for all I knew it was. He had left a few things in the office, so I can only assume his homecoming had not been happy. This left me in charge until a replacement could be found. Suddenly my primary focus was to expedite line pipe manufacture.

The only pipe mill in Indonesia capable of rolling thirty-six-inch-diameter welded steel line pipe to the American Petroleum Institute specification API 5L standard was the Krakatau Heavy Industries spiral-welded pipe mill outside Cilegon in West Java. The only steel mill capable of supplying the steel-coil raw material was Krakatau Steel, not far away in the same industrial estate. Steel is produced from iron ore in a furnace batching process by removing impurities, such as carbon, and adding alloying elements, such as nickel and chromium, to produce a product of the required strength, weldability and durability. The API testing regime for steel-coil manufacture includes chemical testing of molten steel samples from each batch. The primary objective of the chemical test is to ensure residual carbon is within its specified range. The early results from Krakatau Steel were patchy and the mill was forced to reprocess a worrying number of batches, leading to significant delays.

Wisely, Kelsri-Ipco had bid the project with support from an experienced Australian cross-country pipeline contractor, AJ Lucas. Their main role was to second lead-construction personnel to the project and Andy Lukas, their managing director, became a valuable project consultant. One of his specialists, Arthur James, was an experienced pipe mill inspector and within weeks of installing Arthur in the mill at Cilegon, the batch rejection rate had been reduced to an acceptable level.

Arthur was the first of around ten senior field personnel seconded to the project by AJ Lucas. A few, including Fred Rowbotham, were farmers from the Darling Downs, who had acquired their pipelining skills working on Australia's first gas pipeline from Roma to Brisbane, commissioned in 1969. Fred was our nominated construction superintendent. He arrived in late February and after spending a day with him in Jakarta before he went to the site, I knew I didn't have to worry too much about preparations for the start of construction in Kalimantan. Fred knew the other members of the AJ Lucas team and their capabilities so was ready to put them to work as soon as they arrived.

Much to my relief, Ipco found a replacement for George Klause within weeks. Having been a project manager on the Alyeska pipeline and the Channel Tunnel, Carl Strande came with rolled-gold credentials. He and Ray Hodgson arrived at Marangkayu towards the end of March. Charlie Chong was well on the way to finishing the construction camp and

I flew over to meet them. Andy Lukas from AJ Lucas was there as well. We spent two days touring the site, meeting the client and interviewing labour and plant hire contractors. We also spent a lot of time with the AJ Lucas crew. They had had time to settle into their various roles and it was good to see there was an immediate rapport with the new project manager, who simply said it was his job to get them whatever they needed to do the job. In between, we discussed what else needed to be done in Jakarta, apart from expediting the pipe manufacturing and coordinating its transport to site. The main items were engineering drawings and approvals, weekly progress reporting and bookkeeping. As I was leaving, Carl asked when I could close the office in Jakarta. End of June. After two months in the bosom of the Hotel Indonesia, I wasn't sure how I would enjoy a construction camp in the wilds of Kalimantan.

On April 1st, as planned but miraculously nevertheless, the big cats started clearing and grading a thirty-five-metre-wide working space along the entire pipeline route. It was the bare minimum required to accommodate the pipeline trench and the construction equipment required for trenching, welding and lowering in. The first pipe shipment from Cilegon arrived in Marangkayu three weeks later. This allowed the stringing crew to go to work placing single joints of line pipe, each approximately twelve metres in length, along the pipeline centreline. This in turn provided work for the bending engineer and his crew. Pipe strings, even thirty-six-inch-diameter pipe strings, are remarkably flexible. However, in tight situations certain joints need to be permanently bent to enable the pipeline to conform to the right of way alignment and profile. The bending engineer selects these joints and they are bent to measure on the spot by the bending machine, the largest and clumsiest gadget in a cross-country pipeline spread. Hard on the heels of the bending crew comes the all-important welding crew, welding individual joints into pipe strings. Each weld is X-rayed and any defects cut out and repaired.

Once cleared of weld and coating defects, the pipe string is lowered into the trench by a fleet of side booms and buried. We had eight side booms and provided there weren't too many bends, they could handle a string up to 400 metres long. In East Kalimantan, with the ever-present threat of rain, an open trench two metres deep was asking for trouble. So, trenching was only undertaken if its corresponding pipe string could be lowered in and backfilled before nightfall, leaving no more than a pit for the tie-in crew, whose job it was to weld the new string to its predecessor. When welding started in late April, progress was slow, made worse by an excessive repair rate, but by the end of May, Andy Lukas's welding specialists had turned that around and their team was making forty joints a day provided there were no interruptions. Rain was the main culprit, but there were others. On one occasion in June, work stopped for a day when a crowd of angry locals, some brandishing machetes, occupied the site complaining compensation promised by Pertamina hadn't been paid. It was the usual story. Pertamina *had* paid but had given it to the village chief, who had done a runner.

By the end of June most of the engineering issues had

been resolved, including the design of the restraints required to stabilise the pipeline in the swampy area to the north of Badak. The topographical survey had identified the extent of the area and soil sampling had provided the data required for an analysis performed by RJ Brown and Associates. They had recommended concrete saddle weights be placed over the pipeline in the trench before burial. We asked Charlie Chong to manufacture the weights and he agreed to set up a casting yard onsite on the basis we provide the cement, sand and gravel, since it wasn't available in Kalimantan. It would have to come from Sulawesi and we would have to talk to Mrs Yurike Sanger, who had a Sulawesi sand and gravel export licence.

Ibu Yurike had been President Soekarno's wife in the twilight of the founding father's reign. This was presumably why she had the licence. Rent seeking is a national sport in Indonesia but I was curious to meet her, nevertheless. I shouldn't have been concerned as I was soon to discover she was an effective operator. I called her at her offices and she invited me to dinner at the formal restaurant in General Ibnu Sutowo's Jakarta Hilton. She would have known him well. She was punctual, beautifully dressed, fluent in English and accompanied by her second husband, a retired academic. And she knew her business. Her sand and gravel were dredged from the Palu River, three barge days to the east of Marangkayu across the Makassar Strait, and she sourced her cement from Semen Tonasa, who quarried the pure limestone formations to the east of Makassar to provide feedstock for their cement kilns. She offered cement packed in sacks on pallets for US$98 a tonne, bulk sand for US$22 a cubic metre and bulk three-quarter-inch aggregate for US$18 a cubic metre, all CIF Marangkayu, specifications to be provided next day. These prices were well inside our budget, but I had to be sure she would be a reliable supplier. I was expecting her to suggest I head off to Sulawesi with one of her lackeys, but no way. She would accompany me to the quarry in Palu and the cement plant in Tonasa as soon as I was available.

It wasn't possible to go immediately as there were still teething problems at Marangkayu with the supply of spare parts and construction consumables, such as welding rods and cutting discs. I soon became familiar with Jakarta's Chinatown, Glodok, just to the south of Tanjung Priok, where you could buy anything from a carton of Augmentin to a spare motor for a Caterpillar D9. Even so, Indonesian Customs still made shipping from Jakarta to Marangkayu a nightmare. A project like Bontang Train F was a ticket to ride for Indonesian Customs officers. The solution was Ibu Treesye, a freight-forwarding agent whose father was a senior officer in the Indonesian Airforce. She became our air cargo service between Jakarta and Balikpapan, and Customs stayed well away. On a couple of occasions, she even brought in equipment from Singapore.

With supply chain problems improved, I turned my attention to Sulawesi. By now it was mid-July so time was running short. I met Ibu Yurike at Soekarno Hatta and we flew to Palu via Makassar, arriving mid-afternoon. Palu is a small city at the mouth of the Palu River, which drains into Teluk Palu, a narrow thirty-five-kilometre-long inlet leading to the Makassar Strait. This meant there was ready access from the rich freshwater sand and gravel deposits to every port in the Indonesian Archipelago. We went to the depot where they were loading 200-foot transport barges ideal for the trip to Marangkayu, if necessary. The operation could have been better, but so can gravel pits anywhere. Few would have enjoyed more spectacular views—as did the open-air fish restaurant we visited later on. The patron made a great fuss over Ibu Yurike, who was clearly no stranger.

We returned to Makassar early next morning and drove to the Tonasa cement factory directly from the airport. In doing so, we drove through the distinctive karst formations, the Gothic landscape betraying the presence of limestone to even the most junior geologist. Limestone is an essential ingredient in the manufacture of cement and Semen Tonasa was systematically removing all traces of these eerie outcrops. But they were making cement and that was what I was there for. We toured the impressive works with their vast coal-fired clinker kilns and drove back to town to meet Hajj Rasyid, the Bugis who would be shipping our cement, sand and gravel to Marangkayu.

The bogey man of childhood dreams really wasn't a bogey man; he was a Bugis man, and he was from Makassar. The Bugis were adventurous pirates and traders who roamed the seas from Shanghai to Dubai way before Marco Polo discovered the Silk Road. Makassar is 800 miles north-west of Darwin and roughly the same size as Brisbane. Because Makassar has always been a free port, even under Portuguese and Dutch rule, it has prospered. In the colonial era it was famous for its spices, such as nutmeg, cloves and mace. These days its exports, apart from nickel, are less exotic—seed oils, seafood, cocoa and coffee, and Hajj Rasyid was in it up to his eyeballs. He was a real Bugis trader and the crews of his tiny vessels could sail the Indonesian Archipelago blindfolded and were equally as familiar with the Red Sea and the Persian Gulf.

His English was passable so when I told him I had been to Saudi Arabia many times but not to Mecca he just laughed and told me about the pilgrimage that had earned him the status of Hajj. He said it would have been a lot easier if he hadn't taken three wives. Ibu Yurike decided it was time to change the subject and explained the purpose of our visit. He responded saying he had just taken delivery of a new Bugis Phinisi boat from East Kalimantan and his men knew the coast well. He assured me there would be no problem delivering our cargo to Marankayu. His new pride and joy was tied up nearby in Pelabuhan Paotere, Makassar's small boat harbor. Would we like to see it? Of course.

Thirty minutes later we were clambering aboard his modern manifestation of an ancient masterpiece. The traditional Bugis pinisi had a main mast forward and a mizzen to the rear and was built from ironwood felled in South Sulawesi. Timber shortages forced the industry to move to East Kalimantan in the 1960s, and around the same time the mizzen mast was replaced by a diesel engine. The latest edition to Hajj Rasyid's fleet was just over thirty-five metres long and ten metres wide, had a 330-horsepower Yanmar diesel engine and had cost US$150,000.

I had seen enough. I was confident Ibu Yurike could source the concrete raw materials we needed and ship them to Marangkayu. I left her in Makassar and flew over to Balikpapan for another session with Charlie Chong to make sure there were no loose strings. A visit to his depot confirmed he had already fabricated half a dozen saddle weight moulds and was assembling the equipment needed for the casting yard to be established just to the north of Badak.

Next stop Marangkayu. Carl Strande was more or less relaxed. The last load of line pipe from Cilegon had been unloaded, most of it had been strung along the right of way and he had just over thirty-five kilometres of pipe in the ground, with twenty-two kilometres to go. More importantly, as far as I was concerned, ninety-five per cent of the engineering drawings, specifications and construction procedures were either approved or submitted for approval. He had been talking to Ray Hodgson, who wanted me to return to Singapore to assist with a tender for an offshore pipeline in Nigeria. It was the end of July. He gave me a month to transfer the engineering and the accounts from Jakarta to Marangkayu.

By the time I flew to Singapore on September 2nd we had installed nearly fifty kilometres of the fifty-seven-kilometre pipeline and had started work on the tie-ins at Badak and Bontang. I regretted leaving the project before it was finished but had learned a lot and, more importantly, salvaged my confidence. It had also kindled a great love of Indonesia, despite its obvious flaws. But I was keen to go to work on the Nigerian tender too. It involved the installation of a pipeline in the Bonny River for Shell Nigeria. Ipco had located an eighty-five-metre-long flat-top barge and asked me to use it as the basis for the design of a bespoke shallow-water lay barge. This was a project where I could be teacher rather than pupil.

After having been in Singapore for a few days, I met Saeed Khan for lunch. He was agitated. His engineering manager and his office manager had resigned in April and, with backing from an offshore construction company, established a new company, OGI, to compete with RJBA. Saeed had replaced the engineering manager but earlier that very morning, just as things were settling down, his trusted business development manager and colleague had walked in, resigned, cleared his desk and walked out again. The whole thing had clearly been a shabby conspiracy, as the erstwhile business development manager had clearly spent five months working on behalf of OGI while on the RJBA payroll. Saeed wasn't so much angry as sad. He thought they had been friends; he had helped with school fees; he had been betrayed. Then came the eureka moment. Hey Dave, what are you doing? Why don't you come back as business development manager?

My tenure with Ipco was anything but secure and more than likely depended on the success of the Bonny River pipeline tender. And I wasn't sure I wanted to go to Nigeria, where any movement outside secure camps required an armed escort who was paid next to nothing. On the terms of my contract with Ipco I had to give a week's notice, so to use one of Saeed's favourite expressions, I simply said, 'What's the deal?' US$7,000 a month, after tax. Saeed had clearly been rocked by the OGI defections. It was a generous offer. I was enjoying Singapore with its privileged lifestyle for expats, so I accepted on the basis I work out my notice with Ipco and return to England for two weeks to vacate Yew Tree Cottage.

The newspapers offered on the flight back to London were awash with Black Wednesday stories. In essence, George Soros made a billion pounds selling the pound short; the Chancellor of the Exchequer, Norman Lamont, was forced to withdraw Britain from the European Exchange Rate Mechanism, interest rates soared and property values plunged. It was 17 September 1992.

Eleven years, six months and seven days after Joop Veltman had called to say Bligh Engineering had a tax problem in Saudi Arabia, my luck had changed. Perhaps I could even get back into the London property market.

Singapore Again

If I were to return to the London property market, I wanted to be in Holland Park. I had loved my old flat, with its high ceilings and shuttered sash windows and had kicked myself more than once for selling it. Having cleared immigration at Heathrow, I caught a black cab and headed straight for Marsh & Parsons in Holland Park Avenue. They were the go-to agents in the area and their office was across the street from the old flat. It was opening as I arrived and there were no other customers, so I was able to sit down with an agent and explain what I was looking for. I had saved most of the £20,000 I had earned in Indonesia. With any luck, I could secure a mortgage for £115,000 and buy something for around £135,000. There was nothing suitable at that level in Holland Park or Notting Hill, but there was a three-bedroom flat in a mansion block in West Kensington off the North End Road, listed for £140,000, that looked interesting. Would I like to inspect it? It won't hurt to look.

The owner was away but the mansion block came with a porter who could let us in, so we were there in minutes. I had been up and down the North End Road on countless occasions and for me it was more a littered and dusty thoroughfare than a destination. So I was pleasantly surprised to discover one of its branches, Fitzjames Avenue, was an estate populated by nothing but red-brick mansion blocks untouched by the Luftwaffe, forged iron fences, manicured gardens and plane trees aplenty. But the flat was the thing—living room, dining room, anteroom, kitchen, three bedrooms, a bathroom, high ceilings and a fireplace, all in 1700 square feet and 500 metres from the West Kensington Tube station. It was almost too good to be true and so was the letter that arrived three days later. The vendor had accepted my offer of £135,000, subject to contract. I had promised Saeed I would be back in Singapore on October 5th. I had two weeks to make it all happen.

The number one priority was to secure the mortgage. I was concerned my offshore employment would be a problem. My solicitor, Christopher Heal, had the man, Quentin, from Pinks and Co. Don't you worry about that Mr Wilson, everything will be fine. Then there were the letting agents. If I were to secure top dollar, the flat would need a coat of paint and curtains. Peter and Claire Stratton had some investment properties and Claire was managing them. She would be very happy to manage mine as well. Neither of us knew what she was letting herself in for.

Back in Thrumpton it was as if I had never been away, but if I was to be in Singapore for the foreseeable future and Sarah was only there odd weekends, there was no point keeping Yew Tree Cottage. Apart from that the owner, George Seymour, sensed he could extract more rent from new tenants so was keen for us to leave. My last days at the cottage were predictably social and included a day's cub hunting. Shelagh

Morley had a new grey called Jumbo. Would I like to take him to the meet at Great Dalby? I would love to, thank you very much. Of course, I couldn't have known at the time, but after twelve seasons through the eighties and into the nineties, it was to be my last day. Robert Browning said (when I die), *Open my heart and you will see/ Grav'd inside of it, 'Italy.'*[29] For me, it will be the thrill of a huntsman blowing 'gone away'.

Two weeks later, I was 'gone away' and settling down to a return match in Singapore. RJBA was now a far cry from the small band I had left behind when I transferred to The Hague in 1974. It was now closer to a hundred people and outgrowing its offices on the West Coast Highway. Feeding the hungry beast was now my problem and maintaining the status quo required around 130 000 engineering manhours a year. It was a job where you had to kiss a lot of frogs to meet a handsome prince. The territory covered the sixteen or so maritime countries between Muscat and Shanghai, and in the next two and a half years I flew nearly 400 000 kilometres. Fortunately, I was able to make an early contribution.

It was a typically Indonesian story. In 1985, American oil and gas middleweight Atlantic Richfield (Arco) found a substantial gas reservoir in the waters off Pagerungan Island in the Java Sea, just to the north of Bali. To assist with the development, it farmed in BP for a forty per cent interest and then, in an unprecedented act of corporate altruism, opened its arms to include Bimantara, a local company controlled by President Suharto's middle son, Bambang, for ten per cent. The surprises didn't stop there. Much to the alarm of the major shareholders, PT Trans Javagas Pipeline (TJGP), a special-purpose company formed by Bimantara and hitherto unknown Indonesian construction company PT Tranaco won the concession to build, own and operate the 430-kilometre pipeline required to transport the gas from Pagerungan Island to buyers in the Surabaya area.

TJGP awarded an EPC (engineer, procure, construct) contract to Nippon Steel for the 430-kilometre twenty-eight-inch-diameter pipeline on condition that it in turn awarded a subcontract to Tranaco for the construction of the 70-kilometre cross-country portion of the pipeline from Porong to Surabaya. I had learned enough on the Bontang Train F pipeline to know this subcontract would be a handful for even the most experienced contractor. There was a long tidal zone to cross at the Porong end; there were dozens of major road and river crossings; it would have to be drilled under numerous villages; and at the Surabaya end, there was an urban zone where much of the welding would have to be done in the trench rather than above ground.

TJGP had retained RJBA to provide a team to monitor Nippon Steel's pipeline design, procurement and construction, so Saeed Khan knew all this. He suggested I go to Jakarta to talk to Tranaco's president, director and major shareholder, Joseph Dharmabrata, to see what we could do to help. I had spent a lot of time in Indonesia and thought I had seen everything, but this was a new departure. Tranaco didn't have one employee with pipeline construction experience nor one item of pipeline construction equipment, and the job had to be completed in ten months.

It's amazing how things fall into place when your luck has

changed. The Bontang Train F pipeline had been completed and Ipco was demobilising its construction management team. By mid-November they were on the RJBA payroll and seconded to Tranaco. The construction equipment shortage was resolved in an equally serendipitous manner. We heard Red Ru, the legendary South-East Queensland pipeline contractor, had retired. His entire pipeline spread was for sale and available for inspection in his depot in Oakey. Joseph Dharmabrata's partner, Anton Tjahjono, was there within days and bought five side booms and a bending machine and shipped them to Surabaya. Tranaco was at work clearing the right of way for the onshore pipeline outside Porong by the end of November.

Another pressing matter on my return to Singapore was to find somewhere to live. My stopgap was The Tanglin Club. Its tennis courts and swimming pool were good for my health but not so the bar and restaurants. Eventually, I leased a flat not too far away in Robin Road, and having received my bed, some pictures and a dinner service from Yew Tree Cottage and engaged a competent Filipino *amah*, I settled happily into expat life.

One of the pictures was a portrait Stuart Wood had removed from a mansion block he was refurbishing in London's Portland Place. He had bought the property from the deceased estate of a well-known Jewish businessman and arrived one morning to find his works foreman alone. *I'm terribly sorry Mr Wood, but the men reckon that the picture of Mr Green is haunting the place and won't come back until it's gone.* It was a life-sized raw pastel head and shoulders of an imposing figure wearing a black homburg and signed Pinchas Litvinovsky in Yiddish. Woody moved it to his flat in Stanhope Mews but a few days later Nicky, his new wife, sensed the ghost as well and declared the portrait had to go or she would. Without more ado, he took it to his office in Mount Street. I happened to pass by a few days later and having dropped in to say hello, was admiring the haunted heirloom propped up against a wall. Woody recounted the story. *Do you like it, Willy? I certainly do. Then please take it, it's yours.*

Eight years later, and after a brief interlude in Yew Tree Cottage, the portrait had found a new home in Singapore. I had struck up a friendship with a lively group of cigarette traders and Israeli ex-air force pilots whose regular Friday night haunt was The Elvis Bar in Tanjong Pagar. One night I invited them round to Robin Road for cocktails. After arriving and spotting the portrait, Ilan, one of the Israeli pilots became agitated, possibly sensing some sinister plot. Or perhaps he felt a ghostly presence. *David, how is it you have a portrait of our first president? What are you talking about? This is a portrait of Chaim Weizmann, our first president.* No, I said, *it's Mr Green, a Jewish businessman who died ten years ago and haunted his mansion block.*

Days later, I was able to find a photograph of Chaim Weizmann and so had to ring Ilan to apologise. One can only surmise Mr Green was a supporter of Weizmann's Zionist movement in the days leading up to the Balfour Declaration and had hung the portrait in his building's foyer in Portland Place. But why is the ghost of Chaim Weizmann still on the prowl?

Four months after my offer for 12A Fitzjames Avenue had

been accepted, the transaction was eventually completed on January 29th. I had a mortgage of £114,750, with annual repayments of £10,300. I needed a tenant. Fortunately, Claire Stratton was on the job and within weeks her team of painters, plumbers, curtain makers, floor polishers and cleaners had made the improvements requested by the letting agents. This work was funded by the sale of 24 Douglas Street in Mooloolaba, which made AU$147,000. I had paid AU$55,000 for it in 1981. The first tenant moved in to Fitzjames on May 8th, providing an annual rental income of £23,400. Mr Micawber would have been delighted.[31]

Drumming up engineering work can be tiresome, but once in a blue moon it walks through the door. Having a reputation helps and RJBA certainly had that. Trans Java was going well and I had turned my mind to other prospects when our receptionist put a call through from the general manager of Kingsleigh Petroleum in Hong Kong. This was not a name that decorated the oil and gas pantheon but Mr Ng would be in Singapore next week and would like to talk to us. No problem.

It was an interesting story, starting with Richard Nixon's visit to China in 1972 and the 'open door' policy that followed. By 1992, Chinese industry and trade had been transformed to the extent China was importing rather than exporting crude oil. Middle East crude shipped in VLCCs (very large crude carriers, between 150 000 and 275 000 deadweight tonnes) was the cheapest source, but the only refinery that could process Arabian heavy crude was the Maoming Refinery in Guangdong Province, and it didn't have a suitable port.

In the four years since its formation as a trader, Kingsleigh Petroleum had become one of the leading independent suppliers of crude oil to the Maoming Refinery, to the extent that Kingsleigh and Maoming had agreed to form Fortune Oil PLC to install and operate a single point mooring capable of handling the largest VLCC. The money required for the venture was to be raised on the London Stock Exchange and although Fortune Oil was a name designed to warm the hearts of all but the most cynical investors, Shaw & Co, the issue sponsors and stockbrokers, had insisted an independent enterprise evaluation be included in the prospectus. Mr Ng wondered if RJBA was qualified to undertake the appraisal. Is a blue bird blue? RJBA had been involved in twenty-three SPMs, including the Botany Bay and Pulau Bukom projects, in which I had been involved. We agreed a generous fee and a letter summarising our findings was included in the prospectus issued three months later. It raised £9 million and Fortune Oil PLC was the first Chinese company listed on the London Stock Exchange.

By the end of June, the RJBA construction management team seconded to Tranaco had settled in well and fifty-two kilometres of the seventy-kilometre onshore section of the Trans Java Gas pipeline had been installed. It was eventually commissioned in August 1993 and is still feeding the power stations that keep the lights on in East Java.

In the meantime, I was chasing work in Malaysia, India, Thailand and Myanmar and getting nowhere. Just as I began to think my luck had turned sour again, I took a trip to Manila to visit the Asian Development Bank (ADB). The

ADB is traditionally focused on civil infrastructure, such as ports, roads, rail, water, power generation and transmission, so it wasn't a typical RJBA client. However, it had taken an interest in an offshore gas field known as Ping Hu, about 420 kilometres south-east of Shanghai, and this was a real prospect. It operated a complicated contractor and consultant database and my objective was to make sure RJBA was properly enrolled in their system. Since the Vietnamese had discovered a new gas field called Bach Ho in the Mekong Delta, I planned a stopover in Ho Chi Minh City on my return.

The Americans endowed the Philippines with poverty and guns. The poverty fills every nook and cranny between Manila's palatial landmarks, such as the Hotel Edsa Plaza and the ADB campus. These are secured by burly liveried guards bristling with firearms and outside banks these include sawn-off shotguns. Best to be somewhere else when they get nervous. Then there is the problem of getting from one palatial landmark to the next. Manila's traffic jams make Bangkok look good. To be sure of making my 8 am Monday meeting I had taken a Sunday afternoon flight and stayed at the Edsa Plaza, a fifteen-minute walk from the ADB. My meetings there were businesslike but nothing more. I was able to enrol RJBA in their consultant database and it was suggested next time I was in Beijing I talk to CNOOC (China National Offshore Oil Corporation) about Ping Hu. I added the Philippines to my expanding list of wasted journeys.

On to Ho Chi Minh City and an eerie feeling calling to mind my university student view of the war and the associated fear of conscription. Would it be anything like

The Deer Hunter? Probably not since that was more a film about America. I wondered what the Vietnamese reaction to Australians would be. In the event, it was friendly. Apart from the Bach Ho gas field, the only thing I knew about Vietnam's oil and gas landscape was BHP Petroleum had a much larger field called Dai Hung. It wasn't difficult to find their offices just a stone's throw from the Century Saigon Hotel where I was staying. The general manager there was a friend of a colleague and invited me in for tea. Dai Hung was well underway so there was nothing to do for BHP, but he suggested if I were interested in Bach Ho I should go down to Vung Tau and talk to Vietsovpetro and PetroVietnam.

Vietsovpetro, a Russian-managed joint Vietnamese-Russian company, had discovered the field and had installed a drilling/production platform. It was producing around 200 000 barrels a day of crude oil and thirty-five MMscfd gas. The degassed crude was being stored in and exported from a tanker tethered nearby. The separated gas was being flared—very sixties and typically Russian. As I left the receptionist was kind enough to write down the addresses in English and Vietnamese.

Vung Tau is two hours south of Saigon by car. I decided to go early next morning. The hotel arranged a limousine with a driver who could speak some English. He didn't take long to put it to good use. We pulled into a service station to fill up for the journey and he asked me to pay. I was very soon to learn US dollars were the preferred currency and if you didn't have the right change the excess inevitably came back in cigarettes, sweets or dong, which would have been worthless if it weren't etched with a fine portrait of the great liberator.

Vung Tau was reasonably small compared to Ho Chi Minh City so it didn't take us long to find Vietsovpetro. The first clue was a fabrication yard looking more like a scrapyard (never go to sea in a Russian submarine). Their offices were next door. It was my first encounter with citizens of the evil empire. They may not have been able to cut, roll or weld steel but they seemed reasonably hospitable. Perhaps they just wanted someone to talk to. The Russians had hoped for great things in Vietnam following the American withdrawal in 1975. However, most of it had come to naught since they had no money and no business sense. Business is not in the Soviet psyche. I came to understand this on the train from Vladivostok to St Petersburg ten years later. Like Australia, they are good at farming and mining, but that's where it ends. As far as business is concerned, they could be another Central African republic. That's probably why they flared the gas. Anyway, they were good enough to tell me PetroVietnam was handling the project and suggested I talk to Mr Le Huu Lap, manager of gas processing.

PetroVietnam was not so easy to find since they had moved into what appeared to be an abandoned school just outside town on the way back to Ho Chi Minh City. It was hard work but I eventually found Mr Le, who had enough clout to set up a meeting attended by three of his colleagues, including Deputy Director Tran Van Thuc from the Bach Ho project. I had explained to Mr Le I suspected Bach Ho was not dissimilar to the Trans Java Gas project, so I was invited to outline TJGP and RJBA's role in it. Tran responded by outlining PetroVietnam's plan for Bach Ho. They intended to install a 125-kilometre sixteen-inch-diameter pipeline to bring the gas ashore and to use it to fire a 200-megawatt power station to be built at Ba Ria, just outside Vung Tau. The preliminary engineering had been prepared by the Canadian engineering group, SNC Lavalin, and enquiries for turnkey contracts had been issued to the usual suspects, including McDermott, Saipem, Nippon Steel, Bouygues Offshore and HHI, with bids due mid-October.

If PetroVietnam had decided to award turnkey contracts, then there was nothing in the project for RJBA unless we could align ourselves with the successful tenderer. It seemed inconceivable with less than two months to run to the bid due date there would be a contractor without a locked-in engineering partner, but everything is possible so I couldn't get back to Singapore fast enough to discuss our options with Saeed Khan. We agreed HHI was probably our best bet. Saeed knew HHI well and so did I. At CanOcean I had been responsible for the design of the firing line and stinger for their *HC-39* lay barge, and RJBA had designed a stinger for HHI's latest lay barge conversion, *HD-2500*. I called YD Kim. Fortunately, he was in Seoul. *No, we don't have an engineering partner for the project and we would be happy for RJBA to join us on a mutually exclusive basis. By the way, there will be a pre-bid meeting in Hanoi at the end of September. Will you be able to join our team there? Of course.*

Having issued invitations to tender, project proponents often invited tenderers to such a meeting where potential bidders were encouraged to raise questions they might have about the work scope, schedule or the proposed contract terms and conditions. If nothing else, it gave rival contractors an opportunity to enjoy a few beers together.

My earlier visit to Ho Chi Minh City did nothing to alleviate my misgivings about visiting Hanoi. Twenty years on from the Vietnam War, vision from the cynical raids that had smashed the city and its stoic citizens was still in my mind. As far as I knew, Australians hadn't been involved in bombing Hanoi but we did go 'All the way with LBJ', and Richard Nixon was no Jimmy Doolittle. But I had underestimated the Vietnamese. After so many years, there was no sign of the devastation, and as far as I could tell, Hanoi was as beautiful as it had ever been. Indeed, at night as I walked down the tree-line boulevard outside the Hotel Metropole, I might have been in Paris.

PetroVietnam was keen for foreign contractors to maximise local content in their bids and to that end, YD Kim had asked me to rendezvous with the HHI marketing team well in advance of the pre-bid meeting to give us a chance to talk to local suppliers. The senior man in the HHI team was Dr Jo 'Joe', and over the following days we got along well. There wasn't much scope for local content in the offshore pipeline but the eighteen-kilometre onshore section offered opportunities and, with that in mind, we talked to two state-owned companies who had services to offer, particularly in the manpower supply area. All the contractors on the formal bid list were present at the meeting, including McDermott, represented by George T Stapleton II, who I had last seen in Safaniya in 1977. I asked him how he could possibly bid while there was a US embargo on trade with Vietnam. George shrugged it off and the sanctions were removed six months later. As I have always said, time and trade are the greatest elixirs. They worked for Dad and the Japanese. Perhaps it would work for the Vietnamese and the Americans.

PetroVietnam had engaged a team from John Brown Engineers & Constructors Ltd in London to advise their project management team. They ran the pre-bid meeting in English. There were no surprises and one clarification. The Mekong Delta was not just a rich oil and gas province; it was an important fishery. In order to reduce potential damage to fishing nets, the scope of work had called for the pipeline to be installed in a trench of unspecified depth. This was now set at a metre.

Following the meeting, the HHI team needed to assess the impact, if any, of the announcements on their estimate. I was asked to join their meeting and was flattered when invited to review the detail of their calculations. One item that drew my attention was a provisional sum of $5 million for trenching. It looked high to me, so I asked how the number had been generated. It was an estimate from a specialist contractor intending to mobilise a spread from Europe if awarded the job. I suggested RJBA could design and build a reusable submarine pipeline plough for this and future jobs for less. *Please provide details Mr David. Certainly, Dr Jo. Give me a few days back in Singapore.*

On my return, I was delighted to discover Bob Brown and his wife Caroline were in Singapore for a few days. There was a big announcement. RJBA had been sold to Norwegian industrial conglomerate, Kvaerner, and its new name would be Kvaerner RJ Brown (KRJB). Kvaerner, involved in pulp and paper, shipbuilding and hydropower, had risen to prominence in 1966 when the Norwegian sector of the North Sea took off and it added oil and gas development to its portfolio. It remained a local player until 1990, when Eric Tonseth took the helm and embarked on a massive expansion plan, including the RJBA takeover. Bob, now sixty-five years old, would remain with the company as a consultant to KRJB in Houston. I hadn't seen him since leaving RJBA in The Hague in 1975. In the meantime, he had pioneered the design and operation of submarine pipeline trenching ploughs, so his arrival in Singapore at this precise moment was an extraordinary coincidence and more than serendipitous for two reasons. If he hadn't been there, I'm not so sure Saeed Khan would have been too enthusiastic about the plough, since the geotechnical data along the 107-kilometre offshore pipeline route was sketchy and we had no plough design experience in the Singapore office.

Well, we did now, as Bob Brown was prepared to help. He rolled up his sleeves and immediately went to work with a small team of designers. To make up for the lack of geotechnical data and for the purposes of the tender, he opted to make the plough as heavy as possible. It was effectively a scaled-up version of the most rudimentary nineteenth century single-furrow horse-drawn plough, with the horses replaced by salvage tugs and the ploughman replaced by a dynamically positioned tender vessel. The plough variables, such as tine angle and angle of attack, would be hydraulically controlled and the tender vessel would monitor and control the hydraulics via an umbilical. When necessary, the tender vessel had to be able to lift the plough on and off the pipeline. One suitable vessel potentially available for the job was Swire Pacific Offshore's diver support vessel (DSV), *Pacific Constructor*. She could lift 200 tonnes, so for bidding purposes it was decided to opt for a plough of this weight. It was massive, approximately twenty-five metres long, six metres wide and six metres high. Within days, the team had prepared a drawing of sufficient detail to send to a Bataam Island fabricator 'for estimating purposes only'. They came back at just over US$1 million. The hydraulics and controls would add another US$500k, so we offered it to HHI for just under US$2 million, FOB Bataam Island. If they liked the idea, the rest would be up to them.

The tenders were submitted on October 15th. Before long, the bush telegraph had crowned HHI the winner. This was confirmed a week later when they were invited back to Hanoi for clarifications. They asked me to accompany them, so I flew up early in November. Tran Van Thuc was still PetroVietnam's team leader. He had introduced me to the project on my first day in Vung Tau and a month later, during the pre-bid meeting in Hanoi, had warned me of the risk of landmines in the onshore pipeline corridor between Long Hai and Ba Ria. He greeted me as a long-lost friend. *You are a lucky man Mr David. You were last man here, but you won.* That was indeed the case.

One of the important resolutions of the meeting, as far

as I was concerned, was confirmation the pipeline design office would be KRJB in Singapore. HHI's nominated project manager, DK Kim, requested a quote to provide furnished and fully equipped offices for the HHI design liaison team and the PetroVietnam/John Brown project management team. Fortunately, KRJB had just moved from the West Coast Highway to a bigger office in the Singapore Science Park, so accommodating the visitors for three months would be no problem.

PetroVietnam and HHI signed the contract mid-January. This was the trigger for KRJB to go to work on both the pipeline and plough designs. Fabrication and assembly of the plough on Bataam Island commenced in the first week of June and HHI's derrick lay barge, *HD-2500*, began laying the 107-kilometre offshore portion of the pipeline shortly thereafter. The eighteen-kilometre onshore section between Long Hai and Ba Ria was installed by a local subcontractor and both on and offshore sections were completed by the end of August. Everything was going well. All that remained was the trenching and a hydro test of the entire pipeline from Bach Ho to Ba Ria.

The plough and its tender, *Pacific Constructor*, arrived off Long Hai just as *HD-2500* was completing the installation of the thermal expansion loop and riser at the Bach Ho Platform. The first problem arose when the tender couldn't lift the plough off its cargo barge. It might have done so in millpond conditions but not in a three-metre swell that wouldn't go away. The solution was to use *HD-2500*, with its 2500-tonne Clyde crane, necessitating an expensive deployment back to Long Hai.

The problems didn't stop there. The plan was to use *HD-2500*'s anchor-handling tugs to pull the plough, but the geotechnical investigations had completely underestimated the extent of the limestone outcrops encountered along the pipeline route. The anchor-handling tugs couldn't handle limestone, so the job came to a standstill while HHI mobilised salvage tugs from Singapore. These behemoths did the job but severely dented HHI's bottom line. But there's more, *When sorrows come, they come not single spies, but in battalions.*[27]

It will be remembered that throughout this period the Bach Ho platform operator, Vietsovpetro, was producing crude oil for export via a moored storage tanker and flaring the gas that the new pipeline would eventually take to Ba Ria. As the plough was making its tortuous journey towards the platform, unbeknown to either PetroVietnam or HHI, a Vietsovpetro work barge moored alongside it for routine maintenance activities. Unfortunately, as it was leaving, one of its anchors snagged the new pipeline expansion loop, rupturing it as it dragged it 200 feet from the seabed to the surface. For whatever reason, perhaps the prospect of a long holiday in Siberia, the Russian barge superintendent panicked, cut the anchor loose and ran, instructing the crew to say nothing.

HHI first discovered something was wrong when, having finished the trenching and flooding of the pipeline for the hydro test, they couldn't pressurise it. There was obviously a leak and quite a big one. They soon found it and the anchor that had caused it. HHI swore black and blue somebody else had done it, but PetroVietnam would have none of it and instructed them to make the necessary repairs. Fortunately, somebody had the wit to take the anchor serial number and it was traced back to Vietsovpetro. As a result, HHI had a valid insurance claim. A specialist subsea diving company was appointed to make the necessary hyperbaric repair. It took six months and cost six million US dollars. Happily, twenty-five years on and well beyond the pipeline's twenty-year design life, the Ba Ria Power Station is alive and well and still running on Bach Ho gas.

Following the Bach Ho contract award, I resumed my pursuit of new work. Being part of the Kvaerner group had become a mixed blessing rather than the promised godsend. One of our new sister companies, Kvaerner Earl & Wright, had been a household name in the structural engineering field and this gave us an important new dimension. On the other hand, Kvaerner had offices in India, Malaysia and China and from time to time there were overlapping interests. Certainly, in 1994 I chalked up an impressive tally of air miles for little or no reward. Initially, there was no pressure, as Bach Ho was keeping us busy.

It was time for something new. Saeed had sagely introduced a young engineer from CNOOC into the office as an intern. An Weije spoke passable English and was familiar with the Ping Hu project. He suggested I go to Shanghai to talk to both Shanghai Petroleum Corporation (SPC) and CNOOC and was instrumental in making the necessary arrangements. Meetings were arranged in Shanghai and Beijing and I left for Shanghai on a Singapore Airlines flight mid-March.

On boarding the flight and having arrived back from a skiing holiday in Switzerland the day before, I was happy to find an empty row of four seats towards the rear. I had hoped to stretch out and sleep but before I had taken off my shoes a Chinese gentleman appeared and without ceremony settled himself into one of 'my' seats. I didn't hiss, but not even the best of my dirty looks would shift him. Then he wanted to talk to me. This was unbearable. I pretended not to notice, but not to be deterred, he handed me a business card ... 'DJAMALUDDIN, President Komisaris, PT Gunung Garuda Steel Mills, Jakarta and Medan'. And so, over the next three hours, the story came out. It was incredible. Starting from nowhere as a scrap scrounger he had built steel mills outside Medan and Jakarta. The mills recycled scrap steel and the monthly power bill alone in the Jakarta mill was US$500,000. Days later, when I met his bankers in the Portman Shanghai, they confirmed he was the UK's largest customer for scrap steel. He was now taking a tilt at China.

The Chinese Government had offered him a site in a 500-hectare industrial estate on the southern bank of the Yangtze River, however, it needed an 800-metre-long jetty to provide the draft necessary for ships delivering his scrap. *Don't you worry about that Pak Djamaluddin, Singapore is one of the great entrepots of the world and my company, KRJB, has designed many of its jetties and wharves. Did I have time to visit his site? I would love to but have reserved tomorrow for meetings with the Shanghai Petroleum Corporation. Perhaps Friday?*

The flight was over in no time. As we disembarked, my new best friend presented me with a Dior necktie and invited me to dinner the following evening. While I was delighted to accept the dinner invitation, I did my best to refuse the tie, but failed. *What hotel will you be staying in Mr David? The Westin Taiping. I will send a car to collect you 6 pm tomorrow.*

By the time I had checked in to the hotel, it was time for a walk and dinner. The concierge suggested a stroll along the Bund in Pudong, where I would be sure to find a suitable restaurant. Good idea, thank you. The Bund is now a pedestrian thoroughfare that runs for about two kilometres along the left bank of the Huangpu River as it wanders through Shanghai towards the mighty Yangtze. It has an interesting history dating back to 1842, when the Treaty of Nanking ended the First Opium War and set up Shanghai as a free port with foreign enclaves. The Bund effectively became Shanghai's free port and the centre of the British and American enclaves. The party lasted almost a hundred years, until 1941, when the Japanese invasion, recreated in Steven Spielberg's *Empire of the Sun*, cleaned them out overnight.

But the evidence is still there in stunning architecture, beautifully preserved. It was dark as I embarked on my walk but the street lighting was enough to show that a day on the Bund would do more for a student of architectural history than a month in a library. It was all there. As Polonius would have put it, *tragedy, comedy, history, pastoral, pastoral-comical, historical-pastoral, tragical-historical, tragical-comical-historical-pastoral*.[19] Architects are rude about engineers, and it's true we barely know the difference between Gothic and Bauhaus, but I was doing my best when I sensed a shadow, who eventually attempted to catch my eye. Naturally, he received the same reception as Pak Djamaluddin. He didn't look like a beggar but was persistent. Eventually I stopped to find out what he wanted. English conversation, if you would be so kind, Sir. For the second time in the day, I had been mean-spirited. Chastened, I explained I was a newcomer to Shanghai out for a walk and would be happy to talk with him.

Bao Hui Chum turned out to be a knowledgeable guide. Of particular interest was the monumental Hongkong and Shanghai Bank building with its classic dome. It's prominent in one of the early scenes from *Empire of the Sun* and prompted my new friend to relate his story. He was working for the Hongkong and Shanghai Banking Corporation Limited (HSBC) in Hong Kong as an export documentation clerk when the Japanese invaded in 1941. In the ensuing chaos he had jumped from the frying pan and ended up in Shanghai. Over dinner, I told him what I was doing in China and suggested he might be able to help me. Of course. So, I took his address and telephone number and maintained contact with him during subsequent visits.

My meetings next day with the Shanghai Petroleum Corporation Ping Hu development team revealed the project was further advanced than I had been led to believe. CNOOC, the development consortium leader, had already submitted their development plan to the State Planning Department for approval, and a decision was looming. The major elements were a twenty-four-slot eight-leg drilling/process platform producing 20 000 barrels a day of crude oil and fifty MMscfd gas for export to Shanghai, 420 kilometres away, via ten-inch-diameter and fourteen-inch-diameter submarine pipelines. SPC was to be a junior member of the development consortium and responsible for processing and distribution of the oil and gas onshore. With our expanded Kvaerner capability, the entire project was of interest, so I had high hopes for my meeting with CNOOC in Beijing after the weekend. But first there was my dinner date with Pak Djamaluddin.

The car arrived as promised and twenty minutes later I was downtown at the Portman Shanghai. I was expecting dinner with my host and perhaps a few associates, but having enquired at the reception desk, I was shown to a room where around fifty people were seated for a banquet. I could see it wasn't a business gathering as there were women and children. Pak Djamaluddin rose as I arrived and offered me the seat on his right. It was a family dinner. The prodigal son had returned.

It was a happy occasion. Who wouldn't be happy when presented with such a feast? —pork, duck, chicken, fish, shellfish, eggs, vegetables, rice, rice and more rice. There was also tea and rice wine. My host was keen to confirm I was still able to visit his site in Taicang. I was. He wasn't. He had urgent business back in Jakarta but introduced me to two cousins who would accompany me the next day. As the evening progressed and inhibitions waned, a few of the younger members who spoke some English were encouraged to try it out on me. Government policy makers had identified it as essential to economic progress so English had become an important subject in schools.

After dinner there was more. The car was called, and Pak Djamaluddin took me to a night club. I don't know where it was, but it wasn't a seedy hole in the wall. It was stylish and vast with liveried waiters and waitresses, a big band, lavish lighting, disco balls and dancing girls. Who said Chinese girls were short? Not these. They had the longest legs, looked great and could dance. Shanghai wasn't holding back. After the show there was a second car waiting to take me back to the Westin. My host apologised for not being able to accompany me to Taicang City but promised to visit KRJB on his next trip to Singapore.

The drive out to Taicang next morning took two hours. We arrived around 10 am and spent another two hours touring the industrial estate, including the site earmarked for the new steel mill. There were already several household names either occupying sites or intending to. One of them, a large local petrochemical manufacturer with a site on the riverbank, had already built a 1750-metre jetty out to the Yangtze's eleven-metre contour. This was roughly the same size as the jetty project Ken Foss managed in Yanbu in 1981, and that was a US$170 million contract. I didn't think an 800-metre-long jetty was likely to provide the draft Pak Djamaluddin needed for his ships and was worried the cost might be prohibitive anyway.

The last thing I needed for lunch was another banquet, but Pak Djamaluddin had invited a large delegation from the city administration and I sensed he was quite keen for me to be there. I was flattered to think it gave him some face. In the event, I enjoyed it. There was even more variety in the dishes than the night before. Could there have been some dog? I wasn't game to ask but made it back to Shanghai without obvious side effects.

The next day, Saturday, I headed north to Beijing. With a

Sunday to kill, I was able to wander across Tiananmen Square without being run over by a tank, visit a waxy Chairman Mao in his mausoleum and walk a section of the Great Wall. My Monday meeting with CNOOC confirmed everything SPC had already told me about Ping Hu, and following my presentation of Kvaerner's capabilities they undertook to contact me when the tender documentation became available. Culturally if not commercially nourished, I returned to Singapore. An invitation to submit a lump sum tender for the project arrived a month later. Kvaerner decided not to bid. It wasn't my only disappointment. Pak Djamaluddin kept his promise to visit KRJB but only to say he had decided not to go ahead with the project in Taicang. He didn't say why but maybe the jetty was a bridge too far. Nevertheless, given the level of construction activity in China since, I suspect he may have regretted that decision.

Undaunted, I resumed my perambulations and over the next eight months flew more than 50 000 air miles—Bombay, Jakarta, Bombay, Hong Kong, KL, Jakarta, Beijing, Nanjing, Nantong, Shanghai, Hong Kong, Muscat, Istanbul, Abu Dhabi, Muscat, Seoul, Ho Chi Minh City, Seoul, Shanghai, Nanjing, Hong Kong, Bangkok, Seoul, KL, Miri, Manila, Bangkok. A new prospect similar to the Maoming SPM project surfaced during a trip to Beijing in August. For strategic reasons, perhaps old scars from the Opium Wars, the Chinese authorities traditionally located important industrial assets away from the coast. Maoming Refinery was thirty kilometres inland. The Jinling Refinery in the old capital of Nanjing was 400 kilometres inland. It turned

50 000 tonnes of crude oil into gasoline, kerosene, solvent, LPG, asphalt and benzene every day. Its feedstock from the Middle East arrived off Shanghai in VLCCs. They couldn't navigate the Yangtze, so the cargos were transferred into shuttle tankers that could. This was expensive, if not environmentally hazardous. An SPM installed in deep water off Shanghai with a pipeline to Nanjing would reduce costs and obviate a potential disaster. CNOOC's engineering arm had undertaken a feasibility study and suggested I go to Nanjing to talk to Jinling Petroleum about providing a management team for the project.

The Jinling Petroleum team had prepared a detailed presentation so I headed for Nanjing the following day. Their hydrographic survey had found a site for an SPM forty kilometres to the east of the village of Dongsan, across the Yangtze River to the north of Shanghai. It would take a forty-kilometre twenty-eight-inch-diameter offshore pipeline and a 332-kilometre twenty-eight-inch-diameter onshore pipeline to transport crude oil from there to the Jinling Refinery. A major problem for the offshore pipeline would be the installation of the landfall section in a trench across the tidal flats off Dongsan. I had estimated the distance between the high and low water marks at around four kilometres. The problem would be keeping the trench open while installing the pipeline in it. I pointed this out to the project team. *Would you be interested to visit the site Mr Wilson? Certainly.* Arrangements were made and the following day I flew to Nantong, where I was met by engineers from the Nantong Planning Commission and an interpreter.

We reached the proposed landfall just after 4 pm. Murphy's law—it was high tide, so the tidal flats were submerged but the terrain to the west told the story—low lying alluvial plains created over millions of years by sediment transported down the Yangtze and deposited in the delta. The tidal flats would be the same. As I took all this in and discussed my observations with my companions, I sensed trees in the area were vaguely familiar. *They are mulberry trees Mr Wilson.* Of course, they were. There was a mulberry tree in my grandfather's garden in Dalby and he fed the mulberries to the chickens. *They don't do that here Mr Wilson; the mulberry trees are for the silkworms. This is the birthplace of the silk industry.* Could it have been the origin of the Silk Route as well? As it happened, I was in Istanbul a week later, a city that was also an important stop on that ancient trade arterial. Seven hundred years earlier, it had taken Marco Polo three years to reach Constantinople from China.

But the great explorer's journey had been far more fruitful than mine. By year end, the State Planning Commission had decided the Jinling pipeline was not a priority and it was shelved. Much to my relief, however, and at about the same time, we were awarded a contract for the design of a 360-kilometre forty-eight-inch-diameter cross-country LNG feed gas pipeline from Saih Rawl to Qalhat in Oman. Earlier, Shell Oman had sent out invitations for expressions of interest. We were prequalified and submitted the winning bid. It was as simple as that.

Early in January, Claire Stratton called to say 39 Fitzjames

Avenue was for sale. It was a one hundred-square-metre two-bedroom ground-floor flat with high ceilings in the same Victorian mansion block as 12A. Securing a mortgage for a second property was a struggle, but in May I completed the purchase of the fifty-one-year lease for £110,000. With a one-hundred-year lease extension, a makeover and fees, the final bill was £167,000. But it didn't matter because there was no trouble finding a tenant and the resulting cash flow was well and truly positive. More importantly, it was another important milestone in my financial rehabilitation.

Back in Singapore, change was in the air. Much to Saeed Khan's dismay, Kvaerner had set its mind on establishing an entity in Indonesia. This was anathema since Indonesia was an important market for the Singapore office. But the writing was on the wall; local content was the catchcry, so he had to go along with it. Having been in the region since 1974, he had contacts, and in Indonesia these included Aburizal Bakrie, head of Bakrie & Brothers, a manufacturing, mining, construction, shipping, real estate, telecommunications and banking conglomerate. The manufacturing side of the business included pipe mills and a fabrication yard but no engineering. It was a good fit, so Bakrie and Kvaerner entered into an agreement to establish a fifty/fifty entity to represent all Kvaerner's interests in Indonesia.

Richard Wagner's *Flying Dutchman* was doomed to sail the seven seas until saved by the love of a fair maiden. Mine was a far more prosaic salvation, but it was salvation, nevertheless. I was saved from trawling the bars of Asia by an appointment in Indonesia. On 1 August 1995, having transferred the contents of 10 Robin Road into storage, I headed back to my old stamping grounds in Jakarta. The question was, aged forty-eight, did I have the drive to build another engineering company?

Bakrie Kvaerner Engineering

Kvaerner Energy had a 300-square-metre project office in Jakarta with bags of spare space so I was able to concentrate on setting up the new company and looking for work. Makes & Partners, the lawyers, made good progress and on 15 September 1995, PT Bakrie Kvaerner Engineering (BKE) was established with a fully paid-up capital of US$1 million, Kvaerner fifty-one per cent, Bakrie forty-nine per cent. I was confirmed as president director, the grand poohbah of a company of one. If Dick McMahon and I could get Bligh Engineering off the ground in 1976 with £500, then surely a million dollars would be enough for this venture. My plan was to have the company in profit by the end of 1997. So, there was plenty to do.

There was a house in Menteng some called the Rising Sun. A stone's throw from my new office, it was a seedy guesthouse rather than a bordello where they made the beds if you were lucky and could be induced to do your laundry. I knew about it because it was a popular halfway house for transiting construction personnel and seamen. I had been given a generous living allowance so was determined to find a grown-up residence within cooee of work, and that would take time. In the meantime, Jalan Kudus No. 6, Menteng, would do. I engaged a house hunter to arrange inspections. It took four months, but she eventually found an airy bungalow with a proper garden in Senayan, only ten minutes from the office. An English friend with an architectural masonry business in Bali offered to furnish it. A month later, a truck arrived filled with everything and the house was transformed in a day. Jalan Widya Chandra VIII was my home for the next seven years.

It was seven years that saw the end of President Suharto's thirty-year reign and independence for East Timor. But anybody who had prophesied these events in 1995 would have been dismissed as a dreamer. Pak Harto's paternalistic rule had provided fertile ground for the development of a rich resource economy. The change since my first visit in 1974 had been profound—Soekarno Hatta, a modern airport, eight-lane tollways, modern high-rise hotels, office blocks, hospitals, well-stocked supermarkets, international schools, universities, reliable telephones, television and, thanks to the likes of Aburizal Bakrie and Djamaluddin, a thriving industrial sector. Of course, the first family was involved. Madam Tien had seen to that. Her children had and still have substantial business interests, including Bambang's Bimantara Group. It will be remembered they had muscled into Arco's Pagerungan Island development. And then there were the resource giants that provided the seed money—Pertamina (oil and gas), PT Kaltim Prima (coal) and Freeport McMoran (copper and gold). The LNG plants at Arun and Bontang shipped more than a third of the world's LNG in the 1990s.

One of the hot projects in prospect on my arrival in Jakarta was the development of the Terang and Sirasun gas fields. The plan presaged the installation of ten subsea wells in 275 metres of water and a 135-kilometre twenty-eight-inch-diameter submarine pipeline back to the gas treatment plant recently installed on Pagerungan Island. Towards the end of August Arco convened a meeting to brief the local engineering and construction fraternity of their plans for the project. Peter Carver, general manager of PT Calmarine, was there. They had won a contract to bury a 130-kilometre twenty-six-inch-diameter submarine pipeline in the Ardjuna field in the Java Sea and required a stability analysis to determine the required concrete coating thickness.

It was a US$6000 study; no big deal and the work was done in Singapore, but it was done well and done quickly, and word got around. Within weeks, there was an enquiry for another submarine pipeline installation engineering study from French contractor PT Bouygues Offshore Indonesia. Total Indonesie had major expansion plans for its Tunu field in the Mahakam Delta in East Kalimantan. It was one of my old stamping grounds. Tunu had become a major feed-gas source for the Bontang LNG Plant. The plans included a 3000-tonne gas processing platform, five infield gathering platforms together with associated infield and export pipelines. They had issued EPC tender packages and Bouygues intended to bid. The problem was the water depths along the proposed pipeline routes in the shallow waters of the Mahakam Delta were nowhere near enough for a conventional lay barge. Would BKE undertake a study to develop a competitive methodology for the installation and trenching of the pipelines? *Bien sûr, give me a few days to visit the site and I will be back to you with a proposal.*

Arrangements were made with Total and days later I flew into their Tambora Tunu base for a tour of the existing facilities and proposed construction sites. Just a year on from my visit to the mulberry trees in the Yangtze Delta, I was visiting another great delta, although the civil engineer who hadn't been the least interested in geology at university could tell this delta was a much younger formation than its big brother to the north. The Mahakam starts fragmenting into some ten smaller streams around thirty kilometres from the coast, and whereas the flood plains of the Yangtze Delta are dry and arable, the Mahakam Delta is mostly swamp and a difficult environment for construction of any kind. I took photographs, copied tide tables and some sketchy alignment sheets and went back to Jakarta where I called my old boss, Carl Strande.

We had maintained contact since I had finished my work on the Bontang Train F pipeline three years earlier. On completion of that job, Carl had remained in the region and was currently in Manila assisting the National Power Corporation with plans for a gas distribution system for Metro Manila. He had an instinct and thirst for unusual construction problems and readily agreed to give the matter some thought. The upshot was a combination of methodologies, and days later I was able to send Bouygues a proposal to carry out the studies they would need to price the installation of the pipelines across the swamps of the Mahakam Delta.

Bouygues accepted the proposal and with Carl's help I handed them a report three weeks later. They must have been happy because they asked me to submit a bid for detailed engineering for the entire project, platforms and pipelines. We prepared the proposal in Singapore. The work would take 10 000 manhours over nine months at a price of US$358,000. There were four other companies in the race but Total was French and Bouygues was French, so they had to be front runners. If they won and gave BKE the subcontract for detailed engineering, it would be an enormous shot in the arm for a fledgling engineering company, but it would also require an enormous effort to produce a fully functional engineering team from scratch. The Kvaerner project office I was sharing had room for thirty people, and at the time there were only three of us, so if we were lucky enough to win the job then we had the space to accommodate it. It was October and the contract award was expected in March. I may not have had any people, but I did have time to employ a few and be ready to employ the rest should we win the work. I employed Indonesians wherever possible, but I didn't have the time or confidence to go without expatriates entirely.

When Arco's scope definition work on the Terang Sirasun subsea development concluded at the end of October, I heard one of the casualties was a capable process engineer. All oil and gas projects start with a deceptively simple process flow diagram, normally developed by a process engineer, so I called him and asked him to come in for a chat. Leon Kleppe accepted my offer of employment with BKE and turned out to be a more than capable process engineer. He was a methodical engineering manager who created a quality assured culture in BKE that survived long after he left during the Krismon riots in 1998.

Apart from independence, Sukarno's great gift to Indonesia was *Pancasila*, a philosophy of government based on five principles, including social justice for all Indonesians, be they Muslim, Buddhist, Hindu or Christian. One palpable consequence was at least fourteen public holidays a year. So, with Leon in the office, I was able to head home for two weeks over Christmas.

It was a happy occasion with everybody home except Sarah, who was spending every spare penny on the flat she had bought in Battersea after vacating Yew Tree Cottage. I took the opportunity to visit Dick and Pam McMahon, who had quixotically moved from a comfortable townhouse in Sydney's Surrey Hills to a permaculture commune in the Blackall Range, outside Maleny. The last time I had seen Dick was during a stopover in Sydney three or four years earlier. He and Pam may have been living in a commune, but their high-set residence was comfortable, nevertheless. Dick had lost none of his zest and was leading a campaign to persuade the shire council to address a communal grievance.

Seven months later, the shire clerk had agreed to attend a community meeting. To prepare for the occasion Dick had decided to mow the grass around his house, but the mower wouldn't start. I can imagine his reaction. He would have growled and pulled even harder. Whatever he did, it killed him. My best friend, my brilliant partner, who had first suggested Bligh Engineering, had been beaten by a motor mower. The news didn't reach me until well after the event, and even if I had known, it's unlikely I could have left Jakarta and gone to Australia even for Dick's funeral because BKE was working overtime. *Now cracks a noble heart. Good-night, sweet prince, And flights of angels sing thee to thy rest.*[32]

By the time I had returned from my Christmas '95 break, Leon Kleppe had created a rudimentary engineering office. We had drawing boards, workstations, a local area network and an internet connection. An email sent to KRJB in Singapore received a reply minutes later. Amazing. Fax machines had become relics overnight. Apart from Leon, there was a senior piping designer on loan from KRJB, Perth, and a local secretary. The focus was on preparing for the possibility of winning the Tunu detailed design, but there were other prospects as well, including Terang Sirasun. I had proposed an alternative development scenario saving US$70 million on Arco's US$313 million base case. They were interested but needed a buyer for the gas. It was no longer a hot prospect, but when one door closes another opens. Out of the blue there was a call from IKPT. I had worked with them on the Train F project when they were in a joint venture with Chiyoda. They were now in a joint venture with The MW Kellogg Company and had been awarded a contract to install yet another LNG train in Bontang.

Train H would increase overall capacity at the plant from 13.8 to 16.1 million tonnes a year, and this would require another forty-two-inch-diameter feed gas trunkline from Badak. *Would BKE be interested in preparing a front-end engineering design package for the new pipeline? When do you need it? Two weeks. No problem.* There was nobody in Singapore who could help us with a cross-country pipeline project should we win the job, so I approached Andy Lukas of AJ Lucas Constructions (AJL), my old colleague from the Bontang Train F pipeline project. Andy was only too happy to help, and we agreed to pursue the project as a joint venture, pooling the costs and splitting the profit.

There would be subtle differences between the Train H and Train F pipelines but because Andy and I had worked on Train F, we knew what they were. Being a bower bird, I had also retained details of the Train F project on my laptop computer. In other words, it would have been difficult for anybody to have produced a better proposal for the Train H front-end engineering than the BKE/AJL Joint Venture. We received a letter of intent on March 5th, and a kick-off meeting was convened the same day. Little more than a week later I signed a subcontract with Bouygues for detailed engineering design for the Tunu field. This was the project that would be supplying the gas for Train H.

We now had US$700,000 worth of work to be completed over the next nine months. PT Bakrie Kvaerner Engineering was up and running. We still needed to recruit a dozen people, but the site surveys required for both projects provided breathing space and by mid-April we had two functioning design teams.

Andy Lukas assumed leadership of the Train H team and I led the Tunu team. This left Leon free to support both projects, although as his Train H input tapered off he assumed day-to-day management of the Tunu project. Andy couldn't abandon his office in Sydney completely, but his extended visits to Jakarta were enough to keep the client happy. It kept me happy as well because he became a regular guest in Widya Chandra and always arrived with a suitcase full of beef, a scarcity in Jakarta at the time.

One of the key issues for Train H was route selection. The pipeline corridor between Badak and Bontang was crowded. It was nominally one hundred metres wide and there were already three high-pressure gas trunklines in it. Installing another without treading on the incumbents wouldn't be easy. Fortunately, Carl Strande was available to accompany Jim Walsh and his surveyors for a week. In the wake of the Train F pipeline, there was nobody who knew that corridor as well as Carl did, and as a result I was satisfied we had selected the best route possible for the new pipeline.

The rest was straightforward, although having undertaken a risk analysis, it became clear a substantial flare stack would be required to disperse the gas in the event the pipeline relief valves were triggered. And if that event coincided with a failure of the flare ignition system and lightning struck the gas plume, what would happen then? There would be a big bang. The remedy was to ensure regular testing of the ignition system was included in the operation manual. So far, twenty-five years on, it hasn't happened.

Back in England, my property investments were doing well. Claire Stratton sent details of a three-bedroom townhouse off Parsons Green. The 989-year lease had been reduced from £139,500 to £133,500 and they accepted my offer of £130,500. The United Bank of Kuwait offered a £91,000 mortgage and the purchase was completed in May. The house was let shortly afterwards. My annual rental income from three properties was now £58,000, with interest and redemption £27,000. Mr Micawber would have been over the moon.[31]

We delivered the Train H pipeline front-end engineering design reports to IKPT/Kellogg towards the end of July. They were happy. We were happy. The job had been reasonably profitable. The final report included a material take-off and cost estimate. Andy was in his element and our client was delighted with the outcome—US$72 million. It must have been significantly less than they had provided for in their contract because they asked us if we would consider taking on the job. Of course we would, but first we would need formal bid documents and I needed approval from Kvaerner and Bakrie since parent company guarantees would be required.

Saeed Khan was cautious and with good reason. We were engineers not contractors but our new colleagues from Kvaerner were uninhibited and ambitious. So too were my Bakrie board members. Indeed, they were delighted because we had identified a substantial subcontract for another Bakrie subsidiary, Trans Bakrie, who had a fabrication yard not far away from the Krakatau Steel pipe mill. So, the answer was a unanimous and unqualified 'yes'.

There is more to preparing a tender for real money than an estimate for budgeting purposes. First off, the price and delivery of long-lead procurement items, such as line pipe, coatings, pumps, compressors, valves, pipe fittings and instrumentation, must be firmly established. These delivery times form the basis for the entire project schedule and a framework for each and every activity. It is then possible to determine the manpower, construction plant and bulk materials required for each activity, hence overall cost and cash flow. Importantly, a detailed and accurate schedule provides a valuable tool for resource levelling thereby ensuring significant plant items, such as large crawler cranes, are not all required on the same day. By including contractual progress payments into the cash flow it's also possible to ensure the project is cash flow positive.

The front-end engineering estimate had included some of this work but there was plenty more to do. We submitted a bid amounting to $70 million, including a ten per cent markup in mid-August. IKPT/Kellogg undertook to revert by the end of November. Andy Lukas went back to Sydney, and we poured all our resources into the Tunu project. Bouygues had opted to manage the site survey themselves, but their subcontractor had got off to a poor start. Not surprisingly, the platform surveys could be accessed by a small boat equipped with an echo sounder and position fixing equipment, but surveying and marking the pipeline routes across the swamps would have been a different story altogether. There was also another reason for the delays. Total was changing the scope of the work. They wanted two more gathering platforms with associated pipelines. Bouygues, as main contractor, were instructed to take on the extra work, and the engineering fell to BKE. This is normal practice but when I wrote to Bouygues advising them of the schedule and cost impact, they refused to confirm a scope variation. It became a Mexican standoff. That was until I made a new friend.

With the formation of Bakrie Kvaerner, I became an honorary member of the Club Rasuna. Aburizal Bakrie, Ical, was a keen tennis player and had established the club as an upmarket sports club open to all by subscription but gratis to senior Bakrie & Bros. executives. It was just across Rasuna Said from my office and had floodlit tennis courts, coaching staff and ball boys, gym, swimming pool, bar, restaurant/coffee shop and meeting rooms where Pak Ical enjoyed convening Bakrie & Bros. management meetings. It was at one of these meetings I met AD Do, chief operating officer of Bakrie Investindo, Bakrie's property development arm. AD was Vietnamese and although our initial connection resulted from my recent exploits in Vietnam we probably remained in touch because we were outsiders in Bakrie.

The final deliverables for the Tunu project were approved and issued in late September. The BKE overrun was substantial. We had claimed US$140,000 over and above the US$358,000 we had already been paid, hoping to get something like US$100,000. That would have given us a tidy profit, but Bouygues was stonewalling. After work one evening I went over to Club Rasuna for a hit with a coach. AD Do was there and over a beer I related the Bouygues problem. *Is this company related to the French conglomerate Bouygues Construction? Yes, it's a wholly owned subsidiary. In that case, I might have a solution.*

This was the moment AD outlined Pak Ical's plan to build a skyscraper on Jalan Raya Casablanca to house the entire Bakrie & Bros. group, including Bakrie Kvaerner. It would be called Menara Bakrie (*menara* means tower). Bouygues

Construction wanted to build it and Martin Bouygues, its chairman and major shareholder, would be in Jakarta with a delegation to press their credentials the following week. *Don't leave town and when you have a moment, please send me a summary of the outstanding amounts and why.*

Sure enough, the following Wednesday morning AD called inviting me to Bakrie headquarters in Wisma Bakrie to meet the visitors from Paris. It was less than a ten-minute walk from my office and on arrival I was ushered up to Pak Ical's suite on the top floor. He was there, AD was there, Thierry De L'Aulnoit, president director of Bouygues Offshore Indonesia, was there, and M Martin Bouygues was there with four very senior executives. Following the usual introductions, Pak Ical signalled for silence and formally welcomed the French delegation, adding in an impish tone he hoped that while in Jakarta they might help Bouygues Indonesia pay Bakrie Kvaerner's overdue account for their work on the Tunu project.

You could have heard a pin drop. Martin Bouygues turned to a gravely embarrassed Thierry De L'Aulnoit, and in French said, 'Thierry, what does this mean?' There was a huddle and the meeting was reconvened in a conference room. It gave me an opening to return to the BKE office. A week later, we received the entire US$140,000. AD Do was delighted but not as much as I was. Weeks later, I ran into Thierry De L'Aulnoit in a restaurant on Rasuna Said. *David, that wasn't fair.* That's debatable, but the Asian Financial Crisis, Krismon, in Indonesia, struck a year later. The rupiah crashed from IDR2,600 to IDR11,000 to the US dollar. With loan interest and redemption in US dollars and income in Indonesian rupiah, Bakrie & Bros. did well to survive, but Menara Bakrie never got off the ground. Bakrie Kvaerner survived as well, but things would have been different without the US$140,000.

There was silence on the Train H front until late November, when Uray Nazirin, the deputy project manager on IKPT/Kellogg's Train H team, called to invite us for preliminary clarification talks on our tender for the construction of the pipeline. Pak Uray may have been the deputy PM, but he was the senior Indonesian and therefore the link to Pertamina, the client who would have the final say in awarding such an important subcontract. He had been in a similar position on the Train F project. He was good at his job, and I had found him to be a straight shooter. Andy Lukas came up prepared for a wide-ranging session, but the main focus was on line-pipe procurement since there was a concern Krakatau Steel, the mandated pipe mill, might not be able to accommodate the project schedule. Eventually, it was agreed IKPT/Kellogg would seek direct assurances from Krakatau Steel and final contract negotiations would take place with BKE/AJL in February, with a view to award on the 1 March 1997.

That seemed pretty good to me, so I accepted Bill and Jackie Ferguson's invitation to join them for New Year in Cape Town. Bill had been a real estate agent with an office on the east side of Berkeley Square and had a permanent table for lunch at Morton's Club overlooking the square on the north side. Morton's was just around the corner from Bligh Engineering's offices in Bourdon Street. Dick and I didn't have a permanent reservation but it was almost as good as the Guinea Grill, so meeting Bill Ferguson was inevitable.

We became friends to the extent that for my Christmas 1989 holiday in Australia I suggested he come along, and he accepted. Then there was his whirlwind romance with Jackie. It would have been a shame to waste a ticket to Australia, so after a brief stop at the Chelsea Register Office we headed for Heathrow and a honeymoon with the Wilson family on the Sunshine Coast.

Back to New Year 1996, Cape Town is a popular escape for the English over the winter school holidays, and the locals enjoy it since they can let their sprawling mansions for lots of UK pounds and take off to 'Plett' (Plettenberg Bay). The Fergusons had taken a large house in Hillwood Road, Bishopscourt, complete with tennis court, swimming pool, a magnificent view to Table Mountain and more domestics than Buckingham Palace. I wasn't the only guest; we were a dozen or so, counting children, but it didn't matter. We were looked after beautifully.

Two weeks was barely enough in this once-troubled land where, just two and a half years on from Nelson Mandela's election as president and eighteen months on from its triumph in the Rugby World Cup, the rapprochement between black and white South Africans was, to me, miraculous. And Cape Town, endowed as it is with stunning sea and landscapes, has an endless choice of diversions, particularly at year-end, with a cricket test at Newlands and races at Kenilworth, not to mention golf at the Royal Cape, surfing at Llandudno, a walk up Table Mountain, a picnic in Kirstenbosch Gardens, lunch at the Mount Nelson, or just being at Cape Point.

Back in Jakarta, and on a night I will never forget, there

was a call from Mum. It was far too late to be social. It was the saddest news I ever heard. Lock's eldest son, Ben, the twenty-one-year-old grandson she adored, had died following a fall from a balcony. The lioness was devastated, and I couldn't do anything to help except mumble something about being home as soon as possible. Chris came from New York; Sarah came from London. We spent the weekend together, grieving. Perhaps that was the best we could have done for Lock—for all of us. *Here rests his head upon the lap of Earth, A youth to Fortune and to Fame unknown.*[6] The Wilsons and the Knightses had survived two wars; surely these awful events were only for other families.

The Train H clarification meetings resumed shortly after my return to Jakarta. By now, Kvaerner had recognised the project was a real prospect and sent reinforcements. These included engineers from PT Sofresid Indonesia. Hitherto, Sofresid had been a competitor, but with the Kvaerner takeover of the Trafalgar House Group five months earlier, Sofresid had become a sister company and was able to provide support in areas where we were wanting, such as instrumentation and controls. After three weeks of technical and contractual clarifications, we were invited to submit our final price. On the afternoon of March 14th, a Friday, Ron Hogan, IKPT/Kellog's project manager, rang and asked me to come to his office Monday morning to countersign the letter of intent.

It was too good to be true. I spent the weekend basking in the glory of a US$70 million contract. I shouldn't have. Ron called back first thing Monday to say he needed more time. Days later, he rang to ask me if there was room in our consortium for PT Kelsri. They had been Ipco's partners in the Train F contract and were well connected. Alarm bells were ringing. I rang Andy. Because Kvaerner was putting up the performance guarantees, he had agreed to reduce his share in the joint venture to thirty per cent. This would reduce his share to less than twenty per cent. He wasn't happy. Nor was I. I went back to Ron Hogan and said no. Days later, he called back, clearly embarrassed. Kelsri had undercut our bid and he had been given no option but to accept it. Welcome to Indonesia.

There was no time for recriminations. BKE was in a precarious position. For months we had been told the contract was ours, so looking for other work hadn't been a top priority. I wanted the decks clear for Train H. BKE/AJL stood to make over US$7 million from the project, but it was possible to lose this one as well, and the best way to avoid that was to get off to a good start. We needed to restart. Fortunately, my alternative field development proposal for Arco's Terang Sirasun field had struck a chord and we were commissioned to undertake an availability and reliability analysis of the proposed subsea gas gathering system. US-based Kvaerner Subsea projects had developed reliability data for similar developments in the Gulf of Mexico and we were able to use this to develop a model for Arco's project in the Java Sea. The work kept us going for three months. It gave us the time we needed to find something more substantial.

With the completion of Bontang Train H, Pertamina would be exporting sixteen million tonnes of LNG, valued at US$3 billion a year, to Japan. This would require over two billion cubic feet of natural gas daily. Construction of the Tunu project was well underway, but Total had more gas off the coast south of the Mahakam Delta and had decided to develop it as well. With gas reserves of six trillion cubic feet, the Peciko field, discovered in 1983, was almost as big as Badak, discovered ten years earlier. The initial development would involve the installation of two drilling/production platforms, each twenty-five kilometres offshore in fifty-metre water depth and each with a twenty-four-inch-diameter export pipeline. The job was split into two packages: platforms and pipelines.

Total called a meeting in mid-July to brief contractors interested in bidding to install the pipelines. The usual suspects were there—Nisconi, Bouygues, Saipem and Shillelagh. Total had suggested I attend since all the contractors invited would need a local engineering company. After the meeting, Saipem's boss, Fabio Rosso, asked if I would give them a proposal for the detailed engineering. We did, and in August 1977 they won the contract and awarded the engineering to BKE. There was more to come. A month later, we won engineering contracts for multi-product pipelines in Java and Sumatra. The combined contract value for the three jobs was US$820,000, from which we expected to make around US$230,000. We had dodged a bullet and now, with nearly twenty-five people on the payroll, we needed more space. Fortunately, the floor above us was vacant so we were able to carve off a 395-square-metre suite, giving us room for our people as well as clients' representatives.

It was an opportunity to create an efficient, reliable and productive engineering office, and I had the people for the job. Leon Kleppe was a skilled process engineer but, more than that, he was a professional and had created a quality assurance system that gave me a high level of confidence in the work we were producing. Leon had also groomed two senior Indonesian engineers, Budio Tjahono and Agusman Zubir, who were more than at home introducing and applying the latest software tools available to the industry and extracting the best from the younger engineers working for them.

Our library of proprietary computer software programs included process and structural design software, AutoCAD, a design and drafting system and, for project planning and scheduling, MS Project. If that wasn't enough, more software, including spreadsheets and non-proprietary programs for specific applications, was available from Kvaerner Engineering. All this came via a high-speed twenty-seven-gigabyte Pentium server running forty Pentium workstations and a wide range of laser printers and plotters. Everything was backed up daily and stored off-site. The server also connected BKE to Kvaerner's global network, providing access to a suite of equipment and packaged equipment specifications. This allowed our team to employ the most sophisticated and cost-effective tools available for design/engineering, cost estimation and project management. Kvaerner's dream of a worldwide engineering organisation was coming to fruition.

To make sure everybody knew about it, Kvaerner sponsored an entry in the 1997–1998 Whitbread Round the World Race. *Innovation Kvaerner* and the other yachts were due in Sydney for Christmas and I was invited to join a Kvaerner party on the Harbour to watch the start of the Sydney to Auckland leg on January 4th. Why not? Because it's a complete waste of money. We weren't selling beer; we were selling engineering, and the best way to do that is to let your work do the talking. But it had been a busy year and I would be home for Christmas, so accepted.

I took the long road via London and New York. The London highlight was a dinner party at Brooks's for a dozen or so. Sarah was in sparkling form, perhaps because her husband to be, Mark, was there as well. Of course, it wouldn't have been a party without Mr and Mrs Stratty. Claire was still looking after my rental properties and as a result I was now back on my financial feet. It would have been impossible without her. Next stop, New York.

The last time had been three years earlier for Chris's marriage to Catherine Crier, author and television journalist. Chris had retired from shipbroking and set up an emporium for antipodean arts and crafts. He had some great paintings and sculptures but nothing to compare with the Degas exhibition at the Metropolitan Museum. But the highlight in New York was an evening at the Metropolitan Opera, the perfect venue for a Franco Zeffirelli production of *Don Giovanni*. I had missed my opera, but life is a delicate balance. There isn't time to do everything, but there is time to do as much as you can.

A few days later, as I flew into Sydney, I was fortunate enough to have a bird's eye view over Port Botany. When I ran the red light in Ryde twenty-five years earlier it had been a sandpit. Now it was a busy container port. I had enjoyed being an engineer and here at least was something to show for it—certainly more than a submarine pipeline.

After ten days at home and a day's schmoozing on Sydney Harbour, I headed back to a nervous Jakarta. When the Asian financial crisis had hit Thailand six months earlier and the Thai baht lost half its value, there were more than a few smug Indonesians who said it couldn't happen there. But it did and it was worse. The rupiah started its collapse from IDR2600 to the US dollar in August. By January, it had crashed to IDR14,800, eventually consolidating at IDR11,600, a devaluation of seventy-five per cent. Bakrie & Bros., with borrowings in US dollars and income in rupiah, was struggling to meet its obligations but managed to hang on. BKE was okay because we had work, were paid in US dollars and, as a result, our local payroll cost had been reduced by seventy-five per cent. Our expatriate payroll was reduced by fifty per cent as well. Leon Kleppe had married and his wife was expecting their first child. As unrest had begun to spread across the country, Leon, who had been caught in a riot in Banjarmasin a year earlier had decided Perth would be a better place for the arrival of their new daughter. He left behind a twenty-strong engineering group capable of producing top quality work and Budio Tjahono, a worthy successor, but the task of hammering our reports into passable English fell to me.

My cost of living had been reduced by seventy-five per cent as well. It was surreal. The combined salary of my domestic staff of four at Widya Chandra, including Pak Sario, the fierce driver, had fallen from US$500 to US$110 a month. A round of golf went from US$100 to US$20. I bought a two-year-old BMW 528i for US$7500. It wasn't so good for the locals. Inflation rendered most family incomes totally inadequate. At first it was the cost of food. The International Monetary Fund tried to help with an emergency loan but there were strings attached, including outlawing subsidies for basic commodities. It might have been sensible, but it wasn't wise. In the lead up to Krismon, gasoline was IDR700 a litre, equivalent to US$42 a barrel. That was the cost of crude oil at the wellhead. So, on May 5th, the government raised the price of gasoline to IDR1200 per litre. That wasn't so bad because it was mostly a hit on the middle class, but the real problem was kerosene, which was marked up from IDR280 to IDR350 a litre. This was a hit on every lower income household because they all cooked with it.

Nobody could have foreseen the ensuing mayhem. The student demonstrations initiated in the Bandung Institute of Technology swiftly spread to Jakarta. On May 13th, when members of the armed forces, who routinely got away with murdering demonstrators in remote Irian Jaya and East Timor, killed four university students in downtown Jakarta, the city erupted. The following day saw a rerun of the bloodletting accompanying the downfall of Sukarno. As in 1964, the rage was directed at the ethnic Chinese, *orang Cina*. Jakarta's Chinatown, Glodok, was sacked and many of its merchants beaten to death. A thousand people died attempting to escape from a shopping mall set alight in East Jakarta. We all closed our offices and sent everybody home.

Fabio Rosso, boss of Saipem Indonesia, client and friend, was stopped at a barricade erected across the toll road to Pondok Indah. He was mistaken for *orang Cina*, hauled out of his car and would have been beaten up or worse had it not been for his driver, who bravely intervened and persuaded the crowd Fabio was *orang putih* (white). We had two 'Chinese' girls in our office. As I was leaving, I was told the sister of one of the girls had called warning her not to come home. I lived in a relatively secure area close to the office, so suggested Christina spend the night in Widya Chandra, and she did.

By nightfall, the streets were deserted. I had a regular Thursday night squash game in Kemang, and since news of the events referred to above was yet to emerge, I saw no reason not to attend. Most of the regulars were there plus a young English ring-in who thrashed me without conceding a point. Over a beer after the game, I asked him where he came from. Leicestershire. Where in Leicestershire? Upper Broughton. What did you say your name was again? Ben, Ben Dowson. Of course. I knew his mother and father, Ben and Hilary. They were Quorn Hunt subscribers. Tragically, Ben senior had been killed by an avalanche when heli-skiing in Canada not so long before.

Judging by Ben junior's banter with the Indonesian bar staff, he was a competent Bahasa Indonesia speaker. Yes, he was, and as an Oxford classics graduate, he had come to Indonesia seven years earlier as an English teacher. He was now working for a business publisher writing marketing programs, proposals and course outlines in Bahasa Indonesia. *How is that going? Not well. I am paid IDR10,000 (now worth* less than US$100) a month, which doesn't get me very far. Come to work for me and I will pay you US$500 a month. Great. When can you start? I have planned a trip home in July, would the first of August be okay? Yes. My report editing problems were over, and eight years later, Ben was running the company.

It was all over the next day, Friday. Christina's sister rang to say it was safe, so I drove her home. Nevertheless, she laid low in the back of the car as we went through some of the more crowded areas where clean-up operations slowed us down. Afterwards, I took a drive. Downtown Jakarta was a ghost town, save for small groups of police gathered around stationary armoured personnel carriers. You could have heard a pin drop in Glodok as well. But unlike Jalan Thamrin, which was largely unscathed, Jalan Gajah Mada was lined with burnt-out buildings and vehicles. It was the same on Saturday. The government took the opportunity to announce the price of kerosene had been returned to IDR280 a litre. Thursday's death toll eventually settled at around 5000. They had all died for nothing.

On Monday morning, it was business as usual in the office. Not so in Singapore. The news from Jakarta had been sensational. Saeed Khan rang and insisted I get out. I tried to explain everything was back to normal, but he was adamant. Carl Strande had been badgering me to come to Manila to discuss the design of a cross-country pipeline associated with the new Malampaya field, so I agreed to go to Singapore as soon as possible and follow on to the Philippines.

It was impossible to book a flight. Many of the local

Chinese had had enough and were desperate to leave Jakarta. There was no way I could get a scheduled flight, but our travel agent thought it might be possible to get a seat on a shuttle flight to Singapore from the old airport at Halim. I was at the airport first thing Tuesday morning. It was hopeless. If there was a shuttle, there was no way to get a seat on it. I was just about to leave when I ran into Joseph Dharmabrata, affable as usual. When he learned I was trying to get to Singapore he simply said, 'Follow me'. Ten minutes later, I was on Bambang Suharto's private BAC 111 heading to Singapore. Bambang's father resigned two days later. The whole situation could have been nasty and I have no doubt Saeed Khan knew something I didn't. In any event, I was out of Jakarta and although there was no more bloodshed, I was grateful for his concern.

Three days later, I was back in the Edsa Plaza in Manila. At first, I thought the meetings Carl had organised would be preliminary, but to his credit I returned to Jakarta with a 5000-manhour, US$163,000 front-end engineering study for a fifteen-kilometre, sixteen-inch-diameter gas pipeline from Batangas to a power plant at Ilijan. Two years later, when the First Philippine Corporation went ahead with the project, BKE was awarded the route selection survey and detailed engineering as well. It's an ill wind that blows no good.

And so it was with Indonesia's new president. BJ Habibe's big ideas were devolving power to the regions, removing ethnic classifications (long overdue in Australia) and lifting censorship. He also reformed the cabinet and in doing so sidelined Suharto's greedier cronies, including Prabowo Subianto, the ex-president's ruthless son-in-law and commander of Indonesia's Special Forces brigade, whose stock-in-trade was stirring up and brutally quelling civil unrest for political ends. Order was restored and gradually the country learned to absorb the great devaluation.

BKE went through a lull during the troubles but by August we were up and running again. It was time for a party and an excuse to engage Ireng Maulana's Big Band. Only in Indonesia could one afford to have a ten-piece band perform for a party at home. It was a great success but not just because we were still dancing to the Blues Brothers at 3 am. By now, Sofresid, BKE's new sister company in Jakarta, had been renamed Kvaerner Indonesia (KI), and I had invited one of my new colleagues, Andre Decarpentry. He had come with his Indonesian wife and three of her sisters. Much more interesting than a bottle of wine. They were pretty girls with more than passable English. I thought the tallest, Santy, was particularly attractive and as we danced we agreed to meet again.

Afterwards I checked with Andre to establish the propriety for such an endeavour. He advised talking to her father first. That seemed excessive; it was no more than a dinner date, but I agreed anyway. Andre brought Pak Toid round to Widya Chandra days later. An event I had dreaded turned out to be agreeable and interesting. He had been a non-commissioned officer in Sukarno's presidential guard so had known the founding father. He also remembered Ibu Yurike, who had accompanied me to Palu and Makassar six years earlier. We were connected and Santy received her father's permission to socialise with a *bule*.

BKE's 1998 Christmas present was a million-dollar-plus

engineering contract from Australian contractor PT Petrosea. It was a Tunu field expansion and similar to our first tunu field project with Bouygues. It was also my sixth project in East Kalimantan. There had been the Bontang reconnaissance survey for Bechtel in 1973, Train F thirty-six-inch-diameter pipeline construction in 1992, Tunu North detailed engineering in 1996, Train H forty-two-inch-diameter pipeline front-end engineering in 1996, Pecicko Offshore Pipelines in 1997, and now, Tunu Phase 7. Basically, it was two manifold platforms and half a dozen pipelines ranging in size from twenty-inch up to thirty-six-inch diameter. A lesson learned from earlier projects was management of the survey subcontractor by the engineering subcontractor was essential. This had been a large part of the problem with the Bouygues project. When I explained this to Petrosea's project manager, Kim Smith, he was happy to include the survey in our work scope, which is why the contract sum was so much larger. We subcontracted the survey to Jim Walsh's company, Asminco. It was done properly and on schedule, so the project got off to a good start.

It gave me time to concentrate on the Tunu Phase 7 compression module, an even bigger project. But there was a problem—Kvaerner Indonesia. According to the 1995 Bakrie/Kvaerner Joint Venture agreement, BKE was formed 'to provide general engineering and management services in respect of upstream oil and gas production'. The problem arose when Kvaerner acquired the Trafalgar House Group and its Indonesian subsidiary, PT Sofresid, a year later. To make matters worse, Sofresid had been renamed Kvaerner

Indonesia, as already mentioned. There were now two Kvaerner entities in Indonesia—a wholly owned subsidiary and a fifty-one/forty-nine per cent joint venture, chasing the same work. Fine, except the BKE shareholder agreement (between Bakrie & Bros. and Kvaerner) implied BKE was the only Kvaerner entity authorised to operate in the oil and gas industry in Indonesia.

Hitherto, it had been a Mexican standoff, but the Tunu Phase 7 compression platform brought it to a head. There were two main contenders for the project, Gunanusa and TransBakrie. Both had local fabrication yards, but both needed an engineering subcontractor. Years earlier, Gunanusa had done a similar project for Total with Sofresid as engineering contractor, and Total had been happy since Sofresid was a competent French engineering company. It still was, but the problem arose because it had been taken over by Kvaerner and renamed Kvaerner Indonesia. Neither Gunanusa nor Total were concerned, but Bakrie was, because their joint venture company, TransBakrie, would be competing with another Kvaerner company in Indonesia.

There was another problem. The project was too big for BKE. Had TransBakrie won, we would have needed help from Kvaerner Indonesia anyway. I also knew that if Gunanusa didn't win, Kvaerner Indonesia would go broke. I suggested a compromise, which Kvaerner senior management endorsed and Bakrie & Bros. reluctantly accepted. In the event of a TransBakrie win, BKE would subcontract eighty per cent of the engineering to KI and in the event of a Gunanusa win, KI would subcontract twenty per cent of the engineering to BKE.

Gunanusa duly won and awarded the engineering to KI, who immediately tried to break the KI/BKE pre-bid agreement, citing coordination problems. This was rubbish since much of the work was to be done in Paris and KI was now in the same building on the same floor as BKE. Would I accept the profit margin on our twenty per cent, say US$250,000, in lieu? That suited me fine since BKE was busy anyway and US$10,000 a month for doing nothing for two years would provide a welcome boost to our cash flow. So, yes, provided it's paid monthly.

It went smoothly for three months until my great ally in Singapore, Saeed Khan, retired. His replacement was not so happy with our do-nothing fee, and early on 8 June 1999 a delegation of Kvaerner senior managers, including a lawyer, arrived in my office unannounced. *Dave, we have decided to merge BKE into Kvaerner Indonesia and you will become its business development manager. Okay ... Does Bakrie & Bros. know about this? No. Would you like me to set up a meeting for you to let them know? Yes. Give me a few minutes.* They trotted off to Kvaerner Indonesia. I took a few minutes to come off a boiling rage before calling Lukman Arief.

Lukman was the Bakrie & Bros. director on the BKE board. He and Saeed Khan were good friends and over the last four years we had become friends as well. Our board meetings were irregular, but I always let him know what was going on, particularly if I thought it might be of interest to another Bakrie & Bros. company, such as TransBakrie or Bakrie Pipe Industries. He was therefore aware of the result of the Tunu Phase 7 contract and the compensation payments. I appraised him of the Kvaerner proposal and my thoughts on it. I suggested that since Kvaerner was flagrantly in breach of the joint venture agreement, Bakrie & Bros. should demand compensation and Kvaerner's shares in BKE, failing which, Bakrie & Bros. would seek a restraining order on all Kvaerner activities in Indonesia.

The result was never in doubt. Just before lunchtime, Lukman called to let me know BKE was now a wholly owned subsidiary of Bakrie & Bros. and that Kvaerner had agreed to pay compensation of US$90,000. *And by the way, David, you are now on your own. Don't bother asking us for any money.*

Bakrie Engineering

It was a pyrrhic victory. Justice may have been done but it was an own goal for BKE. Before the parting of the ways, the balance owing from Kvaerner Indonesia's US$250,000 compensation settlement was US$196,000. Now, Bakrie Bros. would receive US$90,000 and BKE nothing. BKE was technically bankrupt. Fortunately, we were busy with the Tunu Phase 7 engineering and the client, Petrosea, a subsidiary of the Australian construction company Clough Engineering, paid their bills. I was responsible for the livelihoods of thirty-five employees. We would trade our way through it.

My secret weapon was an accountant who looked after every penny. Merista Pranata, an ethnic Chinese Indonesian, studied at Tarumanagara University, Jakarta, and after two years with Arthur Andersen, joined BKE, aged twenty-four. She was wise beyond her years and feisty; certainly, none of the engineers in the office messed with her, although she did marry one. At any given moment, she knew exactly where we stood financially. Invoices were finalised on the last day of the month and delivered by hand the next. She knew who to chase for money and which bills could be pigeonholed and she didn't hesitate to let me know if my salary had to wait.

And, more than anything, Merista was discreet. I knew there were only two people aware of our precarious situation.

The engineering group was going well too. In the wake of Leon Kleppe's departure, Budio Tjahono had stepped up to the plate and excelled. Leon had left a good engineering system. Budio adhered to it, expanded it and improved it. He was now responsible for productivity, quality, periodic review and engineering recruitment. We tended to pay more than the going rate for new recruits, but applicants were warned not to resign from a current job unless they were sure they were as good as they said they were, because our six-month trial period was strictly observed. Nevertheless, Budio was always there to help and had a way of getting the best from young engineers.

Needless to say, the engineers could do nothing without work and that meant churning out proposals. No proposals, no work, and one of the secrets of success for an engineering company is knowing when to commit to a proposal, because they are expensive and there is no compensation unless it leads to a job. BKE's success rate was about thirty per cent. The proposal that won the Tunu Phase 7 engineering subcontract was a thirty-page document, excluding appendices. It was based on a spreadsheet developed by Agusman Zubir, listing each and every report and drawing required to complete the project with a breakdown of the disciplines required. It was so detailed it included an estimate of the paper required—11 148 sheets ranging from A1 to A4.

Agusman could produce this estimate in two or three days. It then became the framework for work scope and method statement narratives penned by the relevant lead discipline engineers. This is where Ben Dowson came in. He was fluent in Bahasa Indonesia, and being an Oxford University graduate could write reasonable English. His job was to take all these contributions, work with the authors and merge everything into a seamless document. He had worked for a publisher before joining BKE so was no stranger to producing a bound document. And so it was with our engineering reports. Ben became our in-house publisher and as we embarked on the transition from PT Bakrie Kvaerner Engineering to PT Bakrie Engineering, the company could take pride in the quality of the work going out the door under its new logo.

We won our first job without Kvaerner support, or interference, a month later. A fifty-four-kilometre, eight-inch/ten-inch-diameter pipeline exporting crude oil from the Mudi field in central Java to a storage tanker moored off Palang was choking from a build-up of internal wax deposits. We were commissioned to investigate, recommend remedial action and propose measures to increase its capacity from 23 000 to 40 000 barrels a day. It was a US$362,000 contract and would keep us busy well beyond Tunu Phase 7. It gave me time to revisit the Terang Sirasun project. We had completed an availability and reliability study for subsea wellheads tied back to a fixed platform two years earlier. Arco's latest idea was to replace the fixed manifold platform with a floater and they had issued an enquiry for another study. Without Kvaerner support, it was beyond Bakrie Engineering, but the Arco people suggested we team up with Houston-based Alliance Engineering and gave me a contact. I called their top man, who confirmed they would be happy to work with us but, in the wake of the Krismon riots, were reluctant to send personnel to Indonesia. Could I come to Houston? I didn't bother to say I would be happier walking the streets of Jakarta at night but agreed and made the arrangements. It would give me an opportunity to visit my brother Chris in Upstate New York.

It would also be an opportunity to introduce Santy to another of the world's great cities. In the fifteen months since my interview with her father, we had become close and after Andre and Santy's sister, Tari, moved back to Paris, we spent a week there. Apart from fleeting business trips, I hadn't been in Paris for seven years, so in between visits to Giverny, the Louvre, the Musée d'Orsay, the Eiffel Tower and Galeries Lafyette, there were more than a few people to catch up with, including Nicky and Dominique Knowland, real-life models for *La Bohème*'s Marcello and Musetta. Three years later, during one of their routine separations, Nicky was found alone and dead in a garret not far from their home by the opera house. Dominique died three months later—I believe from a broken heart. But those sad events were for the future and being in Paris with Santy had been a novel experience. Becoming familiar with and being able to admire mankind's greatest masterpieces is a privilege and a joy, but being able to observe Santy's delight on seeing the works for the first time was even better. And there was just as much to see in New York, including the Metropolitan Opera. It may have been the early days for the World Wide Web, but in 1999 the Metropolitan Opera had a webpage, and before leaving Jakarta I was able to book four seats for a production of *Mefistofele* on November 24th and pay online. By an extraordinary coincidence, it was to be conducted by Mark Elder who I hadn't seen since Bayreuth in 1981.

We arrived at JFK on a Thursday afternoon and there was a car waiting to take us to Chris and Catherine's grown-up equestrian estate outside Katonah, Westchester County. Save for my two-day trip to Houston, it was to be our base for a week. Santy had said the first thing she wanted to do in New York was to visit the Statue of Liberty. It was something that I, stupidly, would never have thought to do. I would never have appreciated its scale, beauty or the symbolism of its positioning, smack bang in the middle the world's largest multicultural metropolis—possibly why the World Trade Center's towers were not so far away. We visited them as well and took the elevators up to a viewing platform on one of the towers. Don't look down! The symbolism was too much for the perverts who thought mass murder would help them and their loved ones. Two years later the towers were a pile of rubble and the world had descended into a spiral of retribution. But that was for the future.

The sun was still shining next day as we returned to Grand Central for a walk down Fifth Avenue to visit the Frick Collection, with more recognisable masterpieces per metre than anywhere else in the world. Frick made his pile mining coal and turning it into coke for steel making. He was a millionaire by thirty and had already started collecting pictures. When he died, forty years later, he left 137 masterpieces to posterity and a grand villa on Central Park to house them. There is no particular theme or period, but they are all there—Turner, Goya, Gerard David, Boucher, van Dyck, Gainsborough and three of the thirty-six recognised Vermeers. Only three museums, The Met, the National Gallery in Washington DC and the Rijksmuseum, have more.

My appointment with Alliance Engineering was for early Monday morning, so on Sunday afternoon I flew to Houston and checked in to a hotel near their offices on the west side of town. The meeting was constructive, although Alliance was not prepared to send their people to Jakarta. We could live with that, and, if Arco agreed, it would save money. Their work would involve the three-phase (oil, gas and water) process modelling required to develop the process flow diagram, and I didn't think Arco would be concerned since the tie-up was their suggestion. The internet had done wonders for the coordination of work between offices in different time zones, and if this was done well, it could be advantageous. We concluded by agreeing on our respective contributions to the proposal following receipt of the enquiry.

Before leaving for Houston, I had called Bob Brown. He had insisted I make time to see his latest 'toy'. It had been twenty-three years since first meeting my big boss in New Plymouth and six years since he had helped me persuade Saeed Khan we could trench the Bach Ho pipeline with a plough. That's when the complete takeover of RJBA by Kvaerner had been announced. Three years later, in 1996, Coflexip/Stena bought the old RJBA Houston operation from Kvaerner and rebadged it RJ Brown Deepwater. At sixty-eight years old, Bob Brown had stayed on as guru in residence.

Looking back over my professional life, I can claim three original ideas. The first was to look for a route across the Fasht Al Arab for the Zuluf forty-eight-inch-diameter pipeline. It worked and was probably the reason Bligh Engineering won so much work from Aramco. The second was my alternative development plan for the Terang Sirasun field, and the jury was still out on that. The third came two years later during the conceptual design for a crude oil pipeline across Siberia. Three original ideas in thirty years of engineering. Bob Brown had dozens, which is why he will be remembered as one of the industry's greatest innovators. The reason he was able to realise so many of his ideas was his ability to communicate, and he often did that with models.

The first I remember was the *Viking Piper* model in the RJBA office in Rijswijk. The big idea wasn't just a semisubmersible deep-water pipe lay barge; it was its three-dimensional stinger design with massive rams to raise it from harm's way in the worst of North Sea storm conditions. Bankers can't read engineering drawings, but they understand models, and that's the crux of the matter. We produced a great model of the Bach Ho plough and, apart from anything else, it was invaluable for optimising the rigging details. So, as I headed towards RJ Brown Deepwater, I wondered what I was in for. I didn't have to wait long. Bob was there to meet me, perhaps a shade greyer around the edges but no less effervescent, and after a cursory tour of the office to meet a few people I knew by reputation, I was shown to the 'model room'. It was a cavernous well-lit room with a fifteen-foot ceiling, white walls and a white linoleum floor. A model of a semisubmersible production facility was suspended from the ceiling (the virtual ocean surface) and dotted around the linoleum floor (the virtual seabed) were various subsea wellhead models connected to the submersible by coloured chords representing flowlines and risers. The scale was determined by the ratio of ceiling height to water depth. Drilling in the Gulf of Mexico was moving into deeper and deeper water, at that time up to 6000 feet, and this was an ingenious way not only of modelling the developments but of sequencing and refining the procedures required to make the connections between seabed and surface. The operators loved it so, as well as a practical engineering tool, it was a valuable sales aid.

My sister Sarah had arrived from London by the time I got back to New York. I had invited her to *Mefistofele*, and since two of Chris's artists from Kenya were in town, he was hosting a party in his gallery as well. Karen Lawrence painted wildlife landscapes and Denis Mathews created wildlife bronzes. The party was well attended by locals, including old friends Brad and Melanie Garnett, who now lived with their daughters less than twenty minutes away, outside North Salem. Twenty-five years earlier, Brad had arranged accommodation for my first visit to New York in the basement of 'The Little Church Around the Corner' on East 29th Street. He also suggested I take the time to visit the Frick Collection, which I did then and have done so every visit since.

And so, for our night at the opera. Neither Chris nor Catherine was interested in the fourth ticket, so I invited a neighbour, Liberty Howell. She studied languages so wouldn't need subtitles. We arrived in time for a drink and it occurred to me I must have looked a regular Don Juan with three such attractive young women in tow. But in the foyer's dim light I could see Santy was nervous. It was the crowd. Why? She came from the most crowded island on earth. The bells summoning us to our seats didn't help either, so I took her arm and we headed for velvet drapes leading to the stalls. As we emerged from the foyer's subdued light into the vastness of the Metropolitan Opera House's auditorium and the glare of the house lights, Santy froze. *I can't do it, Dave.* I turned and was about to retreat when Liberty, the student from next door who was following with Sarah, simply said, 'Leave this to me, David. You and Sarah go in and we will be with you.' We did, and as the lights went down they joined us. I don't know what Liberty did, but she had certainly earned her night at the opera.

Mefistofele does nothing to dispel the idea opera always ends badly. It's a story of the fickleness of love, the vanity of old men and the triumph of good over evil, but there is lots of collateral damage. Mefistofele, the villain, is the most attractive character and the hero, Faust, being weak, is not really a hero at all. At the first interval, an usher escorted us backstage for a brief catchup with Mark Elder. From what I could gather, he was very busy, but of course that meant spending a lot of time away from home. I knew better than most that is not as much fun as it sounds.

It was time to go home. We were heading for Y2K and, just like climate change, the world was facing Armageddon and another property meltdown. My London properties, now worth £800,000, owed me £450,000, including redecoration expenses and I was not prepared to lose the gain. I decided the middle road was to keep 12A Fitzjames Avenue as a potential future residence and sell the other two. They sold for £420,000, realising a gain of £120,000. I was quite pleased, but Y2K came and went and the London property market powered on. And so will the cost of coal, oil and gas when the world has recovered from its CO_2 narcosis.

This will mean searching for hydrocarbons wherever they are, including a tropical island on the eastern fringe of the Indonesian archipelago with oil as thick as coal. I was sitting in my office one day when who should walk in but Chuck Schwieder, Bligh Engineering's Aramco liaison engineer from Paul Street days. Chuck had joined Kufpec Indonesia, and he and his wife, Sally, had moved to Jakarta. Kufpec wasn't some third-tier wildcatter, it was a wholly owned subsidiary of the Kuwait Petroleum Corporation and had a thirty per cent share in the Oseil field on Seram Island, with a production potential of 18 000 barrels a day. Kufpec wanted to develop the field but there were problems. There was sulphur in the crude; it was as thick as treacle; the field was almost 3000 kilometres from Jakarta; the annual rainfall was 3300 millimetres; and when the natives ran amok, they killed each other. The project would involve a gathering system, a processing plant amounting to a mini refinery to produce high-sulphur fuel oil and naphtha and an export jetty. Kufpec had completed a front-end engineering design and the project estimate was $100 million, with engineering expected to be around $1.5 million. It was the sort of project best left to others, but for such a big prize and with an old friend in the client camp, I had to give it a go. There were also potential benefits for Bakrie & Bros., who could supply the necessary line pipe.

The first thing to do was to find a suitable partner. In the end, that turned out to be two partners. Ballast Indonesia was an experienced civil works contractor, who could take on the camp, roads, pipelines, power distribution, plant, civil works and export jetty. Being Dutch, I thought they would be better than most at handling the rain in Seram. The second partner, Samudra Ferro Engineering, built process plants. They had a 2.4-hectare fabrication and maintenance facility in East Java, with almost two hectares undercover for shop blasting, prefabrication and assembly. They had direct sea access, so we would be able to modularise and skid mount the process plant, build and test it in a controlled environment and ship the modules from there to Seram. This was a good start, but Bakrie Engineering was not up to designing a mini refinery. The preliminary engineering had been provided by Thyssenkrupp subsidiary, Uhde. They had designed a similar plant for Santos in Port Bonython, South Australia, and now had a subsidiary in Melbourne, Shedden Uhde, who could help us. We discussed the project over the phone for a few days, at which point they suggested I come down and visit the Port Bonython plant, which had been running since 1982.

Shedden made the arrangements and I flew down to Melbourne where I spent a day in their Buckhurst Street offices clarifying their work scope before heading for Whyalla with two of their engineers. We flew Qantas to Adelaide, with the onward flight to Whyalla booked on Whyalla Airlines.

Never Fear the Spills

On arrival in Adelaide, we collected our baggage and as advised, called Whyalla Airlines on a dedicated telephone link we found in the terminal. We were asked to wait outside for the company bus. It turned out to be a big old station wagon. The driver, a young man neatly dressed, loaded our baggage and took us to a tiny terminal building a short drive from the main terminal. As we disembarked, he motioned us into the waiting room, took our bags to the rear of the building and in no time was behind the desk checking our tickets. In the dim evening light, I could see a modest twin-engine aircraft parked outside. We were the only passengers, so with all present and correct, he led us out to the plane and helped us to our seats. He then loaded the baggage, brushed himself off, jumped into the pilot's seat, donned a peak cap and flew us to Whyalla, where we spent the night before heading to Port Bonython by car next morning.

We had known it as a mini refinery, and so it may have been, but to me, being used to the sort of process facilities we installed offshore, it was enormous. The main column was around thirty metres high, three metres in diameter and surrounded by a mass of piping, valves and instrumentation, and it was noisy. But the trip had been worthwhile and the photographs I passed on to my new colleagues in Samudra Ferro Engineering provided valuable context for the preliminary engineering drawings included in the tender package.

Having concluded our visit, we returned to Whyalla Airport for our flight back to Adelaide. It was the same pilot, Ben Mackiewicz, aged twenty-one, and the same plane, Piper Chieftan, VH-MZK. I know this because a month later during the evening flight from Adelaide to Whyalla, as the plane commenced its descent, both engines failed. It was a moonless night and being over water there would have been no visual references, but the young pilot made a textbook Mayday call, advising his situation and exact position, before spearing into Spencer Gulf. He was fifteen miles short of his destination. There were no survivors. The plane was recovered more or less intact, and the investigation found dual engine failure had occurred, inferring pilot error. The bureaucrats love doing that. Fortunately, subsequent detailed examination found the right-hand engine had failed first followed minutes later by the left. It was a fundamental flaw in the aircraft engines that had caused the accident and not pilot error. He had been a hero, and if it hadn't been a moonless night, the result might have been different.

Kufpec received six technical bids for the Oseil field development. Four of those, including the Ballast Samudra Ferro Bakrie Engineering joint venture, were invited to submit commercial bids. The deadline was July 3rd and tenderers were invited to attend a bid-opening meeting the following day. Our bid was just over US$88 million. The successful bid of US$62 million, submitted by Daewoo and local contractor, Istana Karang Laut, was less than our estimated cost price. We had spent a lot of money for nothing. It was the same for Terang Sirasun, where the tender process had been shelved for another year.

The Bontang Train H, Kufpec and Terang Sirasun disappointments demonstrated the existence of a perennial problem for Bakrie Engineering. We needed to win construction projects to make real money. But failures were expensive, and I had been advised in no uncertain terms Bakrie & Bros. was in no position to support us financially. They had their own problems servicing a debt, according to *The Jakarta Post*, of US$1.08 billion. Fortunately, there were other projects providing a subsistence income, but our balance sheet was wafer thin. Families were still struggling from the effects of Krismon, and layoffs would be devastating for the victims. If Bakrie Engineering were to survive and thrive, it needed a new partner or a new owner.

The solution, although I didn't know it at the time, had already walked through the door. In April, PT PalAmec won a contract to survey the production platforms in Maxus Indonesia's Widuri and Intan fields and where necessary to update the relevant as-built process and instrument drawings. Their engineering office in Surabaya was more familiar with shipbuilding, so Bruce Young, their general manager, had asked if we could help. We did the job on a fifty/fifty basis; it went well and in August as we divided the spoils, Bruce asked if Bakrie Engineering might be for sale. Naturally, I said no but undertook to talk to Bakrie & Bros. about it.

The sale of Bakrie Engineering was not going to make the slightest difference to Bakrie's financial woes but it would provide job security for my team so, assuming a reasonable offer, I was all for it. I conveyed these sentiments to Lukman Arief, who reverted shortly afterwards, saying Bakrie & Bros. were happy for me to talk to PalAmec and would accept a reasonable offer. Within weeks the office was crawling with Amec executives. Who wouldn't jump at an excuse to escape an Aberdeen winter? It soon became clear it was a little more than that—they were intent on establishing an engineering office in Jakarta, and taking over BKE was an option. Following these meetings, Bruce Young met Bakrie's president director, Irwan Sjarkawi, and conveyed the same message.

The formal negotiations began in late November with the arrival of Amec's heads of legal and commercial services. The early stages were more or less an audit, and although I was irritated by some of the nitpicking as the first week came and went, it was clear there were no showstoppers. Accounts and administration departments passed with flying colours. Shareholder equity in the October balance sheet was US$170,000, so we were comfortable. But work was petering out again and I was therefore keen to move the process along. But it was Christmas and despite there being more Muslims in Indonesia than any other country, nothing was going to happen, so I went home and Santy came too.

By now she had become a regular travelling companion, adding a zest that had been missing for years. Bligh Engineering's erstwhile financial adviser, Barney Cue, had invited us to his chalet in Megev in the winter of '98/'99. There aren't many Indonesian skiers, but after a few lessons Santy became one of them. Then in July she had accompanied me to England. We spent our first weekend in the New Forest with Andrew and Fiona Maconie. Andrew had joined Stuart Wood and me on our first fox hunting adventure to Ireland in 1993 and proved to be fearless if not orthodox across country. With our hunting days behind us, Andrew and I resorted to golf and played Royal Lymington, Andrew's nickname for a nine-hole course just down the road.

Next stop London, where Santy and I stayed with Peter and Renate Nahum in their elegant Bloomsbury townhouse. I had first met them in the early eighties when Peter had established himself as a dealer in nineteenth and twentieth century paintings, drawings and sculpture, and he had been a generous supporter of an emerging Sandy Goudie. We had spent a weekend with them in their house outside Lisieux in Normandy during our first trip to France two years earlier. Peter had given me a copy of *The World of Yesterday* by Stefan Zweig. It planted a sadness in me that is never far away.

When I asked Santy what she wanted to do on her first day in London her reply was even more telling than her response to the same question in New York: go to Greenwich. Why? Because that's where everything starts. How did a twenty-three-year-old educated in the Indonesian public school system learn to think like that? I never found out but if it hadn't been for Santy, I would never have visited the Royal Observatory, the prime meridian or fully understood the role of a chronometer in determining longitude in a ship at sea.

Warana, on the Sunshine Coast, is 153.13° east of Greenwich. As the Earth rotates, the dawn moves 15° west each hour. This is simplified by dividing the globe into twenty-four time zones and Warana is in the +10 zone. As a result, midnight in Greenwich is 10 am, precisely, in Warana.

It was in December 2000 when Santy made her first visit to the Sunshine Coast. Douglas Street was no longer, so we stayed with Lock and Ros, his new wife of seven years, in their house three hundred metres along the beach from Mum and Dad's place. Once again, Santy knew exactly what she wanted to do in Australia. This time it wasn't so surprising. Of course, she wanted to see a kangaroo. Eighteen holes at the Headland Golf Club fixed that. They were so tame there it was often necessary to move them to take a shot. By the time we left for Sydney a week later, Santy had joined the family. She was not a swimmer and neither was Mum, but they enjoyed their beach walks and Mum couldn't wait to take her shopping in Noosa. We then spent a few days in Sydney where we saw Patrick White's *A Cheery Soul* at the Opera House Theatre and, better still, took a return trip to Manly on a ferry.

Back in Jakarta there was no let-up from Amec, who were now talking money. What premium were they prepared to pay over shareholder equity? Shareholder equity was a moving target. At the end of October, it had been US$170,000, but since then the office had been running at a loss, so by year end it had fallen to US$120,000. In theory, they could hold off and the company would be worthless, but fortunately there were two substantial jobs in prospect and either would reverse our fortunes. The first was a Conoco project to develop two subsea gas fields in relatively deep water in the West Natuna Sea. The water depths were typically eighty metres, so it was to be Indonesia's first oil or gas development utilising subsea trees. The second was another pipeline project for Total in the Mahakam Delta, Tunu Phase 8 pipelines.

The combined value of the two projects was US$930,000 and by the end of March it was clear we would win both. Conoco awarded Saipem the West Natuna Sea project early

April and they in turn awarded the engineering subcontract to Bakrie Engineering with a proviso: I had to agree to be design project manager. It was blackmail but I agreed. Two weeks later, we won the engineering for the Tunu Phase 8 pipelines as well. It was a good time for Amec to take over Bakrie Engineering and it was a good time for Bakrie & Bros. to sell. Irwan Sjarkawi accepted Amec's offer of US$280,000 and the contract was signed on May 3rd.

It had not been the investment Bakrie & Bros. had hoped for, although, in Indonesian rupiah terms, they had quadrupled their investment. The company's employees had done well. All were guaranteed their places in the new company with the same pay and conditions and could look forward to a secure future with a committed owner. Bakrie Engineering would become PT Amec Berca Indonesia, Bruce Young would take over as president director and I was invited to stay on for a year in the position of operations director.

That didn't mean I had been relieved of my responsibility for the West Natuna Sea project. It was a pleasure working on such an interesting job without having to worry about funding the payroll. Not only was it to be Indonesia's first subsea development, but would also be the first project to export gas to a neighbouring country, Malaysia. The objective was to develop two subsea gas fields with subsea wells tied back to a mobile gravity base jack-up platform processing 325 MMscfd for export to the Malaysian gas grid via a one-hundred-kilometre, eighteen-inch-diameter export pipeline.

The export pipeline destination was a platform off the Malaysian east coast operated by Petronas Carigali. One of my first tasks was to head to KL to coordinate the design of the modifications required for the tie-in. My taxi ride into KL from the airport took long detours, avoiding demonstrations protesting at the incarceration of the country's former deputy prime minister, Anwar Ibrahim, on trumped-up sodomy charges. They play rough in Malaysia. If that's what they do to one of their own, what chance does a foreigner have?

Fortunately, this foreigner was lucky and Conoco's gas was flowing into Malaysia a year later. Five years later, having returned to live in Australia, I read a muse in the local newspaper suggesting Brisbane's imminent hosting of the International Shakespeare Association's World Conference was proof of a growing intellectual maturity. Yes, tickets were still available, and it was open to all. So a week later I drove down to Brisbane, checked into a nearby hotel and spent the week listening to academics. Like all conferences, it was a curate's egg. However, for me there was an astonishing highlight. The keynote speaker on the third day was Anwar Ibrahim. In September 2004, after six years in solitary confinement, Anwar's conviction had been overturned and he had been released. For his first six months in the clink his only reading material had been the Qur'an. Then he was given a copy of *The Complete Works of Shakespeare*. It sustained him for the rest of his imprisonment. Needless to say, his speech was a heartfelt tribute to the Bard's genius and humanity.

Later that evening, I went to a Sydney Theatre Company production of *Romeo and Juliet*, running at the Queensland Performing Arts Centre in conjunction with the conference.

I arrived early and with nothing better to do went to my seat to find I was sitting next to Anwar and his wife, Wan Azzizah, who were already seated. I introduced myself, complemented him on his address and related the story of my difficulties avoiding his supporters during my visit to KL in 2001. Naturally, he was interested in the West Natuna Sea project and the precedent it had set for gas sales from Indonesia to Malaysia, but he was more interested in what I saw in Shakespeare. It's not simple, but of all my heroes, including Einstein and Mozart, I can at least understand some of Shakespeare.

My new contract of employment with PT Amec Berca Indonesia gave me thirty days annual leave—in effect, six weeks. Keeping the company afloat was no longer a burning issue nor my problem, so I took the leave whenever possible. The Conoco project was well underway and on schedule, so with one of Indonesia's numerous public holidays looming, I spent a week at home. Dad was nearing his seventy-eighth birthday. Over Christmas I had noticed he was withdrawn, and this wasn't easy for Mum, although her irrepressible good humour was never far away. The best thing I could do was to spend more time with them. A week here or a Christmas there was a fine gesture, but why not more? Whether these thoughts came first or the 'For Sale' sign on the house across the street from Mum and Dad, I will never remember.

It was a sad story. The couple who had built the house for their large family had fallen out and been forced to sell. It wasn't exactly my cup of tea, but it was on the beach, less than fifty metres from Mum and Dad, close to my brother

Lockwood and it might come in handy sometime. I made an offer and it was accepted. I went back to Jakarta with the kernel of a plan—a plan to return to Australia. A plan was a new departure for me. In the thirty-seven years since my spur-of-the-moment decision to study engineering, I had done nothing but react to the event of the day. Engineering had been a great decision, some others not so good. My contract with Amec had another ten months to run, so there was time to confirm the plan and time to make it work.

The major obstacle was Santy. She had enjoyed a holiday in Australia but whether she would want to leave her family and friends for good was a different matter. Then, in an extraordinary rerun of what had just happened in Australia, the house next door to her parents in Bintaro came up for sale. I bought it in Santy's name, demolished it and built another. It was finished in less than six months. If Santy wanted to go to Australia she could, and if not, she would be comfortable.

The Conoco West Natuna Sea engineering package was signed off early in November. It was an excuse to engage Ireng Maulana for another party at Widya Chandra. In a sign the work had gone well, the Conoco and Saipem teams were all present and all smiles. Eat, drink and be merry, for tomorrow we may die. An honoured guest, Peter Carver, who had awarded Bakrie Kvaerner Engineering its first contract, hosted a barbecue the following evening. Peter was a New Yorker and his party had barely started when there was news from home. We turned on the TV and watched as the second Boeing 767 flew into the South Tower of the World Trade Center. It was a sad day for everybody but particularly sad for the Indonesian ideal of tolerance across the religious divide. It's not true to say its slide towards Islamic fundamentalism started that day, but the Jemaah Islamiyah attacks in Bali weren't far behind.

Before leaving for home and the Christmas holidays, I packed a container with enough Widya Chandra furniture to kickstart the new house. The clever plan worked and by the time Santy arrived a week later it was habitable. As usual, it was fun introducing Santy to new places. Her favourite was the Saturday market at Eumundi. It was crowded and I suspect made her feel at home. But there was also time for reading and I had yet to reach the end of Dad's Jack Aubrey collection, complete from *Master and Commander* to *Blue at the Mizzen*.

With the holidays gone, I returned to Jakarta wondering how to while away the next four months. I needn't have worried. Amec had an office in Japan and the Nippon Steel Corporation had commissioned a review of a Russian design for a crude oil pipeline from the oilfields in Western Siberia to Vladivostok, from whence it could be shipped to Japan. At the time, it went via the Trans-Siberian Railway. Three years later, while taking the world's longest train journey from Vladivostok to St Petersburg, I saw it for myself—a parade of trains heading east, each around 800 metres long and carrying 5000 tonnes of crude oil. This was expensive, but that wasn't the only problem. Vladivostok was not an ice-free port.

Amec had engineering offices worldwide, some with pipeline experience, so I was flattered when asked to form a team to carry out the work in Jakarta with port design and geotechnical support from the Amec offices in Vancouver and Moscow. The plan was for each office to undertake a preliminary review of the earlier designs, attend a coordination meeting in London in early February and to collate and issue the final report in April.

It was a fitting swansong for the engineer who had never forgotten his first lecture at the University of Queensland: 'Engineers are those that build for ten shillings that which costs everybody else a pound', and that's what we had there. The proposed thirty-two-inch-diameter pipeline was 3985 kilometres long, including through around 1000 kilometres of permafrost and swamp. The Russian design called for the pipeline to be installed above ground in those areas to prevent heat from the pipeline turning them into bogs. The problem with above-ground installations was exposing the pipeline to temperatures down to minus thirty-five degrees Celsius during winter. It would be well-nigh impossible to pump crude at these temperatures. The Russian remedy was a pipeline trace-heating system requiring a billion US dollars' worth of power generation and distribution infrastructure, not to mention substantial running costs.

A similar problem occurred with some pipelines in the North Sea. It was simply resolved by insulation. But as I had explained at my Ipco interview ten years earlier, there are offshore pipeliners and cross-country pipeliners, and never the twain shall meet, certainly not in Russia. We costed the application of insulation, concrete weight coating and burial through the permafrost and swamp and reduced the overall estimate from US$6 billion to US$5 billion, but it wasn't enough. The Trans-Siberian Railway is still carting crude oil from Angarsk to Vladivostok and Bakrie Kvaerner Engineering has undergone its third transformation to become PT Berca Engineering International.

In the two years following my return to Australia, Santy was a regular visitor. On the last occasion, as we were driving home from the airport, she said she wanted to tell me something but only if I promised not to be angry. I asked her how I could do that if I didn't know what she wanted to tell me? This went on for a day or two until I cracked and agreed. 'I want to have a family.' It took a moment for the penny to drop. It was her way of saying she had found somebody else. It was typical of Santy. Rather than tell me over the phone, this gutsy twenty-five-year-old had flown all the way to Australia to tell me face to face. She married her someone else and they went to France to make a family.

Maybe everything is for the best. Having the house across the street from Mum and Dad did come in handy. Two years before Dad died, it became impossible for Mum to look after him, so rather than the tender mercies of aged care, he moved in with me. I had the space and could manage the people needed to look after him. He could walk to the beach and all Mum had to do to visit was cross the road. She came for lunch most days. It was the least I could do for the most generous man I will ever know. Mum and I became the best of friends as well. I walked Polly, her dog, most mornings and we would have tea afterwards. We played bridge together at the bridge club, and after I had learned to fly we often flew out west to catch up with the country cousins. She lived at home alone until a week before she died at ninety-five, which means I still have a long way to go.

Tally-ho!

Bibliography

1. William Shakespeare, *Julius Caesar*, Act 4, 1599
2. Lieutenant TP Chataway, *History of the 15th Battalion AIF 1914–1918*, The Naval & Military Press Ltd and the Imperial War Museum London, circa 1945
3. William Wordsworth, *The Rainbow*, 1802
4. AB Paterson, *The Collected Verse of AB Paterson*, Angus and Robertson, 1895
5. Robert Burns, *To a Mouse*, 1785
6. Thomas Gray, *Elegy Written in a Country Churchyard*, 1751
7. William Shakespeare, *Twelfth Night*, Act 1, 1601
8. Percy Bysshe Shelley, *Ozymandias*, 1818
9. William Shakespeare, *Henry V*, The St Crispin's Day Speech, Act 4, 1599
10. Jerry Jeff Walker. *Mr Bojangles*, 1968
11. William Shakespeare, *Henry V*, Act 1 Prologue, 1599
12. Stefan Zweig, *The World of Yesterday*, 1943, Viking Press (translated from German, *Die Welt von Gestern: Erinnerungen eines Europäers*, 1942)
13. Charlotte Brontë, *Jane Eyre*, 1847
14. Arthur Balfour, Balfour Declaration, 1917

15. Peter Shaffer, *Amadeus*, Orion Pictures (directed by Miloš Forman), 1984
16. Oscar Wilde, *The Ballad of Reading Gaol*, 1898
17. Alexander Pope, *A Little Learning*, 1709
18. Philip McCouat, The Shocking Birth and Amazing Career of Guernica, *Journal of Art in Society*, 2012, https://www.artinsociety.com
19. William Shakespeare, *Hamlet*, Act 2, 1599
20. William Wordsworth, *Daffodils*, 1807
21. Alan Jay Lerner, *My Fair Lady*, 1956, (based on George Bernard Shaw's 1913 play *Pygmalion*)
22. Giuseppe Verdi (composer), Francesco Maria Piave (Librettist), *Rigoletto*, 1851
23. Sir Walter Scott, *The Fair Maid of Perth*, 1828
24. Alexander Pope, *An Essay on Man*, 1733
25. Richard Strauss, *Tod und Verklärung*, 1888
26. Robert Browning, *Childe Roland to the Dark Tower Came*, 1855
27. William Shakespeare, *Hamlet*, Act 4, 1599
28. William Shakespeare, *The Winter's Tale*, Act 4, 1609
29. Robert Browning, *De Gustibus*, 1855
30. Joseph Conrad, *Lord Jim*, Blackwood's Magazine, 1899
31. Charles Dickens, *David Copperfield*, 1850
32. William Shakespeare, *Hamlet*, Act 5, 1599

List of Acronyms and Abbreviations

ABC	Arabian Bligh Corporation; Australian Broadcasting Corporation
ADB	Asian Development Bank
Agip	Azienda Generale Italiana Petroli (Italy)
AGTL	Alberta Gas Trunkline Company (Canada)
AJL	AJ Lucas Constructions (Australia)
am	ante meridiem
AMS	Aramco Materials System
AOC	Aramco Overseas Company
API	American Petroleum Institute
ASAP	as soon as possible
BA	British Airways
BAR	Brown & Root International (USA)
BE	Bligh Engineering
BKE	Bakrie Kvaerner Engineering (Indonesia)
BMW	Bayerische Motoren Werke (Germany)
BODL	Burmah Oil Development Ltd (UK)
BP	British Petroleum
BSc	Bachelor of Science
BTR	Bligh Technical Recruitment
CAD	computer-aided design (also AutoCAD, automated computer-aided design)

CASOC	California Arabian Standard Oil Company (Saudi Arabia)
CBD	central business district
CEGB	Central Electricity Generating Board
CIA	Central Intelligence Agency (USA)
CIF	cost insurance and freight (trading term)
CNG	compressed natural gas (the fuel of the future)
CNOOC	China National Offshore Oil Corporation
CO_2	carbon dioxide
COPE	Compagnie Orientale Petroles des Egypte (Egypt)
CPP	central processing platform
CV	curriculum vitae
DB	derrick barge
DC3	Douglas DC3
DSV	diver support vessel
DWT	deadweight tonnage
DZIT	Department of Zakah and Income Tax (Saudi Arabia)
EEC	European Economic Community
EG&G	formerly Edgerton, Germeshausen, and Grier, Inc., (USA)
ENO	English National Opera
EPC	engineer procure construct (contract)
ETPM	Entreprise Travaux Publics Maritimes (France)
EU	European Union
FMC	formerly Food Machinery & Chemical Corporation
GOSP	gas-oil separator platform

GPS	global positioning system
H_2S	hydrogen sulphide
HAM	formerly known as Hollandsche Aannemings Maatschappij (Netherlands)
HHI	Hyundai Heavy Industries (South Korea)
HQ	headquarters
HRH	His Royal Highness
HSBC	Hongkong and Shanghai Banking Corporation Ltd
HSL	Hindustan Shipyard Ltd (India)
IDR	Indonesian rupiah
IGAT	Iran Gas Trunkline
IHC	formerly known as Industriële Handels Combinatie (Netherlands)
IIAPCO	Independent Indonesian American Petroleum Company
IKPT	PT Inti Karya Persada Tehnik
IMEDE	Institut pour l'Etude des Methodes de Direction de l'Entreprise
Inc	incorporated
IOOC	Iranian Offshore Oil Company
Ipco	International Project Consultants
IRA	Irish Republican Army
JFK	John F Kennedy
JV	joint venture
KFC	Kentucky Fried Chicken
KI	Kvaerner Indonesia
KISS	keep it simple stupid
LBJ	President Lyndon B Johnson

List of Acronyms and Abbreviations

KL	Kuala Lumpur
KRJB	Kvaerner RJ Brown
LB	lay barge (used to install submarine pipelines)
LNG	liquefied natural gas
LPS	Lockheed Petroleum Services
LSTK	lump sum turnkey
MA	Master of Arts
MBA	Master of Business Administration
MBOD	thousand barrels of oil a day
MEA	Middle East Airlines
MEECO	Middle East Equipment Company (Bahrain)
MMBW	Melbourne Metropolitan Board of Works
MMscfd	million standard cubic feet per day
MSB	Maritime Services Board
MSW	municipal solid waste
MTPA	million tonnes per annum
MW	megawatt
Mwh	megawatt hour
NASA	The National Aeronautics and Space Administration (USA)
NGL	natural gas liquids
NIOC	National Iranian Oil Company
NQEA	formerly North Queensland Engineers and Agents
NSW	New South Wales
ODDT	Offshore Data Development Team
P&H	Pawling and Harnischfeger (USA)
P&ID	process and instrument diagram

P&O	The Peninsular and Oriental Steam Navigation Company (UK)
PC	personal computer; politically correct
PES	Project Engineering Services
PFD	process flow diagram
plc	public limited company
PLEM	pipeline end manifold
pm	post meridiem
PM	prime minister
PMT	project management team
ppm	parts per million
PT	Perseroan Terbatas (Indonesian form of limited liability company)
PZE	Palestine Zionist Executive
QA	quality assurance
QC	quality control
QF	Qantas Flight
RADA	formerly known as the Royal Academy of Dramatic Art
RAAF	Royal Australian Air Force
RAF	Royal Air Force
RDF	refuse-derived fuel
retd	retired
RHM	formerly Rank Hovis McDougal
RJBA	RJ Brown and Associates (Netherlands)
RMC	ready-mix concrete
ROH	Royal Opera House
ROS	Ratcliffe-on-Soar Power Station
ROV	remotely operated vehicles

RPS	range positioning system (Motorola)
SA	Sociedad Anonima (similar to a proprietary limited company)
SBM	SBM Offshore (formerly known as Single Buoy Moorings Inc), the company that invented the SPM
SBPT	Shell BP Todd
SCADA	Supervisory Control and Data Acquisition
SCUBA	self-contained underwater breathing apparatus
SERNAP	Servicio Nacional de Pesca y Acuicultura
SIRIP	Société Irano-Italienne des Pétroles (Egypt)
SNTP	Société Nationale des Travaux Publics (France)
SOCAL	Standard Oil of California
SPC	Shanghai Petroleum Corporation (China)
SPM	Single Point Mooring
SW	south-west
Tcf	trillion cubic feet
TJGP	PT Trans Javagas Pipeline (Indonesia)
TL	trunkline
TR	Triumph (UK car manufacturer)
TSHD	trailer suction hopper dredger
UDC	Union of the Democratic Centre (Spain)
UK	United Kingdom
UQP	University of Queensland Press
USA	United States of America
V	Vee
VLCC	very large crude carrier
VP	vice president
VW	Volkswagen

WDA	Westminster Dredging Australia
WTI	West Texas Intermediate
WW1	World War 1 (1914–1918)
WW2	World War 2 (1939–1945)
Y2K	year 2000
ZGOSP	Zuluf gas oil separator plant (Saudi Arabia)

www.ingramcontent.com/pod-product-compliance
Lightning Source LLC
Chambersburg PA
CBHW030031100526
44590CB00011B/155